Tailored Fashion Design

b

Tailored Fashion Design

Pamela Powell
COLLEGE OF DUPAGE AND COLUMBIA COLLEGE, CHICAGO

Fairchild Books
NEW YORK

Vice President & General Manager, Fairchild Education & Conference Division: Elizabeth Tighe

Executive Editor: Olga T. Kontzias

Senior Associate Acquiring Editor: Jaclyn Bergeron

Assistant Acquisitions Editor: Amanda Breccia

Editorial Development Director: Jennifer Crane

Development Editor: Rob Phelps

Creative Director: Carolyn Eckert

Photo Researcher: Avital Aronowitz

Production Director: Ginger Hillman

Production Editor: Jessica Rozler

Copyeditor: Susan Hobbs

Ancillaries Editor: Noah Schwartzberg

Director, Sales & Marketing: Brian Normoyle

Cover Design: Carolyn Eckert

Cover Art: Carolyn Eckert and Tronvig Kuypers

Illustrations (book and pattern pack): Pamela Powell

Graphic Designer (book and pattern pack): Thom Olson

Text Design: Tronvig Group

Page Composition: Barbara Barg Medley

Copyright © 2011 Fairchild Books, a Division of Condé Nast Publications.

All rights reserved. No part of this book covered by the copyright hereon may be reproduced or used in any form or by any means—graphic, electronic, or mechanical, including photocopying, recording, taping, or information storage and retrieval systems—without written permission of the publisher.

Library of Congress Catalog Card Number: 2009926333

ISBN: 978-1-56367-746-5

GST R 133004424

TP09, MC06

Contents

Foreword **xiii**

Preface **xv**

Acknowledgments **xix**

Part I: Design Workshop **1**

CHAPTER 1: Introduction to Contemporary Tailoring **2**

CHAPTER 2: Design Workshop **14**

CHAPTER 3: Looking at Fabric **33**

Part II: Preparation **43**

PART II SIDEBAR: Tools of the Trade **44**

CHAPTER 4: The Pattern **45**

CHAPTER 5: The Fit **59**

Part III: Construction **71**

PART III SIDEBAR: Hand Stitches for Tailoring **72**

CHAPTER 6: The Jacket Front **73**

CHAPTER 7: The Pockets **90**

CHAPTER 8: The Jacket Back **117**

CHAPTER 9: The Sleeve **126**

CHAPTER 10: The Undercollar **142**

CHAPTER 11: The Shoulder Pads **154**

CHAPTER 12: Top Collar, Back Neck Facing, and Front Lapel Facing **163**

CHAPTER 13: The Lining **178**

CHAPTER 14: Finishing the Jacket **192**

Glossary **203**

Bibliography **205**

Credits **207**

Index **209**

Extended Contents

Foreword xiii

Preface xv

Acknowledgments xix

Part I: Design Workshop 1

CHAPTER 1: Introduction to Contemporary Tailoring 2

Chapter Objectives 2

Tailoring and Fashion Design 3

    What Is Traditional Tailoring? 4

    What Do We Mean by "Fashion Design"? 4

    Contemporary Tailoring and Fashion Design 5

The Evolution of Tailored Fashion Design 5

    Emergence of the Informal 5

    Tailoring for Women 6

        Ladies Departments and Home Patterns 7

    The Influence of the Prince of Wales 7

    The Influence of Hollywood 8

    The Influence of World War II 8

    Post-War Style: Italian Influence and "Off the Peg" 9

    Designing a Classic Look without the Classic Rules 10

    The Armani Look 11

    The *Enfant Terrible* 12

    Change and Challenge 13

References 13

CHAPTER 2: Design Workshop 14

Chapter Objectives 14

Finding Your Inspiration 15

Taking Inspiration from History 16

From Inspiration to Design 19

    Silhouette 19

    Scale and Volume 20

    Proportion and Line 22

    Details 24

    Color 27

    Contrast 27

    Texture 28

    Fabric 28

BOX 2.1: Vivienne Westwood 30

Chapter Checklist 32

References 32

CHAPTER 3: Looking at Fabric 33

Chapter Objectives 33

Fabric Choice 34

    Plaids and Stripes 36

        Toile, or Muslin, and Plaids and Stripes 36

        Working a Plaid 37

    Nap Fabrics 37

Bringing Together Fabric and Design 37

BOX 3.1: Linton Tweed 40

    Selecting Linings 41

    Selecting Interfacings 41

        Sewn-In Interfacings 41

        Fusible Interfacings 42

Chapter Checklist 42

References 42

Part II: Preparation 43

PART II SIDEBAR: Tools of the Trade 44

CHAPTER 4: The Pattern 45

Chapter Objectives 45

Taking Measurements for the Jacket 46

The Fit of the Jacket 48

Making the Pattern 49

The Jacket Front 51

    Double-Breasted Jacket 51

    The Jacket Sleeve 52

    The Two-Piece, or Tailored, Sleeve 53

    The Raglan Sleeve 54

    Collars 54

BOX 4.1: Alexander McQueen 56

    Making the Toile 58

Chapter Checklist 58

References 58

CHAPTER 5: The Fit 59

Chapter Objectives 59

Fitting the Jacket 60

    Lapels 60

    Waistline 60

Adjusting for Individual Backs and Bust Lines 62

The Shoulder Line 64

    Low Shoulder 64

    Sloped Shoulders 65

    Square Shoulders 66

Full Bust 66

    Small or Flat Bust 67

    Front Dart 67

BOX 5.1: Satyenkumer 68

Shaping the Jacket 70

    Proportions 70

Chapter Checklist 70

References 70

Part III: Construction 71

PART III SIDEBAR: Hand Stitches for Tailoring 72

CHAPTER 6: The Jacket Front 73

Chapter Objectives 73

Applying Fusible Interfacing 74

Darts, Tucks, and Pleats 76

    Stitching the Waist Darts 76

    Working Tucks and Pleats 77

    Checklist for Tucks, Pleats, and Darts 77

Preparing the Canvas 77

    Adding the Bust Dart on a Woman's Jacket 78

The Chest Piece 79

    Making the Chest Piece 79

        Contemporary Method: Chest Piece 79

        Traditional Method: Chest Piece 80

    Joining Together the Canvas and Jacket Front 80

Pad Stitching and Shaping the Lapels 81

    Pad Stitching 82

    Taping and Shaping the Roll Line 82

    Bound Buttonholes 84

        The Piping Strip 85

    Cutting, Turning, and Finishing the Bound Buttonhole 85

Attaching the Facing 86

Chapter Checklist 87

References 87

BOX 6.1: Yves Saint Laurent 88

CHAPTER 7: The Pockets 90

Chapter Objectives 90

Pocket Placement 91

    Chest Pocket Placement 91

    Hip Pocket Placement 91

Basic Jacket Pockets 92

    The Welt Pocket 92

    The Double-Piped Pockets 97

    The Double-Piped Pocket with a Flap 102

    The Patch Pocket 106

    The Inside-Stitched Patch Pocket 112

    The Inseam Pockets 114

Chapter Checklist 115

References 115

BOX 7.1: Haider Ackermann 116

CHAPTER 8: The Jacket Back 117

Chapter Objectives 117

Constructing the Jacket Back 119

    Stabilizing the Back, Neck, and Armhole Edges 119

    Beginning Construction and Working with a Back Yoke 120

        Constructing the Yoke 121

    Placement of the Back Vent 121

Attaching the Jacket Back to the Front 122

Adding a Half Belt 123

Chapter Checklist 124

BOX 8.1: Jil Sander 125

CHAPTER 9: The Sleeve 126

Chapter Objectives 126

Types of Sleeve Construction 128

    The One-Piece Sleeve 128

    The Two-Piece, or Tailored, Sleeve 129

    Two-Piece Sleeve with a Mitered Vent 130

        Shaping the Two-Piece Sleeve 130

        Making the Miter 131

        Making the Sleeve Cap 134

        Setting the Sleeve 135

        Constructing the Sleeve Heads 137

BOX 9.1: Cristóbal Balenciaga 138

    The Raglan Sleeve 140

        Design Tips for the Raglan Sleeve 141

Chapter Checklist 141

References 141

CHAPTER 10: The Undercollar 142

Chapter Objectives 142

Anatomy of the Undercollar 143

Choosing the Method to Construct the Undercollar 144

    Traditional Method for Constructing the Undercollar 144

    Evaluating Undercollar Fit 146

Attaching the Undercollar to the Neckline 147

    Machine Method for Attaching the Undercollar to the Neckline 147

    Traditional Method for Attaching Undercollar to Neckline 148

        Machine Method for Stitching the Undercollar 148

    Fusible Method for Constructing the Undercollar 149

Constructing the Shawl Collar 150

Constructing a Convertible or Flat Undercollar 151

Chapter Checklist 151

References 151

BOX 10.1: Romeo Gigli 152

CHAPTER 11: The Shoulder Pads 154

Chapter Objectives 154

Constructing the Shoulder Pad 156

The Raglan, or Rounded, Shoulder Pad 159

BOX 11.1: Gianni Versace 160

Chapter Checklist 162

References 162

CHAPTER 12: Top Collar, Back Neck Facing, and Front Lapel Facing 163

Chapter Objectives 163

The Top Collar 164

    Traditional Method for Constructing the Top Collar 166

    Attaching the Top Collar by Machine 168

Constructing the Front Lapel Facing 169

    Shaping the Lapel 170

Constructing the Back Neck Facing 173

Chapter Checklist 176

BOX 12.1: Create-A-Marker, Inc. 177

CHAPTER 13: The Lining 178

Chapter Objectives 178

Types of Linings 179

Constructing the Lining 180

Full Lining Pattern 180

The Lining 182

Inside Lining Pocket 183

"Bagging" the Jacket Lining or Set by Machine 185

Jacket Vent and Hem 185

Inserting the Lining by Hand 188

BOX 13.1: John Rocha 190

Attaching the Jacket Lining without a Back Neck Facing 191

Chapter Checklist 191

References 191

CHAPTER 14: Finishing the Jacket 192

Chapter Objectives 192

Buttons 193

    Measuring the Button 194

    Hand-Worked Buttonholes 195

    Stranding the Buttonhole 196

    Making the Buttonhole Stitch 196

    Machine-Stitched Buttonholes 198

    Marking the Button's Placement 198

Final Pressing 199

Topstitching 200

Attaching the Buttons 200

Giving Your Completed Jacket a Final Evaluation 201

    The Collar 201

    The Lapels 201

    The Front Edge 201

    The Sleeves 201

    The Waist and Hip Area 201

    The Lower Hem Line 201

    The Fabric Design: Plaids, Stripes, or Checks 201

BOX 14.1: Savile Row Jargon 202

Glossary 203

Bibilography 205

Credits 207

Index 209

Foreword

Successful fashion design is based upon the foundations of good craftsmanship and tailoring. Transforming a flat cloth into a three-dimensional form and giving it style and structure requires neatness and precision of sewing. Whether for commercial fashion or haûte couture, good design must employ a practical, clever use of color, shape, and fabric that results in a distinguishing effect.

Written with simplicity and clarity, *Tailored Fashion Design* by Pamela Powell vividly explains how to achieve this. This textbook is an essential tool for fashion design students to propel their understanding of how a garment is made to a higher level.

From concept to completion, detailed steps will help you achieve the intricate skills required to bring your design ideas to life. *Tailored Fashion Design* will open your eyes to the wealth of inspiration surrounding us. It will lead you to seek inspiration from established designers, to use history to predict new shapes for future fashions, and to employ everyday objects—from garment fastenings that take their cue from sliding doors to fabrics the breathe through fish-scale effects. It will show you how to achieve dramatic results through small changes in design, like adding seams or tossing in contrasting color.

As you study the instructions within these pages, you will begin to develop a visual plan of how to perfect your tailoring abilities and, with some guidance, finish your designs to a higher standard and signature style.

Professor Andrew M. Ramroop CMG, OBE
Savile Row Academy, London
(www.savilerowtailor.com)

Preface

Tailoring books typically focus on the construction of tailored garments, beginning with the selection of ready-made patterns and concluding with the assembly of the various pieces. *Tailored Fashion Design* begins a few steps ahead—in the design process. My goal in taking this approach is to inspire you and guide you to make your own patterns for both men's and women's tailored jackets. You will then execute those patterns using contemporary tailoring techniques that the book directs you through to the completion of your own tailored jacket.

Throughout the book, fashion illustrations show you the many silhouettes that the tailored jacket can take. Increasingly, men are opting for a less-structured jacket, making the inner construction similar to women's jacket whereas women's styles have often borrowed from elements of traditionally male garments.

I've included basic jacket patterns with instructions on how to manipulate details within the patterns to achieve a whole new look using three methods of tailoring—traditional (also called classic or bespoke), contemporary, and fusible.

Profiles of professional designers who incorporate tailoring into their collections further highlight the important place that each technique of tailoring—traditionally relegated to strict classic or bespoke methods that required years of apprenticeship to acquire—continues to hold in today's fashion industry. I have also included profiles concerning a few tailoring-related businesses. These profiles include:

- Vivienne Westwood (Chapter 2)
- Linton Tweed (Chapter 3)
- Alexander McQueen (Chapter 4)
- Satyenkumer Patel (Chapter 5)
- Yves Saint Laurent (Chapter 6)
- Haider Ackermann (Chapter 7)

- Jil Sander (Chapter 8)
- Cristóbal Balenciaga (Chapter 9)
- Romeo Gigli (Chapter 10)
- Gianni Versace (Chapter 11)
- Create-A-Marker, Inc. (Chapter 12)
- John Rocha (Chapter 13)
- Savile Row Jargon (Chapter 14)

I encourage you to consider tailoring as a design element, rather than just a method of garment assembly. As a result, you will begin to appreciate tailoring as a viable skill that not only displays your ability to put together garments, but also showcases your creativity as a designer.

I have found that when I'm working on my original design concepts I want to know how to make them work. I'm more open to trying new techniques and experimenting further to achieve the end result. For me, as an instructor, it is a great moment when my students leave their final class wearing their jacket. Although we all know that Savile Row is the home of classic bespoke tailoring, most of the students have never seen a bespoke tailored jacket as they shop at the mall; ready-to-wear, or "off-the-peg," is their concept for both construction and design. Today there are not many people who can afford bespoke tailoring; most designers now work a combination of bespoke and contemporary tailoring techniques. If you can work this combination of techniques, it is easier to understand modern tailoring.

Tailoring should be fun! It is about adding structure to the inside to make the outside work. Adding this structure to the inside means that you can have unlimited design options because this inner structure can be manipulated and changed. Shoulder pads, for example, do not have to be symbols of "power dressing" and intimidation. From my experience as an educator, I have found that students feel disillusioned over the lack of contemporary tailoring books that let them actualize their own visions or those of a particular client. That is why I decided to write this book.

FROM VISION TO CREATION

The book is divided into three parts: Part I: "Design Workshop," Part II: "Preparation" (coving pattern and fit), and Part III: "Construction."

Part I: "Design Workshop," leads you through the process of finding your inspiration—whether from history, observation, or personal experience—and then developing it into a design. How do the various elements of design create a particular style? How will, for example, your choice of fabric articulate your vision?

Chapter 1, "Introduction to Contemporary Tailoring," examines how and why tailoring has evolved and changed. It explores traditional tailoring and contemporary tailoring, which combines hand, machine, and fusible techniques. Chapter 2, "Design Workshop," is a step-by-step look at how to design your own jacket, starting with where you get the inspiration to choosing the right design elements to articulate it. Chapter 3, "Looking at Fabric," shows how fabric, in its various forms and uses, creates particular effects that designers use to create various styles.

After you've chosen the design that will express your inspiration, you need to get it down on paper; to do so you must create your pattern, take precise measurements, and manipulate your pattern working with these measurements. Part II: "Preparation," includes what it takes to do exactly that—Chapter 4 covers "The Pattern" and Chapter 5, "the Fit."

Because it's also important to have the appropriate tools and be able to use them correctly, Part II also begins with a "Tools of the Trade" sidebar, which lists the fundamental equipment used in cutting, marking, pressing, and constructing the tailored garment.

After you have settled on your design, made the pattern, constructed the toile, and discerned the perfect fit, you can begin construction.

In Part III: "Construction," each chapter focuses on a different piece of the jacket. Part III also begins with a sidebar featuring simple directions and an illustration for you to review the basic stitches used in construction. The chapters in this final section are not arranged in any specific order or sequence. This is to give you more flexibility. You can, for example, work your jacket pockets at the machine and then while, say, watching a movie on television, you can pad stitch the undercollar. I also find that by attaching the sleeves before the collar means that you can start to see the finished jacket design sooner. If you are making a raglan sleeve jacket, you have to set the sleeves before the undercollar, which breaks with tradition set by traditional tailoring. Working this way also stops the undercollar and front lapel from getting bent out of shape while setting the sleeves and requiring the undercollar and front lapel to be reshaped.

Chapter 6, "The Jacket Front," covers building and shaping the jacket front. Chapter 7, "The Pockets," demonstrates how these details can be functional or purely decorative. In Chapter 8, "The Jacket Back," you decide if the back shoulder area of your jacket needs to be stayed, taped, or both to give a nice, smooth line and stop any stretching. Here I also look at any other design concepts from single or double vents, yokes, pleats, and half belts.

I go out of sequence with Chapter 9, "The Sleeve," because the collar is normally attached to the jacket before the sleeves; however, I have found it easier for students to set the sleeves before attaching the collar. Chapter 10, "The Undercollar," shows how to interface and shape the undercollar to support the weight of the upper collar and looks at how to attach the collar to the neck of the jacket. Chapter 11 covers "The Shoulder Pads"; Chapter 12, "The Front Lapel, Top Collar, and Back Neck Facing"; and Chapter 13, "The Lining."

Finally in Chapter 14, "Finishing the Jacket," we set the lining into the jacket and take all the final steps to finish the jacket to a professional standard.

Tailoring has a long, rich heritage and in writing this book I hope to inspire you to both design and engage in a fresh new approach to tailoring by blurring the lines between traditional tailoring and contemporary design; blurring the three methods of tailoring; and blurring the genders.

Most of all, my goal is to encourage you to experiment with anything you may be inspired to experience in order to express your own personal vision.

Acknowledgments

Special thanks to Tony Alston, to Roy Peach for accepting me into the program at the London College of Fashion, and to the tailoring instructors there for introducing me to the wonderful art of tailoring and design.

Tailored Fashion Design would not have become a reality if it wasn't for Francesca Sterrlacci of the Academy of Arts, San Francesco. Thank you, Francesca, for encouraging me to do this project.

I'm deeply grateful to Thom Olson for his friendship, illustrations, art direction, graphic design skills, fabulousness, guidance, and patience—all of which have made this book into something special.

This has been a challenging project, and my special thanks to Jaclyn Bergeron, my acquisitions editor, for her support in making my idea a reality. Rob Phelps, my development editor, with his invaluable enthusiasm, guidance, and skill, pushed me further than I thought I could ever go with this project. And to all at Fairchild Books who worked on this book: Jennifer Crane, editorial development director; Amanda Breccia, assistant acquisitions editor; Carolyn Eckert, creative director; Jessica Rozler, production editor; Ginger Hillman, production director; and Noah Schwartzberg, ancillaries editor—it is your skills that have made this happen, thank you.

A special thanks to my acquisitions reviewers: Sandra Tonz, Mount Mary College; Joyce Greening, Harper College and Columbia College, Chicago; Evelyn Pappas, Savannah College of Art and Design; and Meredith Byron, Massachusetts College of Art and Design. And to my development reviewers: Evelyn Pappas, Savannah College of Art and Design; Paula Dancie, Kent State University; Joyce Greening, Columbia College, Chicago.

And to my family, friends, and students for their interest and encouragement—you know who you are. Thank you.

Tailored Fashion Design

PART I

Design Workshop

CHAPTER 1

Introduction to Contemporary Tailoring

It is only shallow people who do not judge by appearance.

—Oscar Wilde

CHAPTER OBJECTIVES

After reading this chapter, you should be able to:

Define traditional tailoring and contemporary tailoring, and identify the differences between these two approaches to garment construction.

Evaluate the relationship between tailoring and design and have a basic understanding of the history of this relationship.

Define the term "tailored fashion design."

Contemporary tailoring is increasingly blurring the line between traditional tailors and fashion designers. Driven by mass marketing, new technologies, and changing lifestyles, the aesthetic of conventional fashion design has changed and so have the choices of construction used in contemporary design. Up until the later decades of the twentieth century, very strict and long-established rules dictated the procedures of tailoring. Before World War I, the tailors of Savile Row in London's West End dressed elegant Englishmen, who never would have purchased and worn ready-to-wear garments. Not only did Savile Row provide the clothing for these gentlemen, but it also furnished the rules of male dress.

For the contemporary designer, these rules have changed.

The aim of this book is to bring together the different methods used to construct a jacket that can be considered a contemporary tailored garment. Our goal is to explore techniques used in contemporary tailoring—as well as those used in traditional tailoring—in order to develop not only your construction skills but also your designer's eye.

TAILORING AND FASHION DESIGN

Designer Pierre Cardin created the image of the Beatles in their boxy, collarless jackets and tight pants. The French tailor Gilbert Feruch inspired Cardin (Figure 1.1). Here was an occasion where the line separating fashion design and tailoring became unclear. Cardin worked as a designer and not as a tailor to construct these suits, but he certainly employed some of a tailor's techniques.

The French designer Jacques Esterel pushed the fashion designer–tailor fusion further by avoiding traditional tailoring techniques in which he was trained, working in non-traditional fabrics, and dressing men in skirts. In the 1960s, when unisex fashion became the trend typically through pushing women to dress like men, Esterel pushed men to dress like women (*The Fairchild Encyclopedia of Menswear,* 2008, p. 137).

Figure 1.1 The Beatles' look in their boxy, collarless jackets and tight pants was created by Pierre Cardin, who was inspired by the French tailor Gilbert Feruch.

What Is Traditional Tailoring?

In traditional tailoring, also called **bespoke** tailoring or classic tailoring, there are no fusible interfacings; all the structure is created based on custom fitting, using precise hand stitching that reinforces and pads, the interfacings, pressing, and shrinking techniques. Savile Row decreed these rules for male dress up until the American influences of the 1920s and Italian influences of the 1950s weakened its power; these influences were largely due to demands for leisure and the need for ease. But many continued to look for quality construction, the finest materials, and the minutest attention to detail.

There are, of course, still men today who can afford to insist upon perfect bespoke, or traditional, tailoring. A voluntary code of ethics was instituted in the twenty-first century that is loosely based on the rules issued by the Federation de la Couture in France, which specify the amount of handwork that must be done on anything designated as a couture garment. The rules of the Savile Row Bespoke Association specify that any suit advertised as bespoke must be handmade and take a minimum of 60 hours to complete—this, again, is in keeping with couture gowns (Savilerowbespoke.com, 2009).

Today, bespoke tailors can still compete with the designer and there is a demand to learn and practice the trade. However we can also employ these techniques in contemporary fashion design, which can freely go beyond strict dictates.

What Do We Mean by "Fashion Design"?

"Fashion design, is almost like mathematics," noted Jane Mulvagh in her biography, Vivienne Westwood, *An Unfashionable Life.* "You have a vocabulary of ideas which you have to add and subtract in order to come up with an equation right for the times."

Figure 1.2 "Jerry in training for a swell," illustration by George Cruikshank.

Fashion is a way that we express ourselves when we dress. It can show what makes us individual and unique. It is also a way to creatively express design—the aesthetic and/or functionality of the garment. Look around you. I'm sure you will see someone that is passionate about her or his appearance and clothing.

Design is important in tailoring a jacket because, as an outer garment, the jacket will make the first impression regarding what you wear and how you present yourself.

Tailoring is a term used to refer to the method of construction rather than design. The two must, of course, come together; for example, you can have great cut, fit, and construction, but you can't achieve these qualities without great design. Design does not have to result in an "over-the-top" show piece, but can remain understated and rely on details and workmanship. Design can be versatile. When we look at the history of tailoring, we can see, for example, that women over the centuries have borrowed design details and workmanship from men's tailoring and vice versa. The jacket provides us with a great example of the blurring of gender through design.

Contemporary Tailoring and Fashion Design

Changing attitudes of society have created powerful consumers. These individuals have defined their status by wearing ready-to-wear, off-the-peg designer fashion labels and, in so doing, created entirely new looks. Both men and women, for example, have begun to wear jeans with a formal jacket, breaking the rules as to how a suit was once worn. In an article in the *Los Angeles Times*, staff writer Betty Goodwin, closed with the following observations:

> Explains Kelli Questrom, who is married to Bullock's and Bullocks Wilshire chairman and chief executive Allen Questrom: "When I wear jeans with Chanel, I'm combining two remarkably classic things—classic jeans with a classic jacket."
>
> Tina Chow, a regular on the best-dressed lists and wife of restaurateur Michael Chow, concurs. She may take a pair of black velvet trousers from Chanel couture and wear them with an oversize man's polo shirt. After all, Chow reasons, "Chanel was the first one who raided the men's cupboard."
>
> True. Chanel did poke through her lovers' closets for ties, boots, shirts and, ultimately, the ideas that were behind all of her innovations. It was Chanel's tailored suits, trousers and the concept of loose-fitting, comfortable clothes that freed women from the bustles and corsets of the day.
>
> Chanel was the original borrower. (Goodwin, 1985)

Contemporary designer labels also show us how contemporary tailoring employs new technologies. Contemporary tailoring mixes fusible interfacings with both hand and machine stitching to give a garment a soft, tailored look—this is the look of the higher-end, or designer, tailor. For most of the tailored garments we wear today, fusible inner structures completely eliminate the need for hand stitching, making the construction very fast and inexpensive—this method is also used for designer garments as well as for the mass market.

THE EVOLUTION OF TAILORED FASHION DESIGN

Tailoring has a long history. Initially, tailored clothing was made only for gentlemen, whereas women had their clothing made by dressmakers. Think of the painter using soft brush strokes and the sculptor using a hammer and chisel. In dressmaking the fabric is draped and wrapped around the body as a painter brushes a canvas; the dressmaker's efforts result in a garment that adjusts to the wearer, taking its shape from the body. The tailor can begin in the same way, cutting the fabric into precise pattern pieces and sewing them together. But then these pieces are reinforced, shaped, padded, and interfaced as the sculptor works his medium. The name tailor, in fact, comes from the French word *tailleur*—one who cuts.

Emergence of the Informal

Men's dress continued to be very formal until 1860, when Edward VII, Prince of Wales, had the tailoring company of Henry Poole make for him an evening suit with no tails. In 1886, American James Potter watched the prince wear his "informal" evening suit at Sandringham, England, had the style copied by his own tailor, and wore it to his club at home in Tuxedo Park, New York. There it became popular and almost a club uniform; this became known as the tuxedo.

For entertaining at home, the smoking jacket was worn. This was a cross between a dressing gown and dinner jacket. Typically it was made of dark velvet, embellished with piping and braid and was never to be worn on the street (*The Fairchild Encyclopedia of Menswear,* 2008, p. 368).

Figure 1.3 The dinner jacket or tuxedo was introduced into women's wear by Yves Saint Laurent in the 1960s and has since become a staple.

The dinner jacket or tuxedo was introduced into women's wear by Yves Saint Laurent in the 1960s and has since become a staple (Seeling, 2000, p. 356).

Tailoring for Women

Before 1675, male tailors manufactured the clothing throughout France. Women were legally restricted to sew unshaped underwear and sleepwear. This, at the time, was the biggest paid occupation for women in France. Some of these women seamstresses began to establish a reputation as dressmakers. The tailors, intolerant of this competition, retaliated by seeking monetary damages and confiscating fabrics. The women petitioned the King for the right to form a guild of female tailors, and the application was approved. This resulted in more jobs, offered more opportunities for women to hone and take pride in their skills, and allowed women to train generations of young girls to become skilled needle workers. The guilds were disbanded in France in 1791 (Crowston, 2001).

Towards the end of the eighteenth century, English women adapted the riding costume worn by men. This tough hardwearing riding coat showed English tailoring at its best. Tailored to the waist, with a high collar and generous skirts, it did not restrain the wearer when riding. Crossing the English Channel, it became known in France as the Redingote. Later, it became the model for the nineteenth-century formal frock coat, worn by businessmen up until World War I.

Figure 1.4 Marie Adelaide de Savoire, Duchesse de Bourgogne, in a riding habit, early 1700s, by Pierre Gobert.

Back in France, the jacket and skirt became the new spirit of the age and the costume of the French Revolutionaries. Women not only wore this jacket for riding sports and walking, but also highly embellished for fashionable wear.

Ladies Departments and Home Patterns

By the middle of the nineteenth century tailors in both London and Paris had "ladies" departments. Women of society had their jackets made by dressmakers such as the English dressmaker Charles Frederick Worth or bespoke tailors such as John Redfern. (The English tailor Redfern is generally accredited for making the first "tailor made" lady's suit.) Women of lesser means purchased the jacket ready to wear or made it themselves from patterns offered in women's magazines. Women's tailoring expanded throughout the nineteenth century, becoming more than a fashionable garment; it was an expression of the new women of independence (Aldrich, p. 16).

Figure 1.6 The Prince of Wales took the world of men's fashion by storm.

Figure 1.5 The women's jacket was to mark the new spirit of the age and the costume of the French Revolutionaries.

The Influence of the Prince of Wales

Before World War I men's clothing was utilitarian and Victorian influenced. This all changed after the war as businesses boomed, particularly in America. It was the English style of dress that American men liked. The Prince of Wales, who was to become Edward VIII (who then abdicated in 1936), was the trendsetter. By the early 1930s, the "drape cut" or "London drape" suit championed by Frederick Sholte, tailor to the Prince of Wales, was taking the world of men's fashion by storm. This new suit was softer and more flexible in construction than the suits of the previous generation; extra fabric in the shoulder and **armscye**, light padding, a slightly nipped waist, and fuller sleeves tapered at the wrist resulted in a cut with flattering folds or drapes front and back that enhanced a man's figure. Clothing industry advertising used his name by claiming "As worn by the Prince" in their advertisements (Flusser, 1985, p. 4). The Prince of Wales was also responsible for the double-breasted jacket with the long roll lapel the tab collar and the Windsor knot.

The Influence of Hollywood

In the early 1930s, men had become increasingly more interested in being in fashion. With the Great Depression, men as well as women turned to the movies for escape. They watched impeccably dressed movie stars who became the trendsetters. Between 1930 and 1936 basic shapes were created that still prevail in menswear today. Men learned that their clothing should conform and flatter the natural lines of the body rather than hide them under bulky clothing and that every man could show his personality and style though his clothing. They also leaned that clothing could be comfortable if the fit was right. At the same time, Schiaparelli was to change women's fashion from soft to hard. She introduced bold color, and by 1933 the emphasis was on the wide shoulders and narrow waists rather than on the hips of the 1920s.

By the early 1940s, Hollywood tailors had exaggerated the drape to the point of caricature, outfitting film noir mobsters and private eyes in suits with heavily padded chests, enormous shoulders, and wide flowing trousers. African American tailors in Harlem re-cut and reinvented the frock coat that emerged as the zoot suit. The zoot suit was to be adopted by musicians and other fashion experimenters.

The Influence of World War II

World War II placed restrictions on the clothing industry. Women began to make as much as possible themselves using what they had at hand. Magazine and pattern companies showed women how to remake men's suits into smart ladies outfits as the men were in uniform and had no use for the suits. Eisenhower jackets became popular with women, influenced by the

Figure 1.7 African American tailors in Harlem re-cut and reinvented the frock coat that emerged as the zoot suit.

Figure 1.8 Returning servicemen were given a suit upon turning in their uniforms at the end of World War II.

military; these jackets were bloused at the bust and fitted at the waist with a belt. In England, the ready-made "demob" suit was issued to all men on their discharge from the armed forces to help them return to "civvy" street (Figure 1.8).

Post-War Style: Italian Influence and "Off the Peg"

In the late 1940s, Savile Row tried to steer men back to a more dandified style, but the mood was for a more casual dress. In Britain, men and women still had to make do rather than dress as they might have wished. But in 1948, the "New Look" took off. Haute couture was to be translated into affordable and reasonably priced copies.

In the 1950s Italian fashion was established as a new standard of men's classic elegance. This brought to the market softer cuts and fabrics, with more of an emphasis on comfort.

In Florence, in 1952, Brioni presented its menswear collection on the runway, thereby inventing the contemporary menswear show. Brioni made its name by reducing the shoulder pad and the amount of fabric used in a suit; this changed the silhouette and simplified the line. It eliminated pocket flaps, pleats, and cuffs. It also used fabrics such as silk Shantung and offered a great choice of color. Brioni perfected a construction system that combined a high amount of hand finishing with quick assembly. This gave the impression of bespoke but was produced at high speed offering convenience of ready-made. Brioni began selling off-the-peg, or ready-to-wear, suits in 1960.

Tommy Nutter, a Savile Row tailor, believed that a man of fashion should change his image and renew his style as frequently as a fashionable woman. It was Tommy Nutter who created the white wedding suits for John Lennon and Yoko Ono, and Mick and Bianca Jagger. Beatles John, Paul, and Ringo were all clients as were their wives. They wore Tommy Nutter for the album cover of *Abby Road*. Nutter would not be restrained by tradition. His jackets had nipped-in waists, flaring skirts, extraordinarily wide lapels, and strongly padded shoulders. Here we see a tailor who brought an innovative designer's sensibility to his work (McDowell, 1997, p. 172).

Figure 1.9a and b Both (a) Pierce Brosnan as James Bond and (b) Donald Trump dressed in Brioni.

Figure 1.10 "Off the peg clothing made acceptable." An advertisement for Tommy Nutters' ready to wear collection 1980.

Designing a Classic Look without the Classic Rules

In the 1970s, Ralph Lauren mass marketed quality clothing to a high standard. Lauren was not trained as a fashion designer but went to college for business studies. He was able to see a commercial potential in menswear by taking a different approach to the other menswear designers at the time. Menswear had become overly decorated, flashy, and influenced by woman's fashion trends. Color, print decoration, embellishment, and fabric had become more important than cut, with some menswear designers going over the top (McDowell, 1993, p. 173). Lauren designed classic nostalgic garments that he understated with a relaxed sporty Ivy League style. In 1974, he dressed the men in the movie *The Great Gatsby* and went on to dress Diane Keaton in the 1977 movie *Annie Hall*. Since then, he has marketed and built an empire as what designer Karl Lagerfeld once called "The American Gatsby-dream designer" (Figure 1.11) (*The Fairchild Encyclopedia of Menswear,* 2008, p. 213).

Figure 1.11 Ralph Lauren is known for his classic lifestyle looks.

Figure 1.12 Armani is known for a relaxed comfortable elegance.

The Armani Look

Giorgio Armani brought men's suits to women's wear in the 1980s. These garments were simply and elegantly cut and became the symbol of relaxed, comfortable, business attire for both genders. Armani achieved this by softening and reducing the internal structure. All age groups could wear the Armani look because there are no gimmicks or fashion fads. But like Ralph Lauren, much of Armani's timeless style relies on his excellent business sense. By total contrast, Gianni Versace injected huge doses of sex and rock 'n' roll into the staid world of the Milan runway. He made it fashionable for both men and women to be flamboyantly sexy. Gianni Versace created distinctive, avant-garde designs. He admired the work of the French designer Paul Poiret, as you can see in his use of theatrical fantasy, luxurious fabrics, brilliant use of color and print that was to become unmistakably his own. Leather, body wrapping for sensuality, a bold silhouette, and over-sizing for comfort accented both Versace's men's and women's wear. Versace played with asymmetry and bias cutting to produce a continuous rotation around the body, rather than a distinctive front and back. Versace's menswear was sometimes criticized as being futuristic with its big shoulders and technological detailing seeming to suggest science fiction. Line was important, and he used lines to define the waist, shoulders, and center fronts of his coats, dress, and suits (Martin & Benét, 2009).

The *Enfant Terrible*

The *"enfant terrible"* Jean Paul Gaultier began his career by working for both Cardin and Jacques Esterel before producing a small women's wear collection under his own name in 1978. He did so because he could find nothing that he really wanted, particularly in terms of sizing, and even unstructured Armani jackets seemed too small. He noticed that men had been buying his women's jackets because of the unusual fabrics and cut, so he began his seminal reworking of the pinstriped suit for both men and women. Gaultier presented his first menswear collection in 1984. He displayed a traditional male wardrobe by redesigning such classics as the navy blazer while dismantling clichés of masculine styling by producing skirts, corsets, and tutus for men. During one notorious catwalk show, female models smoked pipes and men paraded in transparent lace skirts. This acknowledgement of male narcissism and interest in the creation of erotic clothing for men, as shown in the Man-Object Collection of 1982 was to influence designers such as Gianni Versace into mid-1990s (Cox & Raugust, 2009).

In 1996, Gaultier presented a menswear collection that he called "Homme Couture." As Amy M. Spindler put it in a New York Times fashion review:

> [Gaultier] had long threatened to design couture, and finally, he did—for men. Somewhat left of Savile Row and right of a drag show, Mr. Gaultier showed his own classics gussied up in couture style. The show started with strict tailored suits, and the ante kept going up. There was his No. 24, "Nightclubbing," a sparkling black knit suit with a sweater of giraffe and leather, and then there was No. 53, "Mermaids Ball," champagne-color flared pants with tulle beneath. The show ended with "Le Plus Beau Jour," a white bridal redingote. Mr. Gaultier is more than capable of conquering couture, but since no one has yet asked, he did it his own way. (Spindler, 1996)

Figure 1.13 The designer has put this man into a skirt and cropped jacket.

Change and Challenge

In the 1990s Ozwald Boateng became known for body hugging fits and bold colored suits—something that London's Savile Row had not seen since the 1960s. Radical designer Alexander McQueen began his career with an apprenticeship to a Savile Row tailoring company, Savile Row being to men what haute couture is to women.

The influences of fashion and mass manufacturing continue to change both the cut and construction of the jacket. The cost today of producing a hand-tailored jacket means that far fewer hand-tailored jackets are made. Most jackets are mass produced. On one hand, this means that styles are repeated so everything begins to look the same. On the other, we have a design challenge for the contemporary designer.

Figure 1.14 Ozwald Boateng introduced conservative Savile Row to a whole new concept and customer.

REFERENCES

Aldrich, W. (2002). *Pattern Cutting for Women's Tailored Jackets.* New York: John Wiley & Sons.

Cox, C. & Raugust, K. "Jean-Paul Gaultier," Fashion Encyclopedia. Retrieved on October 28, 2009 from http://www.fashionencyclopedia.com/To-Vi/Versace-Gianni.html#ixzz0UKA9b6So

Crowston, C. H. (2001). *Fabricating Women: The Seamstresses of Old Regime France, 1675-1791.* Durham, NC: Duke University Press.

Flusser, A. (1985). *Clothes and the Man: The Principle of Fine Men's Dress.* New York: Villard Books.

Gavenas, M. L. (2008). *The Fairchild Encyclopedia of Menswear.* New York: Fairchild Books.

Goodwin, B. (1985, June 28). "Contemporary Role for Chanel's Classics Stirs Up Controversy," *Los Angeles Times.* Retrieved on October 28, 2009 from http://articles.latimes.com/1985-06-28/news/vw-1524_1

Martin, R. & Benét, S. (2009.) "Gianni Versace," Fashion Encyclopedia. Retrieved on October 28, 2009 from http://www.fashionencyclopedia.com/To-Vi/Versace-Gianni.html#ixzz0UKA9b6So

McDowell, C. (1997). *The Man of Fashion: Peacock Males and Perfect Gentleman.* London: Thames & Hudson.

Seeling, C. (2000). *Fashion: The Century of the Designer.* Cologne: Konemann.

Spindler, A. (1996, January 30). "Review/Fashion; In Paris, Men's Wear Fit for Parody," *New York Times.* Retrieved Oct. 28, 2009 from http://www.nytimes.com/1996/01/30/us/review-fashion-in-paris-men-s-wear-fit-for-parody.html?pagewanted=1

Wilde, O. (1891). *The Picture of Dorian Gray.* New York: W.W. Norton & Co.

CHAPTER 2

Design Workshop

Some people focus on retro, meaning sixties and seventies revivals. Some people stick to very traditional classic clothing, what we call real clothes, very easy to put on, simple clothes. I wanted to create something that didn't belong to any of these categories, and go forward.

—Rei Kawakubo

CHAPTER OBJECTIVES

After reading this chapter, you should be able to:

Determine and express your inspiration.

Take inspiration from history.

Establish the silhouette, proportion, line, scale, and volume of your jacket design.

Use design details in clever ways to create different styles.

Use color and texture to dictate the mood and season of the jacket.

We all interpret fashion differently. This is what marks us as individuals and what makes our designs individual. If I were to give the same basic notch collar jacket pattern to ten different designers to make, it would come back as ten different jackets. Jean Paul Gaultier plays with both gender and sexuality whereas Armani brings an ageless sophistication and faultless technique, ignoring fads and gimmicks. Paul Smith brings combinations of humor, color, and print to his tailoring.

What will you bring to yours?

FINDING YOUR INSPIRATION

You can find inspiration everywhere and anywhere. Designers need to continually look for new inspiration to keep their work looking fresh and contemporary. Two of the best ways to find inspiration are (1) sourcing material such as pictures from magazines, fabrics, or fastenings, and (2) finding and working from a theme or concept. Inspiration can be personal, literal, or abstract.

Sources for personal inspiration may include music, film, screen goddesses from the past, celebrities, art, a favorite movie, and your list may go on and on. Personal inspiration refers to your tastes, personality, background, social standing, and experiences. Literal inspiration may come from military uniforms, travel, world events, something that you have read, and ethnic or folk customs. Literal inspiration means exactly that—literally mirroring social influences tempered by your opinion or objectively interpreted. Abstract inspiration may include a mixture of both personal and literal but in a vague, unclear, dreamy way. For example, let's consider the movie *Lady in White,* based on the book by Wilkie Collins. This is a dark romance with a Victorian edge. What kind of garments might evoke this mood? Your inspiration might come from a period piece, or it might be something that you've seen, read, or simply felt.

Collect images and items that appeal to you and pin them onto a board. In Figure 2.2, we see how Christian Lacroix has found and pinned fabric swatches, photos, and other bits and pieces onto a wall. Here we can see three elements of the design process coming together: the photograph, the fabric swatches, and snapshots of both people and garments from all eras. A close look at the design of the garment in the snapshot reveals that gender hasn't entered into the equation even though this is a women's wear collection.

Figure 2.1 The half-scale suit has become the design detail on the front of this dress.

Figure 2.2 All of the research is pinned up on the wall for this collection in the Christian Lacroix design studio (Mower, 2009).

If you were given the photograph in Figure 2.2, what would have inspired you and how would you have used it?

- What season would you design for using this wall of inspiration?
- Who do you think that the customer would be? To be able to design anything you must know who you are designing for.
- Would you have made gender more important?
- Would you have made the same fabric choices?
- Inspiration can lead you anywhere you choose; it is your eye that will establish the visual connection to an image or object that "clicks."

Inspiration can lead you anywhere you choose; it is your eye that will establish the visual connection to an image or object that "clicks."

Taking Inspiration from History

You can allow history to inspire you from both source material or an abstract theme or concept. Alexander McQueen's "It's a Jungle out There," 1997–'98, mixes religious paintings and the African antelope. The back of this jacket has a detail from the painting "The Crucified Thief" (1410), attributed to the Flemish painter Robert Campin (Figure 2.3). Here you see protruding from the pagoda shoulders a pair of twisted Giselle horns. How would you use this inspiration? Do you think it has something to do with the power of women, or is it more about the victim and the aggressor?

Vivienne Westwood drew from pirates as well as the taffeta-gowned beauties of the seventeenth- and eighteenth-century painters Fragonard and Boucher to inspire different collections. John Galliano has used

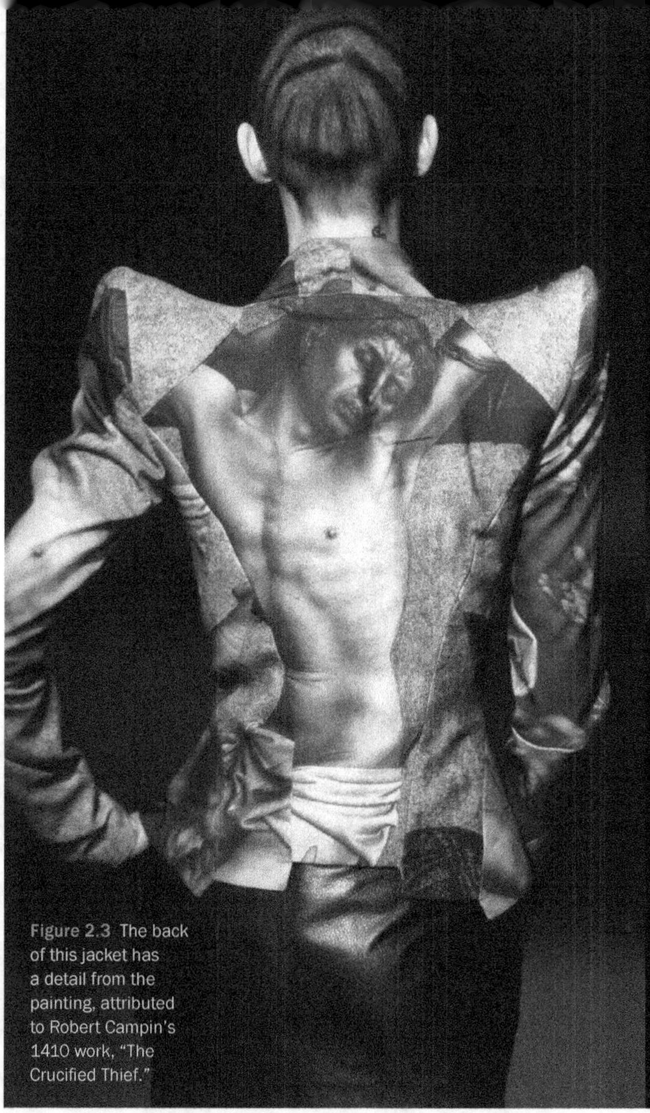

Figure 2.3 The back of this jacket has a detail from the painting, attributed to Robert Campin's 1410 work, "The Crucified Thief."

Figure 2.4 "It came from a research trip to L.A.," Galliano said. "I went around the old houses of Hollywood and imagined how stars like Tallulah Bankhead, Lillian Gish, and Mary Pickford lived" (Mower, 2009).

the circus, the French Revolution, and punk singer Siouxsie Sioux to inspire his work. Figure 2.4 shows a photo from John Galliano's spring 2010 ready to wear show. In this photo, you can see a dreamy parallel with the small part of French history that inspired his degree show in July of 1984 at the St. Martins School of Art. In it, Galliano distorted and exaggerated the clothing worn by the *Incroyables*—a rebellious youth movement that flared up during the French Revolution.

Figure 2.5 is a photograph of a Pourpoint coat that is padded or quilted and would have been worn belted with long hose. Vivienne Westwood used this coat for inspiration in the Man Fall/Winter 1996 collection that was shown in Milan. The quilting was replaced with a beautiful camel hair fabric. The button detail up the sleeve and down the front was removed with the detail now being large patch pockets at hip level, but the silhouette remained the same as was the cut. All that changed was the length. It became a modern coat.

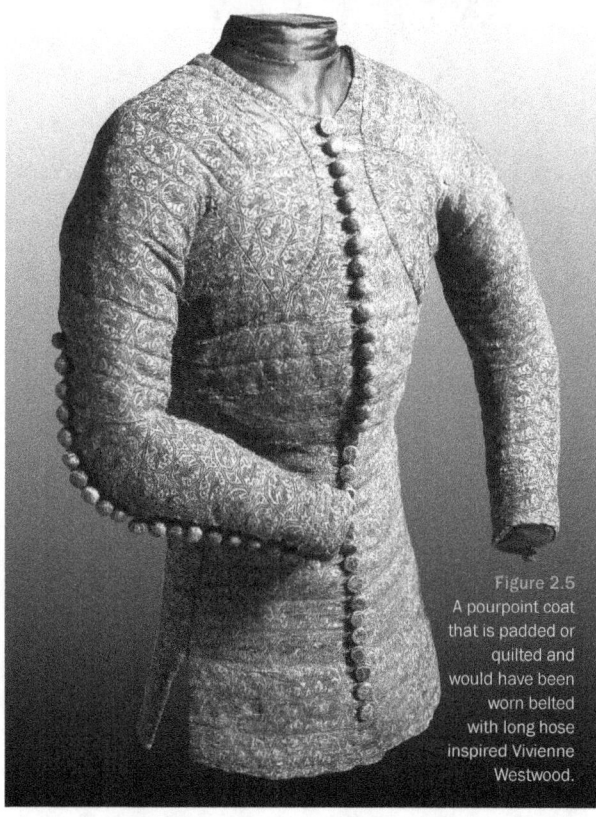

Figure 2.5 A pourpoint coat that is padded or quilted and would have been worn belted with long hose inspired Vivienne Westwood.

John Galliano retained the New Look's spirit and glamour but added a modern fashion ingredient—sex—to Christian Dior's 1947 Bar suit, which encapsulates the spirit of the New Look. (Figures 2.6 and 2.7).

Alexander McQueen refers to historical periods, combining them into postmodern constructions.

Figure 2.6
Dior's famous Bar jacket drawn by Rene Gruau.

Figure 2.7
John Galliano's spirit of the New Look for Dior's sixtieth anniversary, Dior, 2007, Couture.

Figure 2.8
Look at the front of the McQueen jacket from his show "It's a jungle out there." Here you see it representing the African antelope.

FROM INSPIRATION TO DESIGN

Working with your inspiration, you are now going to start to develop your design for a new jacket. As you begin to sketch out your ideas—and continuing right up through your final sketches—keep thinking about how you will use the elements of design to articulate your inspiration. If the elements tie in strongly with your theme to work as a whole, you will make a statement with your designs.

Consider the following examples.

Silhouette

The silhouette, or overall shape of the jacket, should be considered. Determine which part of the body you want to emphasize. Figure 2.9 shows an exaggerated upswept broadened shoulder while keeping all the other proportions correct. Look at what this does to the torso, making the waist and hip appear smaller. Do you see how it has formed a V or wedge-shaped tapered torso? Think of what would happen when you turn the wedge or V upside down, as seen in Figure 2.10. The shoulders appear smaller as the eye travels up the torso from the exaggerated hip.

Figure 2.9 Exaggerated shoulders form a wedge or V shape, which makes the waist and hip appear smaller.

Figure 2.10 Here you see the wedge or V turned upside down, exaggerating the hip line and making the shoulders look smaller.

Figure 2.11
Stella McCartney's jacket silhouette is rectangular.

Figure 2.12
The silhouette of the coat cocoons the body.

In Figure 2.11, Stella McCartney's jacket silhouette is a rectangle shape. The body looks long and lean, whereas Figure 2.12 shows the silhouette of the coat cocooning the body. The classic hourglass silhouette is seen in the Lanvin jacket in Figure 2.13. It is also the silhouette of Christian Dior's 1947 Bar suit (See Figure 2.7).

Scale and Volume

Scale and volume can be taken to extremes; waistlines can be lowered or raised, shoulders narrowed or widened, and hips exaggerated (as seen in Figures 2.10 and 2.11). For the suit in Figure 2.14, the designers borrowed from eighteenth-century male dress. Think how this will

Figure 2.13
The classic hourglass silhouette is seen here in the Lavin jacket. It is also the silhouette of Christian Dior's 1947 Bar suit.

Figure 2.14 Scale and volume can be taken to extremes. Waistlines can be lowered or raised, shoulders can be narrowed or widened, and hips exaggerated.

swing when its wearer walks. Note how the geometric sculpture in the draped grey jersey shown in Figure 2.15 is forming a fluid blouson from under the bust.

Proportion and Line

The proportion is how the body is broken up. Proportion develops from the silhouette and can be vertical, horizontal, curved, diagonal, or articulated through color blocking or fabric. We all like to play with our own proportions; it is a part of dressing. Line is the cut of a garment; this is achieved or can be modified by the placement of darts or seams. Figure 2.16 shows how the proportion is broken with soft curves. In Figure 2.17 the proportion is broken up with horizontal lines, and in Figure 2.18 by blocks of color and fabric. The buttons on the double-breasted jacket in Figure 2.19 give a strong vertical line.

Here are some facts to note about proportion and line:

- Vertical lines lengthen the body.
- Horizontal lines emphasize width.
- Straight lines are seen as hard and masculine.
- Curved lines are seen as soft and feminine.
- Seams and darts can be moved around the body.
- Different hem lengths create horizontal lines across the body.

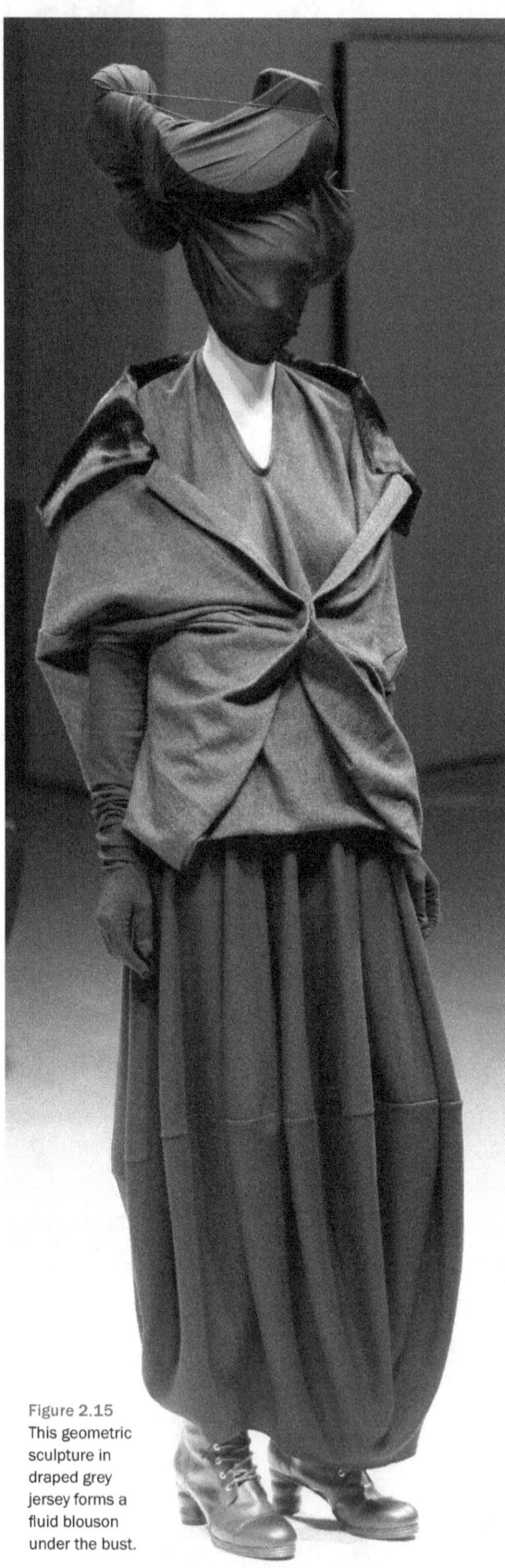

Figure 2.15
This geometric sculpture in draped grey jersey forms a fluid blouson under the bust.

Figure 2.16
Notice how the proportion is broken with soft curves.

Figure 2.17 The proportion is broken with horizontal lines.

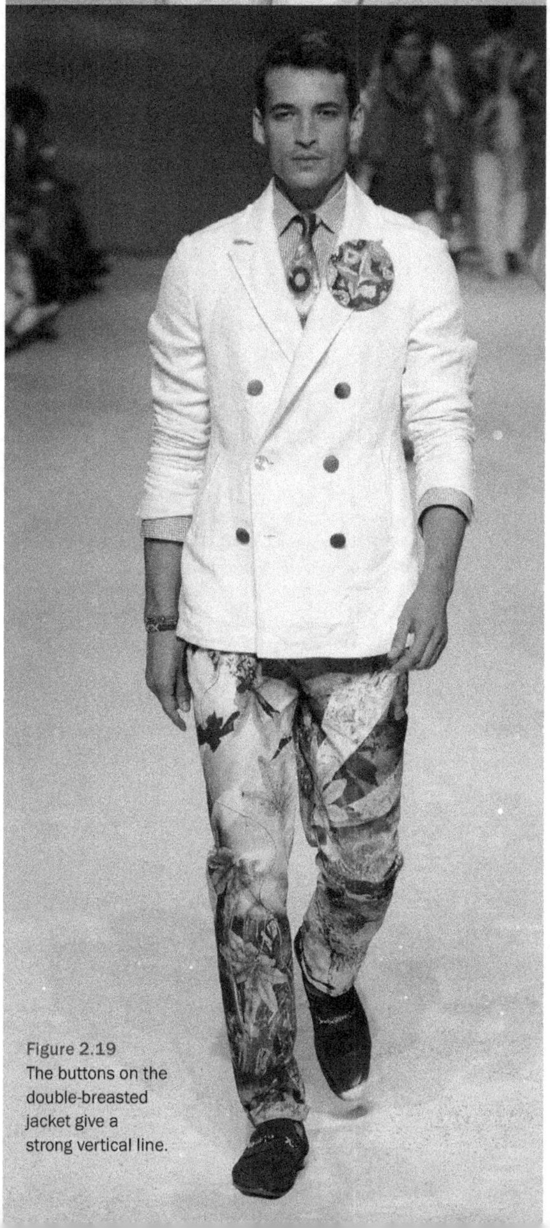

Figure 2.19 The buttons on the double-breasted jacket give a strong vertical line.

Figure 2.18 Here the proportion is broken by blocks of color and fabric work.

DESIGN WORKSHOP

Figure 2.20 Details can create the romantic feeling.

Figure 2.21 The eye is drawn to the pop of color that trims the edge of this classic single-breasted men's suit. This is what makes it stand apart and gives it identity.

Details

A jacket that has a dramatic silhouette and good line must also have great detail.

Clever use of detail can give your jacket identity and make it unique. Look at the details used in the photograph from Comme des Garcons collection, "Here come the brides" (Figure 2.20). The jacket is a Victorian-cropped creation of lace, ruffles, and leg of mutton sleeves. It is the details that create the romantic feeling.

Details are even more important in menswear, which has a more conservative clientele. The eye is drawn to the pop of color that trims the edge of the classic single-breasted men's suit shown in Figure 2.21. This is what makes it stand apart and gives it identity.

The tailoring of the jacket in Figure 2.22 is interrupted by a tie erratically stitched down beside some plaid and Aran knit. This plays skillfully with detail on what would otherwise be sober masculine dress.

Figure 2.22
The tailoring of this jacket was interrupted by a tie erratically stitched down beside some plaid and Aran knit.

In Figure 2.23, Lanvin has made hardware in the form of a hinge into a necklace. What would happen if this became the jacket fastening?

Details are practical considerations. Which fastening or pocket should you choose? Should your garment have top stitching or added braids or trims? Note the mix of color, texture, and trim detail on the pockets in the photograph of the Chanel jacket in Figure 2.24. The inspiration for this jacket and collection is from the

Figure 2.23
In "Hardware," Lanvin used the form of a hinge in a necklace. What would happen if this became the jacket fastening?

DESIGN WORKSHOP

25

Figure 2.24 Details are practical considerations, such as choosing fastenings or pockets, whether to have top stitching, and add braids or trims. This Chanel jacket uses a mix of color, texture, and trim detail on the pockets.

Figure 2.25 There are rules about how certain pockets should look and be made, but these rules can be distorted and reinvented.

British Regency dandy Beau Brummell. So, here again you can see that gender was not an obstacle when researching for inspiration.

There are rules for how certain pockets should look and be made, but these rules can be distorted and reinvented. In Figure 2.25, this is not where we usually expect to see a pocket. We are used to seeing pockets at the hip, not twisted around to the center front. But this adds to the detail of the design. It is original and unique. Remember, in fashion rules are made to be broken!

Color

Today, color is a key factor for both genders. Color hues and values change with every season. Color is one of the earliest decisions to make when designing. We all respond intuitively and even physically to color. White will make you feel cool. Blue and green are calming. Yellow is a sunny, friendly color. Black is slimming, sophisticated, and elegant. Red is seen as sexy and fun. Color is affected by both the season and climate. White and pastel colors reflect heat, so these are more often worn in summer, whereas in winter we are drawn to warm, dark colors that help retain body heat.

Contrast

Contrast causes the eye to re-evaluate the importance of one focal area against another. Looking at the draped black and white jacket shown in Figure 2.26, note how the eye is drawn to the middle section of the jacket where the belt is a contrast of gold and black. There would not have been such a strong impact if the belt had been black and even less so if the belt had been white.

For tailoring, medium to dark colors hide the inner structure of the garment better than light colors, but darker colors can be over-pressed to obtain a shiny surface. Darker colors also hide soil and general wear and tear from handling.

Figure 2.26 Contrast causes the eye to re-evaluate the importance of one focal area against another.

Figure 2.27
This brown woolen jacket looks warm and practical.

Texture

Texture refers to the look and feel of the fabric. Texture can affect the appearance of the silhouette, giving it a bulky or slender look, depending on the roughness or smoothness of the material. The brown woolen jacket in Figure 2.27 looks warm and practical compared to the one shown in Figure 2.28. Here, the jacket is made of heavy satin, and you can see how the light influences the drape. Light affects color by causing the surface to either reflect or absorb it.

Fabric

We will consider fabric choices in detail in the next chapter. However, I hope that while you have been considering how the elements of design affect your final garment, you have been thinking about the fabric for your jacket. If you have already chosen your fabric, knowing what you can design with it is very important. Chiffon, for example, would not be a good choice for a tailored jacket, and leather (unless it is the softest lamb) does not drape well. You should also take season into consideration. Mood and color can be interpreted by fabric, as can texture. Your choice of fabric can alter the silhouette, and you may have to re-think the details.

Figure 2.28 Texture involves the look and feel of the fabric. The roughness or smoothness of the material can affect the appearance of the silhouette, giving it a bulky or slender look.

BOX 2.1 **Vivienne Westwood**

Box Figure 2.1a and b
Vive la Cocotte Historic collection, fall/winter, 1995.

At 17, Vivienne Isabel Swire moved with her family to London from Derbyshire, England, where she was born. Her first husband was Derek Westwood; they were married for three years. In 1965 she met art student Malcolm McLaren. They became a couple.

In 1970, she and McLaren were offered the back area of a store called Paradise Garage located at 430 Kings Road. There they sold second-hand 'fifties records and memorabilia collected from flea markets. Eventually the entire store was turned over to them, and they added vintage clothes and four newly made teddy-boy suits. Westwood started to take the vintage clothes apart and copy them. They renamed the store Let It Rock.

LETTING IT ROCK

For ten years the couple ran the store on the Kings Road together. It was redecorated and renamed many times, and became the center for the growing Punk movement. Westwood continued to work on the clothes, which were distressed and appliquéd with badges, flags, and slogans. To this, rips, zips, porn, slogans, bondage accoutrements, and chains were added that led to the birth of the Punk style. The store was redecorated and reopened to immediate cult status as Seditionaries. McLaren formed and managed the Sex Pistols while Westwood dressed them.

BEYOND THE SEX PISTOLS

Disillusioned after the collapse of the Sex Pistols and working on the fringes, Westwood began researching historical dress and studying art history. Increasingly inspired by art history and the details of past fashion, she rejected her dressmaking approach of the Punk era (Spens, 2006). She found patterns of eighteenth-century men's clothing from research at both the Victoria and Albert Museum and National Art Library and transformed them into the Pirates collection with their first runway show in 1981.

Westwood continued to study the cut of old garments, copying their cut and turning them into toiles, reinterpreting them into her patterns to make them modern. This became the foundation of her distinctive technique that is based on squares, rectangles, and triangular gussets. By adding semi circles and curved seams, inspired by the organic silhouette of animal hides, she found this gave fullness to the fabric while skillful folding created air pockets in the fabric.

EVERYTHING OLD IS NEW AGAIN

Each of Westwood's collections had a name and concept. She began to focus on the classic proportions on English tailoring and with the "Mini Crini" collection, English tailoring became the basis of her work.

A new confidence in tailoring was seen in 1990 as Westwood went on to study the work of French couturier Christian Dior.

Westwood was convinced that fashion is the result of the exchange of ideas between France and England. The English side has the tailoring and an easy charm, and the French side offers solidity of design and proportion that comes from never being satisfied; something can always be done to make it better, more refined (Westwood, 1997).

Westwood continued her scrutiny into tailoring from collection to collection, from the plain eighteenth-century frock coat to the Savile Row suit, from a pink riding jacket to the innovative cutting and piecing of fabric around the body. Some of her suits are molded to the body whereas others form dynamic structures with folds and pleats.

WORLD'S END AND BEYOND

The boutique on the Kings Road, now called World's End, continues to carry Westwood's collections. She remains one of England's most influential designers, influencing designers such as Karl Lagerfeld and John Galliano.

Westwood was advanced from the Order of the British Empire to The Most Excellent Order of the British Empire in the 2006 New Year's Honours List *for services to fashion,* and has thrice earned the award for British Designer of the Year.

Westwood sees fashion as personal propaganda, as an agent of arousal both physical and mental. The way clothes feel is as important as the way they look. To this end, she distorts, exaggerates, and pares away the natural shape of the body, often using the constructions she found in historical costume. She also gives each ensemble an agenda, laden with historical references that, she says, "have a certain type of nostalgia which is how I would define glamour. They are part of the story of human culture" (Westwood, 1997).

CHAPTER CHECKLIST

Before moving on to the next chapter, critique your design. Make sure you can answer the following questions:

- ☐ Is your inspiration reflected in your design?
- ☐ Does the design for your jacket reflect the intended season?
- ☐ Is your design appropriate for the person who will wear the garment?
- ☐ Have you chosen the fabric, color, and texture suitable for your design?
- ☐ Does the silhouette contribute appropriately to your jacket design?
- ☐ Is the line and proportion of your jacket appropriate for your intended design?
- ☐ Is your design original?
- ☐ Have you made clever use of detail in your jacket design?
- ☐ Does your design have too many details? Sometimes the best design is the simplest.

REFERENCES

Dieuzaide, M. (Preface by Morin, E.) (1992) *Etre flamenco*. France: Julliard Paris.

Kawakubo, R. (1997, March 1). *Guardian* magazine.

Mower, S. "Paris," Style.com. Retrieved May 18, 2010, from http://www.style.com/fashionshows/review/S2010RTW-JNGALLNO.

Spens, C. (2006, October 30) "Vivienne Westwood: A Retrospective." Retrieved on December 15, 2009 from www.studio-international.co.uk/reports/westwood.asp

Westwood, V. (1997) *Vivienne Westwood* (memoir). London: Thames & Hudson.

Wilcox, C. (2004) "Vivienne Westwood." Exhibition materials. London: Victoria & Albert Museum.

CHAPTER 3

Looking at Fabric

Fabric not only expresses a designer's dream, but also stimulates his own ideas. It can be the beginning of an inspiration. Many a dress of mine is born of the fabric alone.

—Christian Dior

CHAPTER OBJECTIVES

After reading this chapter, you should be able to:

Determine the correct fabric choice for your jacket design.

Evaluate working with plaid or printed fabrics that have to be matched.

Determine the placement of a dominant stripe in the jacket design.

Use the lining to add visual interest to the jacket design.

Understand why interfacings are important in tailoring.

Know how to make the inner structure work for the design with correct placement.

Evaluate your choice of interfacing.

Your choice of fabric is one of the first decisions to make. You should base your decision on: (1) the type of jacket and its design, (2) its planned use and quality, and (3) the fabric characteristics and performance.

Figure 3.1 A jacket by John Galliano for Christian Dior's Couture collection.

FABRIC CHOICE

For a first tailoring project, I would recommend that you use a woolen fabric. Wool responds well to steam pressing and shaping. Table 3.1 shows different fabric characteristics to consider when selecting your fabrics.

When selecting your fabric to help determine how it will respond to both sewing and wearing, you can test it by:

1. Crushing a corner of the fabric in your hand and releasing it. If it remains creased and wrinkled, it will be difficult to tailor.

2. Pushing the fabric with your thumbs. If the yarns separate and the fabric doesn't recover its shape, it will stretch out of shape when it is sewn or worn.

3. Draping the fabric over the shoulder to see how it falls. Heavy, unflattering folds will be more difficult to tailor.

Figure 3.2 In this photo the tweed herringbone wool fabric has been turned into lace by the designer.

TABLE 3.1
Fabric Characteristics to Consider when Choosing a Fabric for Tailoring

CHARACTERISTICS OF FABRIC	EASY TO TAILOR	DIFFICULT TO TAILOR
Fiber content	• Natural fibers press and shape well. They shrink to reduce excess ease. • Stitches blend or sink into the fabric. • Woolens and tweeds are the easiest because stitches disappear into the texture of the fabric.	• Worsted wools such as gabardine show every flaw. • Synthetic fibers don't press or shape easily. • Manufactured fibers—heat-set creases are hard to remove.
Color	• Medium to darker colors hide the inner construction.	• Light colors—inner construction can show through. • Dark colors become shiny when over-pressed.
Weight	• Medium weight presses and shapes easier.	• Heavy or bulky fabrics are harder to handle and press. • Lightweight fabrics are easily over-worked. The inner structure can shadow through.
Texture	• Surface textures hide imperfections. • Fancy weaves and patterns also help to hide flaws, but may have to be pattern-matched.	• Smooth, hard finished fabrics show imperfect stitching. They are harder to press and shape. • Napped fabrics require special pressing and pattern layout.
Weave	• Medium weaves are more flexible. They hold their shape well and are also easier to manipulate by hand. Stitches tend to blend into medium weaves.	• Loosely woven fabrics stretch out of shape. They are best suited to the fusible tailored method. • Tightly woven fabrics are hard to shape. They can needle mark, and seams can pucker and become hard to press flat.

There are also fabrics made from specialty hair fibers like camel, cashmere, mohair, angora, and vicuna. Linen and silk also work well for contemporary tailoring (Figure 3.3). After you thoroughly understand contemporary tailoring you will find unlimited fabric choices. There are brocades, damasks, boucle, shantung, crepes, and velvet, just to name a few.

Beware of fiber blends, Lycra, and Spandex for your first project. If you must use a blend, make sure that the blend is at least 60 percent wool.

Figure 3.3 The fabric is softly draped on this jacket, giving it a cool, summery look.

Figure 3.4 The plaid fabric has been perfectly matched.

Plaids and Stripes

Working with plaids and stripes can be challenging, especially for the not-so-experienced sewer, because they have to be matched during all the stages of making your jacket. This can take a lot of extra time.

Houndstooth, herringbone, and woven patterned fabrics such as jacquard may also need to be matched, so when purchasing your fabric look to see if there are repeats in rows or color blocks that may require you to match. Having to match the fabric design can also mean that you will need extra fabric. Some fabrics have a random design that does not need to be matched.

At this point, refer to your jacket design. Make a quick sketch, and add the fabric by drawing it in; plan the placement of the plaid or stripe, and remember that darts and seam lines are going to alter the fabric design. Your design may be unsuitable for plaids or stripes—the shaping of your seams may make it difficult or impossible to match.

Toile, or Muslin, Plaids, and Stripes

Make a toile or muslin of your jacket before you cut your fashion fabric, and draw the dominant plaid or stripes onto the muslin. (Refer to Chapter 4 for instructions on making a toile.) This will help give you an idea of how the design will look in your jacket. You can also use this muslin to transfer these lines onto your pattern.

Before you begin, ask yourself:
- Where will the plaid or stripe fall on the body?
- Is there a dominant stripe at the bust line or at the waistline?
- Is the dominant vertical line at the center front and back? Your jacket will look more balanced if it is.

Working a Plaid

When working a plaid:

- Place the center front and back halfway between the two dominant lines.
- Use the shoulder point on your sleeve head in the same way.
- The dominant crosswise stripe usually marks the hemline because this will also balance your jacket.
- If you don't want to draw attention to the hemline, place the dominant crosswise stripe between the two dominant lines. This will draw the eye away from the hem.

Nap Fabrics

Your fabric may have a nap or pile. Check for this by brushing your hand down the fabric. If it feels rough and a dark, rich color appears, you are working against a nap or pile. Now brush your hand back up the fabric. It should feel smooth, and some fabrics will have shine and look lighter in color; this is called working with the nap or pile. In fashion you always work against the nap or pile. Fabrics that have a nap or pile are velvets, woolens, corduroy, some fancy weaves, and some prints and patterns. These usually require more fabric because you will have to cut all your pattern pieces in one direction.

BRINGING TOGETHER FABRIC AND DESIGN

The fabric is going to give a "feel" to the jacket. Let your imagination run wild and free while remembering to work with the inspiration and design elements discussed in Chapter 2. To help you think about choosing a fabric that is appropriate for your design, Table 3.2 lists some types of design, the qualities that characterize these types of design, and the fabrics that work best to express these qualities.

Figure 3.5 Alberta Ferretti, Fall 2009.

TABLE 3.2 Types of Design by Characteristic and Fabric Choices

TYPE OF DESIGN	English Country	Romantic	Smart Casual
CHARACTERISTICS	Slim fitting, hand made. Have a comfortable look to them.	Retro, historical (e.g., Victorian)	Warm, comfortable, career wear, preppy.
FABRIC CHOICES	Woolens, tweeds, corduroy, velvet, tartans, checks, or herringbone.	Textured wool, velvets, wool crepe, brocades, or checks.	Light weight cashmeres, soft tweeds, worsted wool, checks, or stripes.

Table Figure 3.2a Alexander McQueen PFC 2009, Style.com.

Table Figure 3.2b Junya Watanabe, Spring 2010, Style.com.

Table Figure 3.2c Zac Posen, Fall 2009, aStyle.com.

Table Figure 3.2d Prada, Spring 2010.

Table Figure 3.2e Prada, Spring 2010.

Table Figure 3.2f Kenzo, Fall 2009, Style.com.

Military	Global/Ethnic	Evening	Functional
May include braiding, insignias, epaulettes, or metallic buttons.	Patchwork, prints, embroideries, fur, or hobo chic.	Sensual, spiritual, or luminous.	Padded or quilted outerwear or sportswear.
Wool twills, woolens, velveteen, or velvet.	Panne velvets, brocades, woolens, or tweeds.	Satins, velvets, devore (burnout), brocade, specialty fabrics or fibers, light-weight wool, crepe, or lace.	High-tech fabrics, velvets and velveteens, or brocades

Table Figure 3.2g Alexander McQueen, Fall 2008, Style.com.

Table Figure 3.2h Valentino, Fall 2008 couture, Style.com.

Table Figure 3.2i Roberto Cavalli, Spring 2007, Style.com.

Table Figure 3.2j Balenciaga, PF 2009, Style.com.

Table Figure 3.2k Alberta Ferretti, Fall 2009, RTW.

Table Figure 3.2l Roberto Cavalli, Spring 2007.

Table Figure 3.2m Balenciaga, PF 2009, Style.com.

Table Figure 3.2n Raf Simons, Fall 2009

Each season when amazing collections are coming down the runways, remember that it is the fabric along with fantastic design and superb craftsmanship that makes a collection unique.

Think tweed and the double C's of the House of Chanel instantly come to mind. The partnership of Linton Tweed and Chanel is a perfect example of a mill working hand in hand with a designer.

THE FABRIC OF COUTURE

Linton produces more than 600 new fabrics annually and is world renowned for innovative woven technology. The first design samples are still woven by hand before being put into production on a larger rapier loom. The new fabrics are then shown twice a year at Premiere Vision in Paris, exhibits in Milan, Japan, New York, and London, to name a few. Today, Linton shows two fabric collections—Linton and Ullswater. Linton works closely with customers such as Burberry and Max Mara to continue to produce unique fabrics.

Origins of the Fabric

In 1912, Scotsman William Linton started Linton Mill. Initially, he employed two salesmen with ponies and traps to buy wool and sell woolen suit lengths. It was from the woolen tweeds that Linton enjoyed huge European success, since it became the signature look at Chanel. At the time Americans were reproducing the garments being shown by the Paris Couture houses, and Linton began to do massive business in America. From the late thirties and throughout the fifties, Miss Agnes Linton, daughter of William, sailed to the United States many times with trunks of samples. Apart from the war years, business was so good that the Linton Collection was shown to only 10 or 12 privileged American customers each season.

Box Figure 3.1b Inside Linton Tweeds mill.

Box Figure 3.1a Inside Linton Tweeds mill.

Troubled Times

Problems started in 1967 when union difficulties along 5th Avenue caused many of Linton's customers to close their businesses. There were also problems closer to home; the larger more competitive mills in the area were able to produce cheaper cloth. Linton at this time continued to produce 100 percent woolen cloth. Although being prestigious, the market in Paris was not lucrative. The couture houses such as Chanel would order a series of six yard lengths, but use only a few.

A New Vision

In 1969, Leslie Walker became managing director and took Linton into a new and more modern era. He made changes to the product to help make it more unique: new exotic fibers, machinery to make their own fancy yarns, new yarn dyeing, an expanded color range, and the traditional piece-dyed fabrics were redesigned and reduced in weight.

Walker made ground-breaking trips to Japan, America, and Canada to find new customers, and the long association with the Parisian couture houses flourished when the fashion houses began producing ready to wear.

Selecting Linings

The lining gives your jacket its finishing touch. Not only does the lining cover the inner structure, it also protects the garment fabric from wear and tear, stops the jacket from stretching out of shape, and absorbs body moisture.

Linings should be durable because replacing them is a time-consuming process.

Most linings are made from synthetic fibers like Bemberg rayon and acetate-rayon blends because these are more absorbent than other synthetic fibers. This makes them comfortable to wear. Linings should be lighter in weight and softer than the jacket fabric. Their surface should be smooth; avoid fabric that clings or has much texture.

Linings may be part of the inside of the jacket, but today's designers are also turning them into visual statements by using contrast colors, prints, and logos, or choosing a signature color for their linings and placing it in all their garments. This adds visual interest and can be fun.

Selecting Interfacings

Your choice of interfacing will result in either a softly tailored or more structured garment. Your decision depends on your choice of design, personal preference, and acceptance of a fashion trend.

The purpose of interfacings is to:
- Add body and shape to the garment—especially to the shoulder, chest, and armholes.
- Add support to the garment.
- Give line definition to the front edges.
- Strengthen and support buttonholes.
- Strengthen pocket areas.
- Cushion the hem and sleeve cuffs for better wear.
- Help produce a nice smooth roll line in the collar and lapels.
- Add definition to design features.

Sewn-In Interfacings

Hair canvas is a common material for interfacing. There are many different types of hair canvas available; be careful to purchase the best grade of hair canvas for your fashion fabric. You want it to be pliable, non-crushable, resilient, and firmly woven. Hair canvas is a mixture of wool, goat hair, cotton, and rayon. The higher your hair canvas' content of wool, the softer and easier to handle, steam, and shape. You want your hair canvas to cling to your fashion fabric so that the two become one.

A TRIUMPH OF QUALITY AND COUTURE

Today, the world's most influential women wear Linton tweed. First Lady Michelle Obama wore a white coat made for her by designer Thakoon Panichgul when departing for the 2009 European presidential tour, and her mother, Marian Robinson, wore a pink suit to her son-in-law's (President Barack Obama) inauguration.

Hilary Alexander reviewed John Rocha (see Box 13.1) in the *London Telegraph* for the autumn/winter 2009-10 collections in London at London Fashion Week and reported that:

> He opened with his familiar black, with tailored suits, coats, and dresses which had a slight nod to Dior's "New Look" of 1947, nipping in at the waist and then exaggerating the hips with extended peplums, padding, pockets, and gathered details. Linton tweeds, in black and white and lacquered checks, were used for fitted, collarless jackets, detailed with tweed ruffles—a technique which was repeated in the matching "bubble" skirts, in little knickers, and even in a one-piece maillot. (Alexander, 2009)

A reduced-price hair canvas has a higher cotton or rayon content instead of wool. This is why it is cheaper, but it will not be as resilient. It will wrinkle more and be harder to shape.

Your fabric may be an open or loose weave that requires more support. To add more support, add an interlining. Lay your interface on the wrong side of your fabric, and attach it with basting stitches. Interlinings are woven lightweight cotton muslins, mull (cotton fabric used by tailors as an interfacing), or even silk organza. You can also add an interlining to hide seam allowances, darts, and inner structuring from showing through. This can happen when you are working with light-colored fabrics.

Wool domette or cotton flannel is used to give a soft padding to the chest/shoulder area on the front of your jacket. It is also used for the sleeve heads and can be used to add padding to other areas of the jacket, depending on design. It can also add warmth to the garment.

Fusible Interfacings

Fusible interfacings are available in a variety of weights and types. There are four different categories:

- Non-woven—This kind of fusible interfacing is generally less flexible and usually has a crosswise stretch but no lengthwise stretch. Some can feel spongy.
- Woven—This kind of fusible interfacing is stable both cross-grain and lengthwise and will stretch on the bias. Fusible hair canvas is available but is very stiff and may give your fabric too hard a hand.
- Tricot knit—This kind of fusible interfacing has cross- but no lengthwise stretch. It is soft and will give a flexible, supple shape to your jacket.
- Weft insertion—This kind of fusible interfacing has a knitted base with threads added or inserted crosswise. This gives them a firmer hand than the tricot knit. They are stable both cross- and lengthwise and will stretch on the bias. The most suitable for a contemporary tailored jacket is fusible tricot knit and weft insertion interfacings.

Always test your interfacing by cutting a strip or square of your fabric that is big enough to fuse different sample weights and types of interfacing.

CHAPTER CHECKLIST

Before moving on to the next chapter, make sure:
- ☐ You have your final jacket design.
- ☐ You have made the right fabric choice(s).
- ☐ You know the fibers and yarn content of your fabric.
- ☐ The weight of your fabric is appropriate for your design.
- ☐ The color, texture, and weave will all add to your design.
- ☐ You know whether your fabric has a pile, and therefore a nap.
- ☐ Your fabric is matched (e.g., plaid, large print).
- ☐ You have purchased enough fabric for your design.
- ☐ You have chosen your interfacings.
- ☐ You have chosen your lining fabric.

When you have checked off all these items, you are ready to move on and start making your pattern.

REFERENCES

Alexander, H. (2009, February 21) Fashion review, *London Telegraph*.

PART II

Preparation

SIDEBAR 11.1 Tools of the Trade

Selecting tools and using them correctly is very important in tailoring. Try to purchase the best equipment that your budget will allow, and your tools will last a long time.

I have also included a few good tailoring supply companies that I recommend where you can browse through or purchase essential tailoring equipment.

ESSENTIAL TAILORING EQUIPMENT

- **Working surface**—A flat working surface makes cutting easier and stops fabrics from slipping and sliding out of shape. This surface can also double as a large pressing surface.
- **Scissors**—You need good quality fabric shears for careful cutting of your fabric as well as a pair of paper scissors for cutting the paper pattern. If you use your fabric shears to cut patterns, they will become blunt and you will no longer get a nice, clean cut.
- **Paper**—You need paper to make your jacket pattern. Computer plotter paper is inexpensive and easy to find.
- **Pencils and eraser**—You need pencils and an eraser to draft and make your jacket pattern and correct mistakes.
- **Pitt pens or markers**—You use these to write clear instructions on the pattern pieces. Or you can use any fine line marker pen.
- **Ruler**—A flexible see-through plastic ruler is easiest to use. You want it flexible in order to easily bend it around curves. But do keep it away from the iron!
- **Hip curve ruler and French curve**—These are used in pattern making and for creating your curve.
- **Set square**—A large set square with a marked 45-degree angle.
- **Tape measure**—You use this to take body measurements.
- **Tracing wheel**—You use this to transfer markings.
- **Cellotape**—You can also use adhesive tape in the pattern process.
- **Tailors chalk**—You use tailors chalk to mark the pattern information onto the fabric. Use the clay chalk because it can be brushed away easily when you are finished with the markings. Don't iron over the chalk markings because this will make the marks harder to remove.
- **Thread snips**—These are small, sharp, pointed scissors that are used for cutting threads and also give you easy access into corners and trimming curves, etc.
- **Pins**—These include dressmaking pins and silk pins.
- **Needles**—You use needles for hand sewing. "Betweens" are a short, strong needle used in tailoring.
- **Sewing thread**—Match your sewing thread to your fashion fabric, both in color and size. When matching color it is often best to go one shade darker. When determining thread size, look for a thread that sinks into the fabric rather than lies on top as in topstitching. If the thread fails to sink into the fabric, the thread will wear and break down over time, and your seams will open.
- **Muslin**—Use muslin as close in weight to your fashion fabric to make the toile for your design. It is cheaper to use muslin than your fashion fabric at this time to correct any design issues and fit problems.
- **Iron**—These include both dry and stream. The optimal iron is one that is easy to manipulate and offers a powerful surge of steam when needed, but can also be worked dry.
- **Tailors ham**—Tailors ham can be large or small and is used for pressing curves.
- **Pleater or clapper**—This is a woolen block used as a pounding block for flattening bulky edges.
- **Press cloth**—This can be cotton muslin or silk organza. It is used to protect the fabric from direct contact with a hot iron. The pressing cloth can be used on the face of dark fabrics to prevent it from getting shiny.
- **Buttons, hooks, zippers**—Depending on your jacket design.

RECOMMENDED TAILORING SUPPLY SOURCES

Leonard Adler & Co.
3018 W. Montrose Avenue
Chicago, IL 60618
(773) 442-8700
(773) 442-8710, fax

Leonard Adler & Co. stocks everything that you need to start making your garment, from needles and pins to dress forms and paper.

Greenberg & Hammer, Inc.
535 Eighth Avenue – Floor 6N
New York, NY 10018
(212) 246-2835
(800) 955-5135
(212) 765-8475, fax.
www.greenberg-hammer.com

B. Black & Sons
548 S. Los Angeles Street
Los Angeles, CA 90013
(213) 624-9451
(800) 433-1546
(213) 624-9457, fax
www.bblackandsons.com

CHAPTER 4

The Pattern

I never saw any point in stopping at the way in which a conventional wisdom decreed a jacket should be cut. Early on, I realized how important it is just to be curious. You musn't be frightened or hide behind pre-conceived ideas. You have to experiment. You just do it and it's beautiful because you discover an energy there which feeds you. There are no rules!

—John Galliano

CHAPTER OBJECTIVES

After reading this chapter, you should be able to:

Measure the body and transfer those measurements onto the jacket pattern.

Determine the fit of the jacket.

Work from the jacket blocks.

Manipulate the jacket front pattern from single to double breasted.

Alter the length of the roll line.

Manipulate and understand the anatomy of the jacket sleeve.

Design new design details such as pockets and collars.

Add vents to both the jacket back and sleeves.

Make the toile or muslin.

If you don't feel skilled enough to create your own pattern, carefully choose a commercial pattern in a fit that will flatter your figure. Do not choose your pattern by the pockets or if the jacket has a lining; all these details are included in the book. What you will use from the commercial pattern is the basic pattern pieces: jacket front, back, side panels, sleeves, and undercollar. The size of the jacket pattern is determined by the chest or bust measurement.

I have included both men's and women's basic blocks for a fitted and a casual, or easy-fitting, jacket. These blocks have the standard amounts of ease included and have been graded using the measurements given as follows.

TAKING MEASUREMENTS FOR THE JACKET

Figure 4.1 shows where to take the measurements on the male body. Use Table 4.1 as a reference for men's standard body measurements.

Use Table 4.2 to make adjustments for short or tall figures.

Figure 4.2 shows where to take the measurements on a female body.

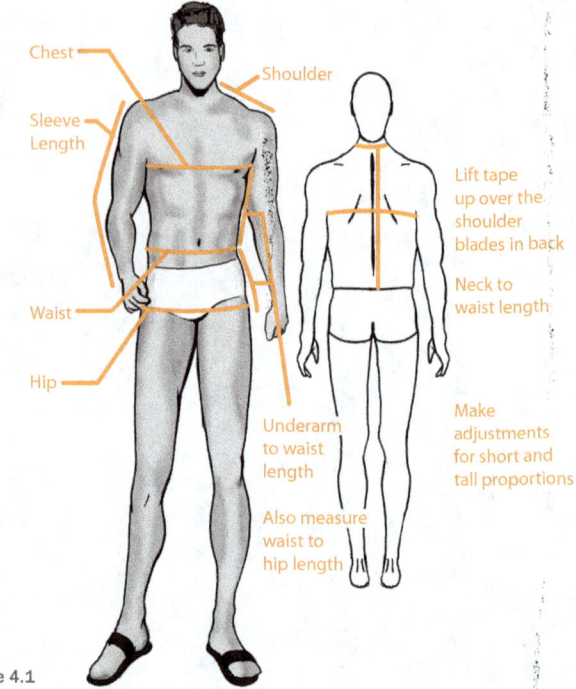

Figure 4.1

Men's Standard Body Measurements

CHEST (INCHES)	36	37	39	41	43	44
CHEST (CENTIMETERS)	92	96	100	104	108	112
WAIST (INCHES)	29	31	33	35	37	39
WAIST (CENTIMETERS)	75	79	83	87	91	95
HIP (INCHES)	37	38	40	41	43	45
HIP (CENTIMETERS)	94	98	102	106	110	114
BACK WAIST LENGTH (INCHES)	17 5/8	17 7/8	18 1/8	18 3/8	18 5/8	18 7/8
BACK WAIST LENGTH (CENTIMETERS)	43.8	44.2	44.6	45	45.4	45.8
SLEEVE LENGTH (INCHES)	25 1/4	23 3/4	24	24 1/4	24 1/2	24 3/4
SLEEVE LENGTH (CENTIMETERS)	64.2	64.8	65.4	66	66	66

Source: *Metric Pattern Cutting for Menswear,* Winifred Aldrich, Blackwell Publishing

TABLE 4.2

Waist Length/Sleeve Length Adjustments for Short or Tall People

	SHORT		TALL	
	5' 4" – 5' 7"		5' 10" – 6' 1"	
	(162–170 cm)			
Natural waist length	–¾"	–2 cm	+ ¾"	+2 cm
Sleeve length	–1"	–2.5 cm	+ 1"	+2.5 cm

Source: *Metric Pattern Cutting for Menswear*, Winifred Aldrich, Blackwell Publishing

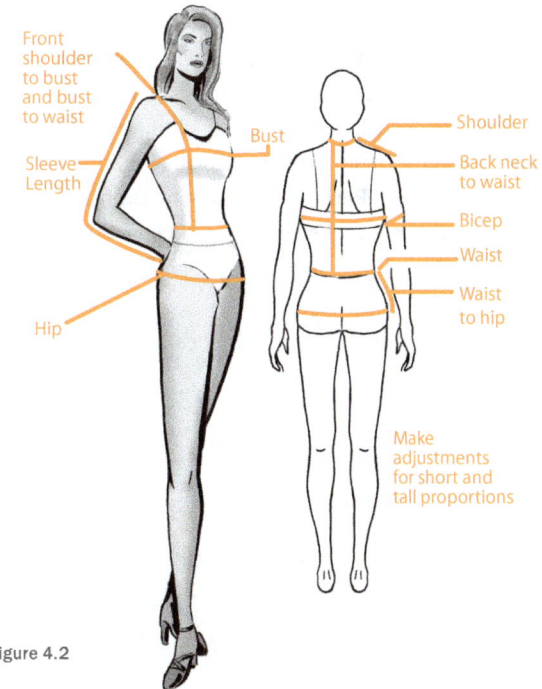

Figure 4.2

TABLE 4.3

Women's Standard Body Measurements

BUST (INCHES)	33 ¼	34 ⅝	36	37 ¾	39 ⅜	41
BUST (CENTIMETERS)	84	88	92	96	100	104
WAIST (INCHES)	25 ¼	26 ¾	28 ⅜	30	32 ¼	34
WAIST (CENTIMETERS)	64	68	72	76	82	86
BACK WAIST LENGTH (INCHES)	15 ¾	16	16 ⅛	16 ⅜	16 ½	16 ¾
BACK WAIST LENGTH (CENTIMETERS)	40	40 ½	41	4 ½	42	42 ½
SLEEVE (INCHES)	22 ¾	23	23 ¼	23 ½	23 ⅝	23 ¾
SLEEVE (CENTIMETERS)	58	58.5	59	59.5	60	60.5
BICEP (INCHES)	10 ¾	11 ¼	11 ⅝	12 ⅛	12 ⅝	13 ⅛
BICEP (CENTIMETERS)	27.5	28.4	29.6	30.8	32	33.2
SHOULDER (INCHES)	4 ¾	4 ⅞	5	5	5 ⅛	5 ¼
SHOULDER (CENTIMETERS)	12	12.25	12.5	12.75	13	13.25
FRONT SHOULDER TO WAIST (INCHES)	15 ¾	16	16 ¼	16 ½	17	17 ¼
FRONT SHOULDER TO WAIST (CENTIMETERS)	40	40.5	41.3	42.1	42.9	43.7

Source: *Metric Pattern Cutting for Menswear*, Winifred Aldrich, Blackwell Publishing

THE FIT OF THE JACKET

The casual, or easy-fitting, jacket has a front, back, and side panel. You can add extra shaping by putting in a front dart. This jacket looks good with either a one- or two-piece sleeve. Think of adding design features, such as a back belt. Play with the pocket design, collar, and lapel. This jacket suits heavier-weight fabrics (Figure 4.3).

The fitted jacket is also cut in panels but is fitted closer to the body. In women's jackets it is fitted to the bust shape and waist. This is a good block to use if you want a convertible collar or no collar. The sleeve is also cut in two or sometimes even three pieces so that it follows the shape of the arm. It is harder to manipulate this jacket block. Think of an evening jacket, suit, or riding jacket. Lighter-weight fabrics are appropriate for this jacket (Figure 4.4).

Figure 4.3

Figure 4.4

MAKING THE PATTERN

Figure 4.5 shows how the patterns will look. There are pattern blocks for both fitted and more casual jackets. Figure 4.5 is for the men's fitted jacket.

Figure 4.6 shows the pattern for a casual women's jacket.

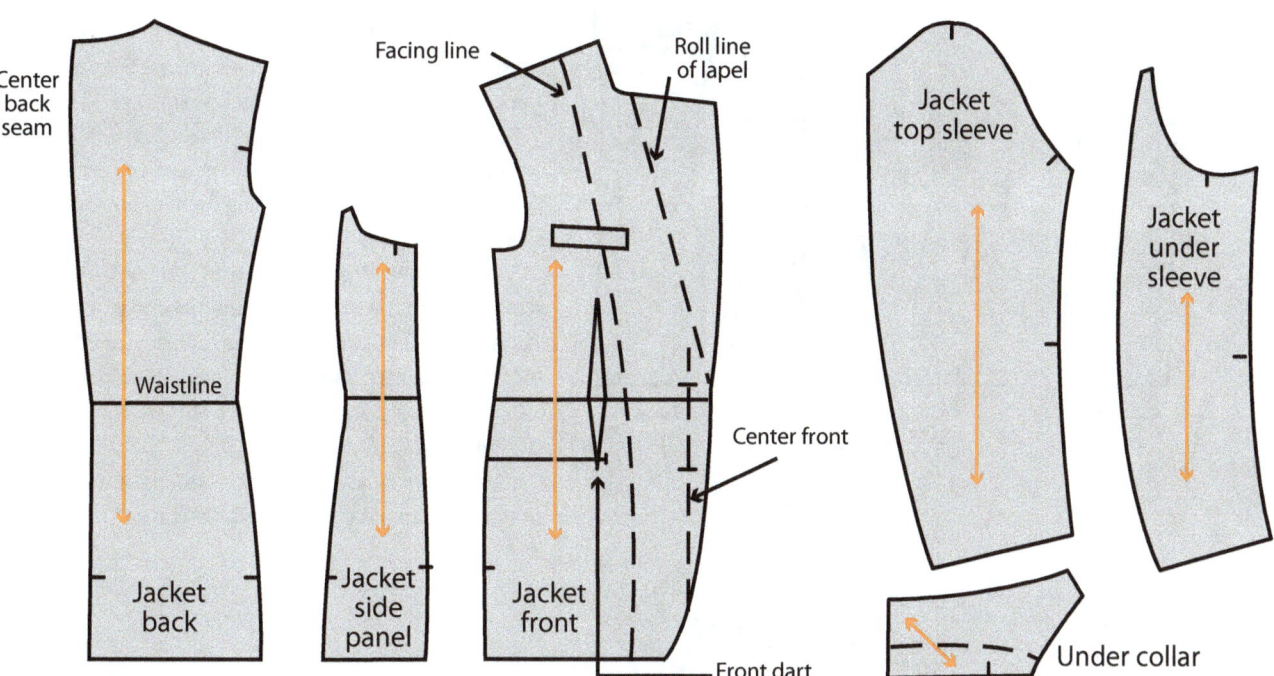

Figure 4.5

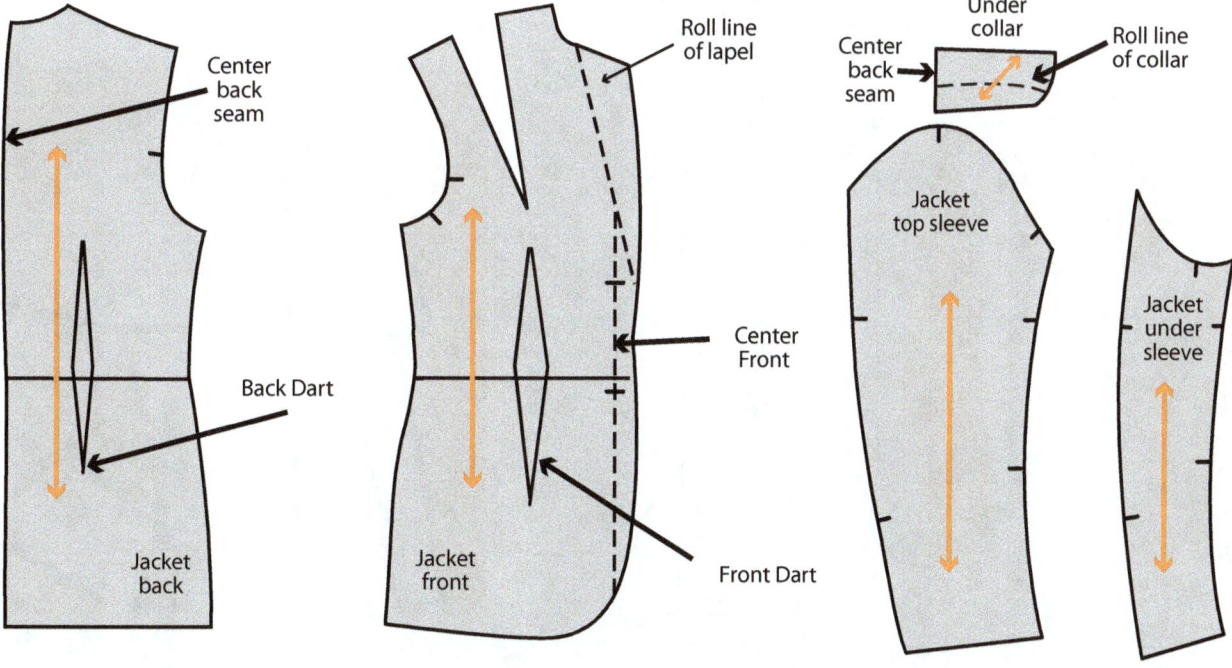

Figure 4.6

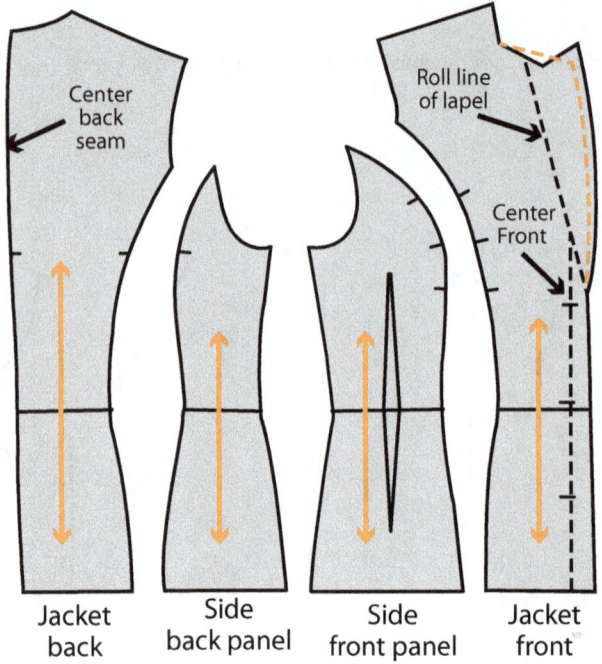

Figure 4.7 shows the women's princess line fitted jacket with a classic notched collar. The dotted line indicates the classic notched collar while the solid line turns the collar into a classic reefer style.

Figure 4.8 shows a shawl collar jacket. Figure 4.9 shows the assembly of the back and front blocks to create the shawl collar. Tip the back block to increase the outer edge; this can even become a cape (Figure 4.10). The collar will have a center back seam.

Figure 4.11 shows a princess line jacket with a funnel collar; manipulate the princess line block by drawing in the raglan style lines and adding them to the top sleeve as shown in Figure 4.12.

The block patterns included with this book are full scale made to the men's measurement chart chest 39 inches (100 centimeters), women's bust size 33 inches (84 centimeters). Draw a line horizontally 4 inches (10 cm) long and cross this with a vertical line 4 inches (10 cm) long.

Your pattern is now ready for you to make any changes to the measurements or length.

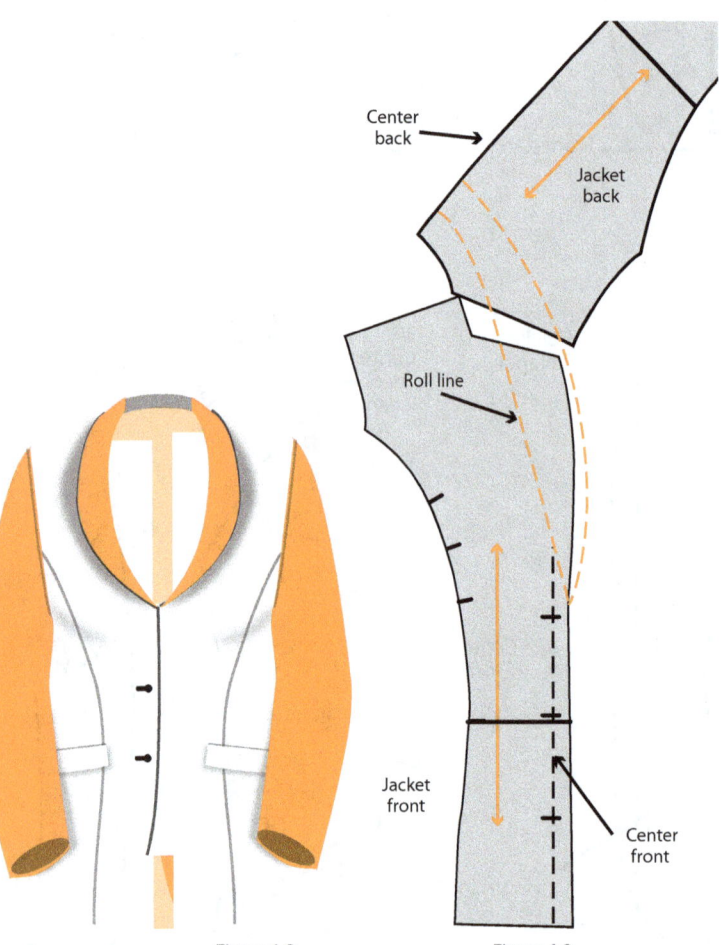

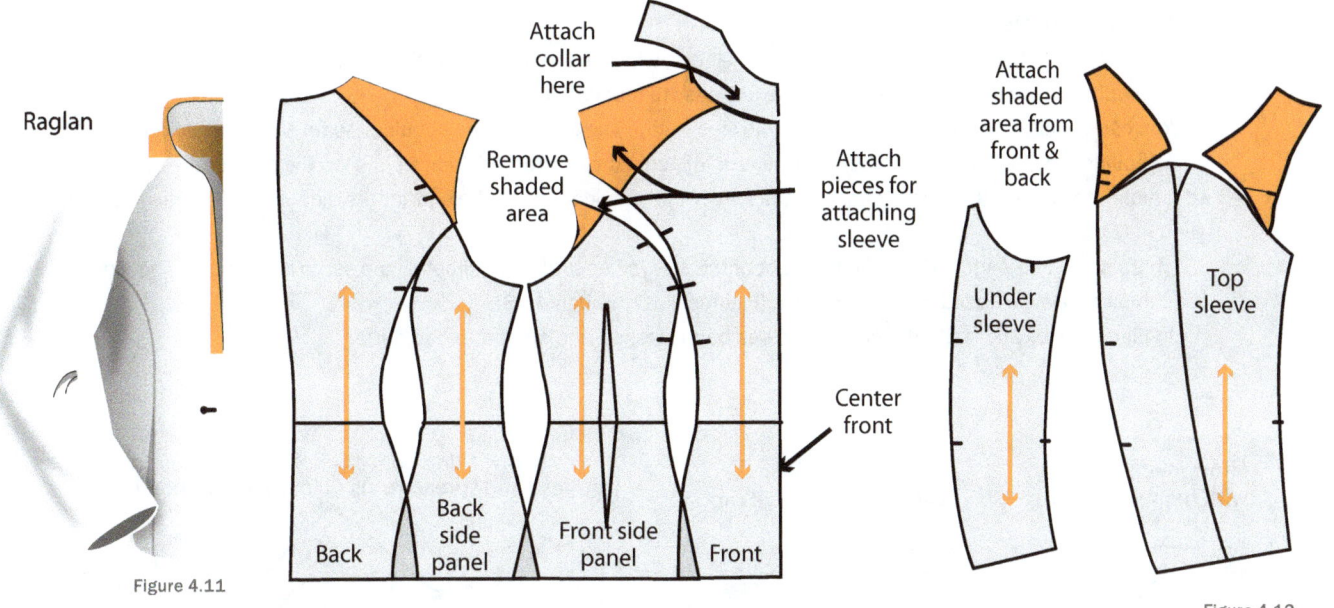

Figure 4.11

Figure 4.12

THE JACKET FRONT

Draw in your front roll line and lapel shape if you are making any changes to the pattern. If you change the lapel you may also have to change the undercollar. Refer to the design ideas showing how to manipulate the pattern in this chapter or the construction chapters. Add a ⅜-inch (1 cm) seam allowance to the pattern and then cut out.

Double-Breasted Jacket

From the center front line add on 2½ inches (6.5 cm). Draw in the roll line and shape the lapel. The top on the lapel can also be shaped as shown in Figure 4.13.

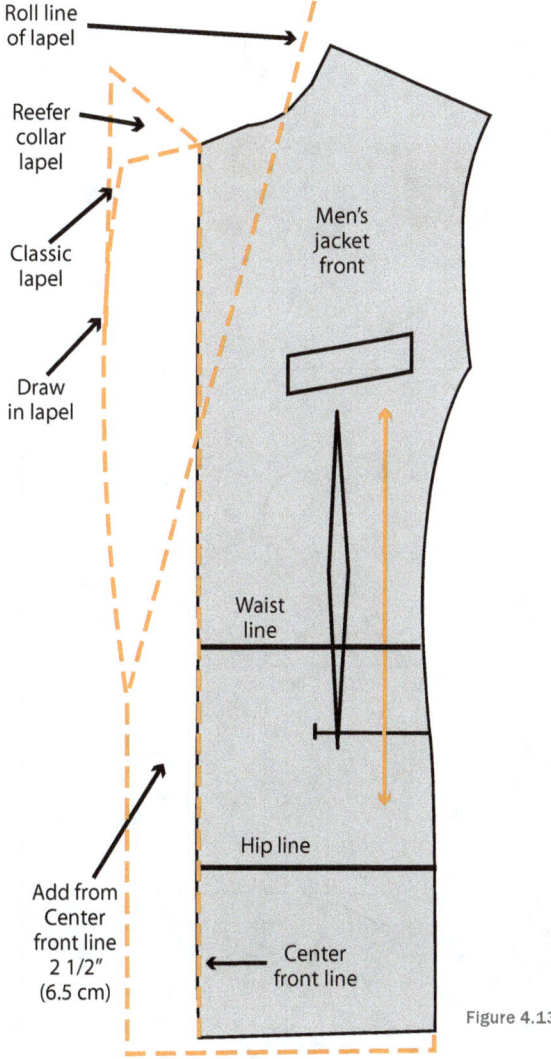

Figure 4.13

The Jacket Sleeve

Figure 9.7 shows the anatomy of the one-piece sleeve, which is the most basic fitted set-in sleeve. It is the foundation for all the other sleeve designs because it is easy to manipulate.

You can change the height and shape of the sleeve cap. The length of the shoulder seam and the height of the shoulder pads affect the cap height. Both are influenced by current fashion trends, so the shorter the shoulder seam, the higher the sleeve cap, and the longer the shoulder seam, the shorter the sleeve cap (Figures 4.14 and 4.15).

There should be 1 inch of ease in the front of the sleeve cap and approximately the same in the back. The sleeve cap must always be eased into the armhole (Figures 4.16 through 4.18).

In Figures 4.19 and 4.20, the sleeve cap has been slashed and spread to add darts.

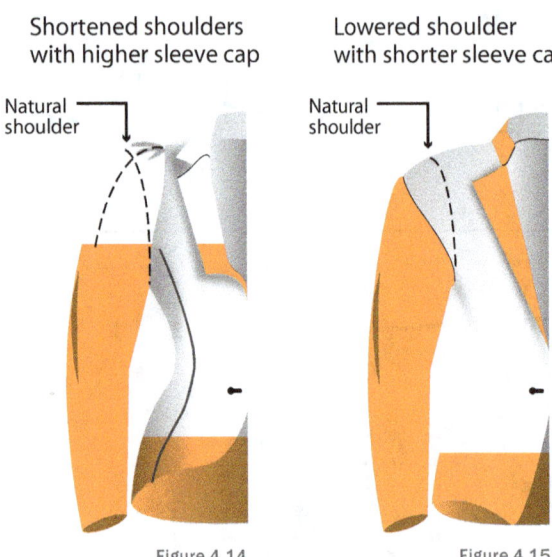

Figure 4.14

Figure 4.15

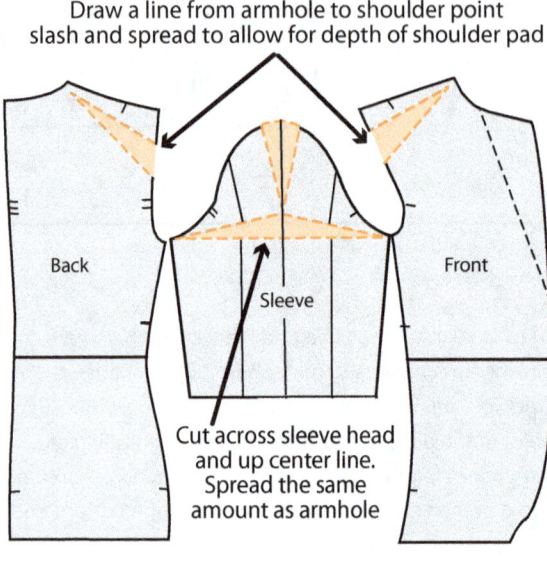

Figure 4.16

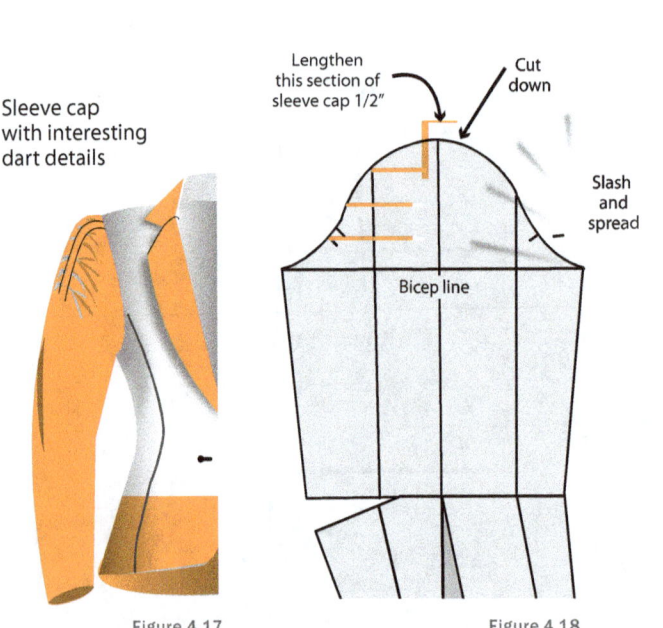

Figure 4.17

Figure 4.18

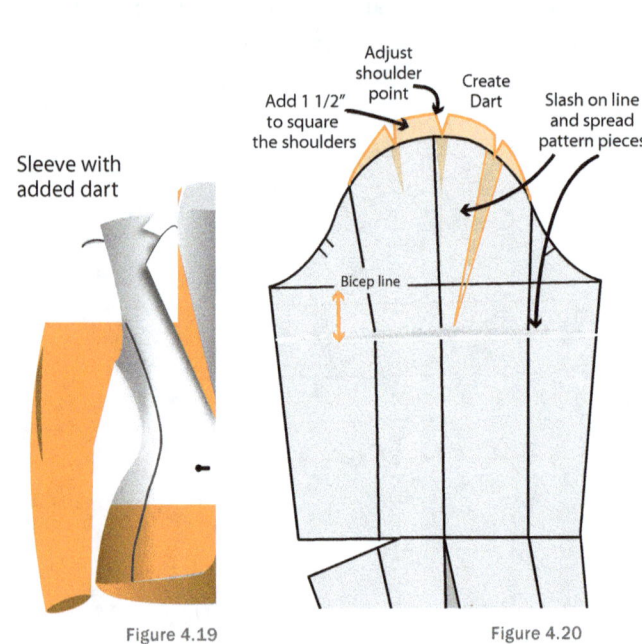

Figure 4.19

Figure 4.20

The Two-Piece, or Tailored, Sleeve

This sleeve is usually used for jackets and coats. The two piece sleeve is composed of a top or upper sleeve and a narrower lower sleeve. The back seam runs down the back of the arm midway between the center of the sleeve and the underarm, whereas the front seam is on the underside of the sleeve front approximately three quarters from the center of the sleeve. (Figure 4.21).

Tape together down the under arm seam line making sure to match the notches. By doing this you have now made the under sleeve pattern piece (Figure 4.17). Measure out from the front 1 to 1½ inch (2.5 cm to 4 cm) and 2 inches (5 cm) at the back (if needed to widen the sleeve at the wrist), and redraw connecting points.

Finish the sleeve pieces by drawing in the grainlines and adding seam allowances, hems, and sleeve vents. If more ease is needed in the upper back of the sleeve piece, add ⅝ inches (1.5 cm) to the length, redraw, and adjust the hem line.

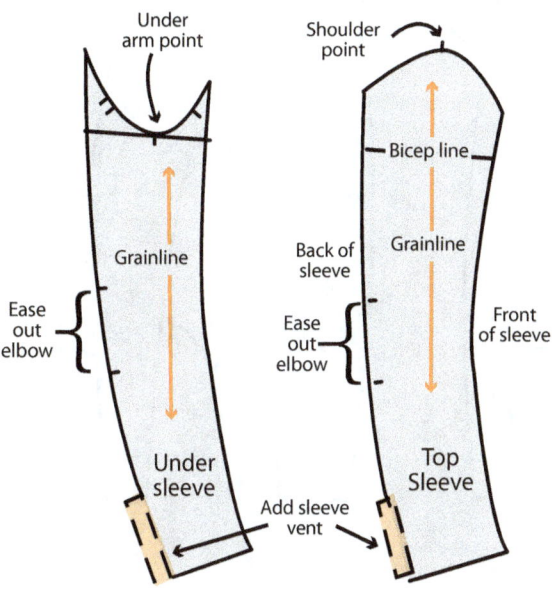

Figure 4.21

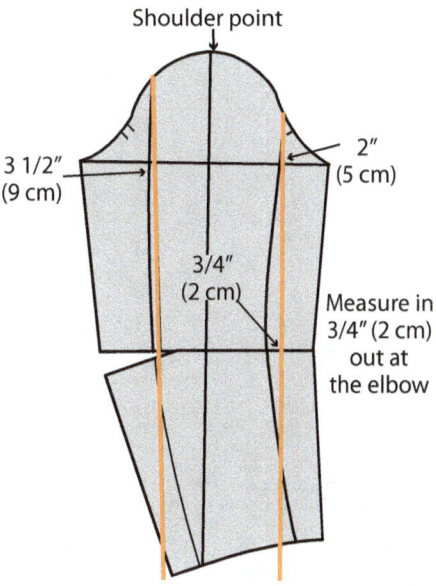

Figure 4.22

Refer to Figures 4.17 and 4.18 to see some design ideas created by manipulating the one-piece sleeve pattern. Note how the sleeve cap has been slashed and spread to create an interesting sleeve cap.

Cutting the sleeve into two pieces enables you to eliminate the underarm seam. It also lets you add more fullness or ease into the back seam over the elbow and a vent at the wrist.

Figure 4.22 shows how to make your one-piece sleeve into a two-piece sleeve.

Working without seam allowances, make a tracing of your one-piece sleeve pattern.

To find the upper sleeve, measure about 3½ inches (9 cm) in at the back bicep line and 2 inches (5 cm) in from the back seam line. Draw vertical lines parallel to the grain from top of the sleeve to wrist line. Measure in at the front elbow line ¾ inches (2 cm) and draw a line that curves in to connect this point. On the back wrist line measure in 3 inches (7.5 cm) and draw a line that connects to this point. Cut down the two vertical lines so your sleeve is now in three pieces (Figure 4.23).

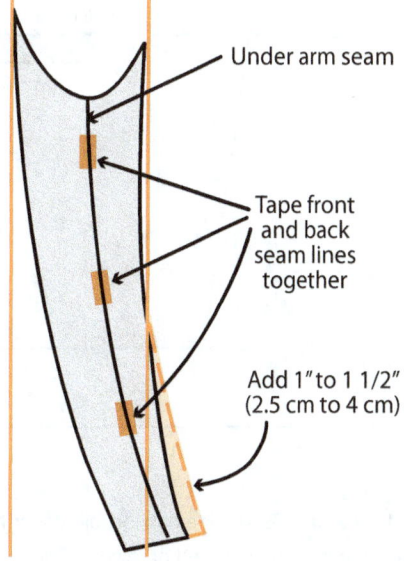

Figure 4.23

The Raglan Sleeve

Figure 4.24 and 4.25 shows a design idea created by manipulating the raglan sleeve pattern pieces.

The sleeve is now three pieces. Find the back line on the back raglan sleeve as you did when making the two-piece sleeve (see Figure 4.25), and draw in the shape. Add facings to the front and back vents.

Figure 4.26 shows how to add a yoke to the back of a raglan sleeve jacket. The yoke can be shaped and attached to the jacket back by buttoning or maybe by adding a buckle. The yoke can also be pleated as shown in Figure 4.27.

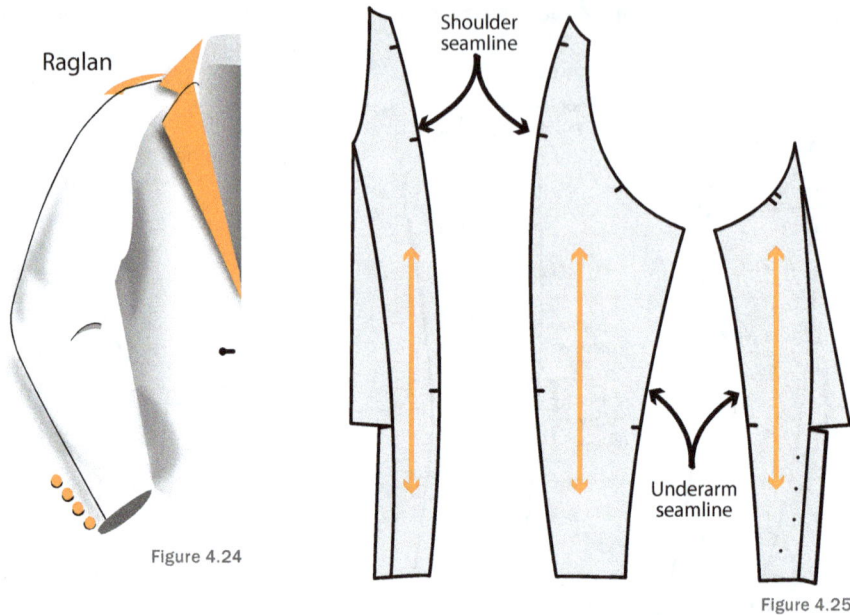

Figure 4.24

Figure 4.25

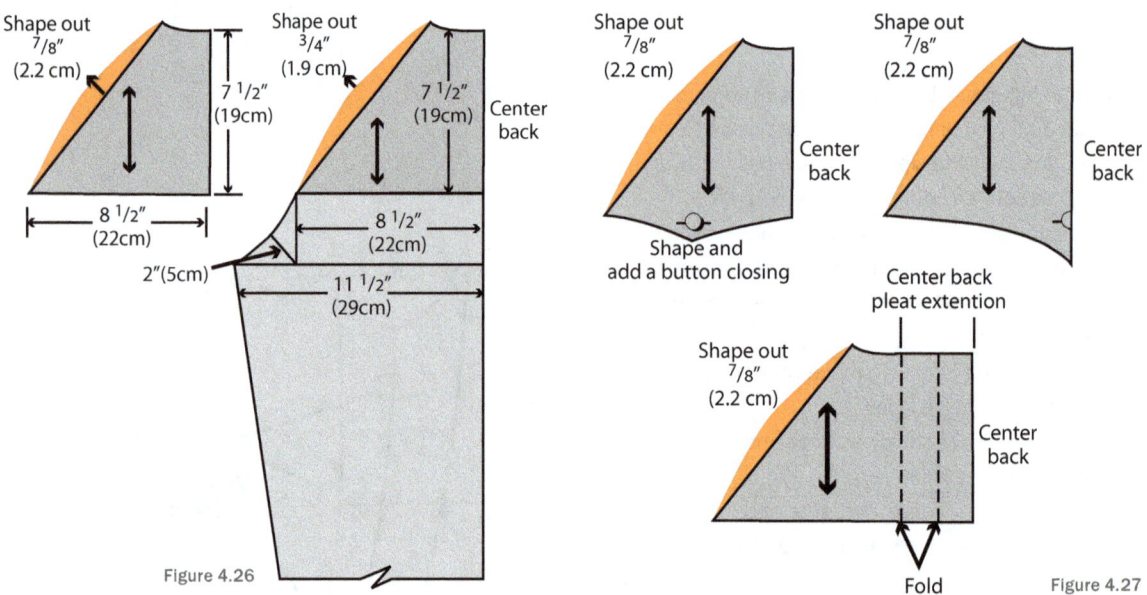

Figure 4.26

Figure 4.27

Collars

Figures 4.28 and 4.29 show a convertible collar based on the measurement of the back and front jacket neckline. If the neckline is to be widened or lowered, do so before taking the measurement—half the neckline measurement; square up the depth of the collar. Find two-thirds of the length and square up. At the front end of the collar measure up ¼ inch (0.5 cm) and mark. Draw in the style line shape at the front of the collar and mark in the shoulder line.

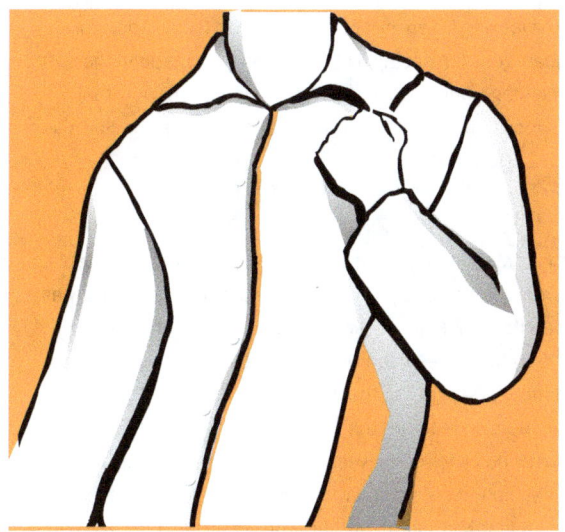

Figure 4.28

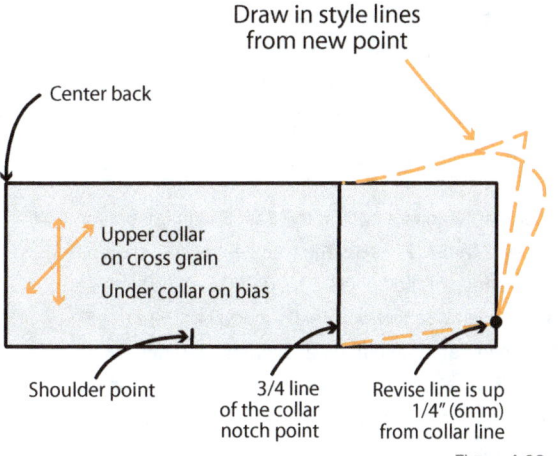

Figure 4.29

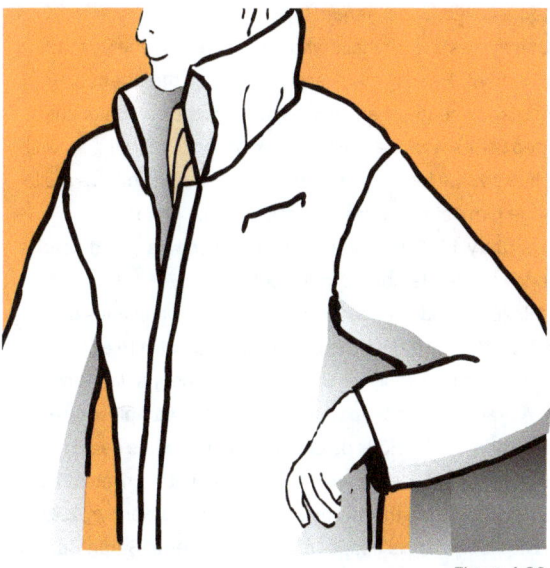

Figure 4.30

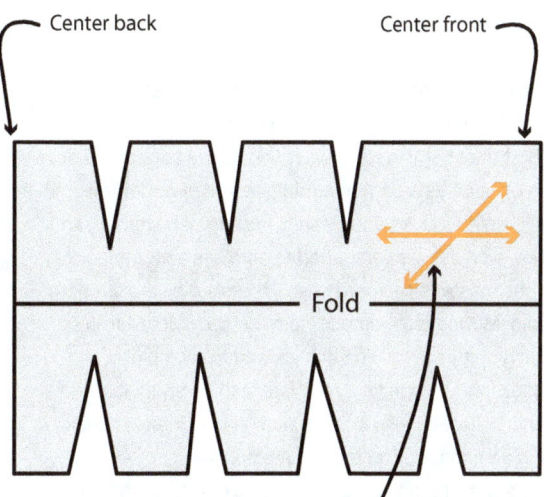

Figure 4.31

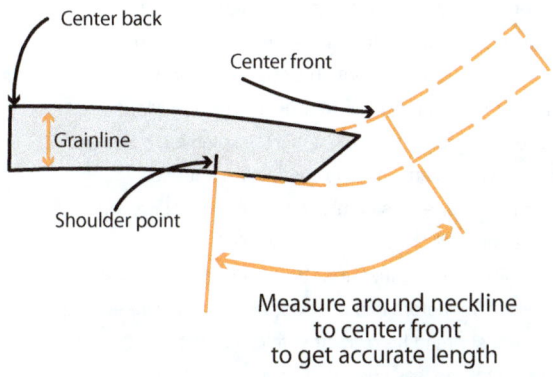

Figure 4.32

Figure 4.30 is a bolster collar. It is shown darted here but can be pleated. Begin by measuring the neck line of the jacket; decide the height of the collar and how full you want the outer edge to be. Draw out the collar on paper to the length of the outer edge and double the height measurement. Draw a horizontal line through the middle of the collar, and add the darts evenly along the outside edges so that the collar neck line matches the jacket neck line. Stagger the darts so that the collar doesn't become too thick at the neckline seam (Figure 4.31). Consider lining the bolster collar with a different color lining.

Figure 4.32 shows an extended collar band.

Alexander McQueen

BOX 4.1

"I'm talking about building a luxury brand from scratch...the new generation of luxury brands like the new Chanel and the new Balenciaga and the new Dior," explained Alexander McQueen of his personal career vision (Foley, 2008).

THE "PINK SHEEP" OF THE FAMILY

Lee Alexander McQueen was born in the East End of London on St. Patrick's Day, March 17, 1969, the youngest of six children. "I was the pink sheep of the family!" McQueen was known to say.

Educated at Rokeby School, where the motto is, "Dare to be best," McQueen left at 16 to pursue a tailoring apprenticeship with the Savile Row Tailoring company of Anderson & Sheppard. He went on to work for Gieves & Hawkes, another renowned bespoke tailoring house down the street, and the famous theatrical costume company, Angels and Bermans. McQueen had said, "It is important to learn the basics of cut and proportion."

Through his apprenticeships, he mastered six methods of pattern cutting, from the sixteenth century to the present. His talented tailoring techniques were well known within the fashion industry.

CUTTING HIS OWN PATH TO SUCCESS

After this rarified education, he went to work for Koji Tatsuno. He then moved to Milan to work as the assistant to designer Romeo Gigli for a short time before returning to London. In London he applied for a position as a pattern-cutting instructor at Central Saint Martin's College of Art and Design. Instead of becoming an instructor, however, he was persuaded to enroll as a student after the head of the master's course was so impressed by the strength of his portfolio. McQueen graduated from Central Saint Martin's with a master's degree in fashion design, and his complete graduate collection was bought by the late fashion stylist Isabella Blow. This final collection also brought him his first international exposure and an enormous amount of press coverage.

Mystery was to surround McQueen, and he developed a reputation for controversy and shock tactics that were to earn him titles such as *enfant terrible* and "hooligan of English fashion." He launched his own line in 1992, dropping his Christian name and using his middle and last names.

DARING TO BE THE BEST

In 1996, he replaced John Galliano as head ready-to-wear designer at Givenchy's Haute Couture. At the same time he also received notoriety by becoming British Designer of the Year. His first collection for Givenchy was, in McQueen's own words, "crap." He also insulted the founder by calling him "[expletive] irrelevant." His time at Givenchy was not a happy one. In an interview in *Arena* magazine, he dared his employers to fire him. However, he stayed until his contract ended in March, 2001.

At the time, McQueen claimed that the contract was "constraining his creativity." But before this contract was over McQueen had sold a 51 percent share in his own label to Gucci, with McQueen the creative director. He was quoted in an article in *Women's Wear Daily* (5 June 2000) saying, "It hasn't been as easy as it seems leaving Givenchy and being able to focus strictly on McQueen. Now I'm seeing all the mistakes we made in the past.... At some stage, you have to grow up. It's important now that people focus on the clothes rather than someone in a clown suit" (Fallon, 2000).

A NEW GENERATION OF LUXURY

Alexander McQueen's clothes are both beautiful and wearable. He won the British Designer of the Year award three times, was awarded the CBE (A Most Excellent Commander of the British Empire) by her Majesty the Queen in 2003, and was named International Designer of the Year at the Council of Fashion awards. He also received the Fashion Directors Award for McQ Menswear designer of the year by GQ in September 2007.

He has boutiques around the world, launched two perfumes (Kingdom and McQueen), oversaw the licensing of his eyewear, signed a deal with Puma in 2005 to create a special line of sneakers, and signed with Samsonite February 2007 to create a collection of luxury cutting-edge luggage. He also more recently designed a collection for Target.

McQueen was a workaholic who brought a new energy to the fashion market. He may have received most of the attention for his outrageous behavior and shows, but it is the genius of cut combined with a working knowledge of bespoke tailoring as well as the fine sewing techniques of the French haute couture atelier that made him not only a fashion designer but an artist.

On February 11, 2010, Alexander McQueen was found dead in his London home; he was 40 years old.

His fall 2010 ready-to-wear collection was shown in Paris on March 9, 2010. It was described by fashion journalist Hilary Alexander as "quite simply, an unfinished symphony to life—and death." Alexander went on to write, "A selection of 16 pieces were shown in Paris, at the Hôtel de Clermont-Tonnerre, the same day the catwalk show would have taken place—in a series of private presentations. The event had the feeling of a requiem" (Alexander, 2010).

In a Style.com article, leader of the design term, Sarah Burton, described how McQueen had turned away from the world of the Internet, which had so powerfully harnessed his last show. "He wanted to get back to the handcraft he loved, and the things that are being lost in the making of fashion," she said. "He was looking at the art of the Dark Ages, but finding light and beauty in it. He was coming in every day, draping and cutting pieces on the stand" (Mower, 2010). The 16 outfits shown had been 80 percent finished at the time of his death.

Lee Alexander McQueen was considered the fashion genius of his generation; this was a sad loss to the fashion world and everyone who knew him.

Figure Box 4.1
Alexander McQueen, [season], 2010.

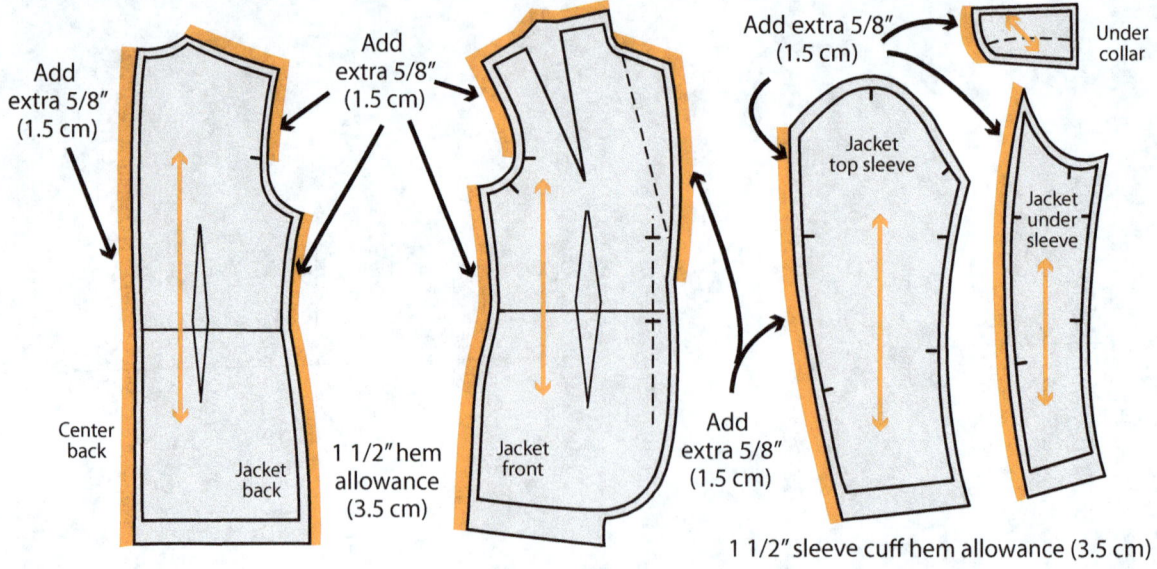

Figure 4.33

Making the Toile

Making a muslin version of your garment allows you to check the fit of the pattern and make any alterations without wasting fabric. This is also the time to make any changes in your proportions and design. Remember, it is a lot cheaper to do this in muslin than in your fashion fabric.

Begin by adding 5/8 inch (1.5 cm) seam allowance to your pattern; also add 5/8 inch (1.5 cm) extra inlay, as shown in Figure 4.33, so that you can make alterations at the first fitting of the toile.

Working on a flat surface, pin the pattern pieces onto the muslin making sure that the grainlines match perfectly. Transfer all pattern markings onto the muslin. To do this you can use a tracing wheel and carbon paper, tailor's chalk, or a pencil, which is the quickest. Mark in the pocket placement; you do not have to make pockets on the toile because their position on the jacket could change. See Chapter 7 for design ideas and pocket placement.

Sew all the jacket muslin pieces together along the seam allowances, pressing the seams open as you work. Press up both the jacket hem and sleeve allowances, and pin or baste in place.

Follow the instructions in Chapter 12 for making the shoulder pads, or have your ready-made pads so that you can pin them to the shoulders of the jacket toile for the first fitting.

Now turn to Chapter 5, and follow the fit instructions. Make any fit adjustments or design alterations to your toile. You may have to make a second toile if you have too many fit alterations and design adjustments. Transfer all alterations and adjustments from the toile to the pattern pieces before continuing.

CHAPTER CHECKLIST

Before moving on to the next chapter, make sure that:
- ☐ The jacket is fitting correctly with no pulling or twisting.
- ☐ You have made all the alterations to your pattern pieces.
- ☐ Your design silhouette is flattering to the body shape.
- ☐ You check that the proportion and line are right for both the design and body shape.
- ☐ You have thought about the details of your jacket design and marked their correct placement.
- ☐ You are happy with your original design before you cut your jacket in your fashion fabric.

REFERENCES

Alexander, Hilary. "Alexander McQueen autumn/winter 2010/11," *Telegraph.* Retrieved March 25, 2010, from http://www.telegraph.co.uk/fashion/paris-fashion-week/7407126/Alexander-McQueen-autumnwinter-201011-Paris-Fashion-Week.html.

Fallon, J. (2000, June 5). "London Finality, Royalty and Rebellion," *Women's Wear Daily.*

Foley, B. (2008, June) "Hail McQueen," *W Magazine.*

Mower, Sarah. (2010, 9 March). "Alexander McQueen," Style.com. Retrieved March 25, 2010, from http://www.style.com/fashionshows/review/F2010RTW-AMCQUEEN.

The Fit

CHAPTER 5

Be daring, be different, be impractical, be anything that will assert integrity of purpose and imaginative vision against the play-it-safers, the creatures of the commonplace, the slaves of the ordinary.

—Cecil Beaton

CHAPTER OBJECTIVES

After reading this chapter, you should be able to:

Evaluate the fit of the jacket on the body.

Understand where to make the fit adjustments.

Evaluate the proportion of the jacket on the body.

Consider if the jacket design is balanced.

Trust in your judgment.

Take these adjustments over onto the pattern pieces.

We all know how uncomfortable it is to wear clothing that doesn't fit correctly. When tailoring the jacket for a client, it is important to watch the client enter your workroom without this person noticing you doing so. This way you will catch your client standing naturally. We all pull back our shoulders, suck in our stomachs, and maybe even puff out our chests in an effort to look better in the garment as we try it on. But after the garment is finished and is being worn, the body relaxes back to its comfortably natural stance. So get the person to relax as much as possible during the first fitting.

FITTING THE JACKET

Fit the jacket over a shirt or blouse, but not a sweater. You do not want the jacket to stick to the undergarment and alter the line and look. Pin the jacket accurately in place. Lap the right front over the left, or vice versa for menswear, matching the center front lines and pinning where you have marked the buttonhole placement. Be critical, trust your eye, and study the jacket for any flaws. First look at the length and make changes by lengthening or shortening the jacket before making any style adjustments.

Lapels

Do the lapels look too wide or too narrow? Or are they too long or too short? (See Figures 5.1 and 5.2.)

Correct by making pencil marks onto the muslin.

Alter the length of the roll line by raising or lowering the top button placement.

Waistline

Make sure that the waistline is in the right place—not too high or too low. This is very important in a jacket that nips in exactly at the waistline. If the waistline is more than 3/8 inches (1 cm) out, a small adjustment will have to be made. Figures 5.3 and 5.4 show a jacket with a waistline that is too high.

Add in fabric to lengthen the jacket if it is sitting above the natural waistline.

Make a tuck in the jacket around the waistline if the jacket waist is sitting below the natural waistline (Figures 5.5 and 5.6).

If you do not have a buttonhole placement on the waistline, make the adjustment.

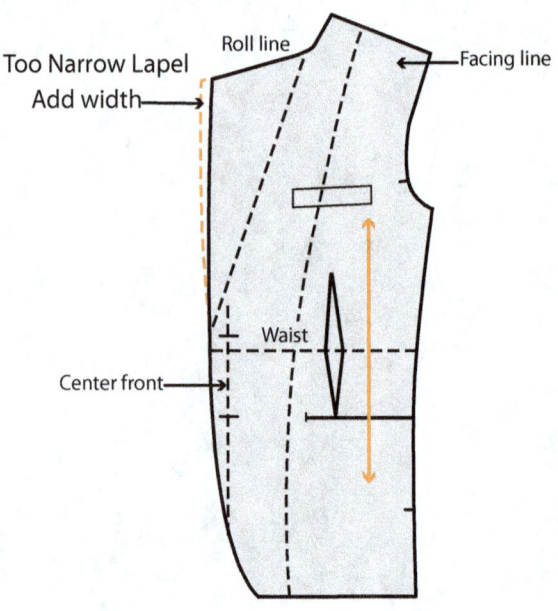

Figure 5.1

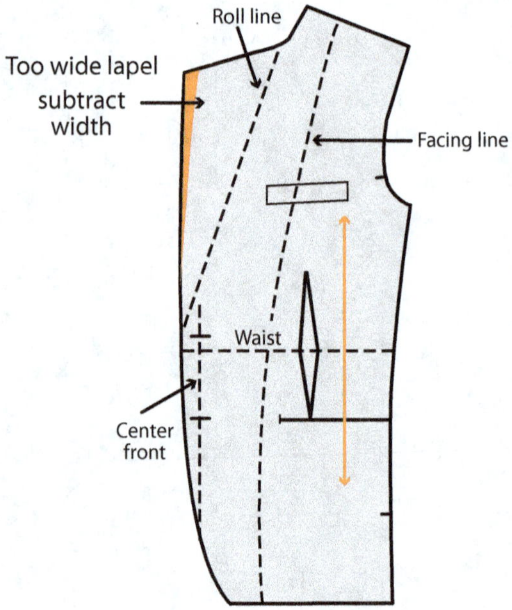

Figure 5.2

Figure 5.3

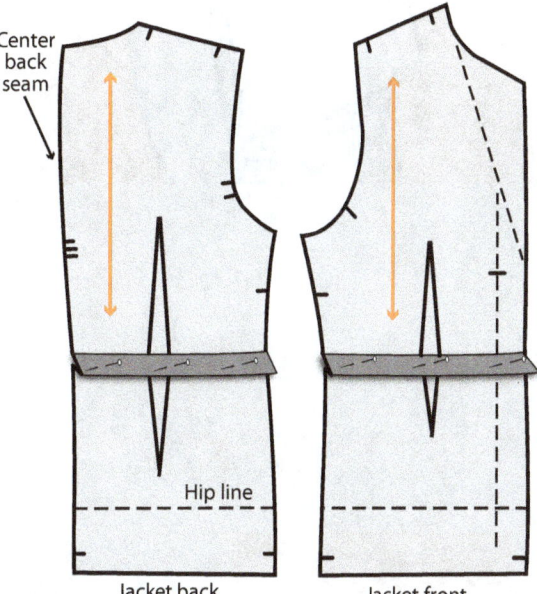

Figure 5.5

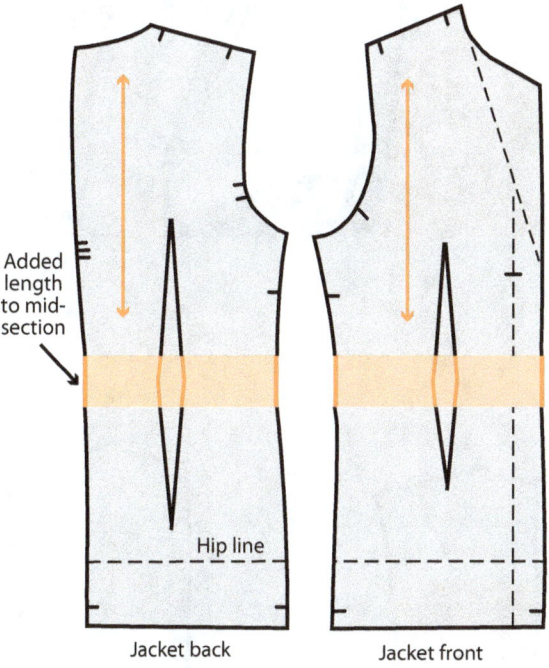

Figure 5.4

Figure 5.6

ADJUSTING FOR INDIVIDUAL BACKS AND BUST LINES

Many of us have sway backs or full bust lines; here you will find that the waist has to be shortened more in the back than the front (Figure 5.7). Adjust your pattern by making a tuck across the back (Figure 5.8).

Check the length and slant of the shoulder line. If the body is stooped or overly erect, or one shoulder is higher or lower than the other, the jacket will not hang correctly.

For a stooped posture the jacket will pull towards the back and upwards (Figure 5.9).

Make a dart in the side seam about 1½ inches (3.8 cm) down from the armhole. The tuck will be between ½ inch to ¾ inch (1.3 to 1.9 cm) wide and tapered across the back (Figure 5.10).

Figure 5.7

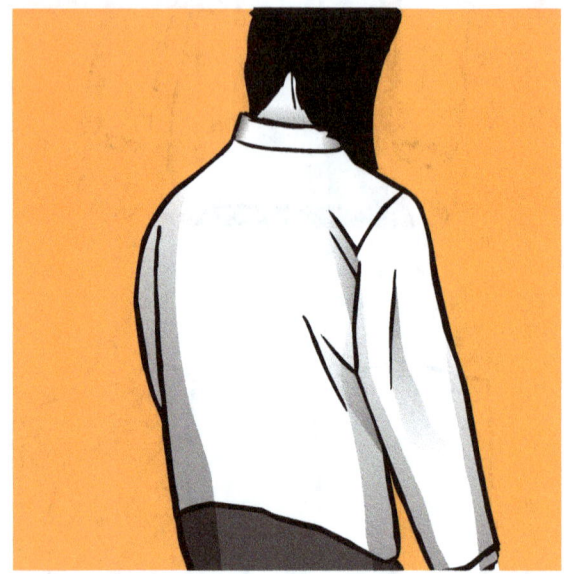

Figure 5.9

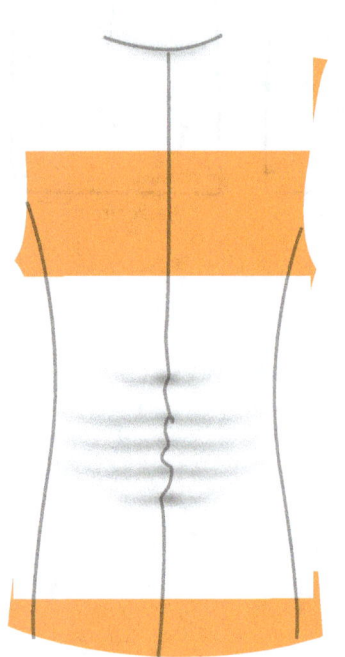
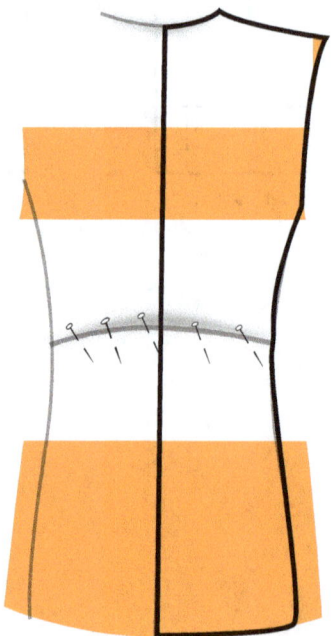
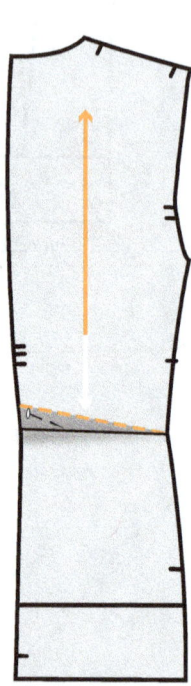

Figure 5.8

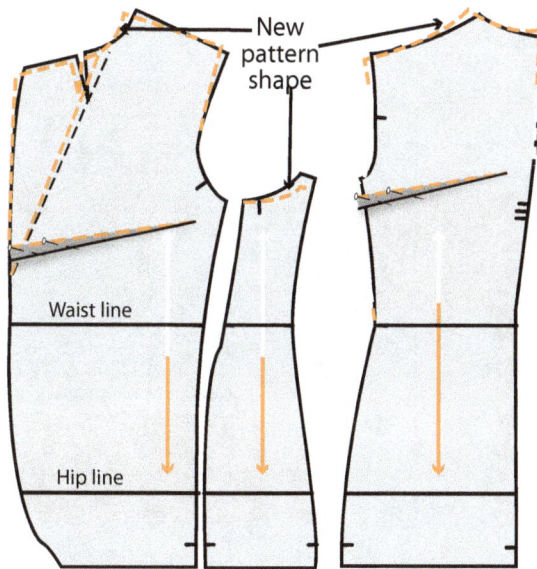

Figure 5.10

Figure 5.12

You may also have to adjust the front at the lapel. Again, make a tuck about 1½ inch (3.8 cm) down from the armhole starting at the lapel edge and finishing about 2 inches (5cm) in from the side edge of the front (Figure 5.11).

The top of the side panel will have to be altered on the pattern. Make sure that the waist notch to armhole match.

A jacket on an overly erect posture will pull towards the front and upwards (Figure 5.12). Undo the seam on the side back seam for about 1½ inch (3.8 cm) down from the armhole. Slash the muslin, beginning at the back side seam, to about 2 inches (5 cm) in from the center back seam (Figure 5.13).

In the front, slash the muslin from the lapel edge to about 2 inches (5 cm) in from the side edge. These slashes should spread apart at the side seam and lapel edge approximately ½ to ¾ inch (1.3 to 1.9 cm). Place a piece of fabric behind this area and pin in place.

Figure 5.11

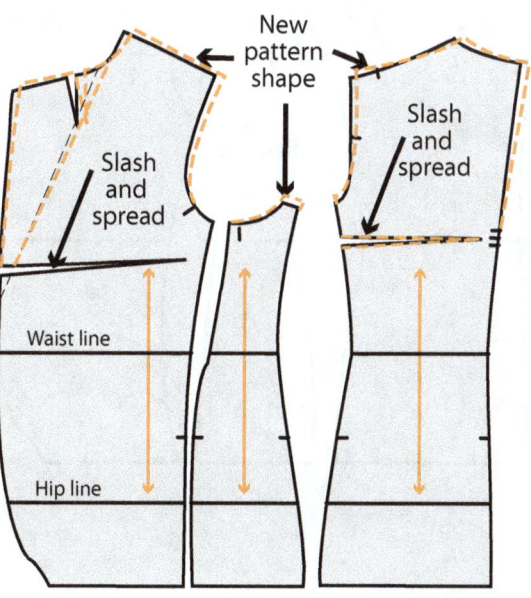

Figure 5.13

THE SHOULDER LINE

If the shoulder line is too long, pin a tuck in the jacket as shown in Figures 5.14 and 5.15.

If the shoulder line is not long enough, un-pick the stitches across the sleeve cap and re-pin the sleeve in the right position. If you still think the shoulder line is too short, extra fabric will have to be added to the jacket shoulder (Figures 5.16 and 5.17).

Make a note on the pattern piece to extend the shoulder line or shorten it.

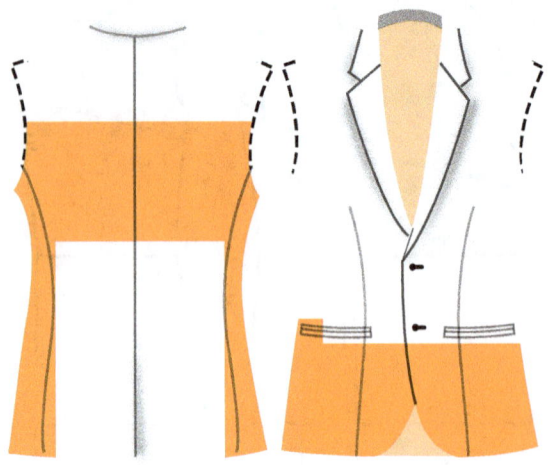

Figure 5.16

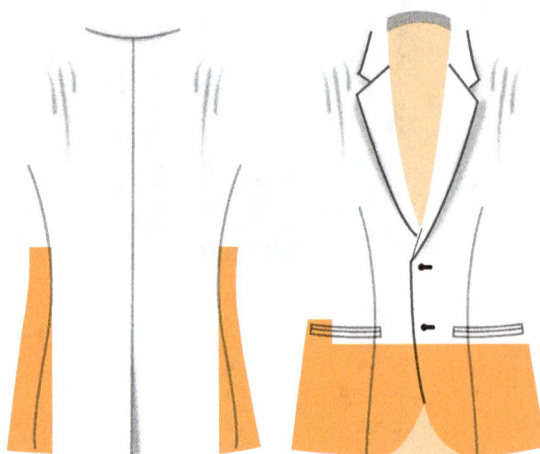

Figure 5.14

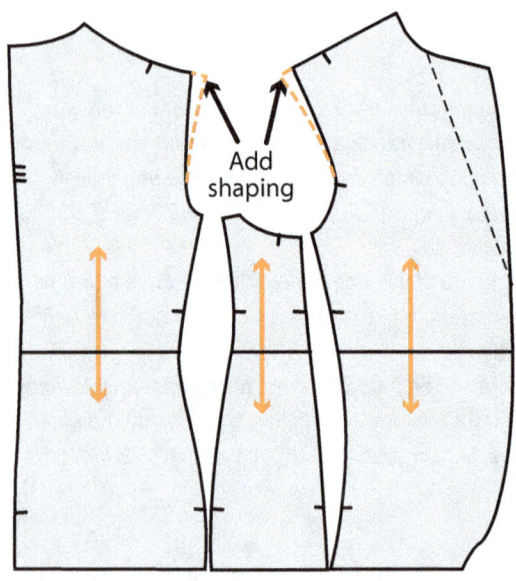

Figure 5.17

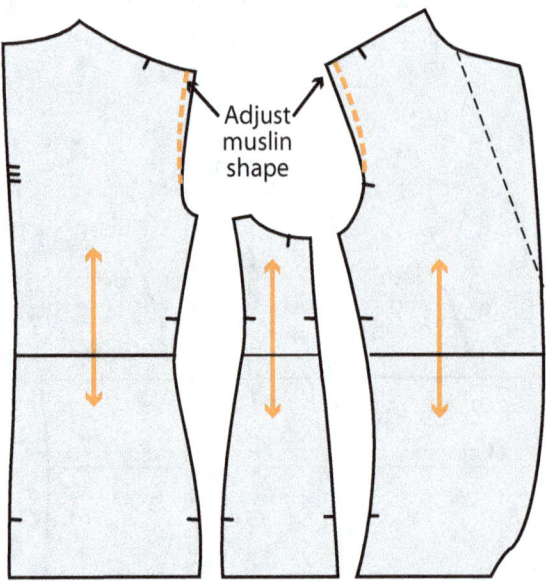

Figure 5.15

Low Shoulder

Many people have one shoulder lower than the other. An indication of this is sagging diagonal creases down only one side of the jacket (Figure 5.14).

Pin the fabric up at the shoulder line until the creases disappear, and measure the amount of fabric you have pulled up to make the adjustment (Figure 5.18).

If you were to remove this fabric at the shoulder line, the armhole size would also change and you would have to adjust the sleeve. The problem is that it is the length of the body from armhole to waist that is mak-

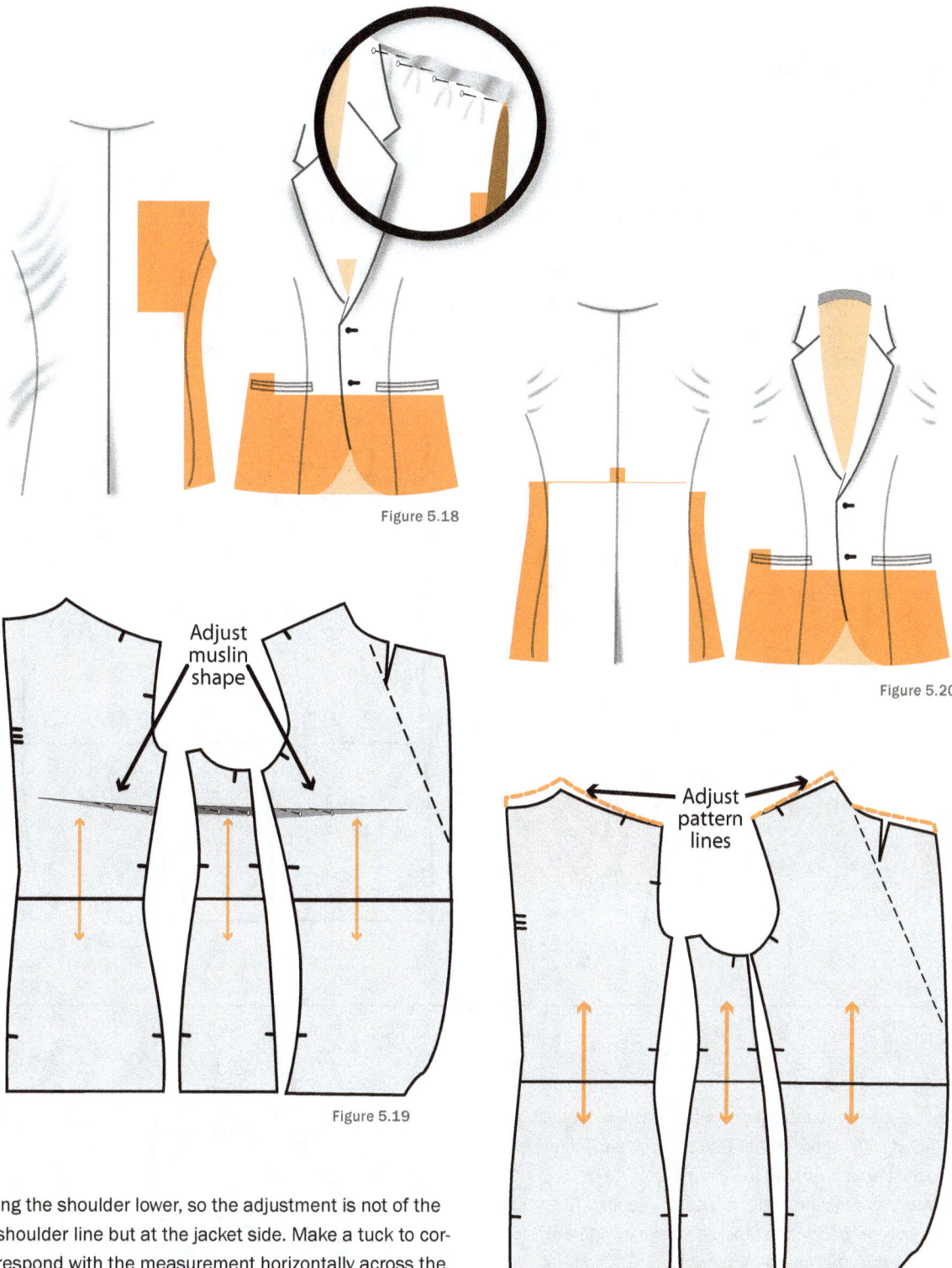

Figure 5.18

Figure 5.19

Figure 5.20

Figure 5.21

ing the shoulder lower, so the adjustment is not of the shoulder line but at the jacket side. Make a tuck to correspond with the measurement horizontally across the jacket as shown in Figure 5.19.

Let the pins go at the shoulder line.

Sloped Shoulders

Sloped shoulders will make wrinkles appear at the bottom of the armhole (Figure 5.20).

To fix this, first try to increase the amount of padding in the shoulder pad. This may eliminate the problem; if not, however, open the shoulder seam and re-pin it to eliminate the wrinkling (Figure 5.21).

Measure the amount of correction at the armhole edge of the shoulder because you now have to make adjustments to the pattern.

Square Shoulders

Square shoulders can cause circular wrinkling at the base of the collar on both front and back (Figure 5.22).

Decrease the amount of shoulder padding, and the problem should be eliminated. If not, remove the undercollar and re-pin the shoulder seams to eliminate the wrinkling (Figure 5.23).

Measure out the amount of fabric removed in the correction and make this adjustments to the jacket pattern front and back down the neck edge of the shoulder. Lower the neck edge and lapel (Figure 5.24).

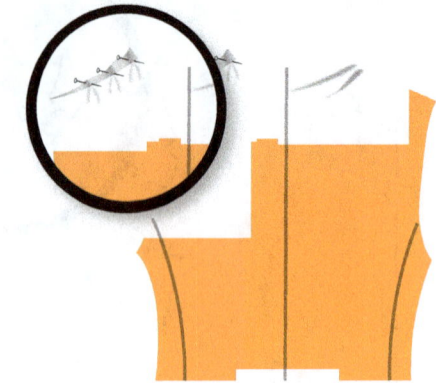

Figure 5.23

Figure 5.22

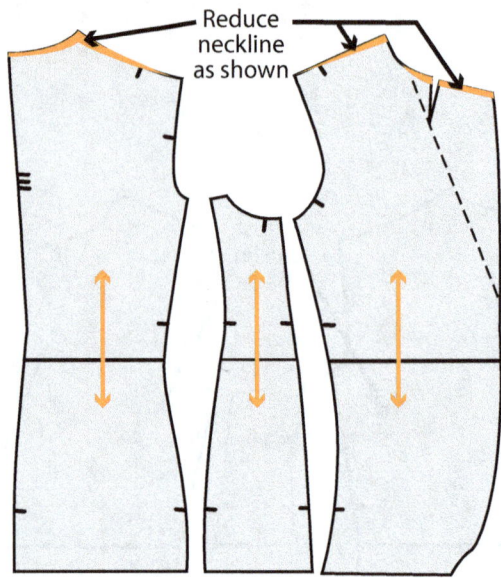

Figure 5.24

FULL BUST

The best pattern choice for a woman with a full bust is a jacket with a princess line, so that you can increase the bust area as shown in Figure 5.25.

You may now find that the lapel is gapping. To correct this, make a dart in the lapel as shown in Figure 5.11. Redraw the lapel shape, if altered.

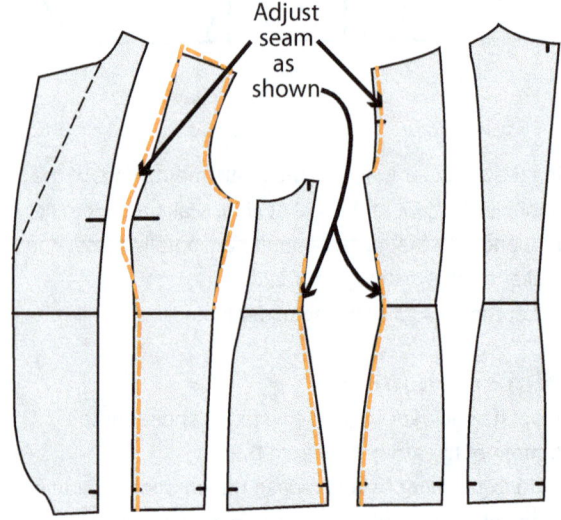

Figure 5.25

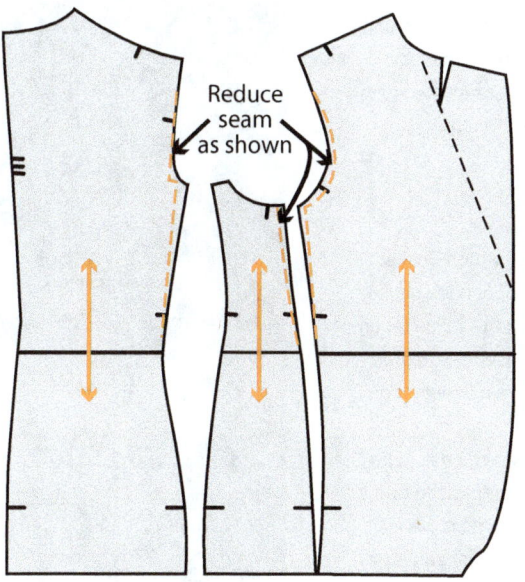

Figure 5.26

Small or Flat Bust

Taper out the excess fabric in the chest area at the armhole edge, the front underarm seam, and the jacket back (Figure 5.26).

Front Dart

If the jacket front dart is not directly in line with the breast, the dart is misplaced and will have to be moved. If you do not move the dart, there will be a restriction in the fabric across the breast and a bulge of fabric at the side (Figures 5.27 and 5.28).

If the dart continues beyond the center of the breast, you will have noticeable pulling in the fabric. Lower the dart so that it ends about 1 inch (2.5 cm) below the bust point (Figures 5.29 and 5.30).

Figure 5.27

Figure 5.29

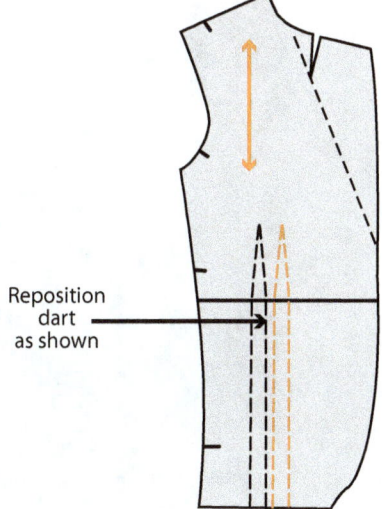

Figure 5.28

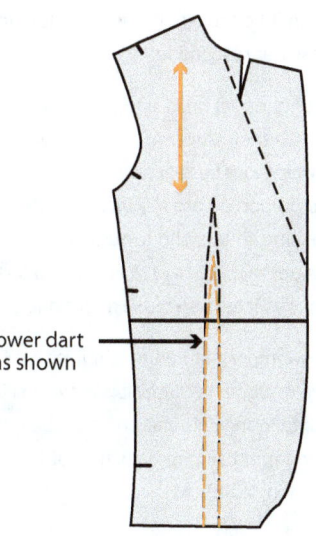

Figure 5.30

Satyen Patel was born in London in 1972 and raised in Gloucestershire, the youngest of three children. As a child he watched his mother and sister making clothes, and this is where his passion for design and creating clothing began. His career started when he enrolled in a class in women's wear in Cheltenham Gloucester, and he says that this is where he learned his pattern cutting skills.

FROM LONDON TO MILAN

He eventually moved from Gloucestershire to London and enrolled in a course at London College of Fashion. It was at the end of the first year of this course that he was given the option to specialize. Satyen choose menswear because he had loved the tailoring classes. He took this all as far as he could, graduating from Central Saint Martin's school of Art and Design with a master's degree in fashion design, menswear in 2001. He then moved to Milan where he worked as a designer on the mainline collection at Versace for four seasons.

Satyen credits London College of Fashion for teaching him his tailoring skills, where he said he would drape and cut on the stand, just doing his own thing and building a portfolio. His style was at times flamboyant, dramatic, and over the top, but as his skills grew his style became more refined and stylish. It was at Central Saint Martin's where he polished his design creativity and style in menswear, where in his final exit collection he used his cutting skills and the addition of couture elements that got him the position at Versace. Versace loved the collection because it was all tailored, uniform, used only a two-color palette, and kept the styling simple.

Satyen then returned to London to work as a consultant for women's wear designer Ashish before starting his own label.

Using his first name, Satyenkumer, he presented his first collection in fall/winter 2006–07. This was well received by both buyers and the fashion editors. It also caught the attention of Harrod's department store, where Satyenkumer was exclusively sold for its first two seasons.

A GRADUAL INTRODUCTION OF TAILORING TECHNIQUES

Satyen has been slowly building his label and slowly introducing more tailoring with each collection. To ensure quality and attention to detail, he manufactures only in the United Kingdom, and sources 90 percent of materials from British suppliers.

In an interview with Oki-ni's Creative Director John Skelton, Satyen said:

> The reason why I never injected a lot of tailoring in my earlier collection was due to sourcing quality production in the UK at a good price, as it is very hard to compete with established designers, so I waited till I found the right factories. But the thing is, in all the pieces that I have done, the element of cut was always there, but it wasn't in a sartorial way; it was kind of in a relaxed kind of sporty way, but in a new way where it wasn't street wear. It was a bit leisure. (Skelton, 2009)

Skelton went on to ask Satyen if he thought it was important for a student to design as well as tailor a jacket, to which the designer responded:

> Design is what makes your garment unique to any other designer. Having learnt the basic principle of tailoring first, it is then easier to design as you understand that there are a lot of elements to tailoring, which can be reproduced in design. Both principles are as equally important, silhouette and proportion are key factors to designing a jacket followed by the shoulder, lapel, and break line. Fabric and texture are important as not only do they change the drape, texture gives a depth to a jacket. A jacket is a special piece in any wardrobe/closet, it has to be the right cut as it says so much about one's look. (Skelton, 2009)

Finally, Satyen was asked how important he thought it is that fashion design students understand and be able to tailor. The designer replied, "It is a dying skill, so it can only be beneficial to understand the principles of tailoring; this skill can then be taken into any design... I hope the reader will enjoy and understand that tailoring is such a valued and respected design principle that should be embraced" (Skelton, 2009).

Figure Box 5.1
Satyenkumar,
Spring/Summer
2010.

If the dart stops well below the center of the breast, you will have too much fabric in the area under the breast (Figures 5.31 and 5.32).

Figure 5.31

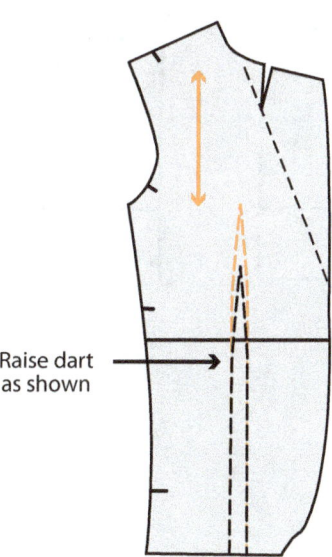

Raise dart as shown

Figure 5.32

SHAPING THE JACKET

The jacket can be altered in size at the side seam or at the darts. These seams can be taken in or let out (Figure 5.33).

If you are taking in the darts to create a tighter waist line, take in both the front and back darts.

The side seam of the jacket should run in a straight line from under the arm to the waist and then follow the curve of the body below the waist.

A good rule of thumb to follow is to see that there is approximately 1 to 1½ inch (2.5 to 3.8 cm) more in the bust, waist, and hip areas than it appears you need at this time.

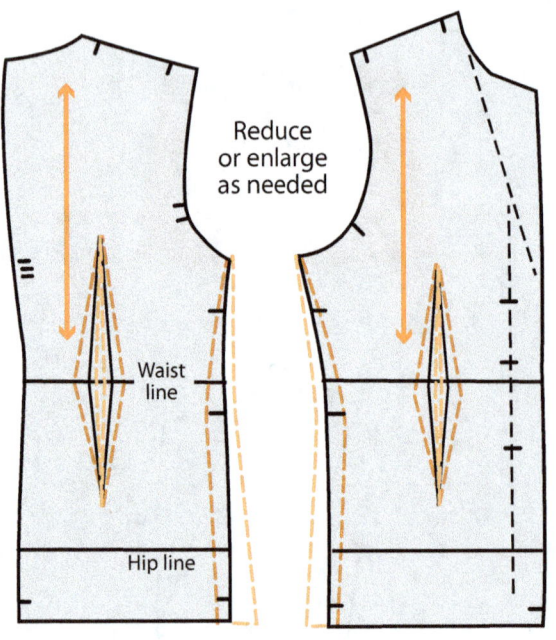

Figure 5.33

Proportions

Look at the proportions of the collar, pockets, and all other parts of your jacket. These can now be altered. If you make changes to the collar, always do so on the outer edge. Body shape will require a change in detail proportion. Pockets may look better lower or higher on the hip, and pockets can be made smaller for someone with very small hands or larger for those with larger hands.

CHAPTER CHECKLIST

Before you are ready to begin construction, be sure to check that:

- ☐ The muslin toile is sitting on the body with no wrinkling or pulling.
- ☐ Your design is in proportion with the fit of the jacket.
- ☐ The jacket looks balanced.
- ☐ You have a button on the waistline.
- ☐ The lapel is not gapping.
- ☐ The back undercollar is covering the back neck seam line.
- ☐ All adjustments have been taken over onto the jacket pattern.

REFERENCES

Skelton, J. (2009, September 25). "New Faces in Menswear." Retrieved on December 15, 2009 from http://00o00.blogspot.com/2009/09/satyenkumar-spring-summer-2010.html

PART III

Construction

HAND STITCHES FOR TAILORING

Pad Stitching

Pad stitching holds the interfacing in place. It adds body and built-in shape that will be permanent.

Pad stitching is worked on to hair canvas interfacing with single thread. Rolling the fabric layers over your index finger, make small stitches that catch only a thread of the fashion fabric will position and hold.

1. Mark your seam allowances with chalk or a soft pencil.
2. Working flat on the table or over your index finger, for both the lapel and collar, take a small perpendicular stitch about ¼ to ½ inch in length.
3. Repeat ¼ to ½ from the first stitch, working down to form a line.
4. Do not pull your stitches too tight.
5. Move your needle to the next line and continue so that you are making rows of chevron stitches.
6. Do not make your stitches too uniform so that you don't show rows on your fashion fabric.

Catch Stitching and Basting

Catch stitching is used to hold seams and the sides of pockets in place.

1. Working from side to side with a single thread, start by taking a small stitch into fabric.
2. With the needle pointing left, catch one or two threads of the garment about ¼ inch in length.
3. Take the next stitch to the right.
4. Keep stitching evenly spaced, and do not pull too tight.

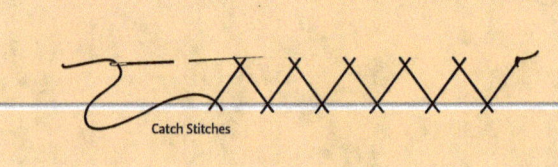

Figure Box III.1c Catch stitching.

Basting stitches are long, loose stitches used to temporarily hold materials together. Refer to the following illustration.

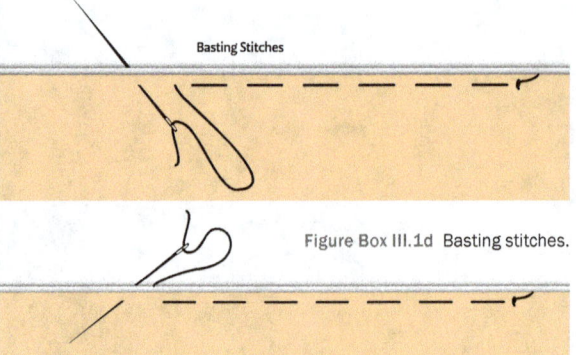

Figure Box III.1d Basting stitches.

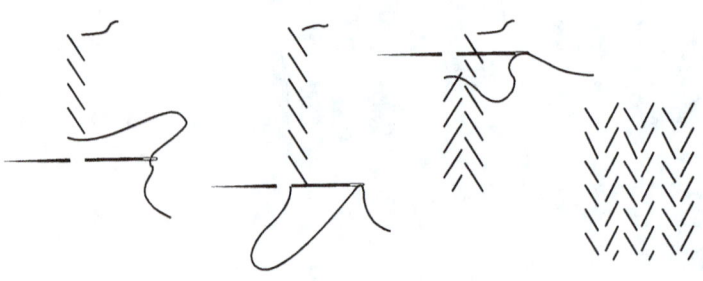

Figure Box III.1a Pad stitching.

Slip Stitching

Slip stitching invisibly joins pockets or the folded edge

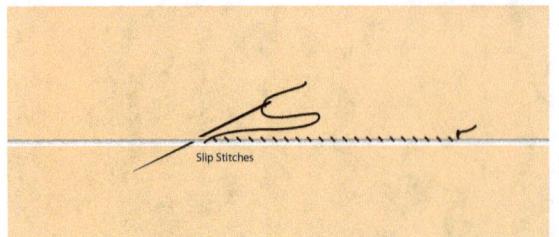

Figure Box III.1b Slip stitching.

1. With a single strand of thread, working through the folded edge, take a tiny stitch.
2. Now work into the garment, catching only a thread or two.
3. Slip your needle into the fold again about ¼ inch and then out to make the next stitch.

CHAPTER 6

The Jacket Front

I'm not that interested in fashion .... When someone says that lime green is the new black for this season, you just want to tell them to get a life.

—Bruce Oldfield

CHAPTER OBJECTIVES

After reading this chapter, you should be able to:

Determine which method to use to add the inner structure to the jacket front.

Cut the fusible interfacings for the front.

Add support to the jacket front by attaching the hair canvas or Hymo canvas.

Understand the importance of adding structure to the chest/shoulder area in the form of a chest piece.

Shape the front with darts, tucks, pleats, or seam lines.

Baste the interfacing to the front so that it becomes one.

Pad stitch and shape the front lapels.

Tape and shape the roll line.

Understand the importance of well-defined front edges.

Mark and construct the bound buttonholes on the jacket front.

This chapter guides you through the construction and shaping of your jacket front. As introduced in Chapter 1, there are three different tailoring methods: traditional (also called bespoke or classic tailoring), contemporary, and quick fusible. Some tailors prefer one method to another, but most contemporary tailors use a combination of techniques to construct different areas of the same jacket. Throughout the remaining construction chapters in this book, you will find instructions for all three techniques. Choose the technique that is best suited to your jacket design, fabric, time frame, and sewing skills. Refer to Table 6.1 for tips to help you choose the method appropriated for your jacket design.

Figure 6.1 This suit is softly tailored, giving it a fresh modern look.

APPLYING FUSIBLE INTERFACING

If you have decided to use contemporary or fusible tailoring methods, this will be your first step in constructing your jacket front. Before applying fusible interfacings, always read the manufacturers instructions. There are three steps to applying fusible interfacings:

- Step 1: Make sure you fuse to the wrong side of your fashion fabric and apply the fusible interfacing.
- Step 2: Remark your darts, roll line, pocket placement, and buttonholes if you have lost these markings in the fusing process.
- Step 3: If using the contemporary tailoring technique, you will now prepare your jacket's canvas.

To complete these steps, follow these instructions:

1. Position the interfacing on the fabric with the resin side down and lightly hand smooth in place.

2. Position a press cloth over the surface.

3. With iron set for wool, hold the iron just above the press cloth and mist with steam to shrink the interfacing. Start at the center and work out to the edges in a fan-shaped pattern fuse for 10 to 15 seconds. Do not slide the iron from one position to the next, but lift move, and place it overlapping slightly to ensure complete coverage.

4. Turn the garment to the right side, and repeat the pressing. It is a good idea to use a new press cloth because you do not want to transfer any resin to the right side of your fashion fabric. Let it cool because interfacing is easily distorted or removed while still warm.

Figure 6.2 shows where to apply fusible interfacing to the jacket pattern pieces in contemporary tailoring; Figure 6.3 shows the same using the quick, strictly fusible technique.

Table 6.1 Three Methods of Tailoring

TRADITIONAL (ALSO REFERRED TO AS BESPOKE OR CLASSIC)	CONTEMPORARY	FUSIBLE
• Time consuming.	• Less time consuming.	• Fast.
• Requires the most hand stitching.	• Most stitching is done by machine.	• Eliminates hand stitching. • May not always fuse securely to all fabrics.
• Retains design shape and character of the fabric. • Firm shape in both collar and lapel areas.	• Soft, tailored look. • Machine stitching may show on the undercollar.	
• This technique has withstood the test of time and is still as appropriate today as in the past.	• Higher end and designer level garments depending on the amount of hand stitching.	• Mass production and designer-level garments mixed with both the other techniques.

Contemporary Tailoring Method

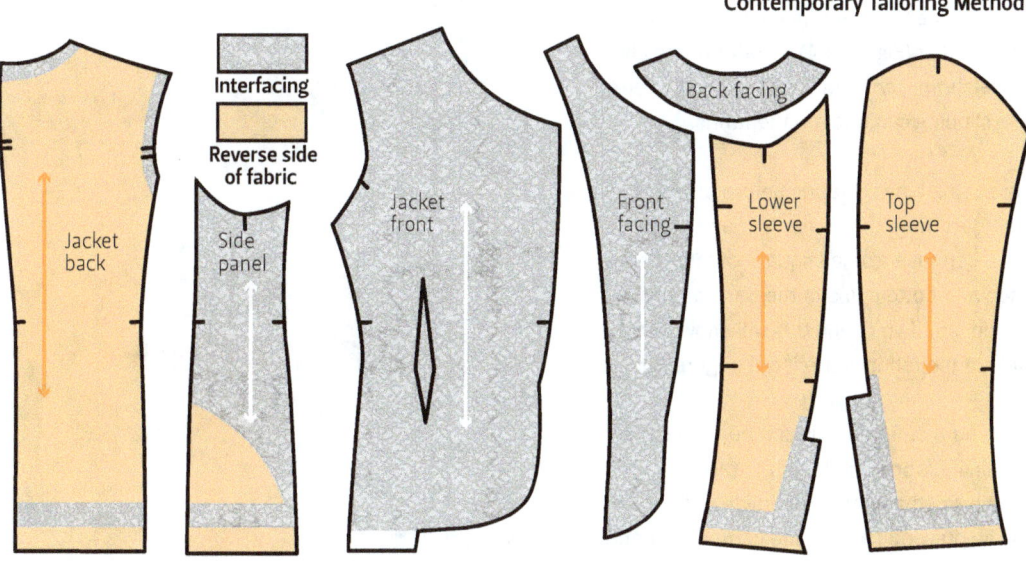

Figure 6.2

Quick Fuse Tailoring Method

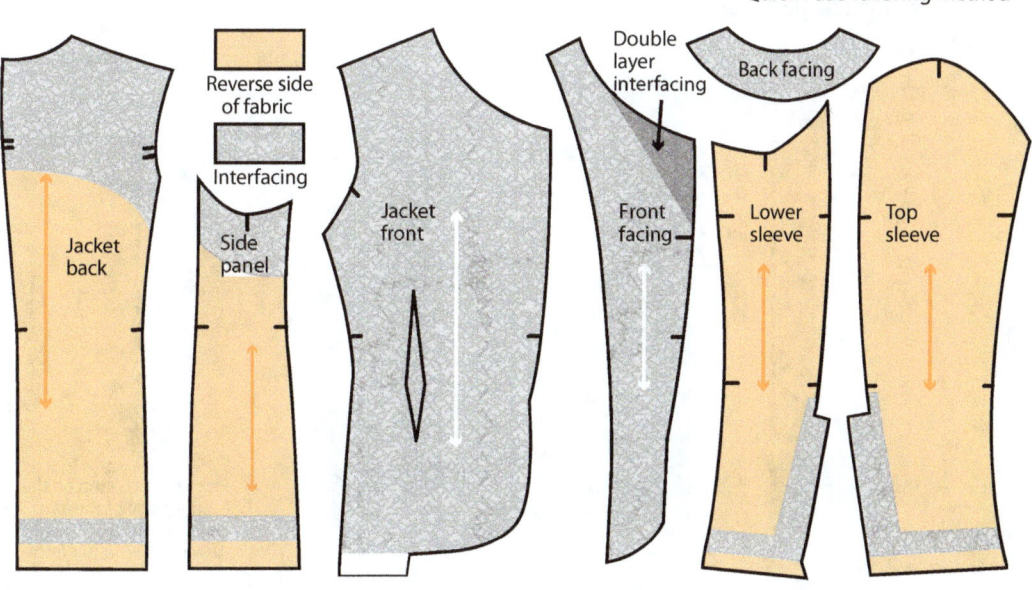

Figure 6.3

DARTS, TUCKS, AND PLEATS

Darts, tucks, and pleats are used to emphasize the body's shape in both men's and women's jackets.

Stitching the Waist Darts

If you are not sure which tailoring technique to use, work a small sample and then decide.

The next step in constructing the jacket front after applying the interfacing is to stitch the waist darts. All darts are sewn from top to bottom or in the direction of the nap, such as velvets and pile fabrics.

Make sure that your finished darts are smooth with no puckers and not showing through to the right side of the jacket front. Figure 6.4 through Figure 6.6 illustrate the three techniques, depending on your fashion fabric.

Be sure to stitch accurately when making the dart.

1. Press the folded edge flat and finish by pressing the dart towards the center front.

2. Your dart may need to be clipped in the center so that it will lay flat (Figure 6.4). I prefer not to clip but to stretch the center of the dart when I iron because clipping can weaken the fabric.

3. If you are using a heavy fabric before pressing, slash the dart down the center fold and press open. You can fuse a small square of interfacing at the top and bottom tips of the dart to reinforce the dart tip, but if you think this will show on the right side of the fabric, leave it out (Figure 6.5).

4. Bias cut a strip of fabric (this can be the fashion fabric or lining fabric) the length of the dart. Place the bias strip on the underside of the dart that will be pressed towards the center front and carefully stitch. This will help to stop a shadowing effect of the dart on the right side of your jacket if you are working with a light-colored worsted wool or linen, a loosely woven fabric, or napped fabric such as velvet (Figure 6.6).

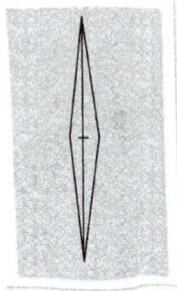 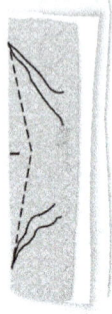 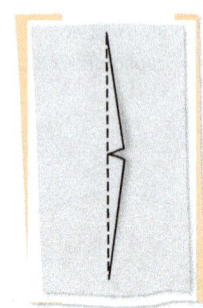

Figure 6.4

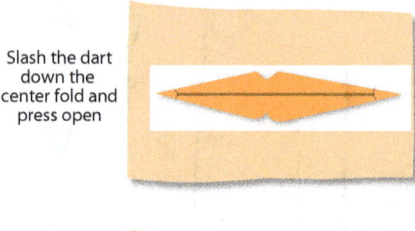

Slash the dart down the center fold and press open

 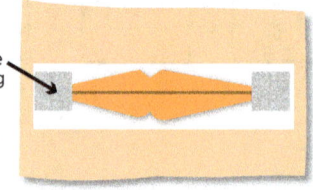

Optional: Small square of interfacing at tips of the dart to reinforce the dart

Figure 6.5

 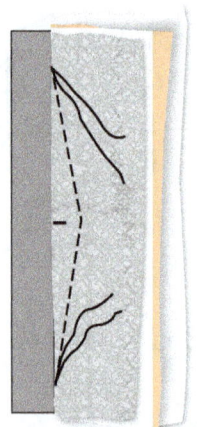 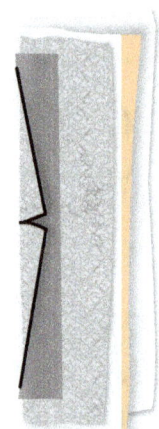 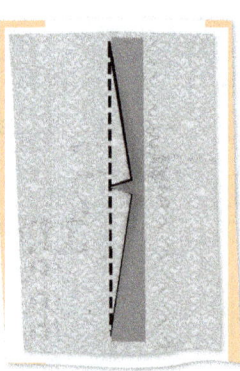

Bias Strip

Place the bias strip on the under side of the dart that is going to be pressed towards the center front

Figure 6.6

Working Tucks and Pleats

Work any tucks or pleats as per your design. Again, be accurate with your stitching because any mistakes or crooked stitching will show on the front of the jacket.

1. With right side to right side, attach the side panels to the fronts of the jacket (as per your design), making sure that you match your notches to keep the ease in place.

2. Press the seams open using a clapper (refer to "Tools of the Trade" sidebar or the Glossary for all references to equipment). You may have to make a small clip at the waistline if the jacket has significant waistline shaping, or stretch the seam allowance with the iron until it is laying flat.

Checklist for Tucks, Pleats, and Darts

Press your jacket front on the wrong side, and check that:

- The darts, tucks, or pleats are balanced.
- The darts, pleats or, tucks are the same length on both your front pieces.
- The darts are not curving into the tip at their top and bottom; this will cause "puckering" on the right side of the fabric that cannot be pressed out.
- The darts, tucks, or pleats are finished at the tips by reverse stitching or by tying the thread so that your stitches don't unravel.
- The seams are pressed open and flat using a pressing cloth to avoid over pressing.
- The side panels are sitting correctly with no tucks, and there is no pulling.
- Both of your front pieces look the same.

Your jacket front is now ready for you to construct the pockets and attach them to the jacket fronts (see Chapter 7).

When you have completed the pockets, add the inner structure to the jacket fronts by following the instructions for preparing your canvas. If you are constructing "fast fusible," move to bound buttonhole instructions later in this chapter, or turn to Chapter 8. Your jacket design may need more structure in the shoulder area (Figure 6.7).

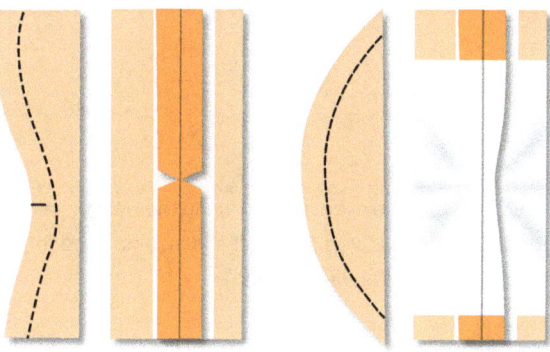

Figure 6.7

PREPARING THE CANVAS

The canvas is cut on the straight of the grain and has no right or wrong side. Use the jacket front as a guide for cutting. Canvas interfacings are used to support the shoulder and front edge of a jacket or coat. The canvas can also add body and define the shape of your design features. The hair canvas can cover the whole of the jacket front.

There is more canvas added to men's jacket fronts than to women's. One of the reasons for this is that you don't want to bring the canvas over the bust point in a women's jacket because of the bust shape; today, we look for a softer feel and look in tailoring. On a man's jacket you may have breast pockets and added lining pockets so men's jacket fronts need more support in this area. Men may also have what is called a hollow, or pirate's, chest that the canvas will help disguise (Figure 6.8).

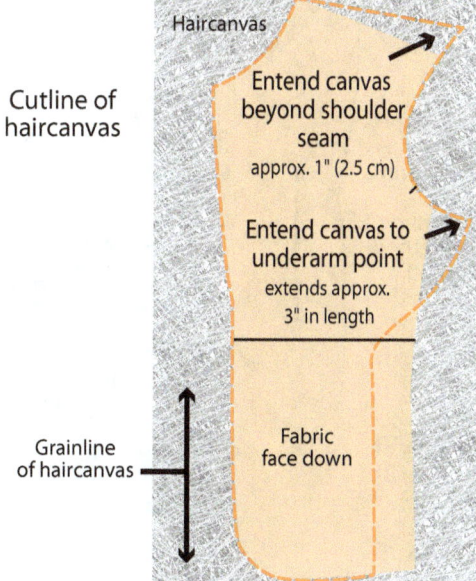

Figure 6.8

If you are creating your jacket using contemporary tailoring techniques rather than bespoke, which will give you a softer, more modern look and feel to the jacket, refer to Figures 6.9 and 6.10. Figure 6.9 shows how I prefer to work most of my jackets.

Adding the Bust Dart on a Woman's Jacket

On the women's canvas, you will have to add a small bust dart at the top of the jacket dart or over the bust point to create this same shape in the canvas.

1. Extend this dart 1 inch (2.5 cm) and redraw the dart on the canvas. Now cut down the center of the dart (see Figure 6.11).

2. Lap this dart closed by placing a strip of fusible interfacing on the wrong side and fusing the lapped dart closed to support this area that you are now going to stitch together. Stitch over the lapped dart, using a zigzag stitch on top of the fusible interfacing (see Figure 6.11).

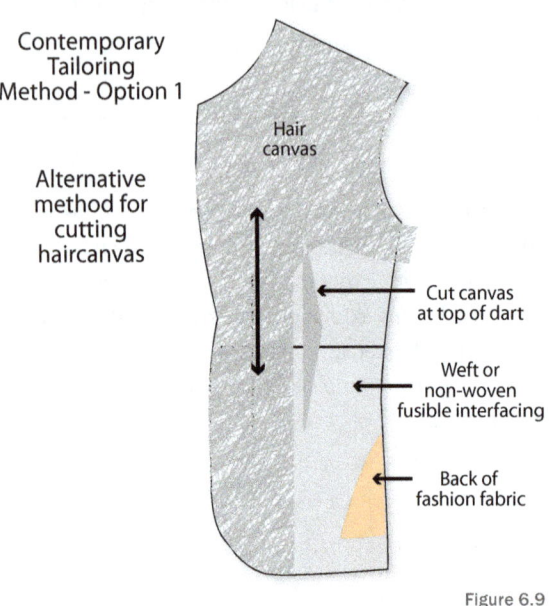

Figure 6.9

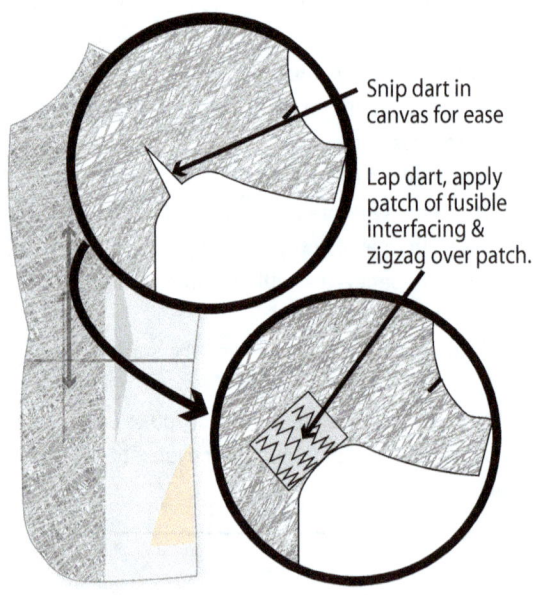

Figure 6.11

Figure 6.10 shows what to do when the design calls for a soft, unstructured look that can also be used for the fast, fusible tailoring method.

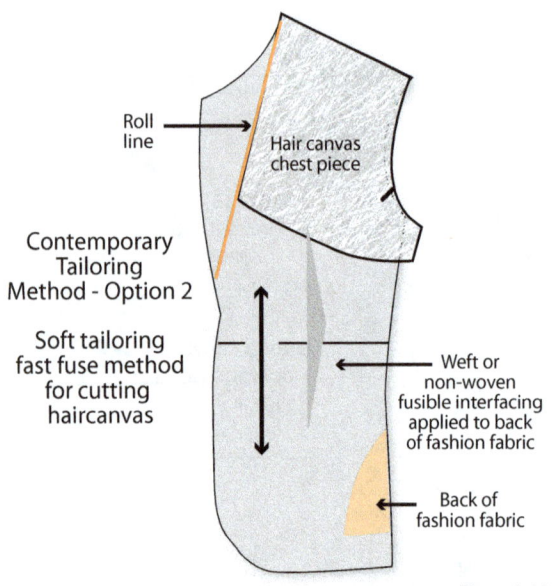

Figure 6.10

If you are using the fusible method for your jacket, you are only going to add canvas to the chest area, as shown in Figure 6.12.

I also add the chest piece, attaching it with zigzag stitching (refer to Figure 6.12). This will still give you a nice rounded line from shoulder to chest. Figure 6.13 shows how to cut the canvas for the fusible method for a collarless jacket.

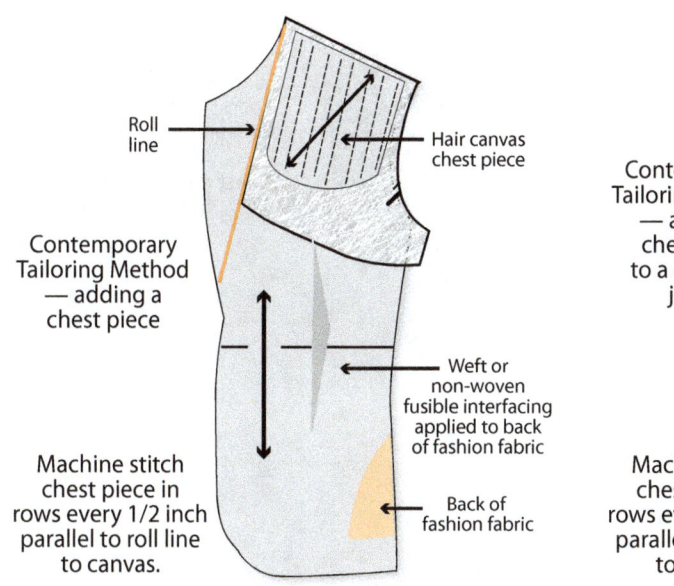

Figure 6.12

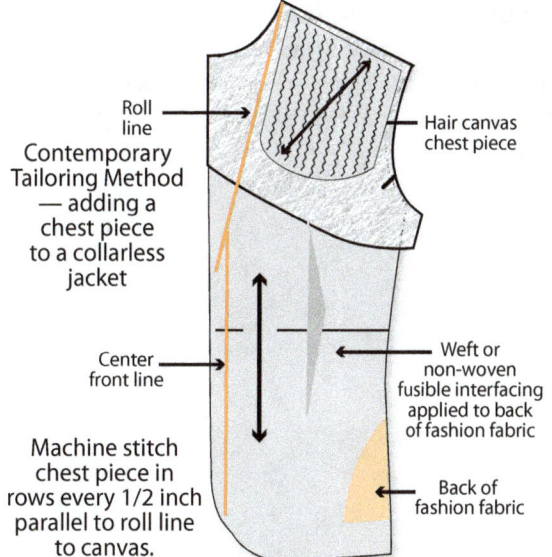

Figure 6.13

THE CHEST PIECE

The chest piece is also known as the chest shield, and it can be single or multi-layered. It is used to help maintain the shape of the upper front of your jacket, rounding out the hollow that occurs between the shoulder and the chest. Most jackets tend to stretch in the neck area when worn; the chest piece can help alleviate this problem.

For a man's jacket, the chest and front of the shoulder are built up with padded layers of canvas interfacing, haircloth, French canvas, and wool flannel (domette). But for a woman's jacket, this forms a solid chest piece that is far too heavy and unflattering; therefore, for women's jackets, use only one layer of wool or cotton flannel (domette) to give a softer feel and look while still reinforcing the front of the shoulder. The finished chest piece should give a nice rounded shape from the shoulder to the bust point or chest area of your jacket front.

Making the Chest Piece

For the women's jacket, working on the bias, cut a piece of wool (domette) or cotton flannel. The neck edge of your jacket will be virtually on the straight of the grain. This is what stabilizes the neck line, while the bias section will give a little bit of ease across the chest. The chest piece has no seam allowances.

Contemporary Method: Chest Piece

For the contemporary method, place the chest piece on top of the canvas with the front edge along the roll line, and position the rest of the chest piece along the seam line of both the shoulder and armhole. Approximately every 1½ inches (3 cm), work a row of machine zigzag stitching. This will hold the chest piece in place and also pad it slightly (Figure 6.14). The reason for using zigzag stitching is that it will not show through as lines of stitching on the right side of the jacket front.

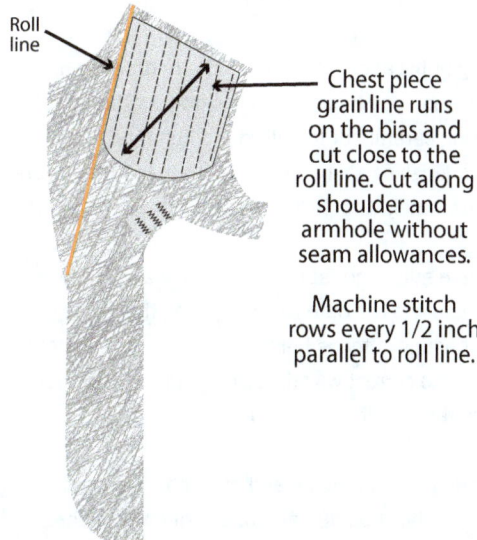

Figure 6.14

Traditional Method: Chest Piece

For traditional (classic or bespoke) tailoring, place the chest piece on top of the canvas and pad stitch in place by hand, as shown in Figure 6.15.

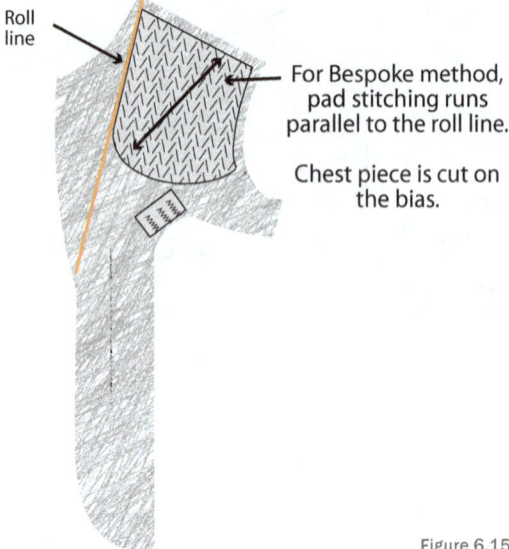

Figure 6.15

Joining Together the Canvas and Jacket Front

The canvas and jacket front are now ready to be joined together. Baste together the canvas and the jacket front so that from now on in the construction of the jacket they are handled as one piece.

1. On a smooth, flat surface, place the canvas onto the wrong side of the jacket front with the chest piece on the top facing you. Be sure to match the darts (Figure 6.16).

2. Flip it over so that the right side of the jacket front is now facing you (Figure 6.16).

3. Beginning about 3 inches (7.5 cm) down from the shoulder, baste down the front of the jacket, being careful not to pull your stitches too tight and finishing at the hem line. The stitches are approximately 1 to 1 ½ inches (2.5 to 3.8 cm) long.

4. Baste stitch the fabric across the waistline from the dart to the outer edge. Placing this short row of basting stitches here will also make it easier to find the correct waistline and balance when you are ready to fit your jacket.

5. Smooth the fabric up and out from the waist to below the shoulder, and baste stitch from the shoulder down over the dart to the hem.

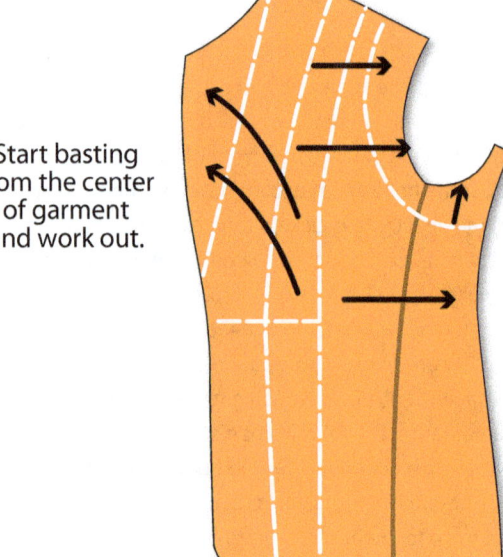

Figure 6.16

6. Chalk mark the roll line on the right side of the jacket. Smooth up and out over the lapel, and baste stitch the roll line.

The last row of basting runs from the armhole end of the shoulder, and traces down the armhole, remaining about 2 to 3 inches (2.5 to 7.5 cm) away from the edge.

You are now ready to pad stitch and shape your jacket's lapels.

PAD STITCHING AND SHAPING THE LAPELS

Pad stitches will show through onto the underside of the lapel in the finished jacket like tiny pin pricks, so make sure that you choose a color thread that matches your fashion fabric.

1. Draw a chalk line around the outer edge of the lapel and down the jacket front on the canvas to mark the seam allowance. If you are working a peak lapel, add a line across the bottom of the peak.

2. On the canvas side, begin pad stitching, with the first row of stitching about ¼ inch (.75 cm) in from the roll line. (See "Pad Stitching" later in this chapter as well as Figure 6.19, or refer to the "Hand Stitching for Tailoring" sidebar.) Hold the lapel in one hand between finger and thumb, rolled back over the jacket front so that it's positioned as it will be when finished (Figure 6.17).

3. Continue working in rows across the lapel, keeping parallel to the roll line. Do not pull your stitches too tight, and try to keep an even tension. Staggering the stitches helps to avoid ridges and puckers that will be obvious through the facing of the finished garment.

For softer lapels, make the stitches longer and the rows farther apart, but as you come to the lapel point or peak, work with smaller, shorter stitches that are more tightly grouped to give a firmer point that will hold its shape, rounding back close to the jacket front without rolling forward or drooping (Figure 6.18).

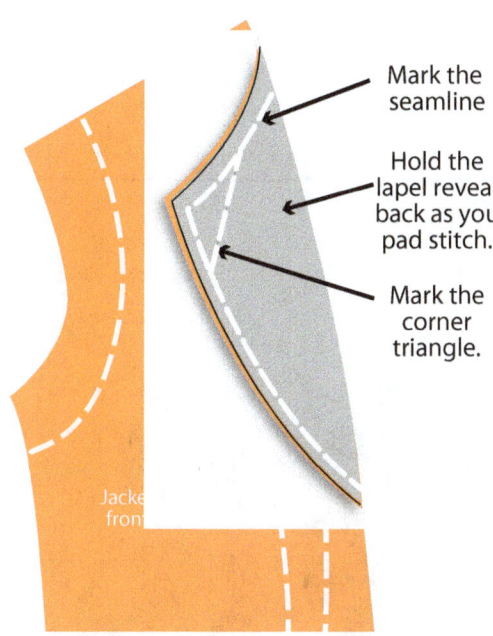

Figure 6.17

- Mark the seamline
- Hold the lapel reveal back as you pad stitch.
- Mark the corner triangle.

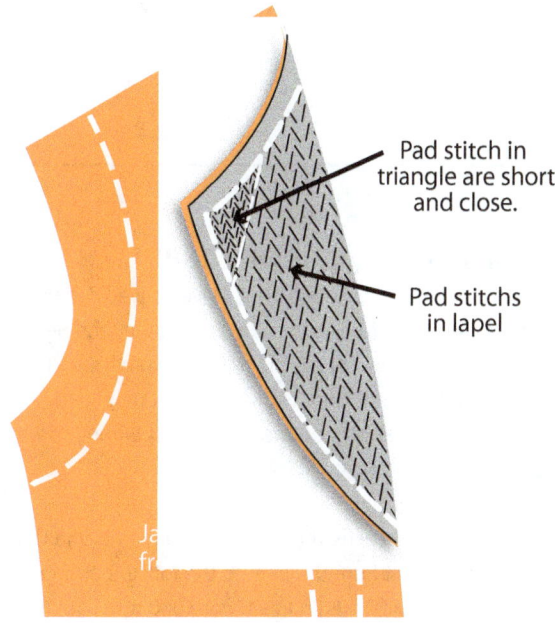

Figure 6.18

- Pad stitch in triangle are short and close.
- Pad stitchs in lapel

Pad Stitching

The pad stitch is a diagonal stitch that is staggered from one row to the next. The reason that you stagger this stitch is so that it doesn't show as "lines" on the shoulder of your finished jacket. Your pad stitches are about ⅜ inch (1 cm) in length. Work loosely so that your work does not pucker and form ridges between your rows, which will happen if the stitches are pulled too tight (Figure 6.19).

Figure 6.19

Taping and Shaping the Roll Line

Taping the front edge of the jacket gives a well-defined edge to the jacket front, stops any stretching, and helps preserve the shape. Taping the roll line, which is on the bias, gives additional support, stops stretching, and fits the roll line to the contours of the body without any gapping.

1. Begin by drawing the seam allowance around the jacket front from the hem to the roll line on the hair canvas. You did this before pad stitching the lapel, but the stitches will have pulled and slightly distorted the canvas so now you recheck the seam allowance and chalk in a new line.

2. Using ⅜-inch (1 cm) cotton or linen plain weave tape, pin the tape to the interfacing side of the top of the lapel starting at the roll line. At the lapel tip, twist the tape, and continue down the front edge to the break line or the bottom of your roll line (Figure 6.20).

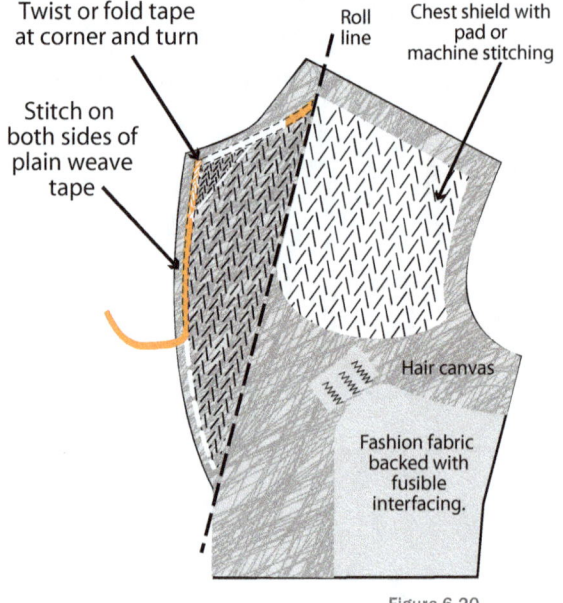

Figure 6.20

3. At the bottom of the roll line, place ⅜-inch (1 cm) ease in the tape, so that the lapel will be free to fold over without restriction. Pin the tape to the jacket front edge down to the bottom button. The tape should be smooth but not taut to this point. Now, hold the tape taut as you continue down to the hemline.

4. Compare the two front edges to make sure that they are the same and that they hang straight. Slip stitch both sides of the tape to your jacket front. Cut the hair canvas from the seam allowance up the front of the jacket and across the top of the lapel, being careful not to cut your stitches holding the tape in position. Do not cut the fashion fabric seam allowance off.

5. Apply the tape beyond the roll line, through all layers of fabric. Pin the tape at the top of the roll line and then pull the tape taut for the next 3 inches (7.6 cm) or so. You will get a rippling effect on either side of the tape. Continue to tape to the end of the roll line. Pulling the roll line tape creates the equivalent of a dart, shaping the roll line to the contours of the body (see Figure 6.21).

6. Starting with the roll line tape, slip stitch or cross stitch along the tape, stitching through all layers of fabric. The stitches should be at the very edge of the tape to prevent it from curling up. If you are using slip stitch, work both sides of the tape (Figure 6.22).

7. Next, press the lapels carefully with the interfacing side up, positioning the roll line along the edge of the pressing stand and the lapel hanging off the stand. Press only the roll line. This builds a curve at the roll line. Press the other lapel.

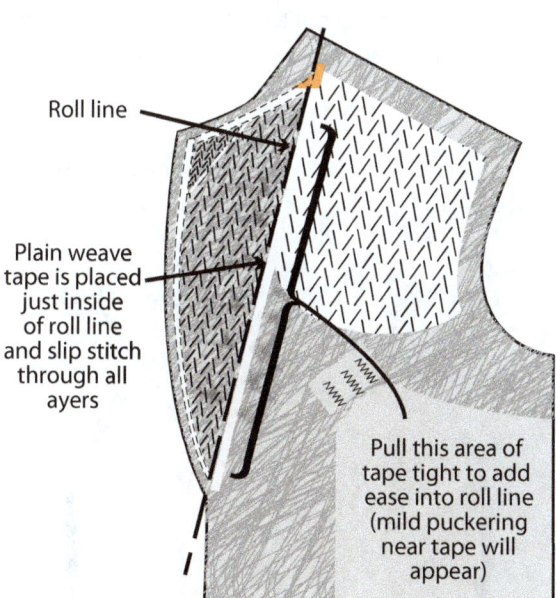

Figure 6.21

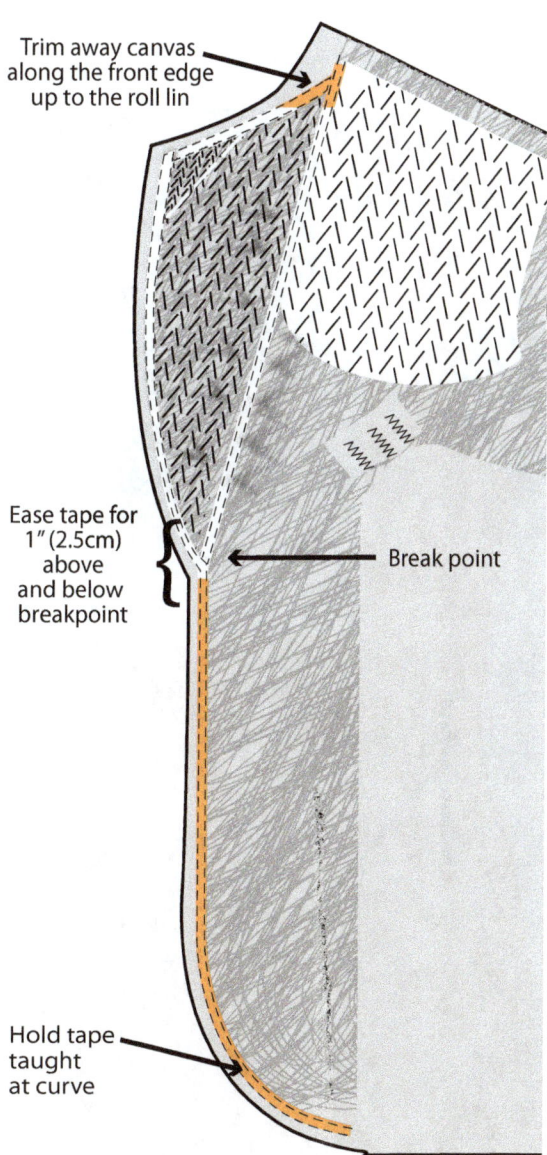

Figure 6.22

You do not have to tape any edges if working fast fusible, but you will get a better finish to the jacket if you tape the roll line. If you use a loosely woven fabric, taping the front edges will help prevent any stretching during wear.

At this stage, shrink the side seam, if you have one at the waistline as shown in Figure 6.23. You can also steam stretch the front to shape the bust; if you are smaller across the front shoulder, steam shrink this area.

The next step is to mark and make your bound buttonholes. If you are making machine buttonholes, mark the buttonhole placement and turn to Chapter 8.

Bound Buttonholes

The following method for constructing a bound buttonhole is easiest if the steps are carefully followed. Always begin by making a sample buttonhole using your garment fabric.

Buttons slide toward the outer end of the buttonholes when the coat is being worn, so that almost half of the button lies outside the buttonhole towards the edge of the garment. Because of this, the buttonholes are not centered on the center front of the garment. The buttonholes need to be positioned far enough back from the edge of the garment so that the buttons will not extend over the edge of the garment.

1. To find the correct position for your buttonhole placement from the finished front edge of the jacket, add together half the measurement of your button plus ⅜ inch (1 cm).

2. Mark on the center front of your jacket, if it is not marked (see Figure 6.24). Mark the ends of the buttonholes with two vertical lines of basting stitches.

3. Mark the line of each buttonhole with a basting stitch that extends well beyond the two vertical lines. This basting stitch will be on the weft grainline of the fabric.

Figure 6.23

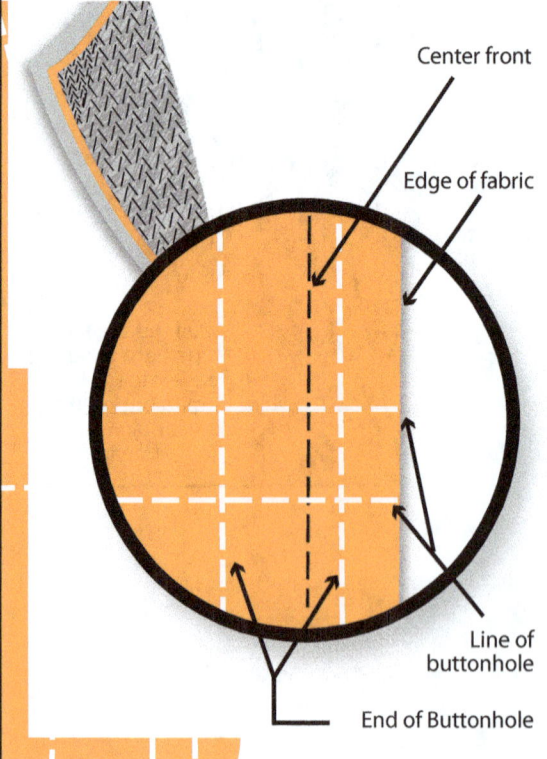

Figure 6.24

The Piping Strip

Your buttonhole will now need a piping strip.

1. Cut a strip of fabric either on the lengthwise or true bias grain about 2 inches (5 cm) wide and 2 inches (5 cm) longer than your buttonholes. Use a basting stitch to mark through the center of the strip.

2. With the wrong sides of the fabric together, make a lengthwise fold ¼ inch (6 mm) back from the center mark. Stitch across ⅛ inch (3 mm) in from fold line to form piping. Mark 1 inch (2.5 cm) in on both ends (see Figure 6.25).

3. Place the strip on the garment, right sides together matching the center of the strip with the line of the buttonhole. The strip will extend 1 inch (2.5 cm) at each end. Baste this strip into place along the center line.

4. Stitch the strip onto the garment ⅛ inch from the folded edge, starting and finishing exactly in line with the ends of the buttonhole. Start your stitching three to four stitches in from the edge of the buttonhole and back stitch to the line, sew across and sew back three to four stitches (see Figure 6.26).

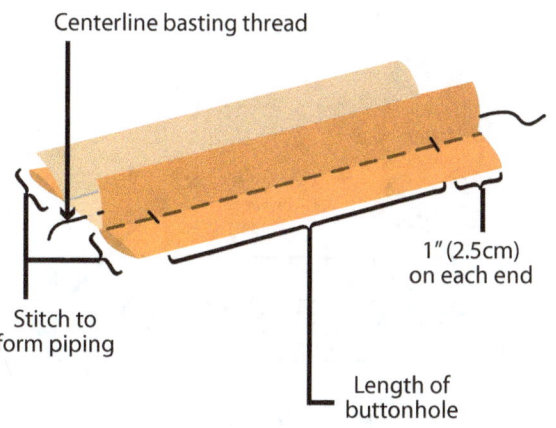

Figure 6.25

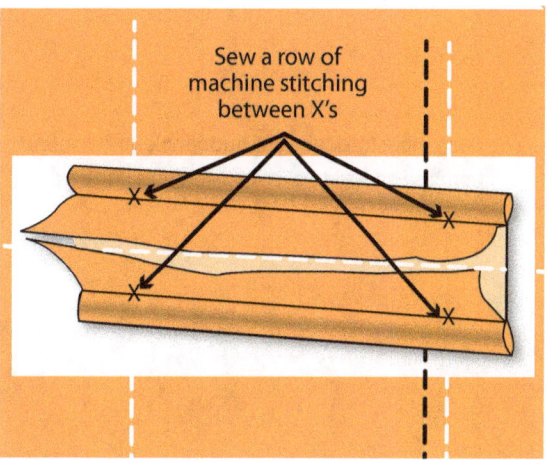

Figure 6.26

Cutting, Turning, and Finishing the Bound Buttonhole

You are now ready to cut, turn, and finish your bound buttonhole.

1. Cut the buttonhole along the center line, stopping about ¼ inch (6 mm) from the end. Then cut up to the stitching on an angle as shown in Figure 6.26 to form a triangle at each end of the buttonhole. It is best to cut from the wrong side of the garment, holding the ends of the piping away from the scissors. Cut exactly to the stitching, but not beyond.

2. Cut away the hair canvas (Figure 6.27).

3. Pull the piping piece through to the wrong side, flipping the triangles to the back. Lightly press on the right side of the garment.

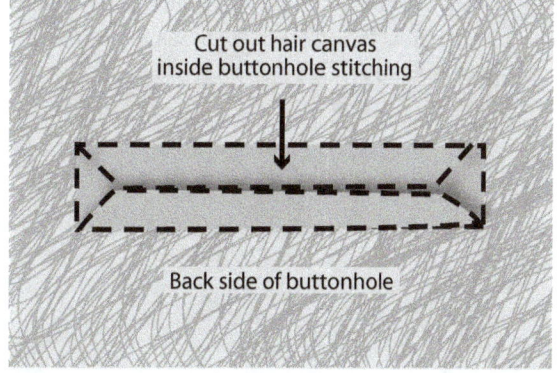

Figure 6.27

At this point, you can overcast stitch the buttonhole piping together.

ATTACHING THE FACING

After the front facing of the jacket has been attached, the facing is then used to finish the buttonhole. (See Chapter 12 for attaching the front facing.)

1. Baste stitch around the buttonhole, going through all layers of the garment front and the front facing (Figure 6.28). This will hold all the layers in place so that the front facing buttonhole position can be accurately marked.

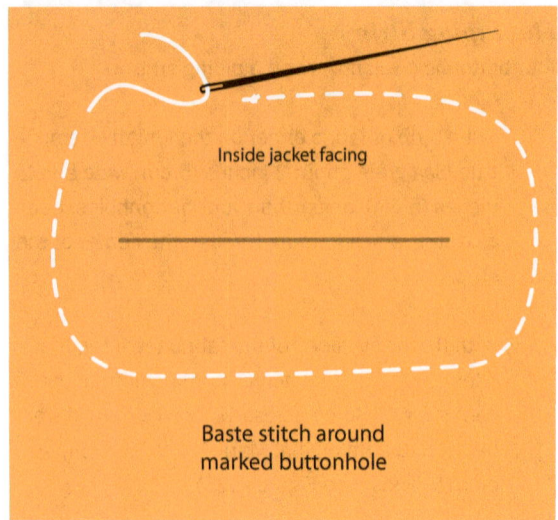

Figure 6.28

2. Push a pin through your buttonhole at each end from the right side of the jacket front (Figure 6.29).

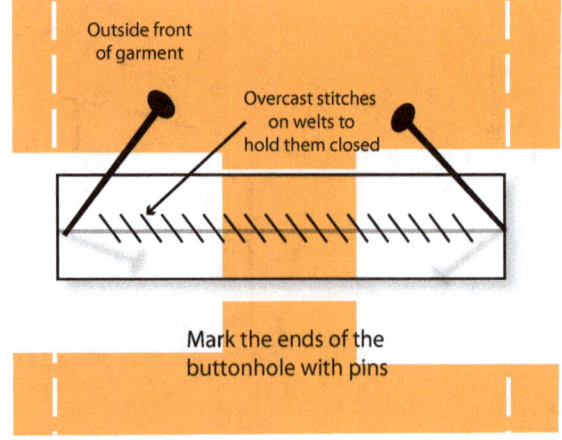

Figure 6.29

3. Mark by drawing a line at the buttonhole position on the front facing exactly between the two pins (Figure 6.30).

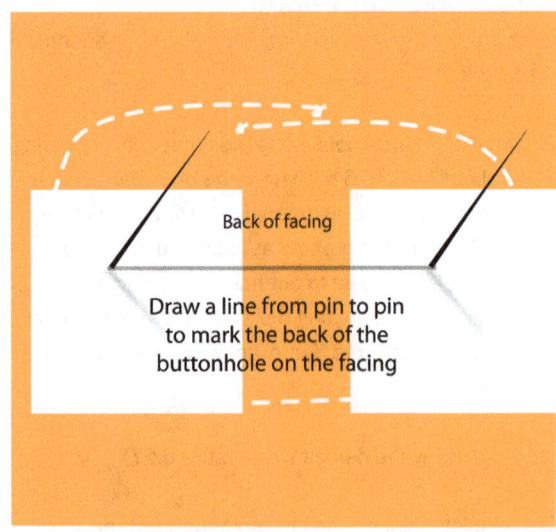

Figure 6.30

4. Cut a straight line along the mark on the front facing, cutting exactly as the buttonhole was cut with the two triangles at each end (Figure 6.31). Be careful that you don't cut the piping. Turn under each side, the triangle ends, and slip stitch around the buttonhole (see Figure 6.31). Finish by pressing with a clapper.

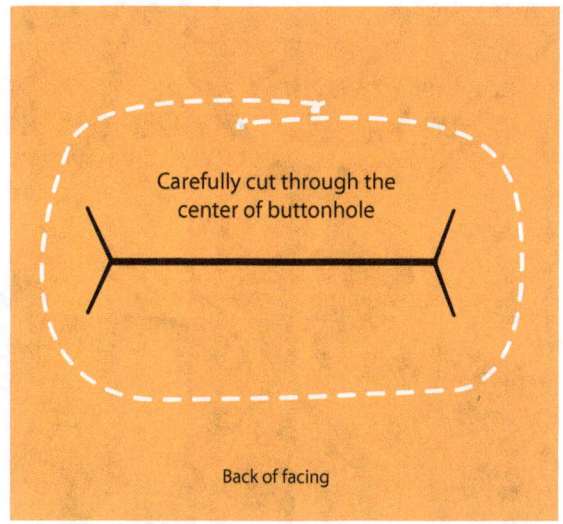

Figure 6.31

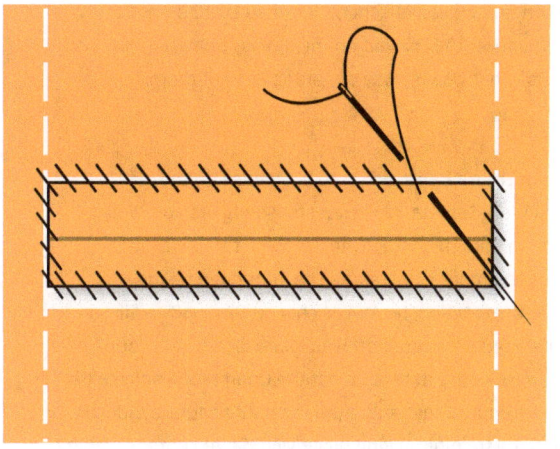

Figure 6.32

CHAPTER CHECKLIST

Before you are ready to begin construction, be sure to check that:

- ☐ The method of adding structure to the front of your jacket is working for both your design and fabric.
- ☐ The inner structure and front are acting as one piece, held together with basting stitches. There should be no pins.
- ☐ The lapel is steamed and shaped.
- ☐ The roll line is steamed to shape.
- ☐ There is a nice, rounded shape from the shoulder to the bust/chest line.
- ☐ The front is shaped and the excess has been shrunk.
- ☐ If including bound buttonholes, you have made them and will finish them when you have attached the front facings (refer to Chapter 12).
- ☐ If you are making machine or hand-worked buttonholes, you have marked their positions.

REFERENCES

Seeling, C. (2000) *Fashion: The Century of the Designer 1900–1999.* Cologne: Koneman.

Topping, A. (2009, June 2) "Yves Saint Laurent, legendary designer and Pied Piper of fashion, dies aged 71," *The Guardian.* Retrieved on December 15, 2009 from www.guardian.co.uk/lifeandstyle/2008/jun/02/fashion.france1

BOX 6.1 Yves Saint Laurent

Yves Henri Donat Mathieu Saint Laurent was born in 1936 in Oran, Algeria, which at the time was the capital of a French département. Saint Laurent was the oldest child and only son of one of the most prominent families at the time in Oran. Unlike most French children he was not directly affected by WWII, but he was picked on and bullied at school. It is said that he once told a reporter, "Whenever they picked on me, I'd say to myself, 'One day I'll be famous.' That was my way of getting back at them."

SUCCESS AT SEVENTEEN

In 1953, Saint Laurent entered three sketches into the International Wool Secretariat contest for young fashion designers. He came in third and was invited to Paris for the awards ceremony in December of the same year. Although he may not have won the competition, he met Michel de Brunhoff, editor on chief of Paris *Vogue*. De Brunhoff was impressed by the young designer and suggested that he study at the Chambre Syndicale de la Couture, the council that regulated the haute couture industry and provided the training. Taking his advice, Saint Laurent began his study there, but left after a few months.

He entered the International Wool Secretariat competition again and this time he won, beating Karl Lagerfeld and Fernando Sanchez. Again, he took his sketches to de Brunhoff, who showed them to Christian Dior, who hired him on the spot. Yves was only 17 years old when he began to work at Dior, and in 1957 at the age of 21 he became head designer for the house of Dior when Christian Dior died from a heart attack.

Saint Laurent's first collection, The Trapeze line, was a hit, and it was only a few days later that he was lucky in love and found his long-time partner Pierre Berge.

INTO A NEW ERA

In 1960, Saint Laurent found himself conscripted into the French army and suffered a nervous breakdown after the stress of being hazed by other soldiers. He was admitted to a military hospital where he underwent treatment. This was the beginning of the mental and drug problems that followed him for the rest of his life. Berge shielded and protected the fragile, shy Saint Laurent.

Saint Laurent was one of the first to sense the beginning of a new era. He showed black polo sweaters under leather jackets and short skirts, like a biker or beatnik. This was the total opposite of the elegant tradition of the House of Dior, and there, for the first time, street fashion entered haute couture. Saint Laurent wanted to dress the young, free-spirited women of the 1960s. In 1962 he was released from Dior to start his own label, YSL, with his partner Pierre Berge.

Figure Box 6.1a
Yves Saint Laurent, Spring 2000, Couture collection.

Together, they went on to open The Rive Gauche boutiques, ready-to-wear, and haute couture collections. His first customer was Catherine Deneuve, who remained one of his muses. Other muses included Loulou de la Falaise, the daughter of a French marquis and an Anglo-Irish fashion model; Betty Catroux, the half-Brazilian daughter of an American diplomat and wife of a French decorator; and the beautiful and exotic Talitha Dina Pol Getty. Yves Saint Laurent likened the Getty's to the title of a 1922 novel by F. Scott Fitzgerald "beautiful and damned."

MODERN INFLUENCES

St. Laurent continued to stretch and introduce new elements into women's wear, such as his Le Smoking Jacket, pants suits, safari jackets, and transparent tops and dresses. He made it respectable to wear retro and ethnic looks, and combined a color palette like no other designer dared, combining yellow with purple or orange with red or pink. The inspiration for his collections came from ancient China and the Ballet Russe to Russian peasants. He was influenced by the art of Mondrian, Matisse, Picasso, and his good friend Andy Warhol. He gave women the choice of dressing as a Russian peasant one day and wearing a color-blocked Mondrian dress the next, or a mini skirt followed by a chiffon maxi with a bomber jacket.

Yves shocked his critics in 1971 when he posed nude for the advertising campaign for the first YSL men's fragrance, Pour Homme. He again shocked the critics in 1977 with the launch of Opium perfume.

AESTHETIC PHANTOMS

When he announced his retirement in 2002, Saint Laurent referred to addictions that blighted his life and, more movingly, the lives of those near him. "Every man needs aesthetic phantoms in order to exist," he said. "I have known fear and the terrors of solitude. I have known those fair-weather friends we call tranquilizers and drugs. I have known the prison of depression and the confinement of hospital. But one day, I was able to come through all of that, dazzled yet sober" (Topping, 2008).

A few days before his death from brain cancer, Yves and Pierre Berge were joined in a same-sex civil pact of solidarity. Saint Laurent's body was cremated and his ashes were scattered in Marrakech, Morocco, in the Majorelle Garden, a botanical garden that he often visited to find influence and refuge. His partner Bergé said during the funeral service, "But I also know that I will never forget what I owe you, and that one day I will join you under the Moroccan palms." His funeral was attended by Empress Farah Pahlavi, Jacque Chirac, French President and his wife Madame Bernadette Chirac.

Figure Box 6.1b
Yves Saint Laurent, Spring 2000,
Couture collection.

CHAPTER 7

The Pockets

Fashion anticipates, elegance is a state of mind ... a mirror of the time in which we live, a translation of the future, and should never be static.

—Oleg Cassini

CHAPTER OBJECTIVES

After reading this chapter, you should be able to:

Identify the different types of pockets for a tailored jacket.

Understand the appropriate application for each pocket.

Select an appropriate pocket for your design.

Alter the size and shape of the pocket.

Correctly position your pockets on the jacket front.

As a highly visible design detail on the front of a jacket or coat, pockets can be functional, purely decorative, or hidden away in a seam. They can define the look of a season, expressing a particular style (e.g., military, safari). They may also be embellished with braids and fringes, beading, embroideries, contrasting colors, textures, and zipped or buttoned closures.

This chapter includes illustrated construction details for pockets from the pattern to the finished pocket. Take the time to practice because any construction error or distortion will call attention to itself.

Attention to detail and careful, accurate stitching are crucial.

POCKET PLACEMENT

The placement of the pocket is important because you want your pocket detail to flatter the figure by following the contour of the body. It is also important that pocket pairs be identical in size, shape, and position. If the pocket on one side of your jacket is higher or lower than the other, it will alter the balance of your jacket.

Pockets should be placed at a position that is both comfortable and flattering to the figure. Large patch pockets will add too much bulk at the hip line of a plus size, whereas welt or piped pockets set at an angle will make the hipline appear narrower and, therefore, more flattering. Dior used pockets to round out the hip; this resulted in a waist that appeared smaller.

Chest Pocket Placement

You can design and make the pocket whatever shape you want, but be sure to keep its placement in mind. Figure 7.1 shows placement of a welt pocket on the front of a man's jacket front. For a woman's jacket front, I raise the placement line 2 to 3 inches (5 cm to 7.5 cm), depending on the bust measurement, so that the pocket will sit better and look more attractive.

Hip Pocket Placement

Figure 7.2 shows where to place the pocket on the lower jacket front, whether the pocket is welt, piped, patch, or shaped to your own design. The pocket is angled up at the side of the jacket to follow the body shape; this gives you the most flattering line. The pocket bag should finish 1 inch (2.5 cm) above the finished hem line. You do not want the pocket bag to get caught up in the hem.

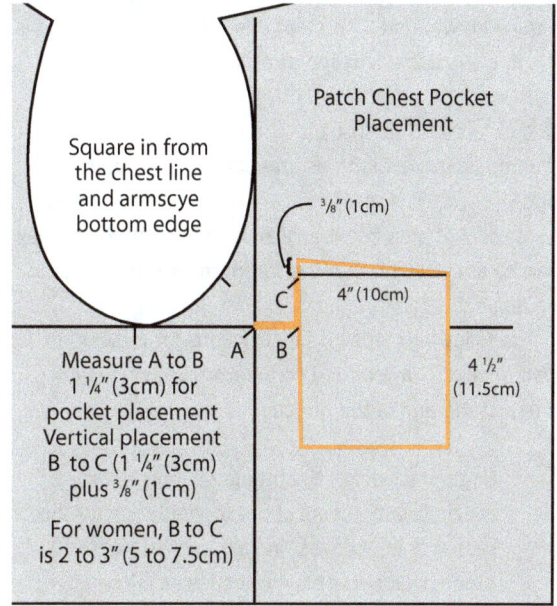

Figure 7.1

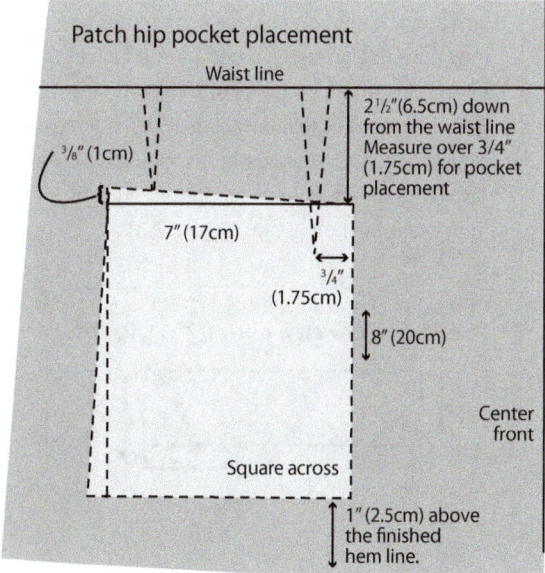

Figure 7.2

BASIC JACKET POCKETS

Basic jacket pockets include the welt, double-piped, double-piped with a flap, patch, inside-stitched patch, and inseam pockets. Remember that you can change the shape, size, and style of all these pockets.

In the following instructions for cutting the pattern and constructing the pockets, the seam allowances have been staggered so that you will have no bulk to cut away. They will sit flat onto the jacket front with no seam ridges or stitching showing. Of all the pocket techniques I have tried, I find that this is the easiest and it is the one that I first learned as a tailoring student.

The Welt Pocket

Welt pockets are found as breast pockets in both men's and women's jackets. They can also be placed in the lower pocket area between waist and hip. Although they can be set straight, they are far more flattering if set at an angle.

The following steps give instructions for making a welt pocket. I have added some examples of design ideas at the end of the directions.

1. Begin this pocket by cutting the interfacing on the crossgrain using either the template for the breast or hip pocket. The finished size of the breast welt pocket is 4½ inches (11.4 cm) by 1⅜ inch (3.5 cm), and the lower pocket is 6 inches (15.2 cm) by 1⅜ inch (3.5 cm). You can change these measurements to make the pocket smaller or larger, and narrower or wider. You may have designed a shaped welt; if so, cut the interfacing to the shape or size that you want. Remember that the interfacing is cut to the exact measurement and shape of the finished pocket. Then draw a line across the bottom edge of the interfacing ⅜ inch (1 cm) (Figure 7.3).

Figure 7.3

2. The breast pocket is placed on a ⅛-inch (1 cm) slant that is higher towards the armhole. The finished pocket will look straight when worn. You can also place the lower pockets on the same slant to slim the figure. Trim away ¼-inch (6 mm) diagonals from each side of the interfacing, if you are going to place the pocket on a ⅜-inch (1 cm) slant (Figure 7.4).

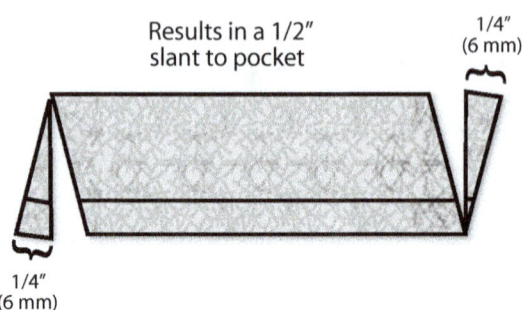

Figure 7.4

3. You are now going to fuse the interfacing onto the wrong side of your fashion fabric, making sure that your fabric is straight of grain. Now mark your seam allowances: ⅜ inch (1 cm) at each side and ¾ inch (1.9 cm) at the top. There is no seam allowance at the bottom edge. Cut out your pocket welt. If your fabric has a stripe or check, you must match the stripe or check of the pocket with your jacket front. To do this, match the pattern using the ⅜-inch (1 cm) line that you have drawn across the bottom of the interfacing (Figure 7.5).

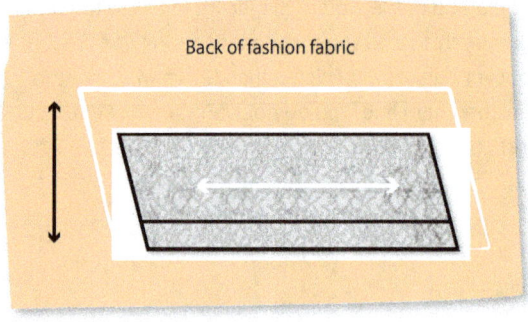

Figure 7.5

4. You now need to cut your pocket bags. Cut two pieces of pocketing 6 inches (15.2 cm) square. If you are making the slanted pocket, cut a ½ inch (1.3 cm) diagonal off the top of each. You now have all the pieces cut for your pocket, and it is time to begin sewing (Figure 7.6).

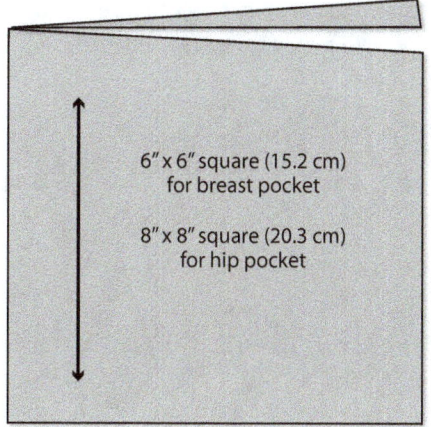

Figure 7.6

5. Place the pocket welt on top of one piece of pocketing. You will have ¼ inch (6 mm) of pocketing on each side. With a ¾-inch (1.5 cm) seam, attach the top edge of the fabric to the top edge of the pocketing (Figure 7.7).

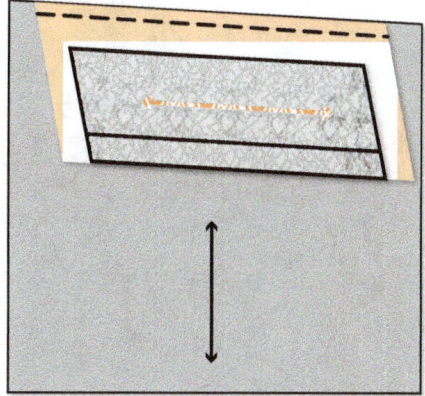

Figure 7.7

6. Press the seam open (Figure 7.8).

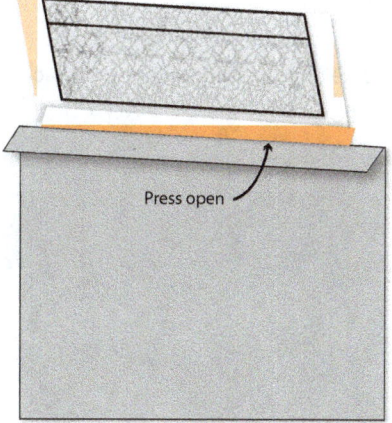

Figure 7.8

7. Fold the fabric right sides together along the edge of the fusible interfacing and pin in place (Figure 7.9).

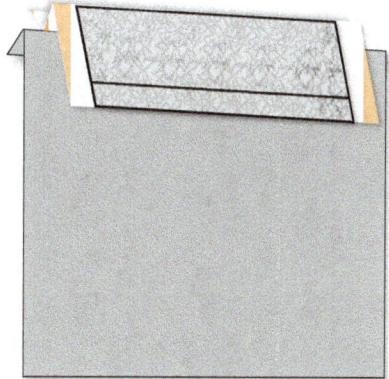

Figure 7.9

8. Using the fusible interfacing as a guide on either side, sew the welt to the pocketing finishing at the drawn line, making sure that you back tack (Figure 7.10).

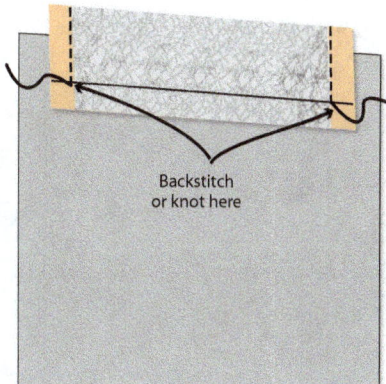

Figure 7.10

9. So that the finished welt sits nice and flat here, you need to remove all the bulk. Clip across the top corners to take out the bulk. Next, slash into the stitching line at the bottom of the welt on both sides. Then trim back the sides to ¼ inch (6 mm) (Figure 7.11).

Figure 7.11

10. Press the side seams open, and turn the welt to the right side (Figure 7.12).

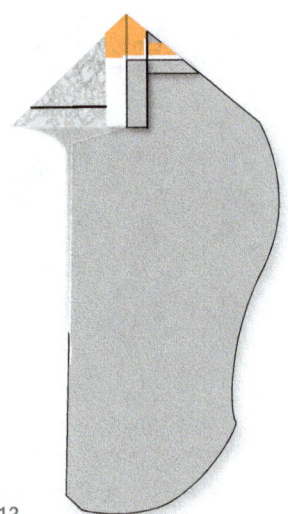

Figure 7.12

11. Gently work the corners of the welt before pressing (Figure 7.13).

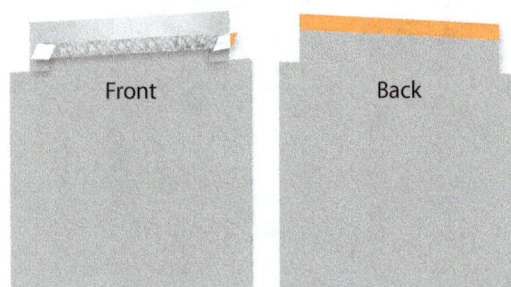

Figure 7.13

12. It is now time to attach the welt to your jacket. Place the welt face down on your jacket front, matching the stitch line (drawn on the fusible material) to the placement line (drawn on the jacket). At this stage, the welt will be upside down. Pin or baste in position before machine stitching the welt to the jacket front. Start your stitching approximately ¼ inch (6 mm) in from the edge and reverse back to the edge, then stitch to the other side and reverse back ¼ inch (6 mm) (Figure 7.14 and 7.15).

Figure 7.14

Figure 7.15

13. Trim the corners of the welt seam allowance (Figure 7.16).

Figure 7.16

14. Place the other piece of pocketing under the welt seam allowance and stitch into place, making sure that you stitch very close to the edge of the welt seam allowance. Your stitching line is going to be ¼ inch (6 mm) shorter at both ends than the welt seam. Make sure that you begin by reverse stitching, and finish again with reverse stitching (Figure 7.17).

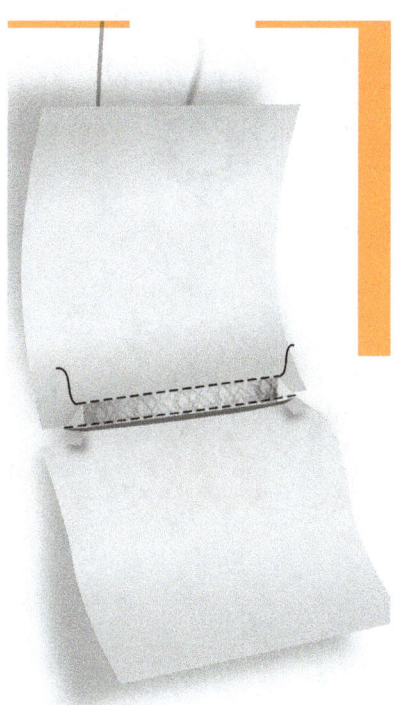

Figure 7.17

15. Working from the wrong side of the jacket so that the two rows of stitching are clearly visible, slash thought the interfacing and fabric down the center. Be careful not to cut the seam allowances of the pocketing. Now carefully clip up to the stitching at each corner. Be careful to clip to the stitching without cutting the threads or clipping over the stitches (Figure 7.18).

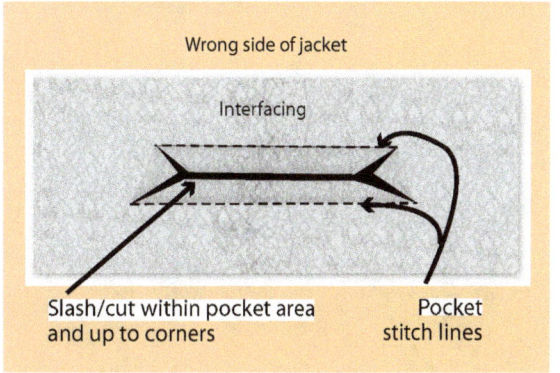

Figure 7.18

16. Reach through the slash and pull the pocketing to the wrong side. Press open the seam. Attach the welt to the jacket with small slip stitches or a diagonal hand stitch from the wrong side (Figure 7.19).

Figure 7.19

17. Machine stitch the pocketing pieces together to form the pocket bag (Figure 7.20).

Figures 7.21a–c and 7.22a–c show a few design ideas for the welt pocket.

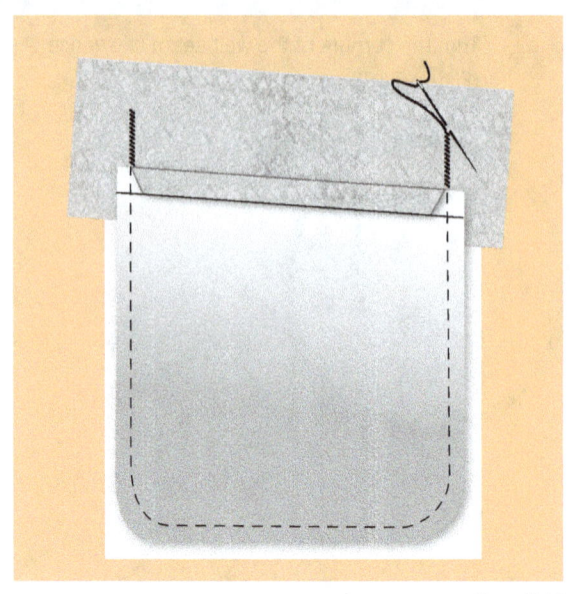

Figure 7.20

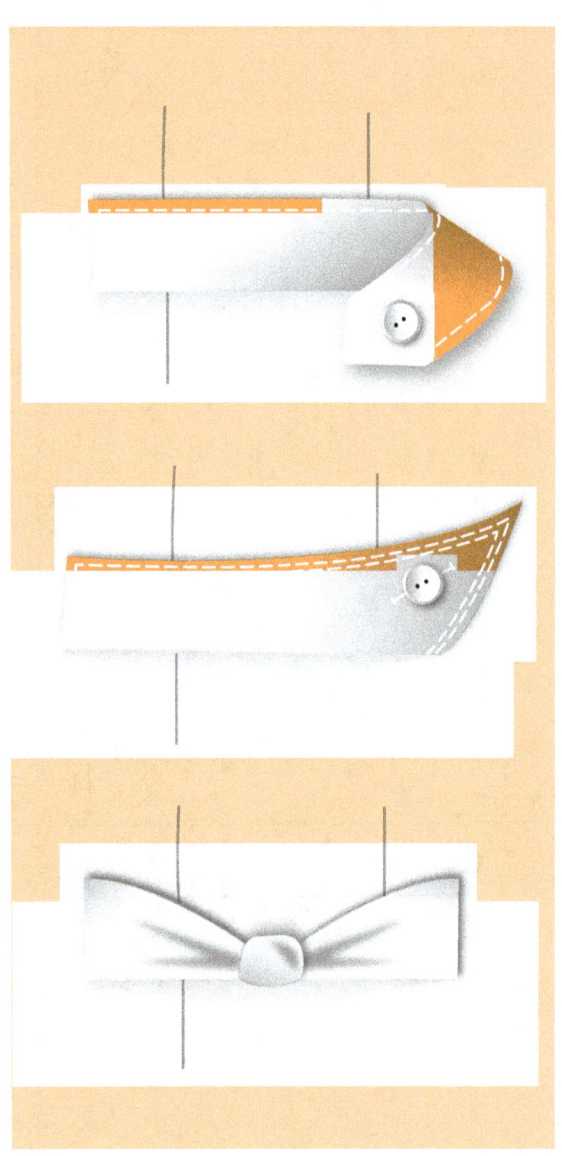

Figure 7.21a–c

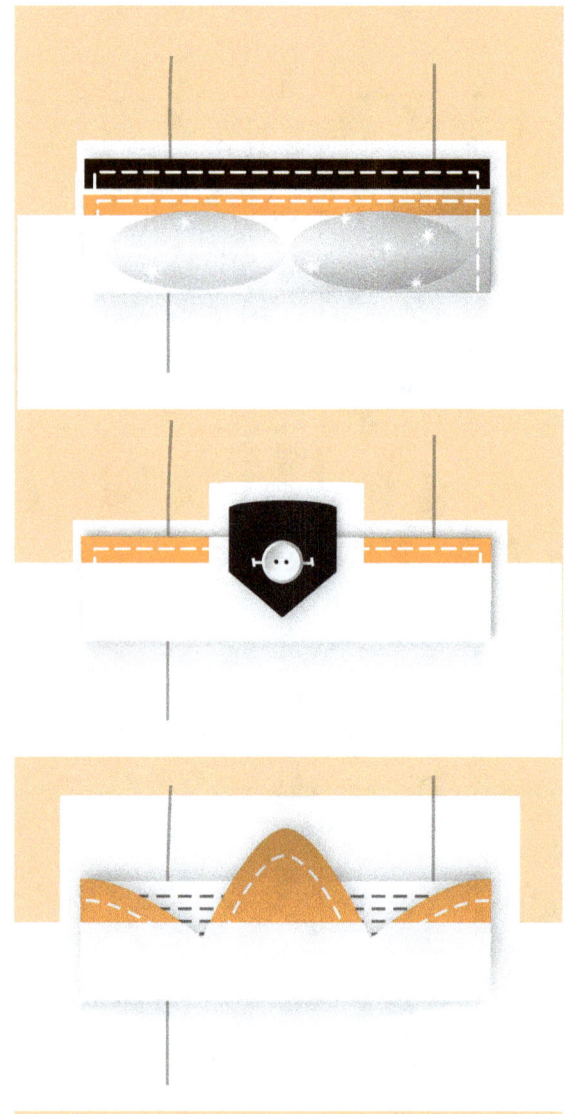

Figure 7.22a–c

Double-Piped Pockets

This pocket is known by many different names, including double welt, jetted, besom, bound, buttonhole, and kiss. The double-piped pocket is the most commonly used pocket on both men's and women's jackets and coats.

It is made with two piped lips at the opening, which are the same length and size. The piping can be cut from contrasting fabric such as velvet or leather, contrasting colors, or cut on the bias if your main fabric is a stripe or plaid to make the pockets a prominent design feature.

To construct a double-piped pocket, follow the next 15 steps.

1. Begin by cutting out your top and bottom piping from your fashion fabric, plus the pocket back, from the pattern pieces. This is for a 6-inch (15.2 cm) finished pocket. Measure over the back of your hand to determine the correct size for your pocket, and make any changes to the pattern pieces. All pattern pieces are 2 inches (5 cm) longer than the finished pocket measurement. For Figure 7.23a, pattern pieces for the double-piped pocket, the top pocket piping should be 8 × 1½ inches (20.2 × 3.7cm). For Figure 7.23b, the lower pocket piping, the measurement should be 8 × 2 inches (20.2 × 5 cm). For Figure 7.23c, the back of pocket, the measurement should be 8 × 3 inches (20.2 × 7.5 cm).

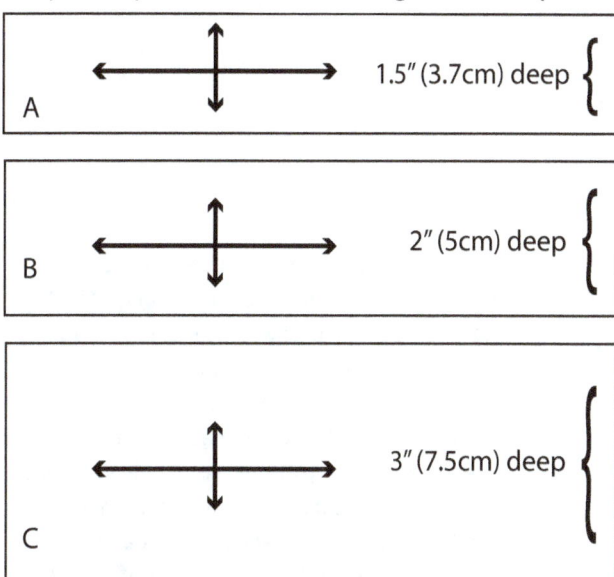

Figure 7.23a–c

2. Mark your pocket on the right side of your jacket—6 inches (15.2 cm) long by ½ inches (1 cm) wide—or the finished length of your pocket as shown in Figure 7.24.

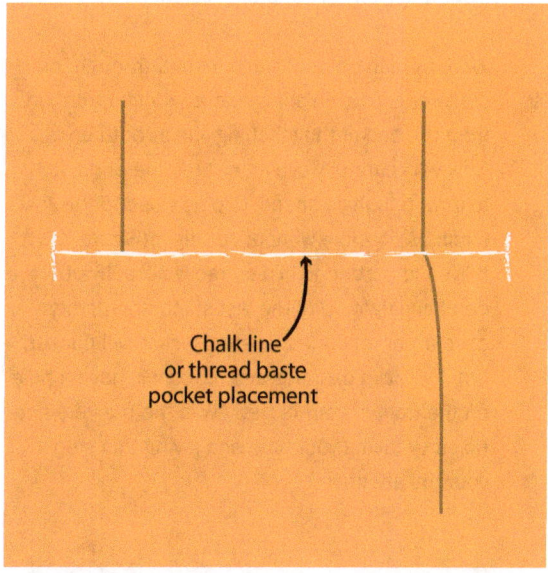

Figure 7.24

3. Place your top and lower piping pieces onto the marked placement line on the right side of your jacket front, and pin in place. Pin or chalk mark the beginning and end of your pocket (Figure 7.25a).

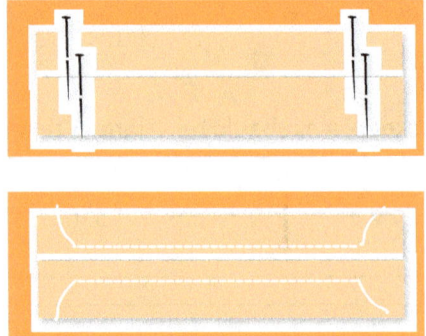

Figure 7.25a and b

4. You are now going to stitch these to your jacket using a ¼-inch (6 mm) seam allowance. Start stitching approximately ¼ inch (6 mm) in from the end of your pocket and backstitch back to the pin or chalk line. Now stitch to the end and then backstitch for approximately ¼ inch (6 mm). Repeat for both piping pieces, making sure that you sew a straight line. It is important that you pay attention to detail and perform careful, accurate stitching (refer to Figure 7.25b). It is also very important that the two ends of the stitch line are directly aligned; if they are not, correct them now because this will make your finished pocket slant and look very unprofessional.

5. Work from the center slash, or cut, through the placement line, finishing about ⅛ inch (1 cm) in from the end of the stitching line at both ends. Now very carefully clip in towards the end stitch to form a triangle shape. Clip as close to this last stitch as possible without cutting it (Figure 7.26). It is so important to clip correctly here. If you don't clip right up to the last stitch, the corners of your pocket on the finished jacket will pucker; but if you clip past this stitch, you will have a hole on the front of your jacket. Avoid the puckers and holes by taking your time and giving this step your full attention.

Figure 7.26

6. A lot of what it takes to make great pockets is in the pressing. Pull the top piping to the wrong side and press the seam open (Figure 7.27).

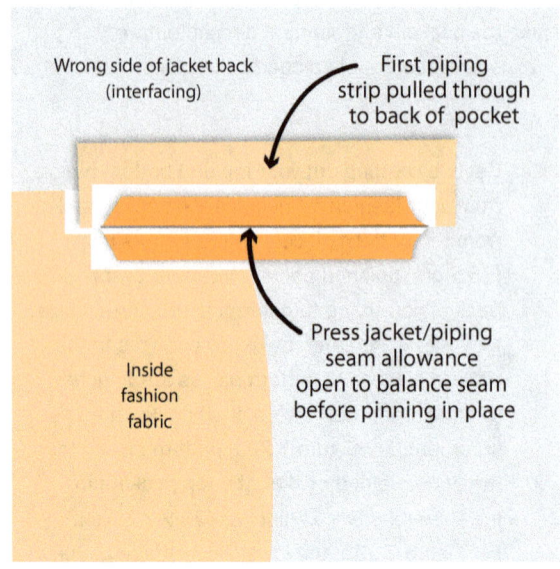

Figure 7.27

7. Now fold the piping back over the seam line and press using the seam allowance and the triangle as a guide. Carefully turn your work so that one side of your seam allowance is showing above your piping, and pin in place (Figure 7.28).

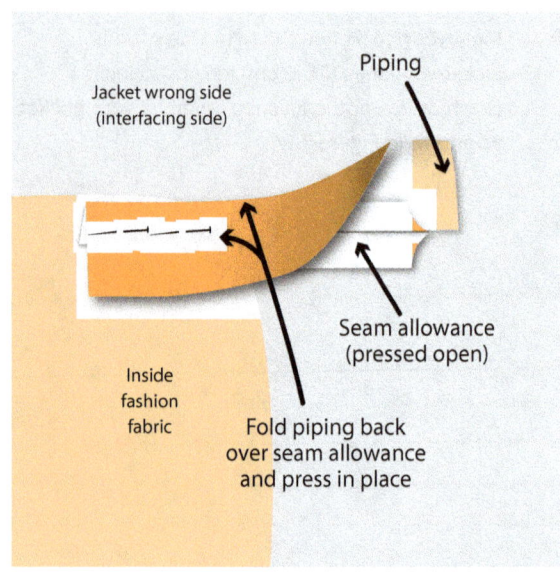

Figure 7.28

8. Sew along the seam line, being careful not to sew over into the piping, and backstitch both ends. Press. Repeat with the lower piping (Figure 7.29).

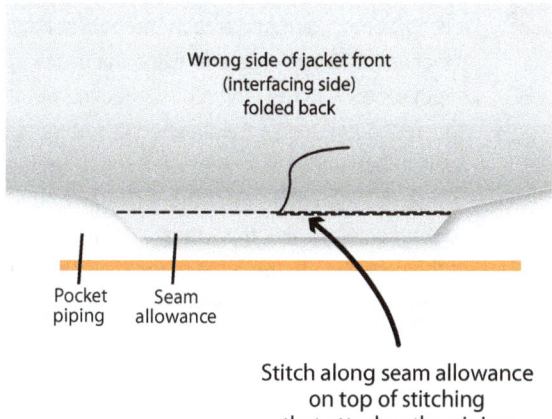

Figure 7.29

9. Your piping should be even on both the top and bottom with no stitches showing. Steam press the pocket on the right side using a press cloth, and ignore the triangles at each corner for the moment (Figure 7.30).

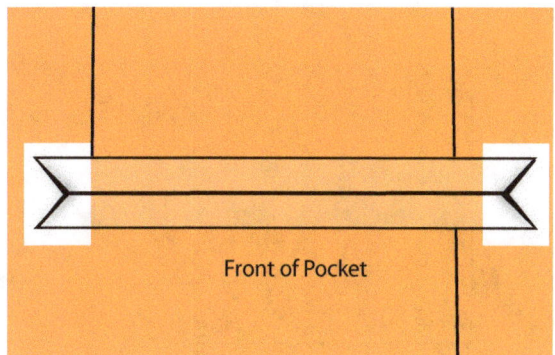

Figure 7.30

10. Whipstitch the piping closed so that it will not shift, but don't stitch into the triangles on each end (Figure 7.31).

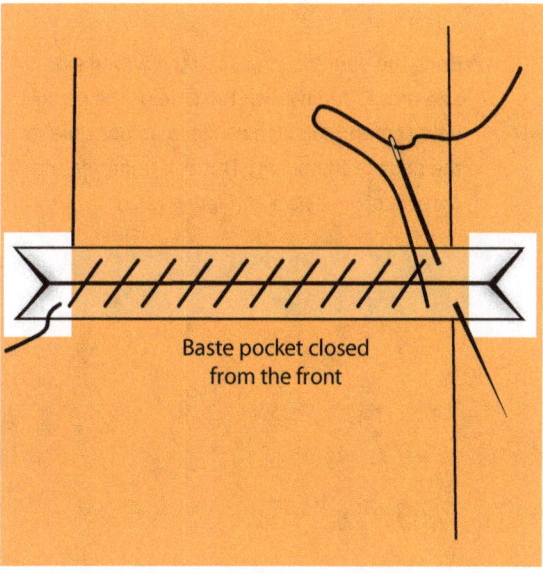

Figure 7.31

11. It is now time to cut and attach the pocket bag. Cut a piece of pocketing 8 inches (20.3 cm) wide and twice the depth of the pocket. The pocket depth varies with the length of the jacket, but the pocket must end about 1 inch (2.5 cm) above the finished jacket hem. Fold the lower edge of the pocket back under ¼ inch (6 mm), place on top of the pocket bag about ½ inch (1.2 cm) down from the top edge and topstitch into place. With the pocket back touching the wrong side of the jacket, attach the bottom edge of the pocketing to the edge of the lower piping using a ¼-inch (6 mm) seam. Press the seam open (Figure 7.32).

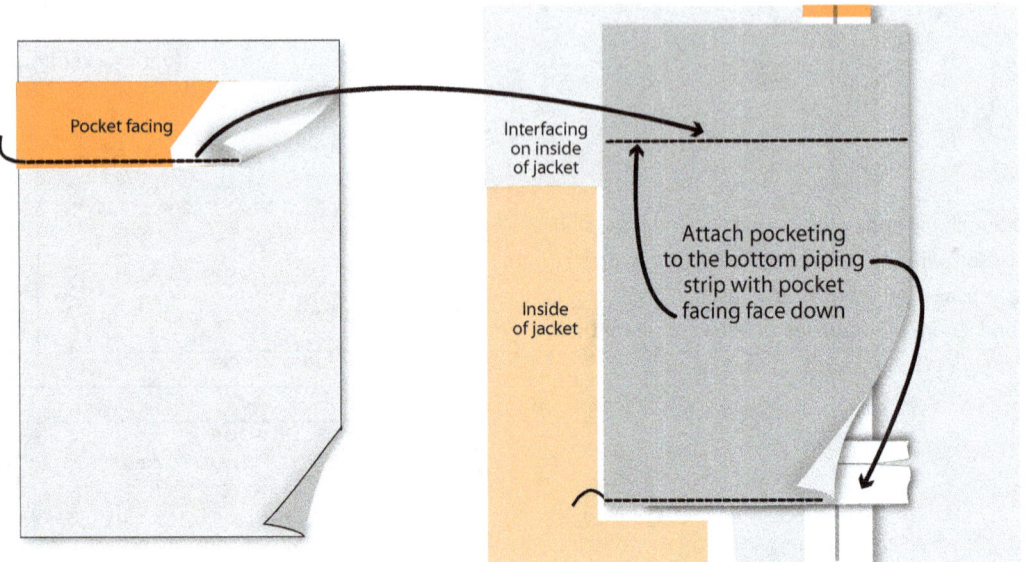

Figure 7.32a–b

12. Bring the corner triangles to the wrong side and press. Stitch down the side of the pocket, being careful to stitch as close as possible to the ends of the piping. This will reinforce the corners of your pocket (Figure 7.33).

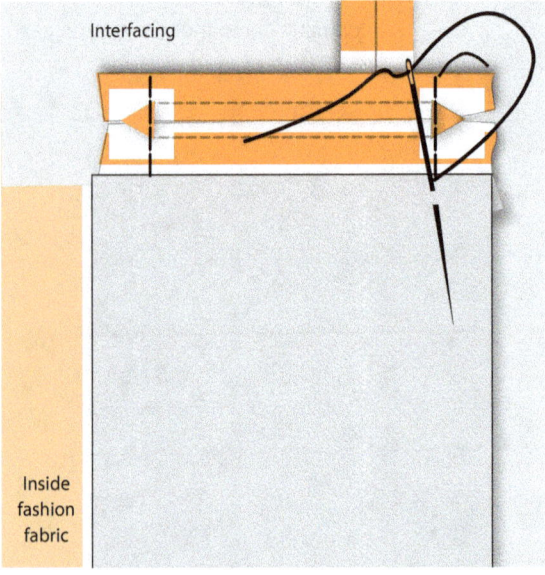

Figure 7.33

13. Bring the top edge of the pocketing up to the top piping, matching the top edges. Stitch along the stitching line (Figure 7.34).

14. Stitch down the side of the pocket bag, across the bottom and up the other side, stitching over the reinforcement stitching from Step 12 (Figure 7.35).

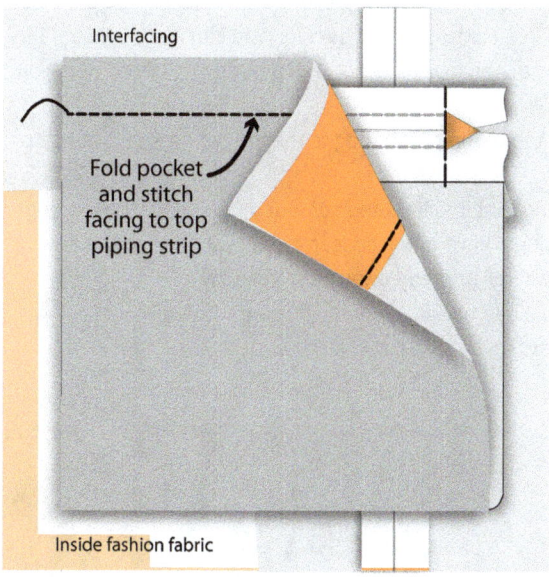

Figure 7.34

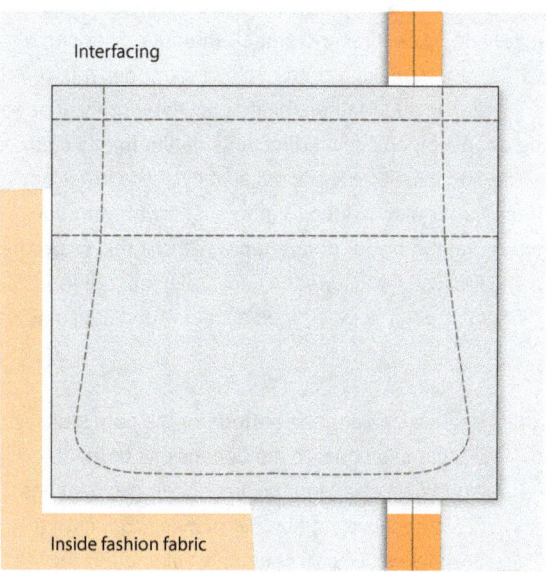

Figure 7.35

15. Cross stitch across the top of the pocket, being careful to catch only the interfacing of the jacket front and down each side to the bottom piping. This will hold the pocket in place (Figure 7.36a).

Your finished pocket should have nice, squared corners and even piping, measuring the same width from end to end and no stitching showing (Figure 7.36b).

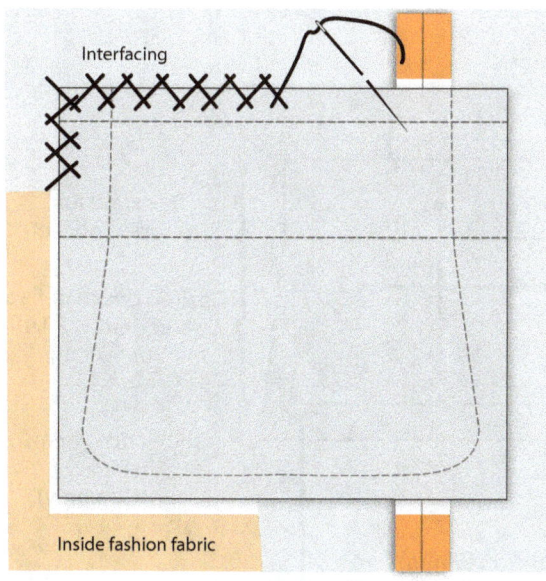

Inside finished pocket

Figure 7.36a

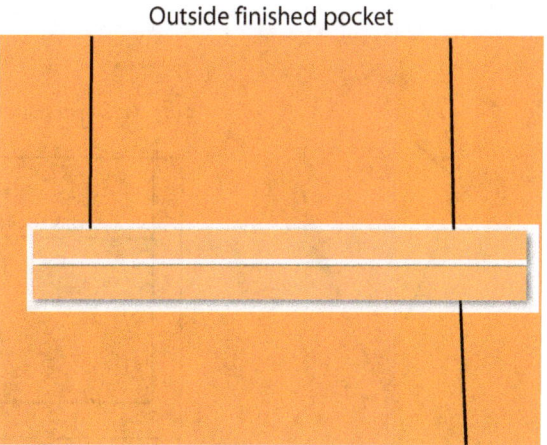

Figure 7.36b

Double-Piped Pocket with a Flap

Figure 7.37 illustrates a flattering placement for a jacket at the hip line. If you are adding a ticket pocket, place this at the waistline mirroring the angle of the hip pocket placement. If your fabric has a stripe or check weave or pattern, draw the stripe or check onto your pattern pieces before you draw the pocket flap. This way, when you cut the flap in the fashion fabric, it should be easier to match up with the stripe or check on the jacket front. Flaps can be cut on the bias when using a stripe or check. They can also be made in a contrast fabric or color. You can also topstitch the edge, adding quilting and embellishments. They can also be attached to the pocket with a button, in which case you would have to make a buttonhole in your pocket flap.

The flap is added to the piped pocket before you attach the top of the pocket bag to the top piping (see Step 12 of the double-piped pocket directions earlier in this chapter).

The flap usually extends out slightly at the lower back edge so that it follows the contour of the body. The top edge of the flap is also ⅛ inch (3 mm) larger than your pocket opening. This creates ease, making your pocket flap sit flat and rounds with your body shape. Without this ease, the flap will roll or stand away from the body.

The flap usually follows the nap, grain, and the fabric pattern. It can be self, contrast, or lined with the jacket lining. To construct a double-piped pocket with a flap, follow the next seven steps.

1. Begin by making the pattern for the flap. Make a rectangle equal to the dimensions of the finished pocket—if your pocket opening is 6 inches (15 cm), this would be 6⅛ inches (15.3 cm); a 5½-inches (14 cm) opening would be 5⅝ inches (14.3 cm) by 2¼ inches (5.7 cm). At the lower right corner, extend the rectangle by ¼ inch (6 mm). Add ⅜-inch (1 cm) of seam allowance to the two sides and bottom edge. Add 1 inch (2.5 cm) to the top edge. Now use this pattern to cut the flaps from your fashion fabric, making sure that you follow the straight of grain or that the fabric nap is down. Cut your lining fabric (Figure 7.38).

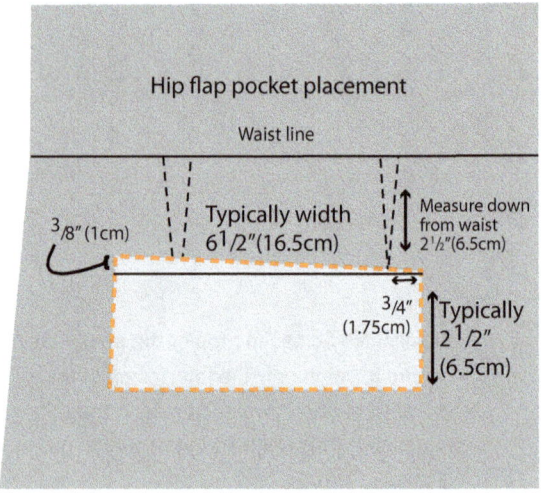

Figure 7.37

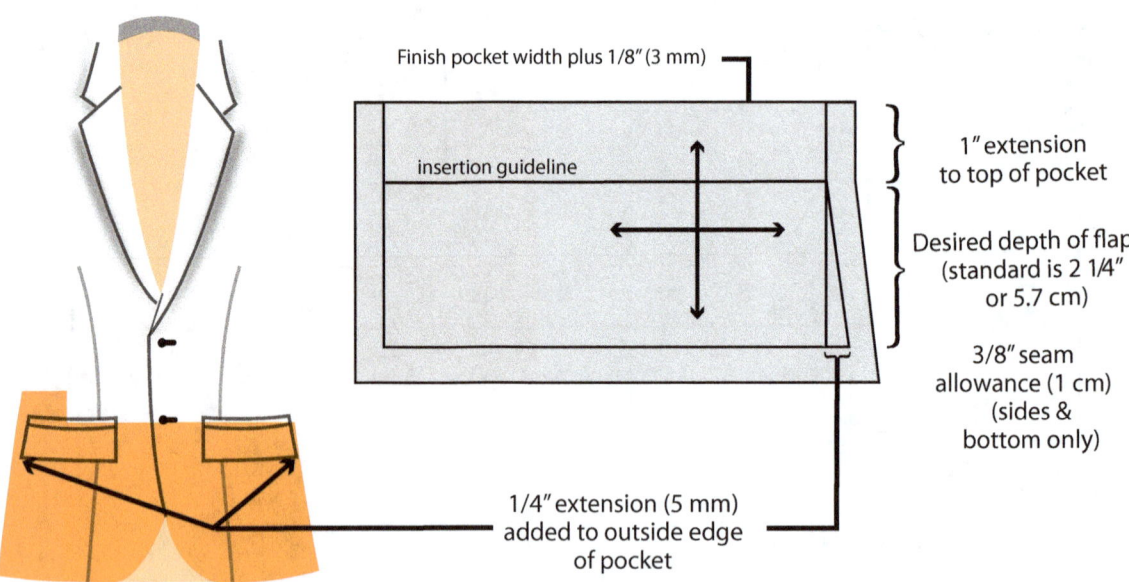

Figure 7.38

2. With the right sides together, pin or baste around the flap edge, easing the fashion fabric in from the lining slightly. This makes the lining slightly smaller and ensures that it will not show at the edges of the finished flap. Sew around the edge of the flap with the lining side up. This helps stop any slipping. Clip away the excess fabric at the corners (Figure 7.39).

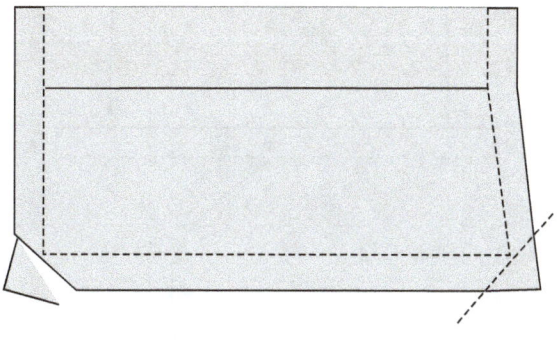

Clip corners and press

Figure 7.39

3. Turn the flap to the right side and press. There should be a border of fashion fabric visible on the under or lining side.

4. Baste or draw a chalk line 2¼ inches (5.7 cm) from the bottom of the flap. This is a guideline for inserting the flap into the pocket opening (Figure 7.40).

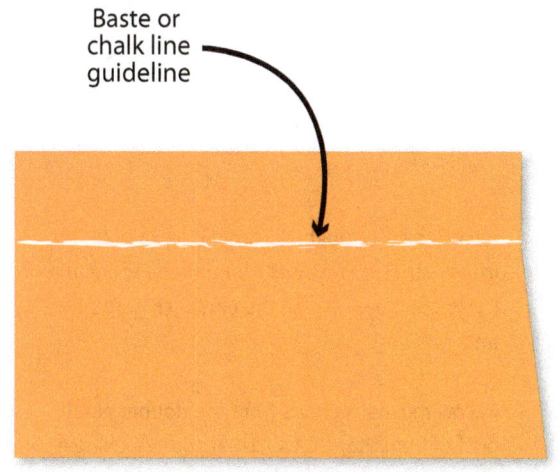

Baste or chalk line guideline

Figure 7.40

5. Now insert the flap into the pocket opening using the chalk line on the flap as a guide (Figure 7.41).

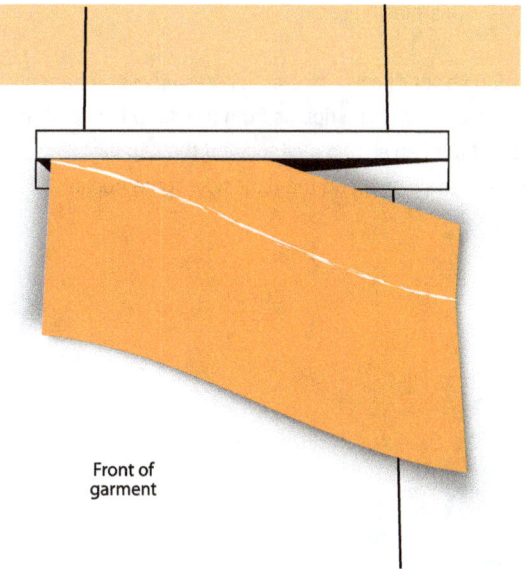

Front of garment

Figure 7.41

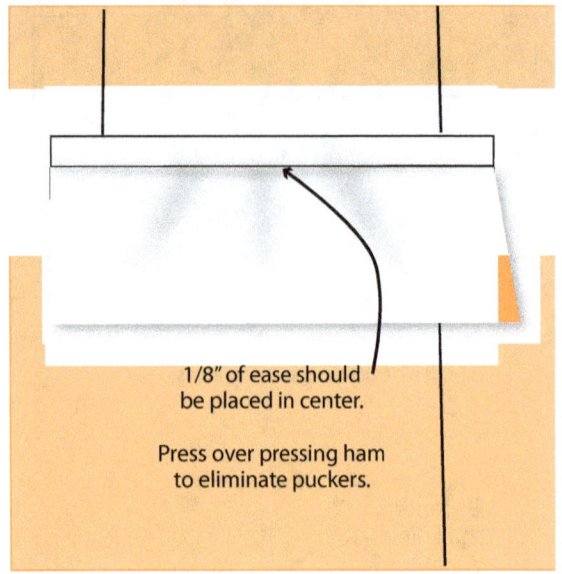

Figure 7.42

Figure 7.43

6. Pin or baste through the top piping to hold the flap in place. The 1/8-inch (3 mm) of ease in the flap should be towards the center (Figures 7.42 and 7.43).

7. Follow the instructions from the double-piped pocket from Steps 11 to 14. If you are using a bulky fabric you can eliminate the pocket back that you attached to the pocket bag, or you can replace this with lining fabric. Because of the flap covering the pocket opening you will not need this piece (Figure 7.44).

Finish your pocket by steam pressing over a ham on the wrong side. The ripples from the added ease at the top of the flap should disappear. If the flap is still rippling, steam press again on the right side of the pocket.

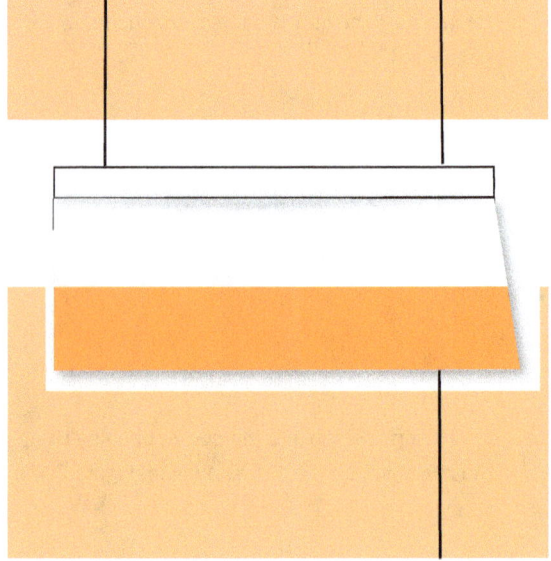

Figure 7.44

In Figure 7.45, the side front panel of this women's jacket has been extended to incorporate the pocket flap. The lower pocket is piped, and the pocket bag attached to the piping. The pocket bag is not sewn into the jacket seams.

The pocket flap here is an extension of the lower front side panel (refer to Figure 7.45). You can see that I have also drawn the pocket on an angle to flatter the body, but this also allows me to exaggerate the flap or play with the design shape (Figures 7.46 and 7.47).

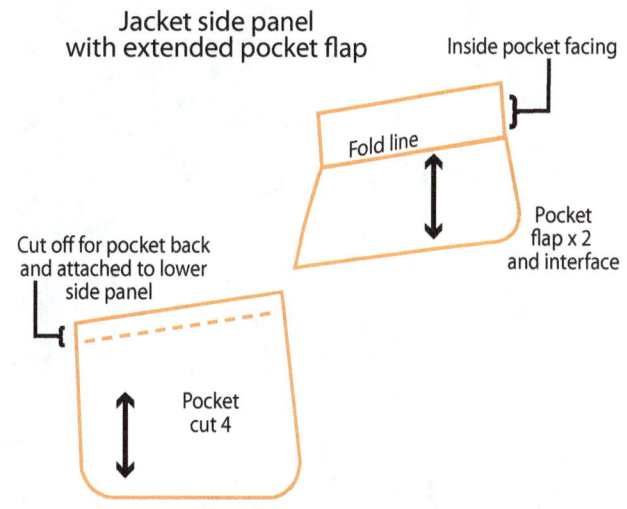

Figure 7.46

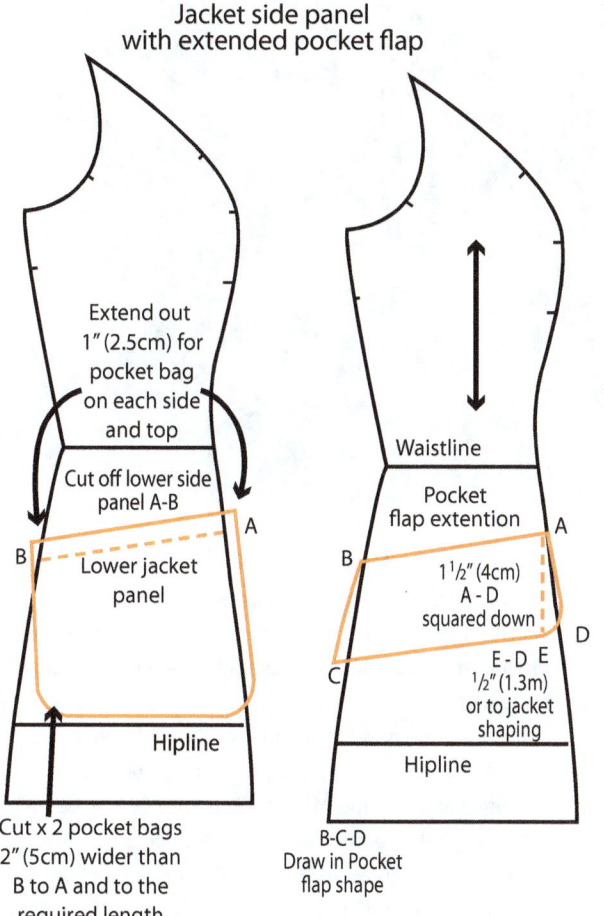

Figure 7.45

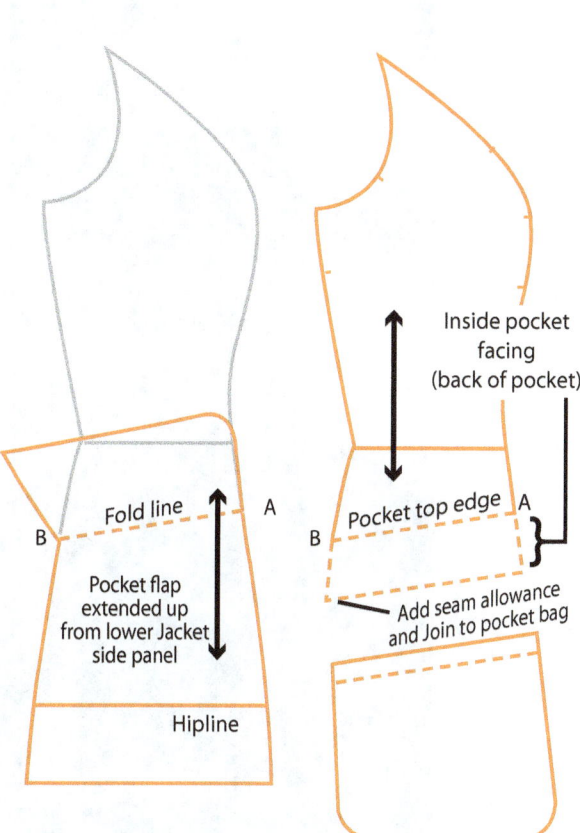

Figure 7.47

Figure 7.48 The designer has exaggerated the size of the patch pockets on this jacket.

Figure 7.50 Tweed suit with embellished pockets.

Figure 7.49 These featured patch pockets have a shape that suggests spilled liquid on a jacket.

The Patch Pocket

Patch pockets can give a more casual look to a jacket; for example, Figure 7.48 shows how Alexander McQueen (Fall 2006) used oversized patch pockets on his jackets.

Figure 7.49 shows that you can play with the shape of these pockets. Patch pockets can also be pleated and have added flaps. You can add embroidery, beading, or any other embellishment. Patch pockets can be made for decoration (Figure 7.50) or as functional pockets (Figure 7.49).

Patch pockets follow the grain or match the pattern of your fabric. They consist of three layers—the jacket fabric, the interfacing, and the lining. If you are working with a loosely woven fabric, the patch pocket is the best pocket choice.

To construct a patch pocket, you will first need to make a pattern and then follow the next nine steps. I have included some design ideas for the patch pocket following the instructions. This pattern has a 1-inch (2.5 cm) hem above the lining (Figure 7.51 a–c).

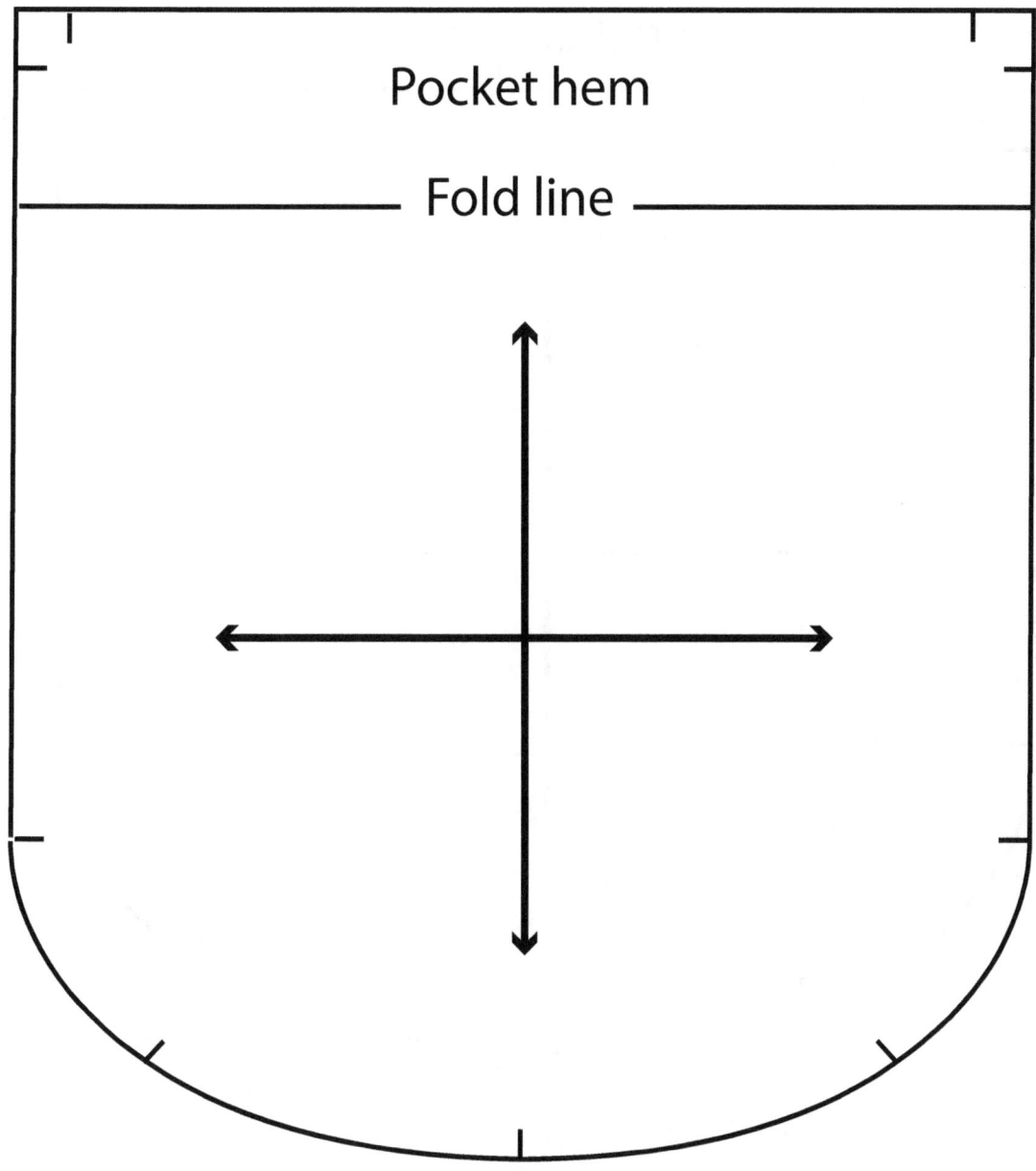

Figure 7.51a

Pocket Lining

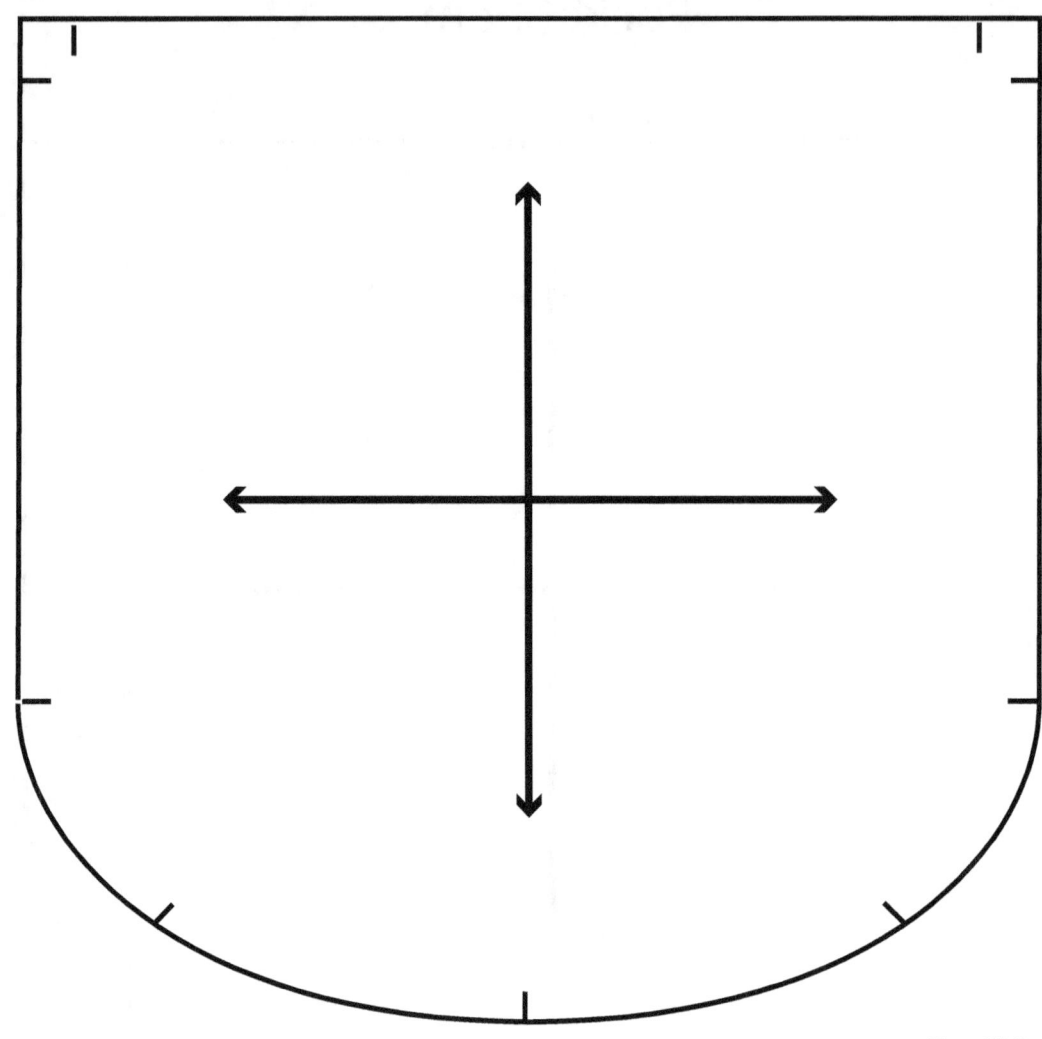

Figure 7.51b

Pocket hem (interfacing)

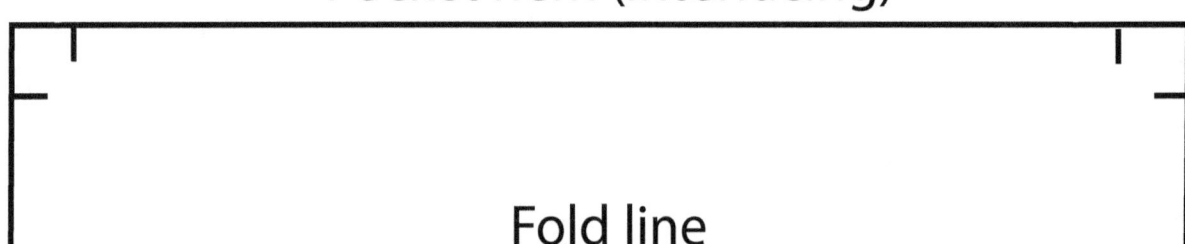

Fold line

Figure 7.51c

1. Fuse the interfacing to the pocket hem; or, you can fuse the interfacing to the entire pocket (Figure 7.52).

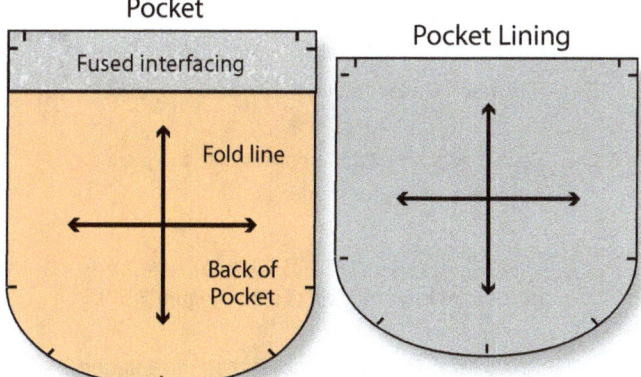

Figure 7.52

3. Fold the hem down at the notches with right sides together. The lining should be ⅛ inch (3 mm) shorter than the pocket. With the lining side face up, backstitch a ⅜-inch (1 cm) seam around the pocket finishing (see Figure 7.54).

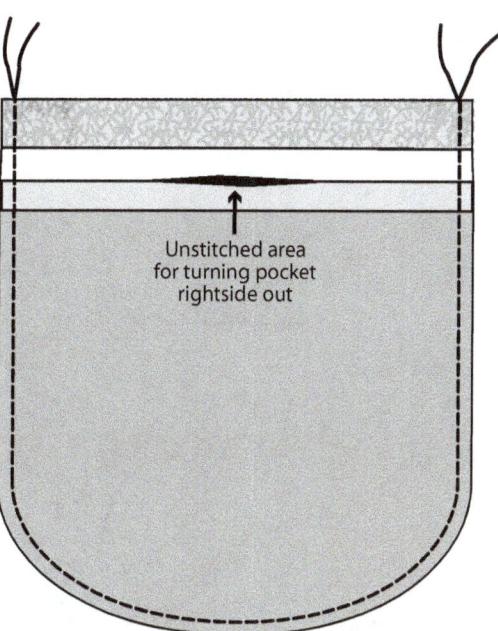

Figure 7.54

2. With right sides together, stitch the top of the pocket hem to the top of the lining leaving approximately 1½ inch (4 cm) gap at the center for turning (Figure 7.53).

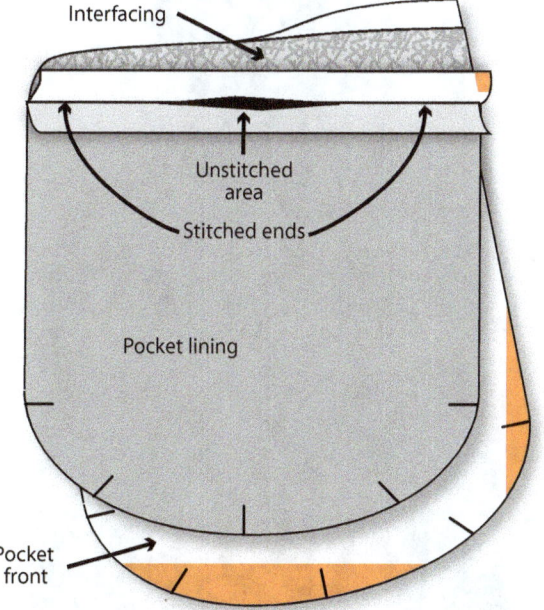

Figure 7.53

4. Clip the curves (Figure 7.55).

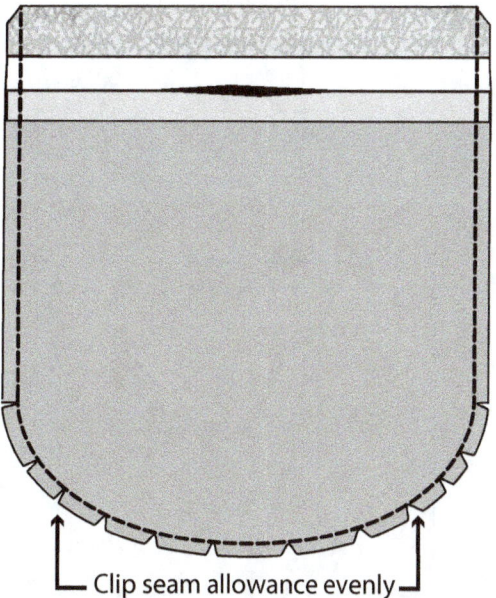

Figure 7.55

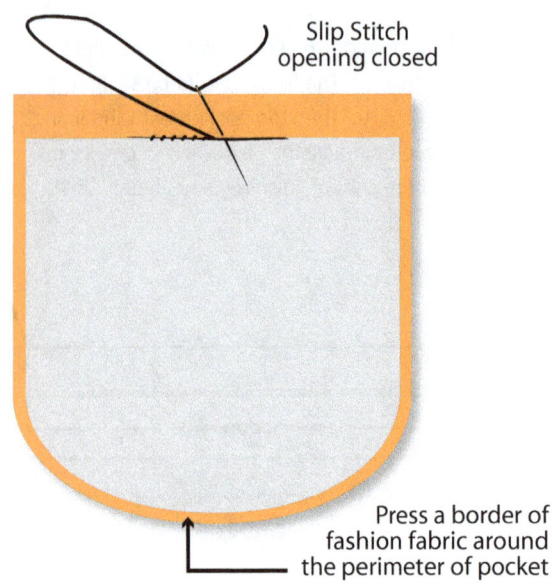

Figure 7.56

5. Turn the pocket by pulling it through the un-stitched section at the hem.

6. Roll the seam line with your fingers and press. There should be a border of fashion fabric visible on the under or lining side (Figure 7.56).

7. Slip stitch closed the unstitched hem.

8. Face side up, place the pocket onto the jacket front matching your markings.

9. Edge stitch in place or slip stitch by hand if you don't want any stitching to show (Figure 7.57).

Figure 7.59 shows a safari pocket that has a button down flap.

The Bellows, Pleated Patch, and Gathered Top are three kinds of patch pockets that you can choose to incorporate into your jacket design (Figures 7.60 through 7.62).

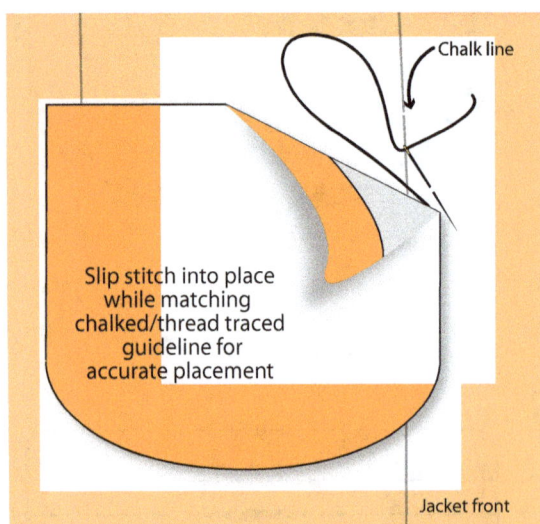

Figure 7.57

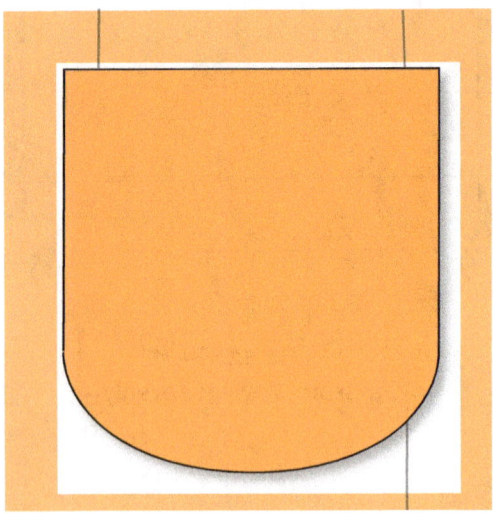

Figure 7.58

Figure 7.59 Safari jacket with buttons down the flap in contrasting color.

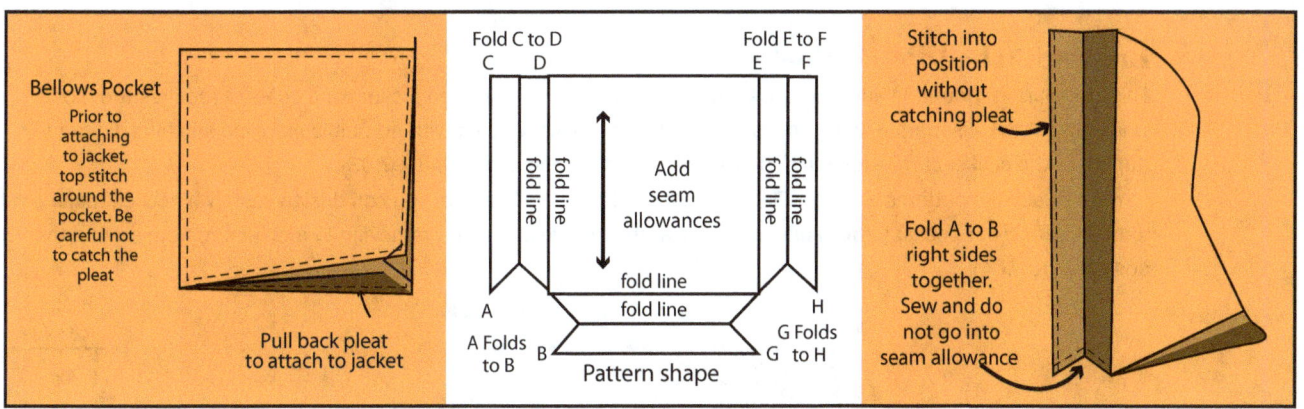

Figure 7.60

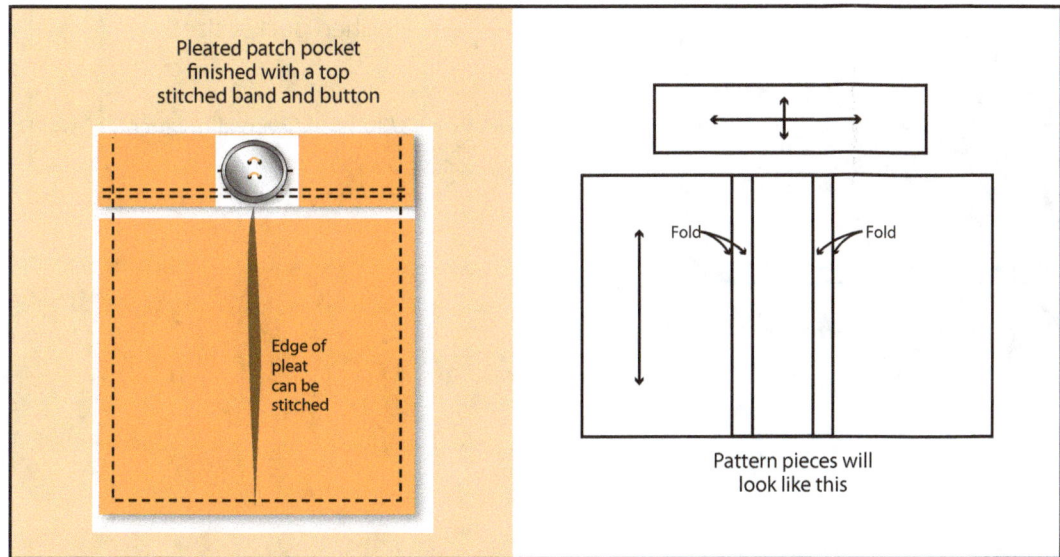

Figure 7.61

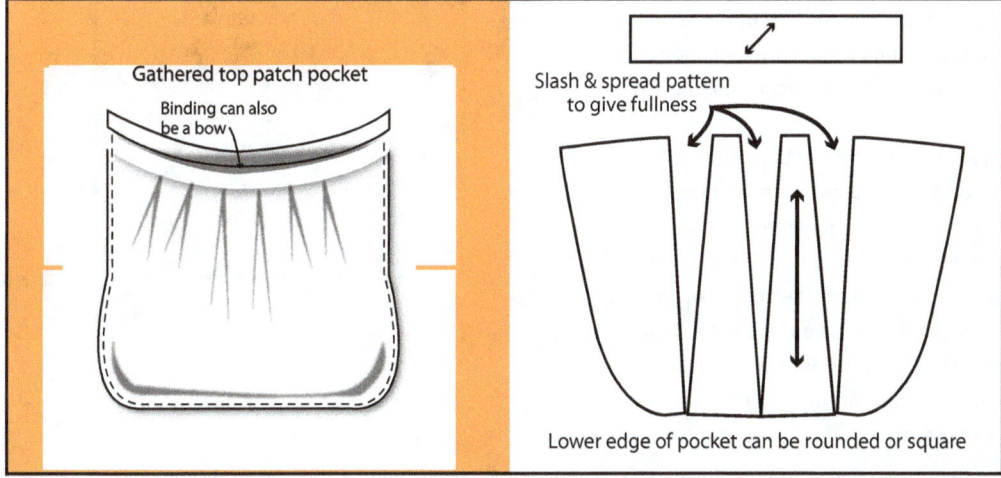

Figure 7.62

Inside-Stitched Patch Pocket

This pocket is very durable and found in both men's and women's tailored jackets and coats. It requires the most skill to set. It has a separate lining and is attached to the jacket or coat with no visible machine stitching. For added durability, the pocket can be topstitched ⅜ inch (1 cm) from the edge (Figure 7.63).

You can use the patterns given for Figures 7.51a and b for the lining, or you can design your own pocket. Make a template from your pocket pattern piece starting at the hem fold line and removing ¼ inch (2 cm) from around the edge (Figure 7.64).

Figure 7.63

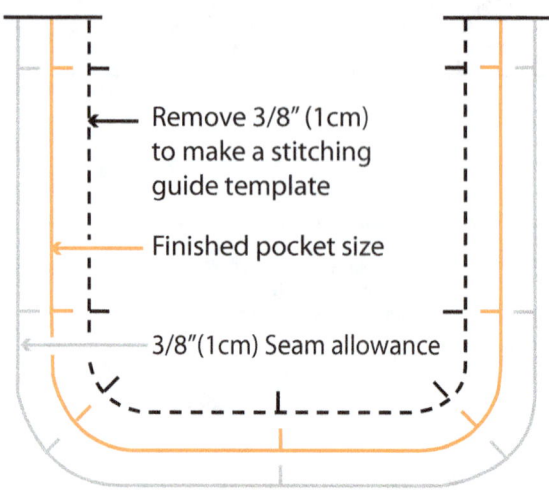

Figure 7.64

To construct an inside-stitched patch pocket, follow the next five steps.

1. With the template face side up, place it on the garment front so that the corners at the top are ¹⁄₁₆ inch (1.5 mm) above your pocket placement markings. Chalk around the template, making sure that you trace mark all notches (Figure 7.65).

2. With the right sides together, stitch the pocket hem to the top of the lining. Press seam open and, with the wrong sides together, fold the pocket down at the hem fold line. Press. With the lining side up, stitch around the pocket edge, and pull up stitching to ease the curves at the bottom of the pocket (Figure 7.66). To make sure that your corners are equal, fit the pocket around the template and press.

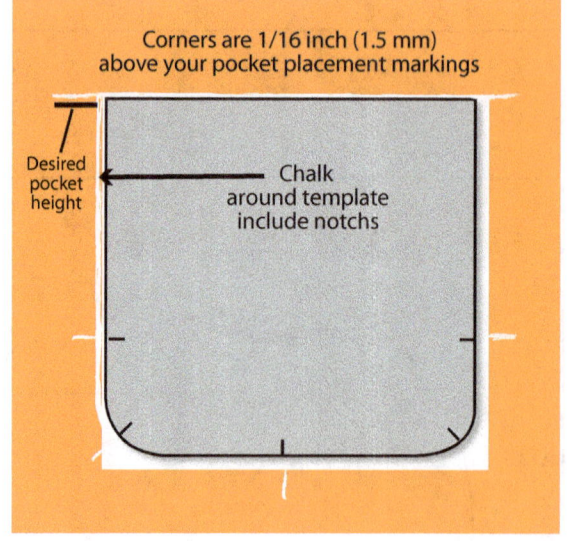

Figure 7.65

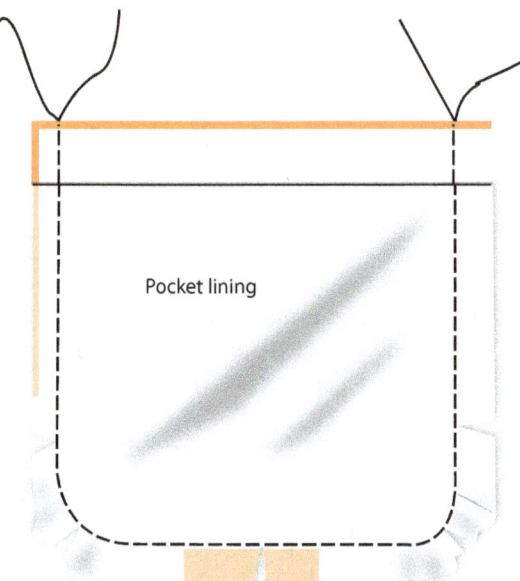

Figure 7.66

4. Place the pocket on the jacket, right sides together to the left. If the pocket stretches as you go around the bottom curve and the notches don't match at the center of the pocket, rip your stitching back to the last notch that matches and re-stitch. Press the pocket right side up lightly using a pressing cloth. At the top corners, fold the seam allowances down so that they form a triangle.

5. With the face side up, topstitch around the edge of the pocket. Pull the tread ends to the wrong side and tie off. You can also just topstitch small triangles at the top corners (Figure 7.68).

3. Place the pocket on the jacket with the right sides together to the left of the traced pocket. Match the raw edge of the pocket to the chalk tracing on the jacket. Begin at the upper left corner of the pocket, back tack, and stitch ⅜ inch (1 cm) from the edge (Figure 7.67).

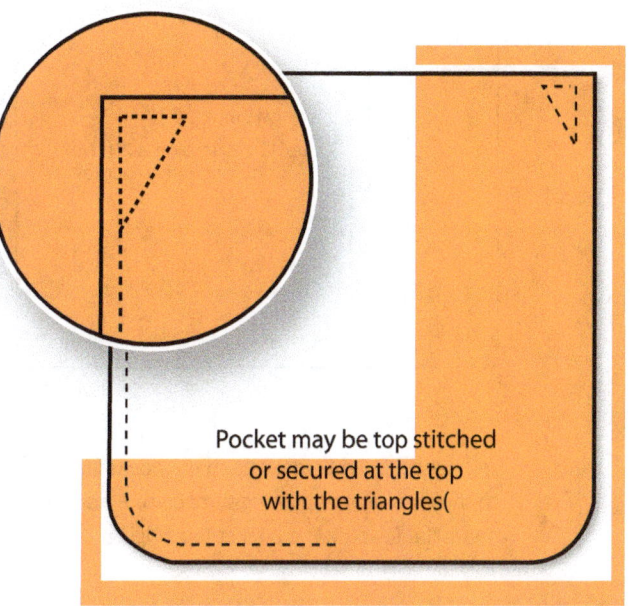

Pocket may be top stitched or secured at the top with the triangles(

Figure 7.68

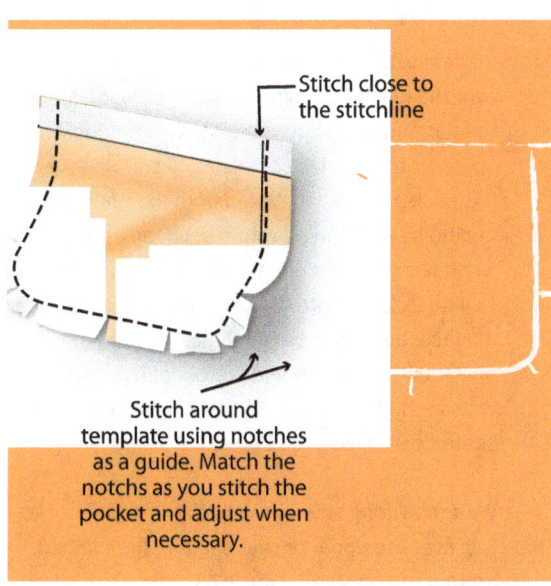

Stitch close to the stitchline

Stitch around template using notches as a guide. Match the notchs as you stitch the pocket and adjust when necessary.

Figure 7.67

The Inseam Pockets

Inseam pockets are located in the seam lines or darts of the jacket or coat. They are both practical and inconspicuous, and can be made with or without an extension. Working with an extension means that you will not have to add a pocket back piece because the extension prevents the pocketing from showing when the garment is being worn. If you want to add a welt to this pocket, make it without the extension.

To construct inseam pockets, follow the next five steps.

1. Add a 1⅜ inch (3.5 cm) extension to the pocket opening that is 6¼ inches (16 cm) in length. The extension is 2 inches (5 cm) longer than the pocket opening (Figure 7.69).

2. Cut two pocket bags. Shape them so that they are narrower at the top and deeper and wider at the bottom so that you can easily get your hand in and out (Figure 7.70).

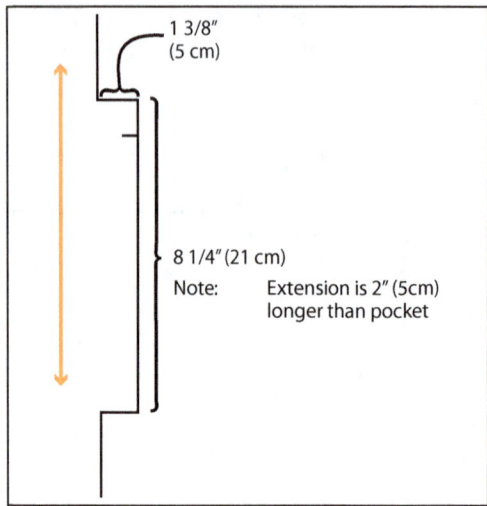

Figure 7.69

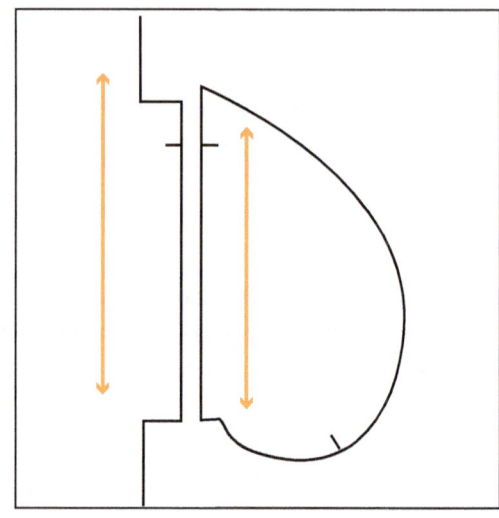

Figure 7.70

3. Right side to right side, attach the pocket bags to the extension, matching the notch. Press the seam flat towards the pocket bag (Figure 7.71).

4. Right side to right side, place the top extension over the lower extension and pin in place. Pin the garment seam from the hem to the pocket opening; this will be 1½ inches (4 cm) up into the pocket extension. Stitch from the bottom up, beginning and ending with a back tack. Now, working from the top of the garment seam to ½ inch (1.2 cm) into the pocket extension, pin in place, and stitch beginning and ending with a back tack. At the top and bottom of the opening clip the back seam allowance and press the seam open (Figure 7.72).

5. With the wrong side up, smooth the under pocket bag over the upper pocket bag and then stitch around the pocket (Figure 7.73).

Press the finished pocket. This pocket can also be made with a welt.

Figure 7.71

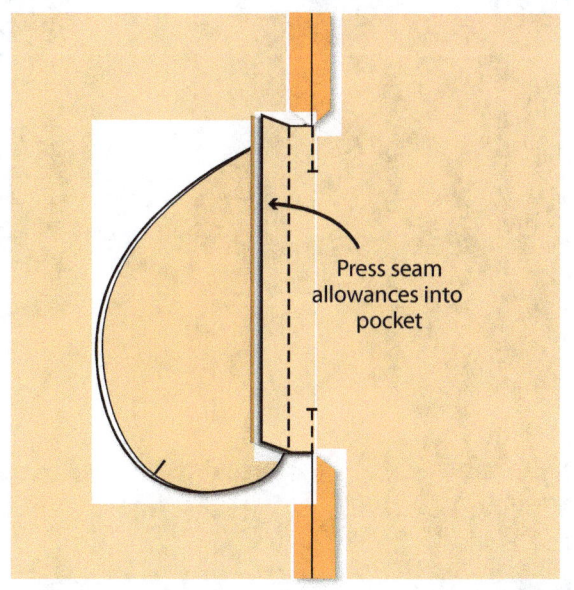

Figure 7.72

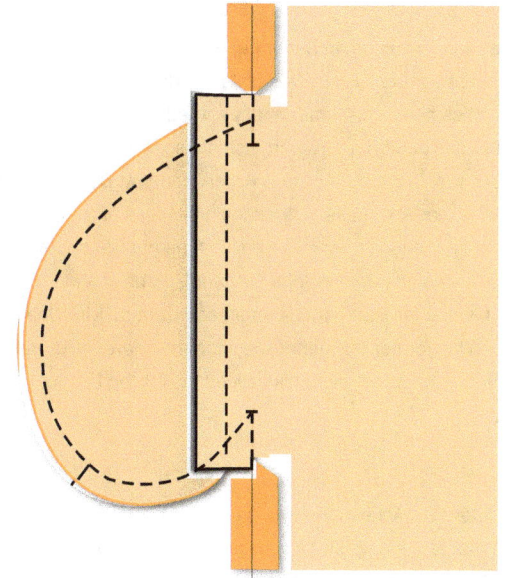

Figure 7.73

CHAPTER CHECKLIST

Before you are ready to begin your jacket construction, be sure to check that:

- ☐ Your pockets are the same size and length.
- ☐ The pockets are positioned on the fronts at the same height.
- ☐ Your pockets look balanced.
- ☐ If you have added them, your pocket flaps are rounding to the shape of the jacket front.
- ☐ Both pocket flaps are the same size.
- ☐ If you have made welt pockets, you cannot see any stitching, and you have not cut too far into the jacket front and created a hole.
- ☐ If you have made double-piped pockets, both sides of the piping are the same size.
- ☐ Your pockets are sitting flat, and one side of the piping is not longer than the other.
- ☐ If you have top stitching around your patch pockets, the stitching is even and straight.

Before moving on, make sure that you like your pockets and that they add detail to your jacket design. When you have checked off all the checklist items, you are ready to move on.

REFERENCES

Maze, E. (2009) "Interview with Haider Ackermann," NNM. Retrieved on December 15, 2009 from www.noname-magazine.com/?page_id=86

BOX 7.1 Haider Ackermann

Haider Ackermann was born in Santa Fé, Bogotá, in 1971. He was adopted by a French family and, as a child, lived in several European and African cities before his family finally settled in the Netherlands.

Ackermann decided on a career in fashion, so in 1991 he left home to study fashion at the Antwerp Royal Academy. But after three years he had to leave because of financial difficulties and wasn't able to complete the fourth year. During his time at the Academy he had also worked as an intern in John Galliano's Paris office.

In 1998, his first job was working as an assistant to Wim Neel, who had been his former teacher at the Academy. Here, Ackermann worked on both men's and women's collections for the Belgium designer.

TAKING THE PLUNGE INTO FASHION

In a recent interview, Ackermann was asked, "When did you really understand that fashion would be your future?" He responded, "I didn't know if it would be my future, but I knew I had to try. Why else would I have played with fabrics in my childhood and observed all those African Giacometti women in their meters of cotton" (Maze, 2009).

Taking the money he had saved and encouragement from his friends, among them Raf Simmons (designer for Jil Sander), Ackermann finally took the plunge and presented his first, self-financed women's collection in Paris for Fall/Winter 2002. This was a sensuous, soft collection that impressed both the buyers and the press. It also impressed the Italian leather manufacturer Ruffio Research, who hired him as head designer just two weeks later. They commissioned Ackermann to create two collections for them while he continued to work on his own collections. He was asked what this experience was like, and why he thought that Ruffio Research, a company specializing in leather goods, chose him. "To work with a company and factory standing behind you, and the awareness of this, is a luxury, especially when you've just done a collection with lots of leather because of the attraction of a second skin and smell. You learn a lot and are thrown into things. It's an enriching experience" (Maze, 2009).

VALIDATION

The real turning point came in 1994 when Haider Ackermann won the Swiss Textile Award, the richest and most prestigious fashion award in Europe, and 100,000 Euros at the Grand Fashion Festival. When asked how he spent the money, he replied, "I concentrated on putting together a collection and a défilé in Paris, though the times were difficult. But I was convinced of not losing my visibility."

Ackermann does not see himself as an avant-garde designer but would rather leave the definition open for others to interpret it as they feel. Nor does he see himself as a revolutionary designer, but more about being discreet, searching for a certain luxury of not caring, a mix of high and low culture, elegance and street life. He is intrigued by cultural differences and forces, the simple purity of aesthetic forms mixed with the vitality of life itself.

If he was given the choice of designing and reinventing a historical fashion brand like Nicolas Guesquiere has for Balenciaga, he thinks it would be exciting if this were Madame Grès.

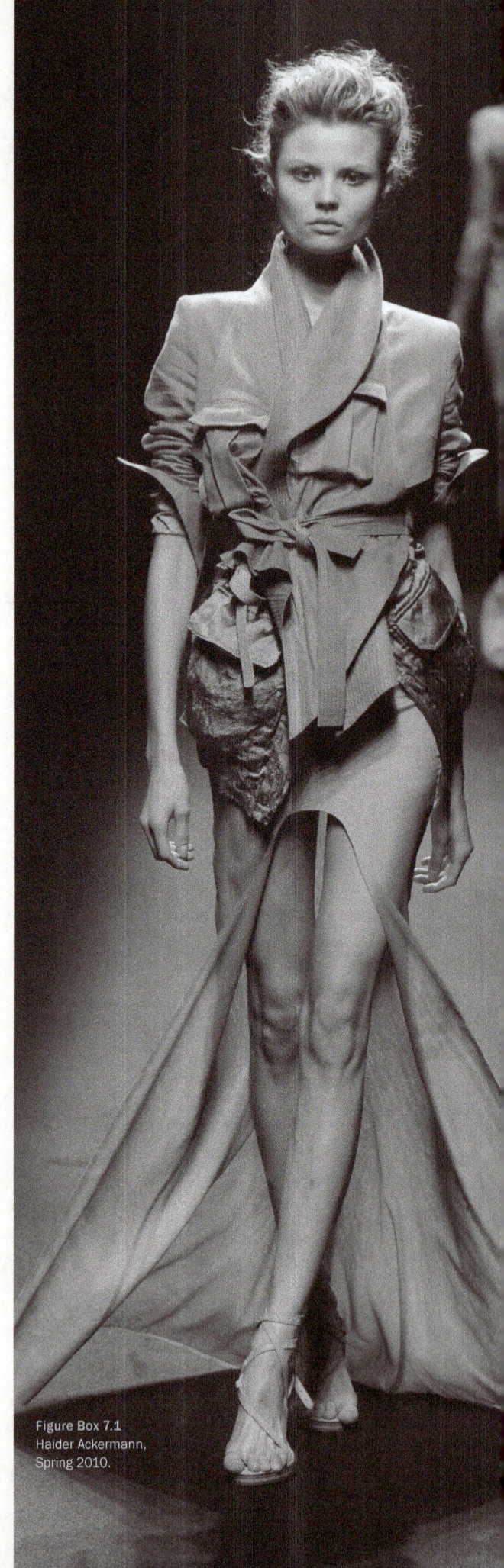

Figure Box 7.1
Haider Ackermann,
Spring 2010.

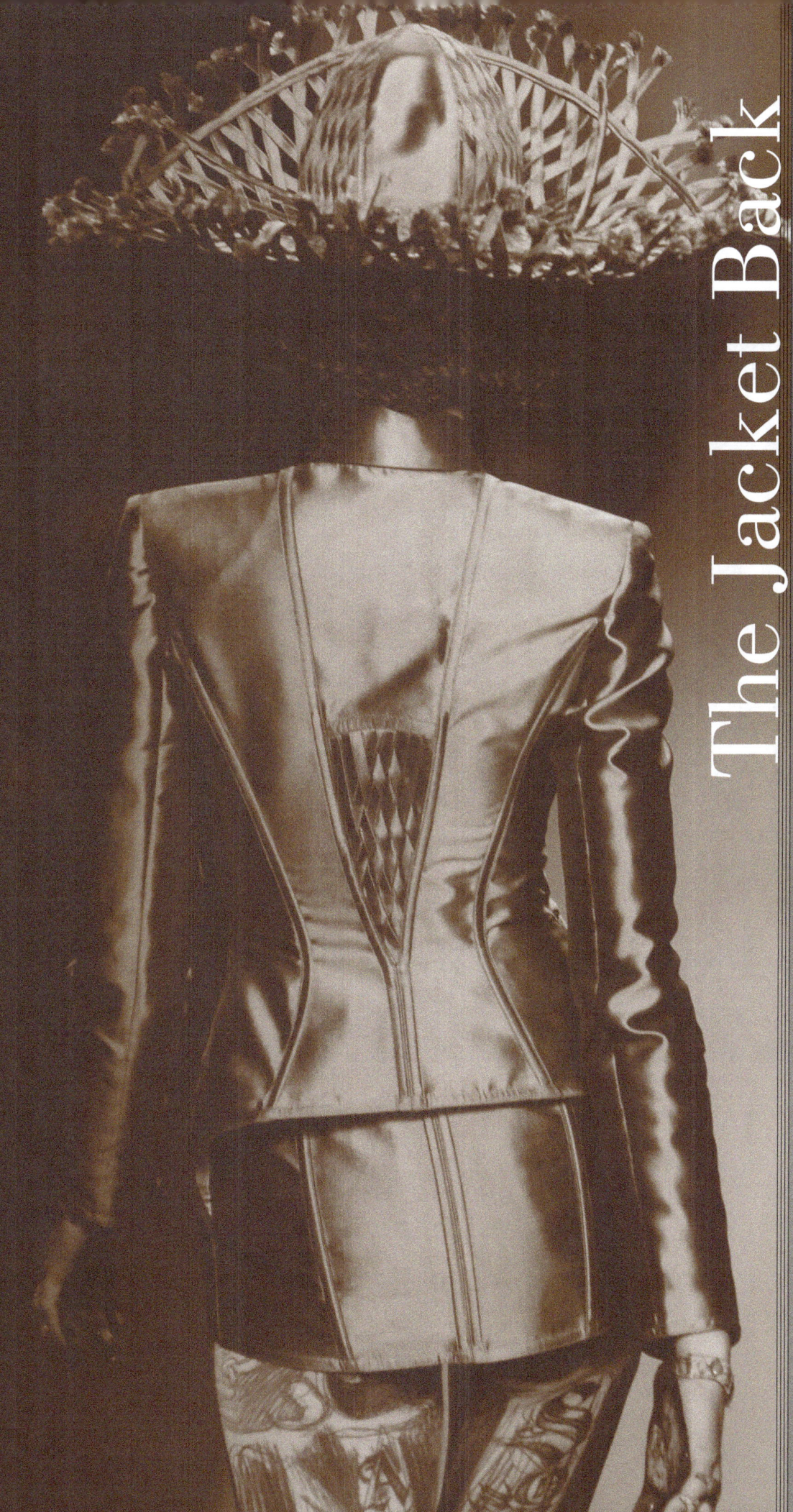

CHAPTER 8

The Jacket Back

My work has never been out of date, it is only a matter of time until it becomes a new look again.

—Charles James

CHAPTER OBJECTIVES

After reading this chapter, you should be able to:

Evaluate the use of design details in the jacket back.

Determine where the back needs to be stabilized.

Know how to add ease to the jacket back.

Work with a back yoke.

Make a back vent.

Add a half belt.

Understand different style, line, and design options.

There is nothing more interesting in a jacket than a simple front and a back that
explodes into something completely different when the one wearing the jacket turns to face the opposite direction (Figure 8.1). The back of the jacket can have a yoke, a vent or vents, a bustle or peplum, tails, pleats, be finished with a half belt, and more. Jean-Paul Gaultier adds a tab at the top of the back center seam that is now a signature. Other designers have used embellishments such as those seen in the back of Charles Frederick Worth's fur-collared jacket from 1885 (Figure 8.2).

Figure 8.1 There is nothing more interesting in a jacket than a simple front and a back that explodes into something completely different when the one wearing the jacket turns to face the opposite direction.

Figure 8.2 The jacket back has been embellished with small wooden beads wrapped in silk, braid and ribbons. The neck is trimmed with silk cut threads that follow down the front and on the sleeve cuffs.

CONSTRUCTING THE JACKET BACK

The jacket back is usually cut with a center back seam and two side panels or two back waist darts. I cut my jackets with a center back seam because this allows me to add more shape and ease, if needed. I can use this seam to add a center back vent at the hem.

Stabilizing the Back, Neck, and Armhole Edges

Before you begin construction of your jacket's back, you must stabilize the back, neck, and armhole edges.

1. Begin by cutting ⅜-inch (1 cm) wide strips of fusible interfacing long enough to fit along the neck edge and around the back armholes. Be careful not to stretch the fabric as you hold a strip of fusible interfacing taut. Fuse along the edge of your jacket back neck and around the armholes. This will stop these edges from stretching (Figure 8.3).

2. If you are working with a heavy fabric, or the design of your jacket needs more support across the shoulder area, add a back stay. This will prevent strain across the shoulder blades and support the fabric (Figure 8.4). The back stay can be made from cotton batiste, muslin, or silk organza and is cut on the bias. The stay is attached after the center back seam has been stitched together. You may also refer to Chapter 6 for instructions on how to apply fusible interfacings, and fuse a back stay to your jacket back.

3. Fuse a 2-inch strip of fusible interfacing along the hem line about ⅛ inch (1 cm) up from the bottom edge. Continue to add fusible interfacing up the vent extension and extending past the end of the vent for 1 inch (2.5 cm) if adding a vent to the jacket back as explained in the instructions for making the mitered sleeve vent in Chapter 9.

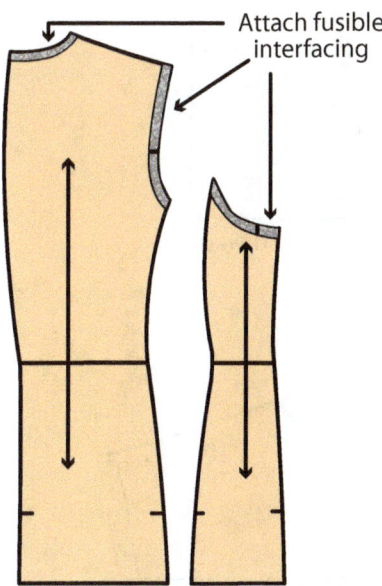

Figure 8.3

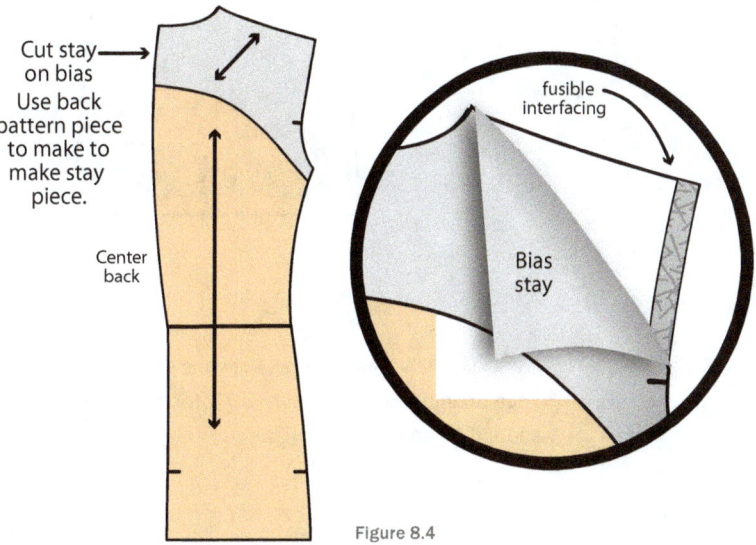

Figure 8.4

4. If you are not working with fusible interfacing but constructing your jacket using the classic or bespoke method, cut a 2-inch (5 cm) bias strip of muslin or pocketing and baste stitch in place, keeping the strip about ½ inch (1 cm) up from the hem edge of the jacket. Attach with baste stitching a 2-inch (5 cm) bias strip to the vent extension extending past the end of the vent 1 inch (2.5 cm) for both strength and to help support the vent.

Beginning Construction and Working with a Back Yoke

After you have stabilized the back, neck, and armhole edges of your jacket, you are ready to begin construction.

1. Pin and stitch the two center back pieces right sides together. Press the seam open (Figure 8.5). If the jacket has a vent at the bottom of the center back seam stop stitching ⅜ inches (1 cm) down from the top of the vent. Remembering to back stitch so that your seam will not unravel.

2. Make any darts or pleats in the two back pieces. If the jacket has a back yoke, attach to the lower jacket back cut matching the notches, and being careful to keep the built-in ease in place (Figure 8.6). The stay is attached after the center back seam has been stitched together (Figure 8.5).

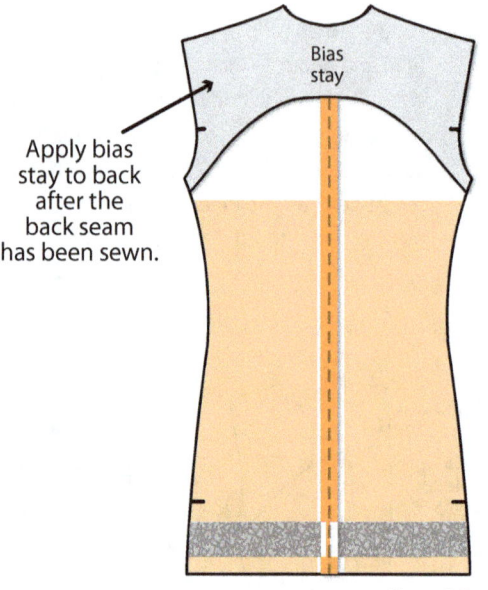

Figure 8.5

Figure 8.6

3. If working with a yoke, press the yoke seam allowance up into the yoke (Figure 8.7). Topstitch this seam if adding.

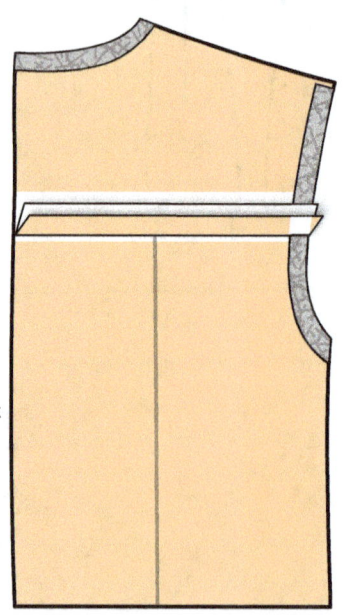

Figure 8.7

Constructing the Yoke

The yoke is not always attached to the jacket body at the lower edge but can hang free, as with a trench coat or jacket. Refer to the illustration of the raglan sleeve jacket with a back yoke in Chapter 4. You can also use a set-in sleeve. The yoke will be either lined or cut with a self facing. Make the buttonhole(s), if in the design, before basting to the jacket back at the armhole and neck edges. With the right sides together, pin the side panels to the center back, being careful to match up the notches that are controlling the built-in ease. Stitch together and press the seam allowance open (Figure 8.8).

Remember that as with the jacket front, you can shrink the seam allowance through the waist and stretch it around the hip and shoulder areas to make it press flat.

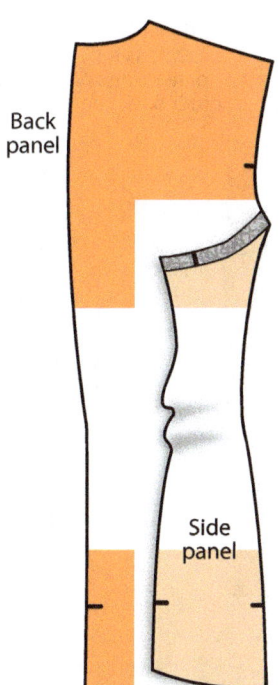

Figure 8.8

Placement of the Back Vent

For a man's jacket vent, the left side overlaps the right side; for a woman's, the left side also overlaps the right but is finished as a single center back vent (Figure 8.9).

Vents in the back of the jacket can be at the center as in Figure 8.9, at either side of the center back panels, or at the side seam. If you decide to make a vent in the jacket, the instructions remain the same.

1. The vent starts 6 inches (15 cm) down from the waistline and is two inches (5 cm) wide. Alter the pattern piece as shown in Figure 8.10. On a women's or shorter jacket, make sure that you start the vent at least 2 to 3 inches down from the waist or where the body straightens out so that the vent will sit together and not try to follow the contour of the body.

2. Make a miter at the hem on the left side of the jacket back for men and on the right side for women for a center back vent or on both sides of the back if you are making a double-vented jacket. You will make the miter on the front side seam if the vent is at the side of the jacket. Follow the instructions for making the miter in Chapter 9.

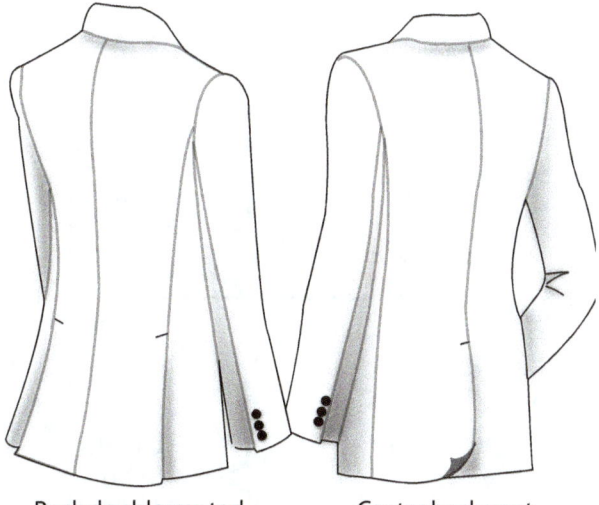

Back double vented jacket for either a mans or woman's jacket

Center back vent in a men's jacket
(left side is overlapping the right)

Figure 8.9

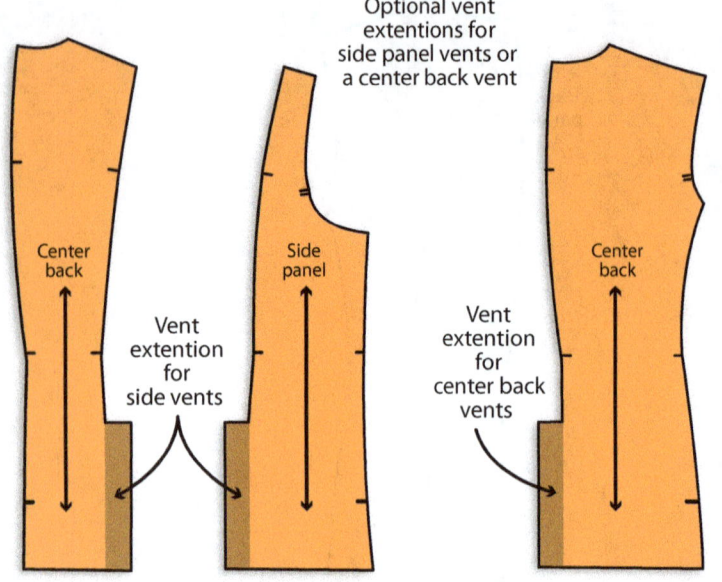

Figure 8.10

Ever thought of adding buttons or a tab to the vent? See Figure 8.11.

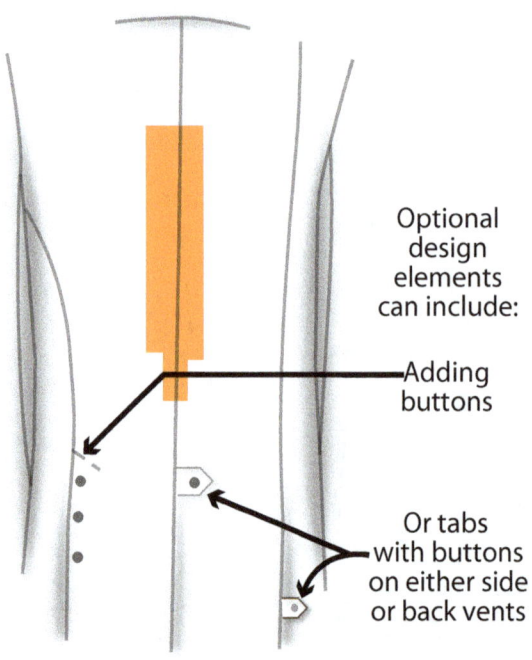

Figure 8.11

ATTACHING THE JACKET BACK TO THE FRONT

Because more fullness is needed to fit the back shoulder due to its rounded shape, you will find that ease has been built into the back shoulder seam allowance.

1. Pin the back shoulder seams to the front shoulder seams with the right sides together, matching the notches and taking care to preserve the ease in the back seam allowance. Also it is important not to catch the front interfacings into this seam because you want this to roll back over the shoulder seam. If you attach the interfacings into the seam allowances, the seam will not lay flat and will add bulk to the shoulder (Figure 8.12).

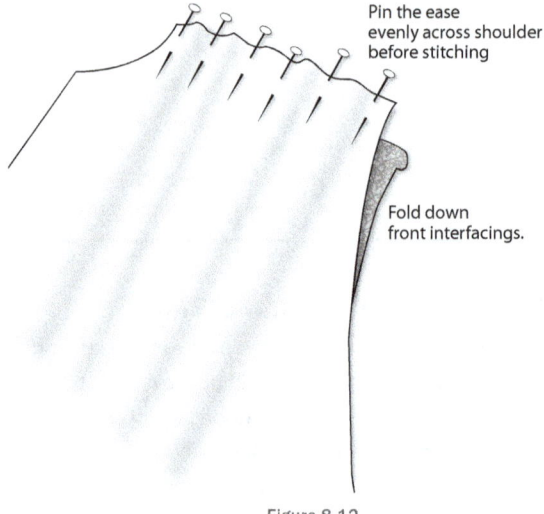

Figure 8.12

2. Press the seam open over a tailor's ham.

3. The shoulder seam can also be taped to help keep the shape of the garment to the body and also to prevent any stretching. At this point, the shoulder seam may not appear to be straight but curved; this curve will disappear when the garment is on the body.

4. If your jacket has a side seam, attach the back to the fronts at the side seams. These seams are curved; they will not lay flat after you have pressed them, unless your jacket has very little shape. Rather than clipping into the seams, it is better to stretch them by rounding them into shape while pressing. Clipping into the seam will weaken it.

Adding a Half Belt

This is a design feature that is very easy to add to the jacket back.

1. Begin by measuring across the back waistline to the side seam on your back pattern piece less 1 inch (3 cm). The width of the belt is your decision plus seam allowance (Figure 8.13).

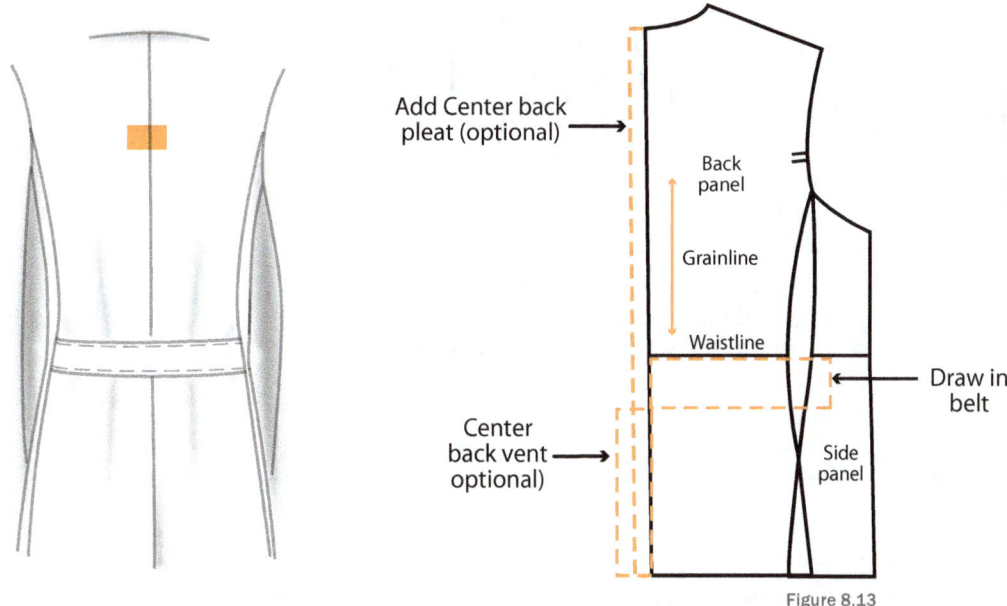

Figure 8.13

2. The back belt can also be part of the jacket construction by adding asymmetrical curved seam lines across the back. (This can begin at the front of the jacket, if you want). You can then add additional flare to the sections as shown in Figure 8.14.

3. Add extra flare between the back and side panels from below the waistline and tighten a little at the waistline and you will have a closer fitting jacket at the waistline with flare at the hip line. You will see this in a classic riding jacket.

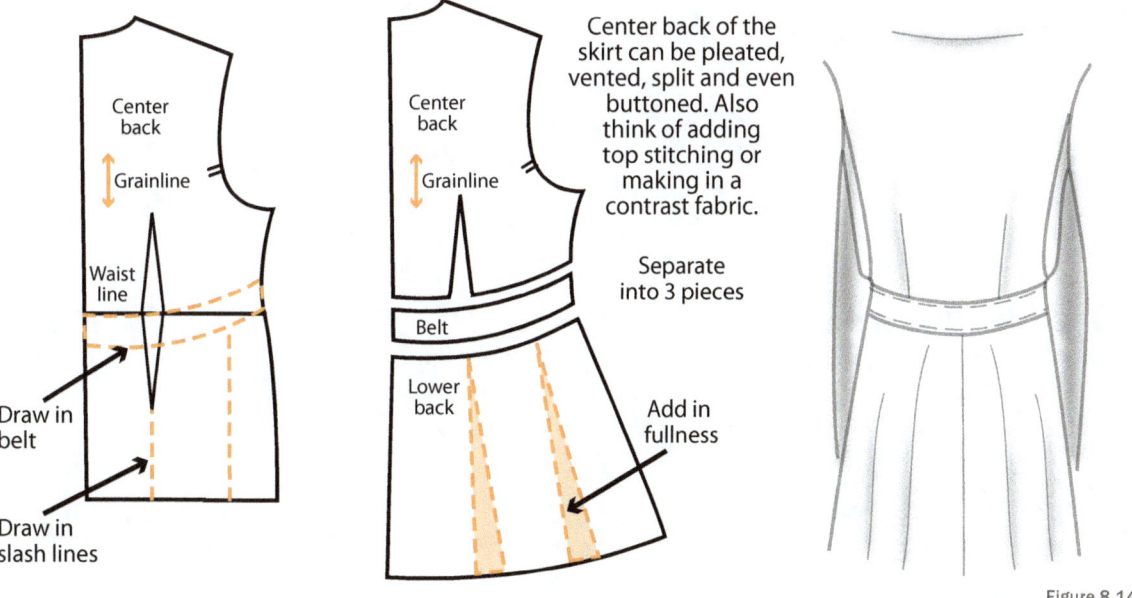

Figure 8.14

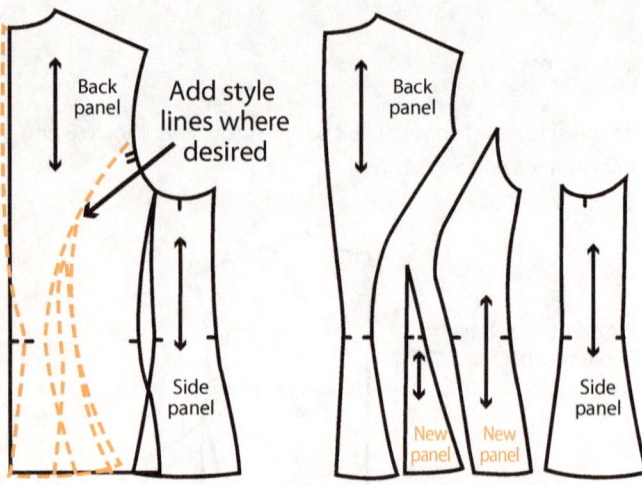
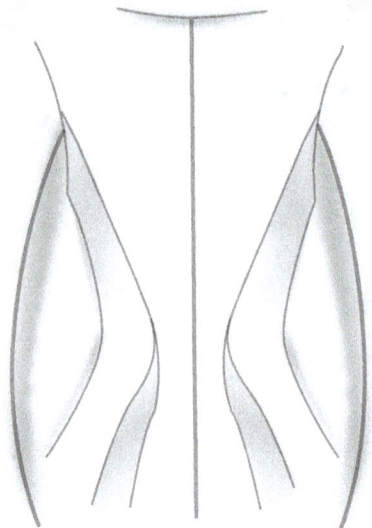

Slash and spread. Make another panel adding fullness at the hemline but keeping the shape at the waist line.

Figure 8.15

CHAPTER CHECKLIST

Before moving on to the next chapter, be sure that:
- ☐ Your jacket has enough fullness across the shoulders. There should be no pulling or strain.
- ☐ The shoulder seam curve follows the shape of the body.
- ☐ You have not lost the ease in the shoulder seam allowance.
- ☐ The side panels or side seams fit smoothly with no pulling or wrinkles.
- ☐ The back vent does not open because it has been set too close to the waistline and is following the contours of the body.
- ☐ You have finished any style details that you wanted to add to the back of your jacket.

Heidemarie Jiline "Jil" Sander was born in 1943 in Wesselburen near Hamburg, Germany. She studied textile design in Krefeld; during this time was an exchange student at University College in Los Angeles for two years before graduating as a textile engineer in 1963. Following graduation she worked as a fashion editor for Petra, a German women's magazine, before opening her first boutique in Hamburg in 1967. Here she mixed her own designs with those of French designers Thierry Mugler and Sonia Rykiel. This led her to form Jil Sander GmbH in 1978.

SUCCESS FROM FAILURE

Sander showed her first collection in Paris in 1975, and it proved to be a complete failure. At the time fashion was dominated by lavish, colorful, glitzy style designs with broad shoulders. Jil Sander's collection focused on fabric quality, with a minimalist slim-fitting style.

In the 1980s Sander began to show in Milan to try to win over the international market and, as a result, her sales grew.

This contemporary, austere look was originally intended for women entering the executive business world. She enjoyed an almost cult-like following because her fashions could easily be coordinated, focused on elegant, high-end fabrics and refined tailoring. Sander created what was to be called "onion look," or in German the "zwiebel-look," layering various pieces of clothing to create one outfit.

CONTEMPORARY AUSTERITY: A STYLE FOR THE TIMES

It took until the 1990s for her style to become a hit. In 1989 Jil Sander AG went public and was sold to shareholders on the Frankfurt stock exchange. Sander was among the first fashion houses to take this step. She used this capital to expand into Asia and North America. Sander opened a store in Paris in 1993—more than 9,000 square feet and four floors—to show the Jil Sander collections. This store was at 52 Avenue Montaigne, and had once been the atelier and showroom of Madeleine Vionnet, whose work had always influenced Sander.

Jil Sander's success continued into the mid-1990s. She showed her first menswear collection in 1997, which was praised by the critics. It was described as "precision cut with the emphasis on light fabrics."

CHALLENGED BY SUCCESS

In 1999 the Prada Group bought a 75 percent share of Jil Sander AG. Sander remained as creative designer and chairwoman. Six months later, in January 2000, Sander left after confrontations with Prada CEO Patrizio Bertelli. Unable to compromise, Sander had refused to use cheaper fabrics and bring her traditionally slim fits into line with standard sizing demanded by Bertelli. He also insisted that she give up her workshops in Germany and use those owned by Prada. After Sander resigned, the fashion house struggled both creatively and financially. She returned to the company in May 2003 as head designer, and once again her Jil Sander signature with a more feminine look was a hit with both customers and critics. She was to resign again in November 2004 and withdraw from the fashion world. Sander's fashion label still exists today but has been carried on without her involvement since 2004.

In early 2009, Sander announced the creation of her own fashion consultancy and her employment by Uniqlo of Japan (Onward Holdings Co press statement regarding Jil Sander consulting agreement, 17 April 2009). Jil Sander was awarded the Bundesverdienstkreuz by the Federal Republic of Germany for her achievements in the fashion industry.

Figure Box 8.1 Jil Sander, Fall 2004.

CHAPTER 9

The Sleeve

Perhaps one of Balenciaga's greatest desires was the search for the perfect sleeve. He believed that a sleeve should adhere to the body, be its natural extension, and fall without the slightest flaw. It should be supple enough to allow movement but without dragging on the rest of the silhouette.

—*Pamela Golbin and Fabien Baron, Balenciaga Paris*

CHAPTER OBJECTIVES

After reading this chapter, you should be able to:

Describe the different sleeve silhouettes and design features for the tailored jacket.

Identify and describe the parts of the sleeve.

Ease and shape the sleeve to the curve of the arm.

Evaluate the fit and hang of the sleeve.

Complete a mitered sleeve vent.

Set two balanced sleeves.

Construct and place sleeve heads.

The set of the sleeve
plays a big part in the ultimate success of your jacket or coat. A badly set sleeve will distract from the final appearance of the design. It also influences the comfort and freedom of movement. There are endless sleeve silhouettes and styles but only two basic categories of sleeve to choose from:

- Set-in sleeves: Sleeves that are made separately and then attached to the body of the jacket (see Figures 9.1 and 9.2).
- Cut-on sleeves: Sleeves that are cut as one with the body of the jacket; for example, raglan or kimono (see Figures 9.3 and 9.4).

Figure 9.1 In this photo you can see a perfectly set sleeve into the armhole.

Figure 9.2 The black and beige plaid wool tweed is cut on the bias, but you can see the plaid on the jacket body and set-in sleeve match perfectly.

Figure 9.3 Madame Grès has shortened the shoulder and extended the sleeve cap for this brocade jacket.

Figure 9.4 Vivienne Westwood, Erotic Zone collection, 1994.

Silhouettes include the bell, bishop, and leg of mutton. We also describe sleeves by their length, such as long, short, full, or close fitting (see Figure 9.5 and 9.6).

The sleeve cap can be gathered, darted, pleated, draped, or fitted smoothly into the armhole of the jacket body. The bottom of the sleeve can be finished with a self hem, facing, cuff, binding, or vents. Sleeves can be made from one, two, or three pieces. Although they are usually cut on the straight of grain, sleeves can also be bias cut or even made to spiral around the arm.

Figure 9.5 Martin Margiela.

Figure 9.6 Christian Lacroix, fall/winter 2004–2005.

TYPES OF SLEEVE CONSTRUCTION

Types of sleeve construction include the one-piece sleeve; the two-piece, or tailored, sleeve; the two-piece sleeve with a mitered vent; and the raglan sleeve.

The One-Piece Sleeve

We begin with the anatomy of a one-piece sleeve (Figure 9.7). This is the most basic fitted set-in sleeve, and it is the foundation for all the other sleeve designs.

Looking at Figure 9.4, you can see that when the sleeve is laid flat the grainline runs from the shoulder point as a straight line to the elbow, dividing the sleeve down the middle. Below the elbow line the grainline moves apart from the centerline, moving over towards the back wrist.

The bicep line defines the base of the sleeve cap and marks the crossgrain. The cap line runs midway between the bicep line and the shoulder point.

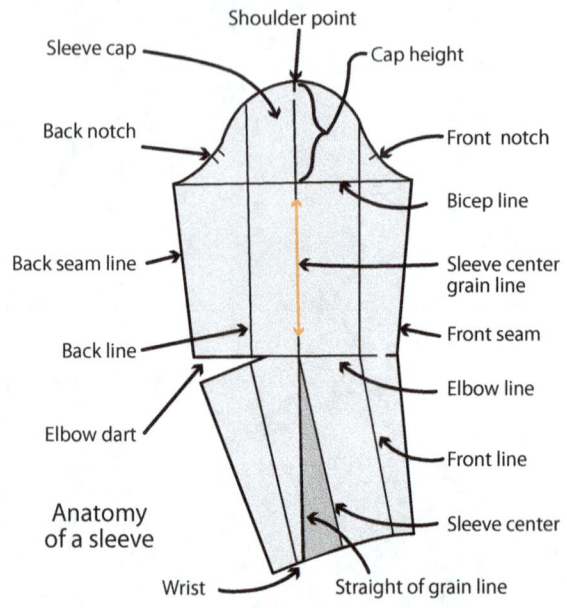

Anatomy of a sleeve

Figure 9.7

The length of the shoulder seam and the height of the shoulder pads affect the cap height. Both are influenced by current fashion trends. So the shorter the shoulder seam, the higher the sleeve cap; or the longer the shoulder seam, the shorter the sleeve cap.

There should be 1 inch of ease in the front of the sleeve cap and approximately the same in the back. The sleeve cap must always be eased into the armhole.

The elbow line is also on the crossgrain. The elbow is darted so that the sleeve follows the curve of the arm and also provides fullness so that the wearer can bend his or her elbow. This dart can become ease.

Other important vertical lines on the sleeve are the front and back underarm seam lines, the front forearm line, and the back line.

The Two-Piece, or Tailored, Sleeve

This sleeve is usually used for jackets and coats. The two-piece sleeve is composed of a top or upper sleeve and a narrower lower sleeve. The back seam runs down the back of the arm midway between the center of the sleeve and the underarm. The front seam is on the underside of the sleeve front approximately three quarters from the center of the sleeve.

Cutting the sleeve into two pieces allows you to eliminate the underarm seam. It also allows you to add more fullness or ease into the back seam over the elbow and to add a vent at the wrist.

Follow the instructions in Chapter 4 for drafting your two-piece sleeve.

When making your toile or muslin, make sure that you mark by drawing both the bicep and elbow line as well as the grainline so you can check that your sleeve is fitting and the hang is perfect. The sleeve cap should fit into the armhole smoothly with no pulling or creases. When you have the sleeve balanced, the grainline will hang straight from the shoulder point and be perpendicular to the floor, and the crossgrain (bicep and elbow) will be parallel to the floor. If the sleeve is twisting out of position, alterations must be made and the sleeve reset (Figure 9.8).

The height of the sleeve cap can be altered, too. You can release some of your seam allowance to increase the cap height, or turn under more seam allowance to decrease the cap height.

The length of the sleeve can also be corrected, if necessary. The finished length of a tailored sleeve is a matter of preference, as comfort should be your main concern, but your sleeve should end somewhere just below your wrist bone. If the sleeve looks too big on the arm, make a narrower sleeve by taking in the back and front sleeve seams.

When all your corrections are made, use this muslin to transfer all the fit alterations to your paper pattern or to make a new paper sleeve pattern. This is now your pattern for cutting both your fabric and lining for your jacket.

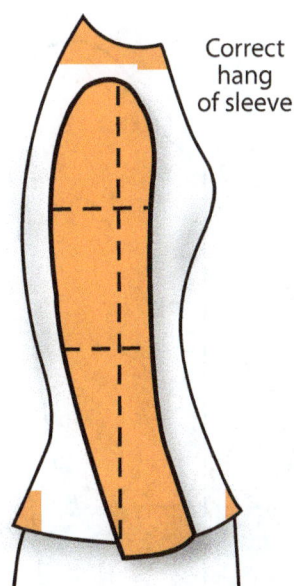
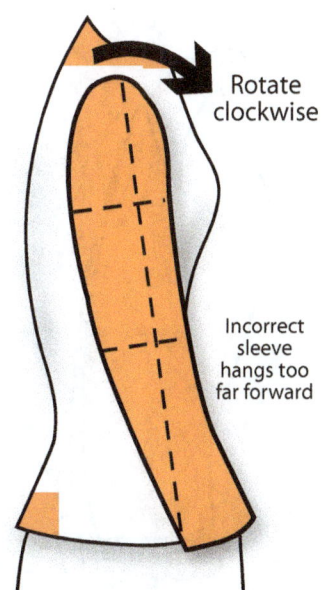
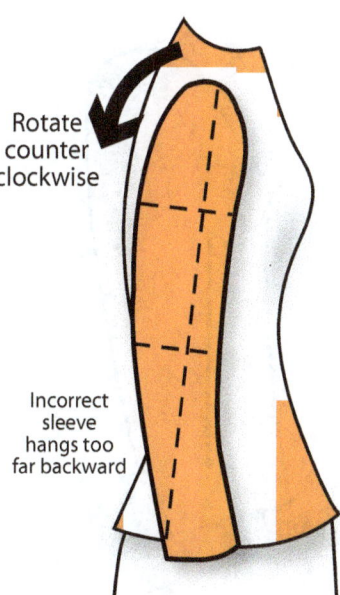

Figure 9.8

Two-Piece Sleeve with a Mitered Vent

When making your sleeve vents, add an extension of 1½ (3.8 cm) out from the fold line of the back seam on both the top and under sleeve patterns. You can make the vent length into a fashion or design statement.

Shaping the Two-Piece Sleeve

Because we want the sleeve to curve in the shape of our arm instead of wrinkling in the elbow area, which is not very attractive, you have to shape the upper sleeve. Both the upper and under sleeves have notches above and below the elbow line. Notice that the notches on the upper sleeve are closer together than the under sleeve.

1. Using the iron, stretch the upper sleeve to match the longer edge of the under sleeve. To do this, lay your two upper sleeves on top of each other, right sides together. Stretch both sleeves together so they are identical in shape. Using steam, or a damp pressing cloth, working up from the wrist edge, press from the edge as you stretch with your other hand. Turn the sleeves over and repeat the process (Figure 9.9).

2. Cut a piece of fusible interfacing long enough to extend from vent edge to vent edge and 2 ½ inches (6.5 cm) wide. Now cut two more pieces of fusible interfacing 2 ½ inches (6.5 cm) by the length needed to cover the length of the vent. Fuse into place with ½ inch (1 cm) extending into the hem. Traditionally, you would have used bias cut pocketing instead of fusible interfacing (Figure 9.10).

3. Pin together under the arm seam, right side to right side, matching notches, and machine stitch (Figure 9.11).

4. Press open the underarm seam (Figure 9.12). Stretch the seam allowances as you press them open. I prefer to stretch the sleeve between the notches than to ease because I find that you get a better shape to your sleeve.

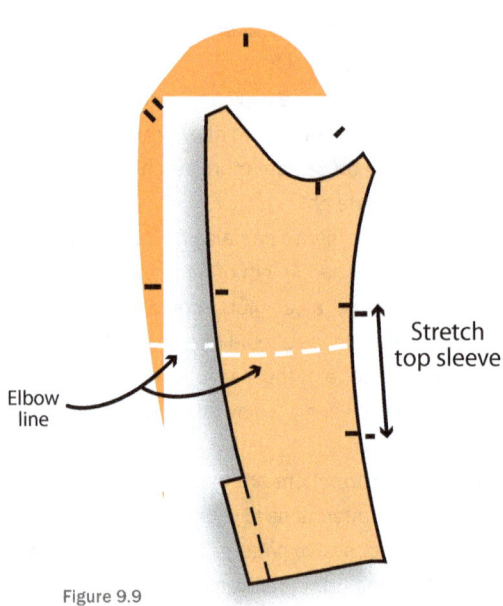

Figure 9.9

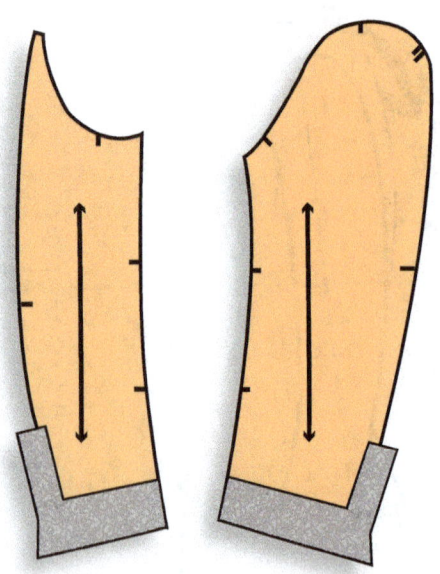

Figure 9.10

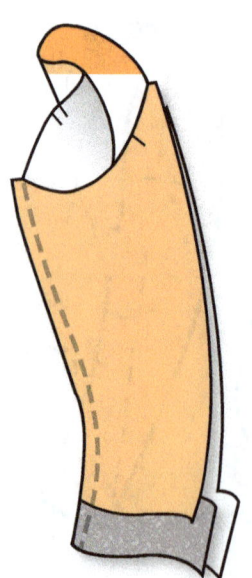

Figure 9.11

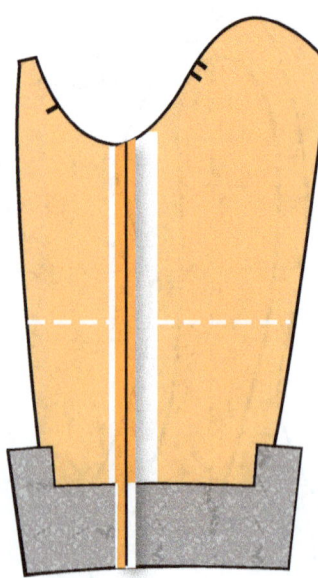

Figure 9.12

Mark and make your buttonholes in the top back sleeve. These buttonholes will begin 1 inch (2.5 cm) above the hem fold line and ½ inch (1.3 cm) in from the fold line at the edge of the vent. The buttonholes are placed ¾ inch (1.9 cm) to ⅝ inch (1.6 cm) apart, so that the buttons are almost touching.

Making the Miter

There are 12 steps to constructing a miter for a sleeve.

1. Press up the hem and press over the vent (Figure 9.13).

2. Mark the point where the sleeve vent and hem allowance cross with a clip from the points of your scissors. Make sure that your scissor tips are pointing in towards the point of the sleeve vent (Figure 9.14).

3. Unfold the vent and hem allowance (Figure 9.15).

4. Draw a line on the wrong side of the fabric, from clip mark to clip (Figure 9.16).

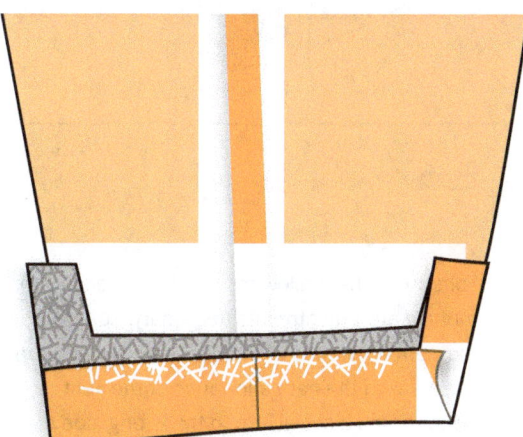

Figure 9.13

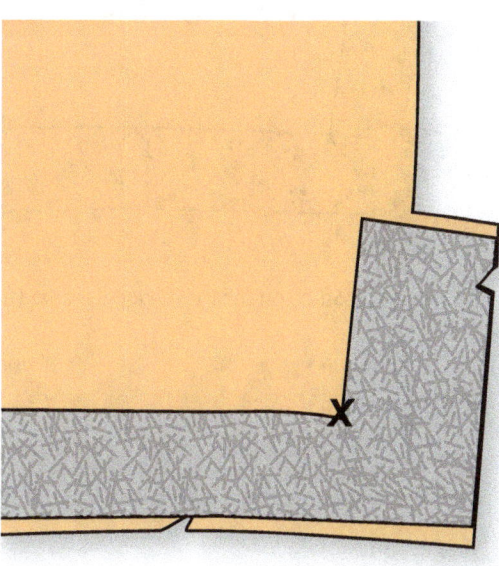

Figure 9.15

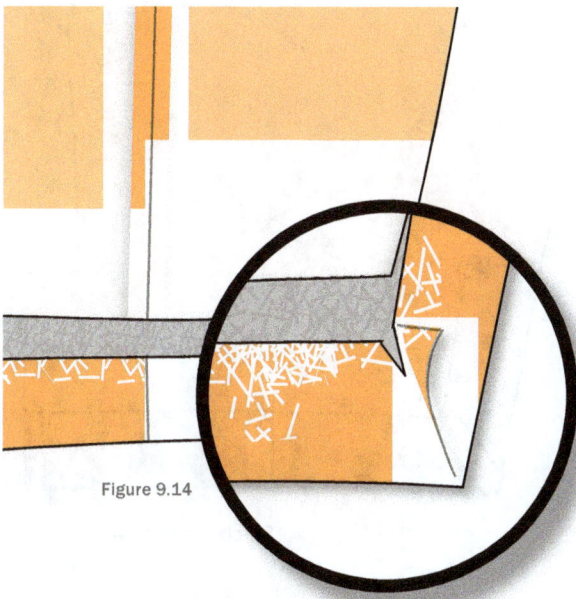

Figure 9.14

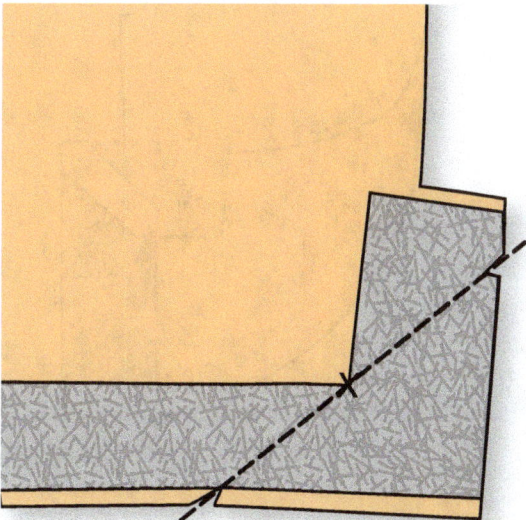

Figure 9.16

5. Pin the hem allowance of the vent to the bottom of the sleeve, with the right sides together, and sew on the line from the clip point (Figure 9.17).

6. Trim away excess fabric, leaving about ½-inch (1 cm) seam allowance and cutting a V shape at the point of the vent to eliminate bulk (Figure 9.18).

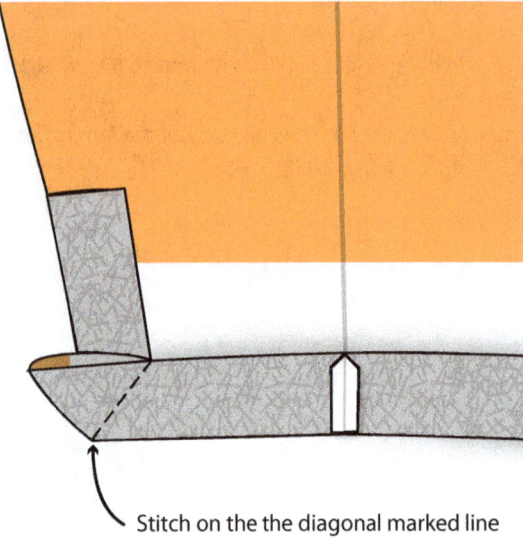

Stitch on the the diagonal marked line

Figure 9.17

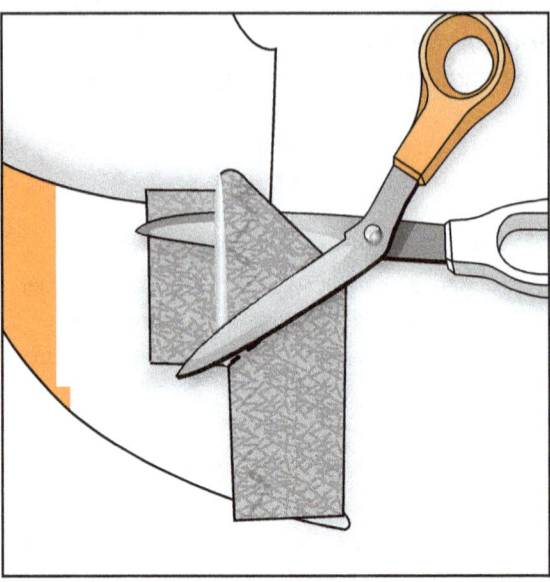

Figure 9.18

7. Press open the seam allowance (Figure 9.19).

8. Fold up the hem allowance of the under sleeve making any adjustments necessary, so that the hem allowance of the under sleeve lines up exactly with the hem allowance of the vent on the upper or top sleeve. Turn to the wrong side of the under sleeve and fold up the hem allowance and sew the vent seam (Figure 9.20).

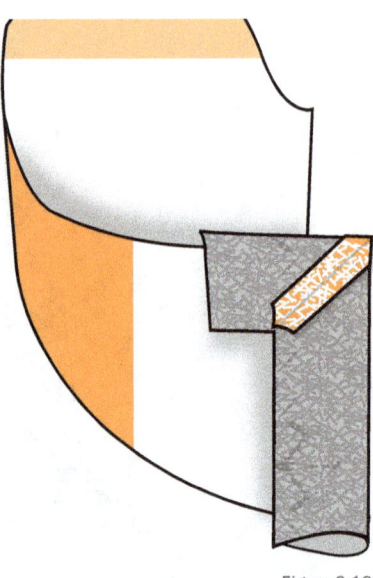

Figure 9.19

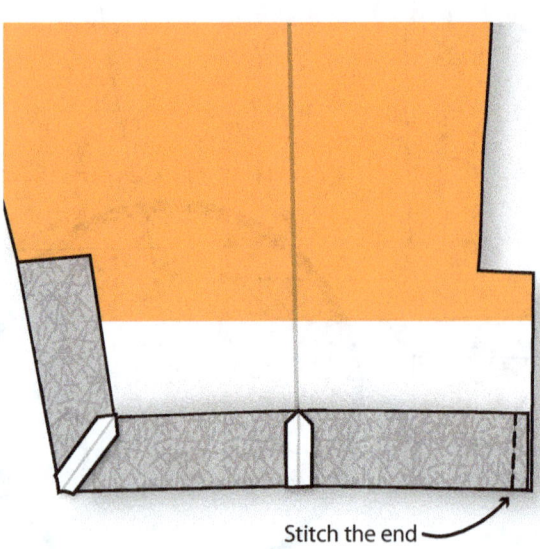

Stitch the end

Figure 9.20

9. Press open the seam allowance, clip in the V shape at the fold line to eliminate the bulk, turn to right side, and press again.

10. Baste the hem into place close to the hem fold line (Figure 9.21).

11. Bring the back seam together right side to right side. The top vent should be a fraction longer than the under vent. Slip stitch the vent closed (Figure 9.22).

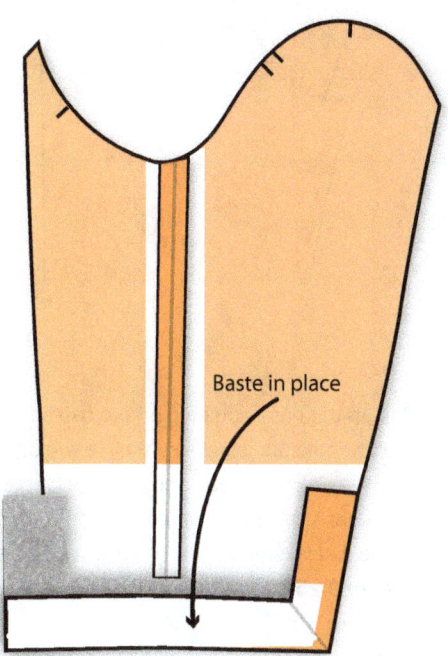

Baste in place

Figure 9.21

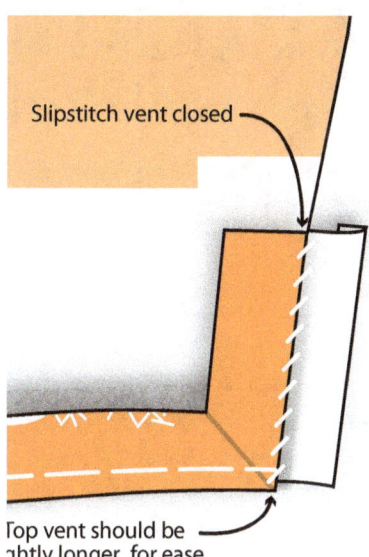

Slipstitch vent closed

Top vent should be slightly longer for ease

Figure 9.22

12. Pin the back seam, making sure that you keep the ease between the two notches. The top sleeve should be about ¼ inch (6 mm) to ⅜ inch (1 cm) longer than the under sleeve. Steam press out any puckers in the seam, and press the seam open, making a diagonal in the seam allowance just above the vent instead of clipping into the seam allowance and weakening the fabric (Figure 9.23).

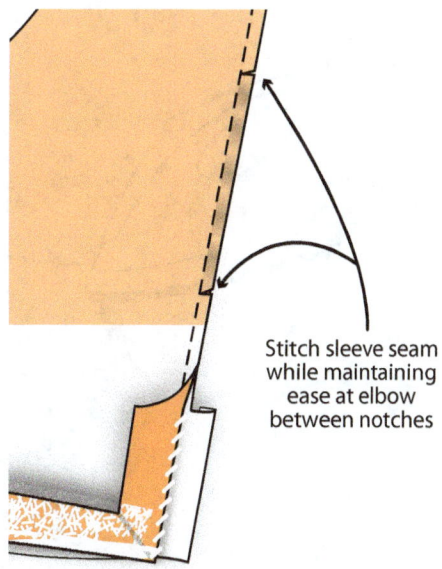

Stitch sleeve seam while maintaining ease at elbow between notches

Figure 9.23

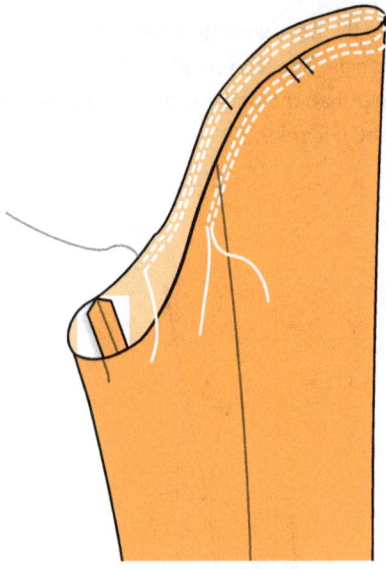
Figure 9.24

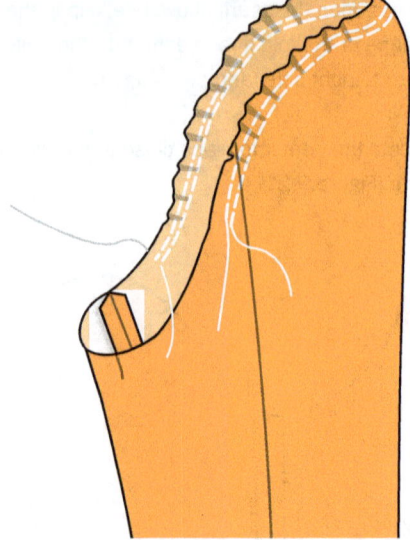
Figure 9.25

Making the Sleeve Cap

The sleeve head, as stated earlier, is about 2 inches (5 cm) bigger than the armhole of your jacket, so it will be eased in to fit.

1. Run two rows of ease stitching, one ⅛ inch (3 mm) in from your seam line and the other just on the seam line from notch point to notch point (Figure 9.24).

2. Pull up the ease stitching on the cap so that the armhole and sleeve seam line are equal in length. I like to keep about 1 inch (2.5 cm) on either side of the shoulder point [md] top of the sleeve smooth with no or very little ease (Figure 9.25).

Arrange the cap right side up on to a tailor's ham. Steam or cover with a damp press cloth and shrink out the excess fullness. Shrink from the edge of the seam allowance inward, moving the iron no more than 1 inch (2.5 cm) over the seam line to keep from shrinking out to much of the fullness there for distorting the hang of your sleeve. Let the sleeve cap completely dry before removing from the ham (Figure 9.26). Check that both sleeve heads are the same size. By shrinking out the extra fabric in the seam allowance, the sleeve will be easier to set.

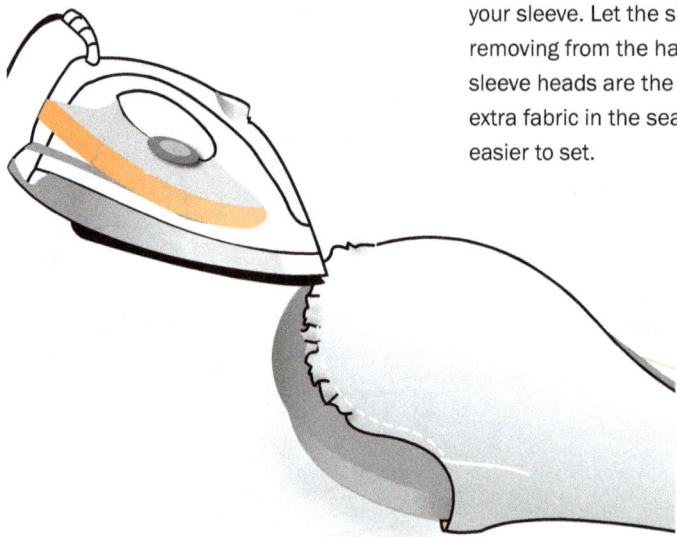
Figure 9.26

Setting the Sleeve

It is now time to set the sleeve into the armhole of your jacket.

1. With the right sides together and working from the sleeve, match the shoulder point of the sleeve to the shoulder point of your jacket and pin in place; now match underarm notch to underarm notch on the jacket body. From the underarm, work up towards the front notch, being careful to ease and pin the sleeve to the armhole as you go. Repeat from the underarm, ease the sleeve up to the back notch, and pin in place (Figure 9.27).

2. Continue to pin your sleeve into the armhole of your jacket. Baste along the seam line with short, even basting stitches, removing the pins as you go and making sure that you are evenly distributing the ease (Figure 9.28).

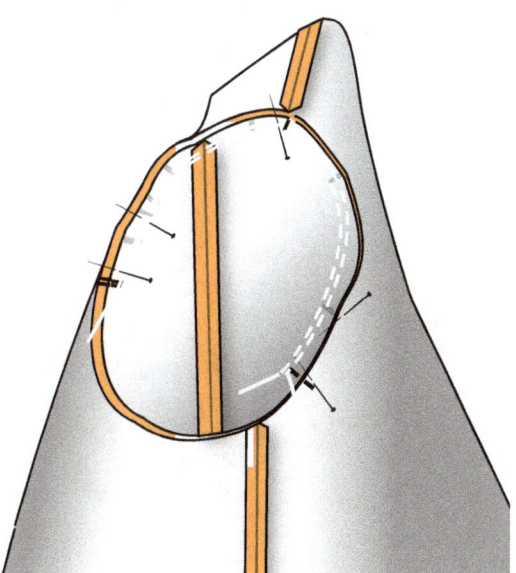

Figure 9.27

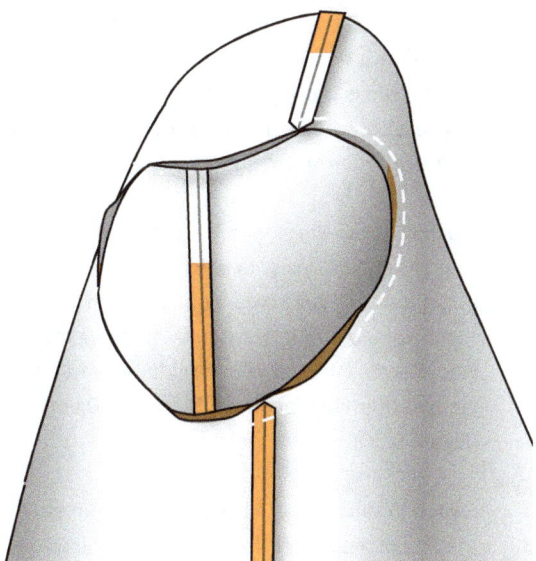

Figure 9.28

3. If you are working in plaids, stripes, or other patterned fabric that needs to be matched, work over a dress form so that you can baste with a fell stitch on the right side of the garment, keeping the fabric pattern aligned. Then remove from the dress form and, working from the wrong side, evenly baste the armhole seam for a second time to make sure that both layers are securely positioned.

4. Now evaluate the hang of the sleeve and ease and smoothness of the sleeve cap by refitting your jacket, putting it on a dress form, or simply by putting your fist into the sleeve cap with the shoulder of the jacket over your forearm (Figure 9.29).

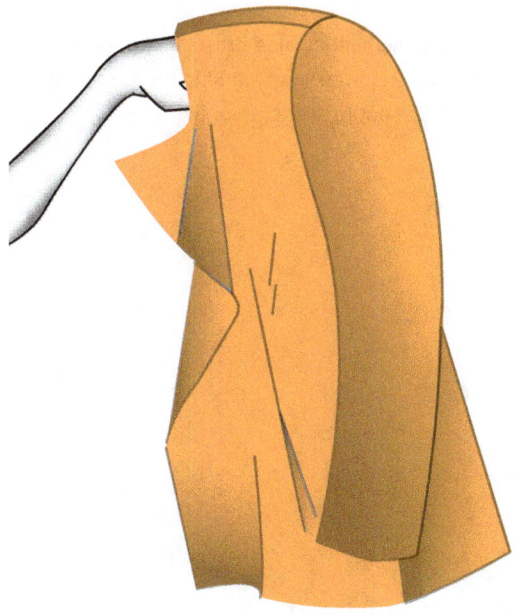

Figure 9.29

5. Hold your arm forward so that the jacket hangs naturally straight, without any wrinkling. Repeat setting the sleeve into the other armhole, pin in shoulder pads, and check the fit of the sleeves on the figure, making any changes that may be necessary. Before permanently attaching the sleeve into the jacket body use the following check points and make sure that you are completely happy with both the drape and fit of the sleeve. This is a focal point. Here is what you need to check:

- The sleeve cap should have no pleats or gathers in the seam line.
- The cap should look smooth and free of dimples. (Some dimpling will be removed when the sleeve head is set and pressed.)
- If the cap is pulling up or too short, reduce the sleeve cap seam allowance. This will also help to reduce unwanted ease.

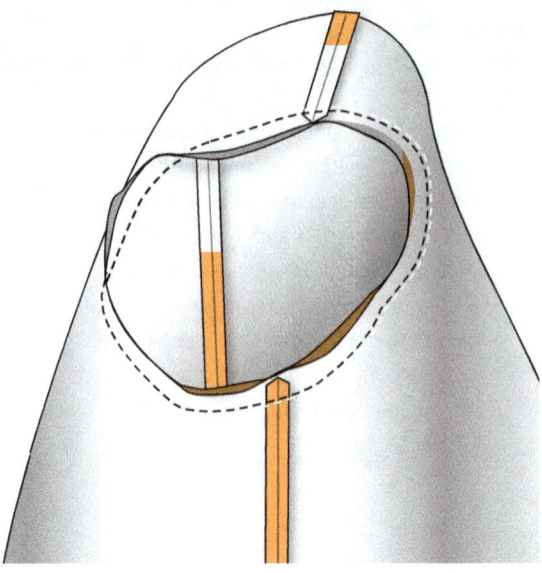

Figure 9.31

6. Machine stitch the sleeve into the armholes of your jacket. It is easier to stitch with the sleeve upper most. To get a nice, straight seam across the top of the armhole, begin by stitching the sleeve across the top from front to back with the jacket uppermost for about 4 inches (10 cm) (Figure 9.30).

7. Switch to stitching with the sleeve side up around the rest of the sleeve (Figure 9.31). Making sure that your first and last stitch are accurately placed on top of the last stitch, as shown in Figure 9.27, so as not to make a tuck.

8. Remove the basting, and press the seam allowance flat as it was sewn working over the ham. Be careful not to over press.

Figure 9.30

Constructing the Sleeve Heads

The sleeve head will fill out and give added shape to the cap of the sleeve and create a graceful fall to the fabric at the top of the sleeve. Place them into the sleeve caps from the front notch to about 2 inches (5 cm) below the back notch. You can buy or make your own sleeve heads.

1. To make your sleeve heads, cut a bias strip of muslin 2½ inches (6.5 cm) wide by 16 inches (41 cm) long. You may need to lengthen this to 18 inches (45 cm) for a man's jacket or coat. Cut a piece of wadding or fleece to the same measurements. For a more subtle increase in the size of your sleeve head, or to support a high sleeve cap that you want well defined, you can add hair canvas, cotton batting, lambs wool, or soft wool, any of which can also be cut wider—consider what your design may call for.

2. Lay the wadding or fleece on top of the muslin strip. Fold the strip lengthwise over 1 inch (2.5 cm) so that one long edge is ½ inch (1.2 cm) wider than the other, and machine baste along the length, ⅜ inch (1 cm) in from the folded edge (Figure 9.32).

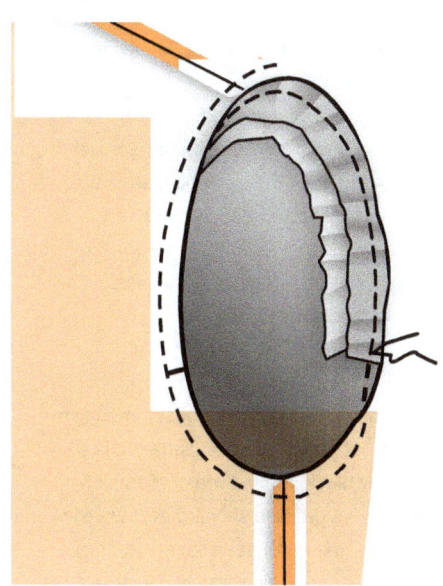

Figure 9.33

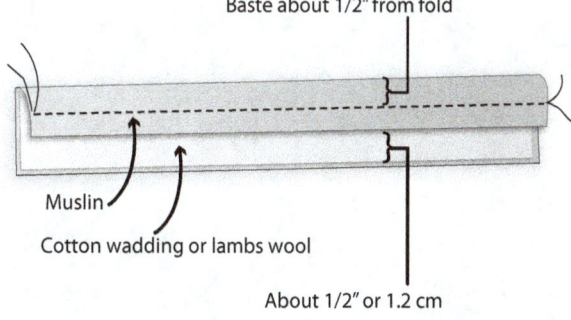

Figure 9.32

Figure 9.34

3. Fold the sleeve head in half to find the center and mark. Place the centered folded edge of the sleeve head on the armhole seam line at the shoulder point. Pin in place with the wider side of the sleeve head against the sleeve. Work over the top of the sleeve and down to both the front and back notch points, pinning in place. Machine stitch to the sleeve seam allowance, being careful not the cross over the seam line into the sleeve (Figure 9.33).

4. Turn the seam allowance towards the sleeve. The sleeve head will have a double roll. Steam press as shown (Figure 9.34).

BOX 9.1 Christóbal Balenciaga

A couturier must be an architect for design, a sculpture for shape, a painter for color, a musician for harmony and a philosopher for temperance.

Balenciaga—*Vogue,* March 1968, pg. 201, interview by Gustave Zumsteg

Fashion photographer Cecil Beaton famously said of Balenciaga, "He has established the future of fashion."

Balenciaga, the son of a tailor, was born in 1895 in the Basque region of Spain. This meant that he was considered both Spanish and French. He opened his first boutique in San Sebastian at the age of 24. This was followed by boutiques in both Madrid and Barcelona, all named "Eisa" after his mother Martina Eisaquirre.

In 1937 he opened a couture house in Paris with the support of Spanish friends. This was an immediate success.

AN EDUCATION OF A LIFETIME

Self taught, he worked for years to refine his techniques, through a relentless simplification of cut that has become legendary. His stark designs in somber colors, mainly black, remind you of pieces of sculpture or architecture. He always dressed simply, never wore jewelry—not even a wrist watch—and was never seen to carry money.

After a visit to the United States and seeing ready-to-wear clothing, he determined never to use machines, and individual items continued to be made by hand in his workrooms. He was also offered lucrative licensing contracts in the United States, to which he replied "What would I buy? I have a car and too many houses."

The House of Balenciaga had five tailoring, three dressmaking, and two millinery workrooms. He trained all his staff and approved all promotions. Each seamstress had an apprentice and created the garment from start to finish. There were notices on the walls that read "Copying is stealing" and the motto of the house "No waste."

The *vendeuses,* or sales ladies, were not paid a salary, but received a percentage of sales, with each being responsible for the salary of staff working under her.

AN ENDURING LEGACY

At the age of 73, and nearly half a century after opening the doors of his boutique in San Sebastian, he closed the doors of the House of Balenciaga in May 1968. It was a turbulent time in France and because of a postal strike his employee's didn't get their redundancy notices until after the event.

Mlle Renee, who had been the director in charge of all aspects of the business, took over the management of the boutique until after his death in 1972 when his family took over the business. From a signature, after his death, his name was transformed into a brand, a trademark label that was to become the surviving trace of its founder.

Andre Courreges and Emamuel Ungaro both trained under Balenciaga, as did many other designers. Hebert Givenchy and Christian Dior called him their master.

From a modest beginning, he was able to establish both financial and worldwide professional success through his passion, discipline and hard work. He was able to transform the way others looked at things, their vision of fashion, and his influence touched many creative people.

Figure Box 9.1
Balenciaga, worn by Lisa Fonssagrives-Penn. Photo by Irving Penn.

Figure 9.35 Armani Privé Spring couture, 2009.

Your sleeve head may be gathered, pleated, or darted as in a pagoda sleeve, in which case you are going to have to add more support (Figure 9.35). You can cut and shape the sleeve heads, but if you are working with really exaggerated sleeve heads you are going to need more support. Cut and interface the shape of the sleeve head with fusible interfacing, and if you are going really extreme, follow this with canvas as shown in Figure 9.36.

But remember that you cannot make darts in canvas, so you are going to overlap them as you did in Chapter 6, in Figures 6.2 and 6.3. Adding interfacing in this way was very fashionable back in the 1980s, and you can even see this in YSL jackets without exaggerated sleeve heads. Behind gathers and pleats you can cut a football-shaped bias-cut support from silk organza or pocketing. Attach to the sleeve head before pulling up the gathers or making the pleats.

For me, this is all very interesting and fun to try and see what happens. If you don't like the finished look, it is easy to remove.

The sleeve can also be set by hand using tiny fell stitches, but today unless you are being paid a lot of money for your finished jacket, I attach the sleeve to the body using the previously described technique.

Cut interfacing to match the shape of the sleeve cap. Cut on the bias and fold in half such that the finshed shaped is like a football.

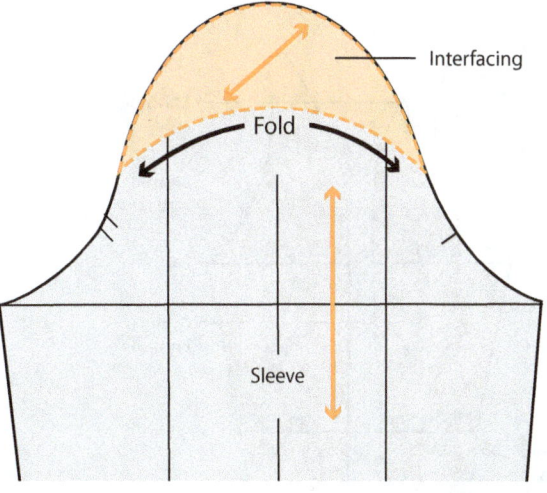

Figure 9.36

The Raglan Sleeve

Lord Raglan lost an arm in the Crimean War. To make dressing easier, he tailor made a short coat with a simple diagonal sleeve seam that extended from the neck to the underarm. It allowed much more mobility for Lord Raglan, and so the sleeve was named after him. The raglan sleeve (Figure 9.37) has a relaxed fit that makes it comfortable to wear. You will find raglan sleeves in sports jackets and coats in both men's and women's wear.

The raglan sleeve extends to the neckline and is attached to the front and back of the jacket with a long diagonal seam running underneath the arm (Figure 9.38).

The raglan sleeve has a shoulder seam that rounds down over the shoulder area into the arm of the sleeve. To support this area using your pattern pieces, cut a stay from muslin or other tightly woven fabric. Draw a line across both your front and back raglan sleeve pattern pieces about 8 inches (20.5 cm) below the neckline, and mark in the bias grainline. Baste the stay to the wrong side of the raglan sleeve edges (Figure 9.39).

Figure 9.37

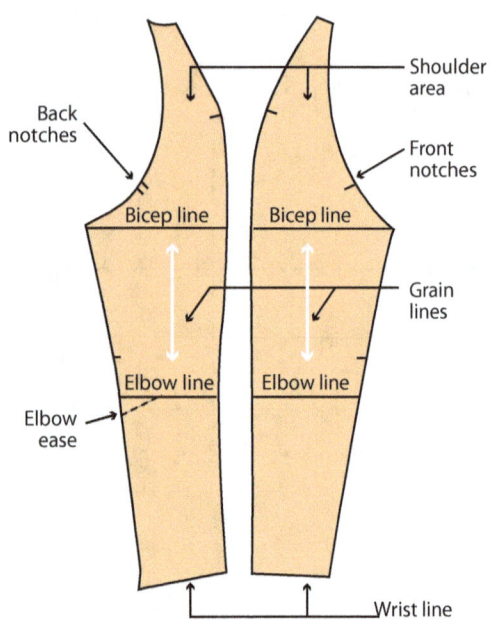

Figure 9.38

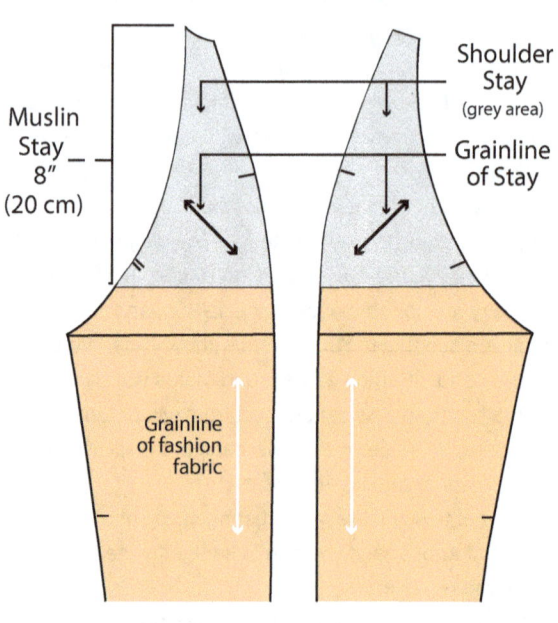

Figure 9.39

1. Begin by interfacing the sleeve hems.

2. Attach the shoulder seam, making sure that you keep all the ease in place. Press all seam allowances open as you sew.

3. With right side to right side, pin together the under seam, carefully matching the notches.

4. Now set the sleeve into your jacket body matching all notch points. Turn up the hem and baste about ½ inch (1.2 cm) up from the fold line. Now evaluate the hang of the sleeve as before with the two-piece sleeve. Pin in raglan shoulder pads, check the fit of the sleeves on the figure, and make any changes that may be necessary.

5. Machine stitch your raglan sleeve to the jacket body along the seam line. Press the sleeve as it was sewn in the underarm area, clip in at the front and back notches, and press the seam open up the neckline.

Design Tips for the Raglan Sleeve

Think of details that you can add into the raglan seam line, such as piping in a contrast color or gathered and pleated ruffles. Pockets can also be added to the front seam line of a raglan sleeve, as can flaps. The raglan sleeve can include a front and back yoke. You will find some design and pattern manipulations in Chapter 4.

CHAPTER CHECKLIST

Before you are ready to begin construction, be sure to check that:

- ☐ Your sleeves are sitting correctly with no gathers or pleats, unless these are part of the design.
- ☐ Both sleeves look the same.
- ☐ Both sleeves are balanced and hang forward in the shape of the arm.
- ☐ The vents at the hem of the sleeve sit correctly.
- ☐ The fit is correct.
- ☐ The sleeve heads are placed correctly.
- ☐ The sleeves are pressed and the hem finished.

REFERENCES

Golbin, P. & Baron, B. (2006). *Balenciaga Paris*. London: Thames & Hudson.

CHAPTER **10**

The Undercollar

My inspiration is not scholarly, it is more instinctive. I always look ahead. The past is just an excuse for experiments. Classical means contemporary to me.

—*Gianni Versace*

CHAPTER OBJECTIVES

After reading this chapter, you should be able to:

Describe the different parts of the undercollar.

Identify and apply appropriate method for its design and fabric.

Identify the different types of undercollar construction.

Shape the undercollar.

Evaluate undercollar fit.

Identify technique used to attach the undercollar to the jacket body.

There are many different tailored collars, but the notched collar and the shawl collar remain the most popular. Figure 10.1a shows a notched collar, and Figure 10.1b shows a shawl collar.

The preparation of the undercollar is important; if the set of the collar and shoulders is good, it gives style to the entire jacket or coat. The undercollar is interfaced to add both body and shape; this enables it to support the weight of the upper collar. It is attached to both the neckline and lapel of the jacket. A good example is the collar of a jacket from John Galliano's Fall/Winter 2005-'06 ready-to-wear collection for Dior (Figure 10.2).

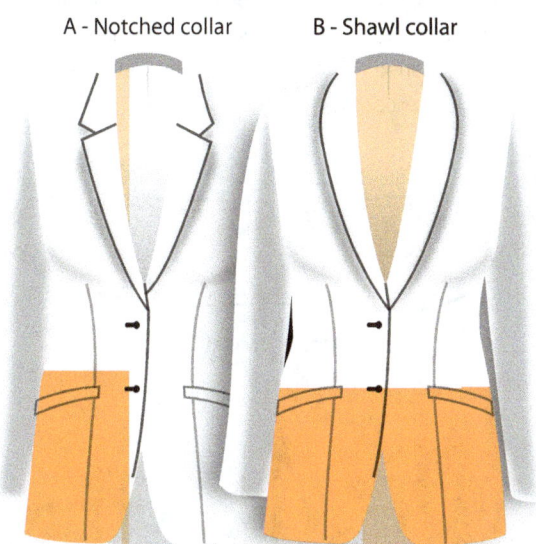

Figure 10.1

Figure 10.2 John Galliano's Fall/Winter, 2005-'06.

ANATOMY OF THE UNDERCOLLAR

Looking at the different parts of the undercollar, you will find that the center back seam is on the true bias so that the gorge line is on the warp. The roll line is the dividing line between the stand and the fall. The stand is shaped to hug the back of the neck and holds the collar at its correct height. The fall is shaped to curve and gently roll towards the collar points. The collar notch is the angle formed where the collar joins the lapel, and the gorge line is the seam line that joins the collar to the lapel (Figures 10.3 and 10.4).

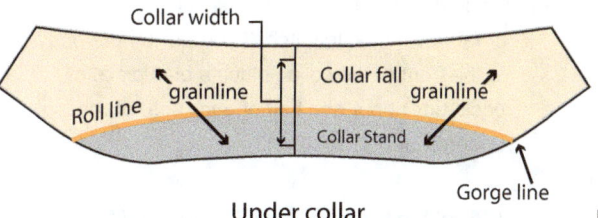

Under collar

Figure 10.4

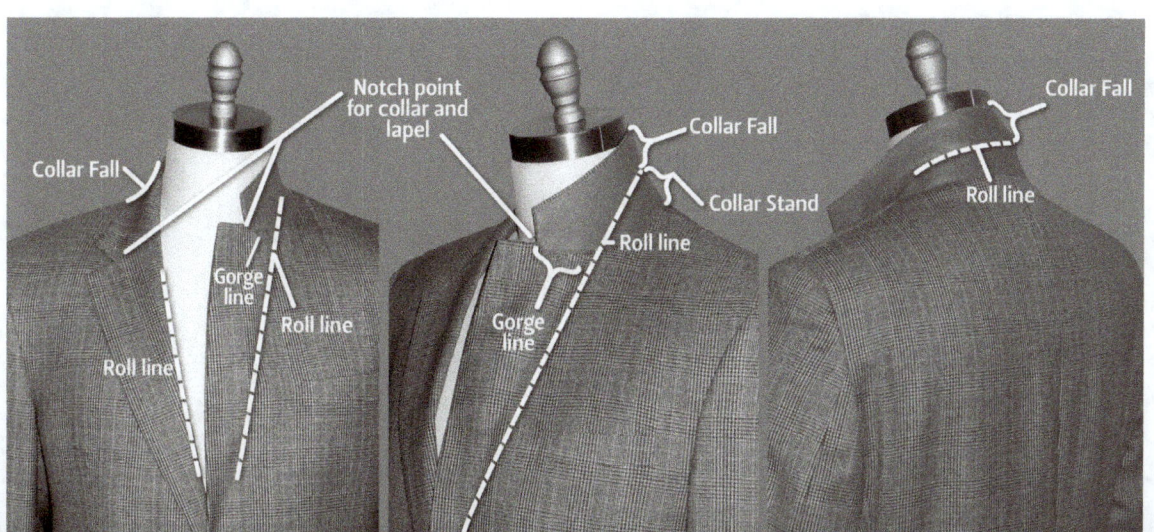

Figure 10.3

143

CHOOSING THE METHOD TO CONSTRUCT THE UNDERCOLLAR

Consider the fabric and the available time when choosing the appropriate method to construct the undercollar. There are three methods shown in this chapter: traditional, machine, and fusible. All three of these will give you good results, but I feel that working the traditional or machine methods will give you more control, which you may need to hold the shape of your collar. Also, think of what you will apply or what materials you will use to create embellishments to the top collar, as in the collar in Figure 10.3. You may want to test the methods to find which is the most suitable for both your fabric and design.

Traditional Method for Constructing the Undercollar

The undercollar is constructed in layers, starting with your fabric or melton. Cut two bias pieces of undercollar from your fabric or melton. If you are still not sure about the design of your collar, cut your two collar pieces much larger than your pattern. It is very easy to redraw the collar after it has been attached to your jacket, making sure that it works with your lapel shape and everything looks balanced. Then trim the excess away.

1. Machine stitch the center back seam and press open (Figure 10.5).

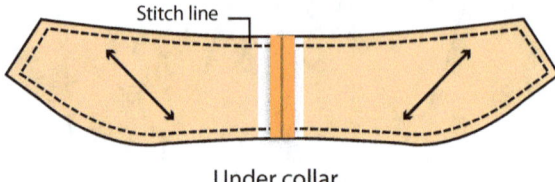

Figure 10.5

2. Using the same dimensions as for the collar, cut two bias undercollar pieces from canvas. Overlap the center back seam and then machine stitch (Figure 10.6).

Figure 10.6

3. Place the canvas on the wrong side of the melton or fabric and baste stitch. If you want more body in the front of the collar, place a bias piece of pocketing about one half of each side of the undercollar (Figure 10.7).

4. The canvas is now pad stitched to the melton or fabric, joining them together so that they remain flexible enough to be shaped with the iron. Now, draw in your seam allowance.

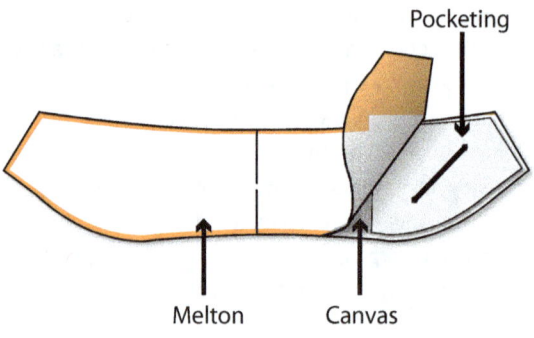

Figure 10.7

5. There are two ways of working your pad stitches, as illustrated in Versions 1 and 2 in Figure 10.8.

   a. For Version 1, pad stitch the stand, working parallel to the roll line and working small ¼-inch (6mm) stitches. Then using slightly bigger stitches, pad stitch the fall on the crossgrain. Draw a semi circle at the neck edge stitch line that is a radius of about 2 inches (5 cm). Pad stitch inside the semi circle and then beyond, creating a circular pattern of stitches. Do not pad stitch out into the seam allowance, and make sure that your thread is well matched to your melton or fabric. (Refer to Figure 10.8, Version 1.)

   b. In Version 2, work smaller tighter stitches about 1 inch (2.5 cm) in from the collar points, holding the collar rolled over your hand. (Refer to Figure 10.8 Version 2.)

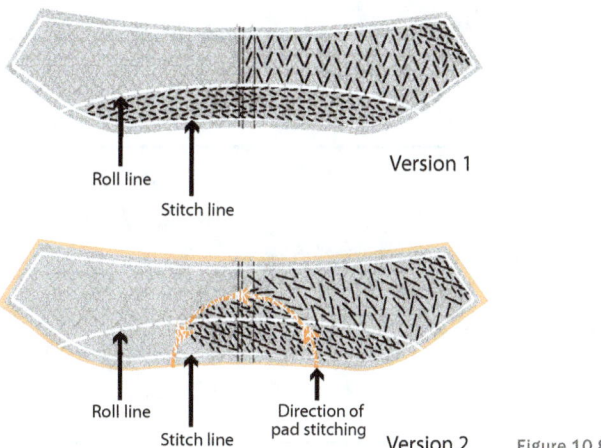

Figure 10.8

6. If you are making the undercollar using melton, some stretching may occur in the pad stitching. Place your paper pattern over the melton undercollar and trace the outline. From the melton side, draw in your seam allowance; then trim away the seam allowance completely. Trim a small margin of the canvas back from the edges (Figure 10.9).

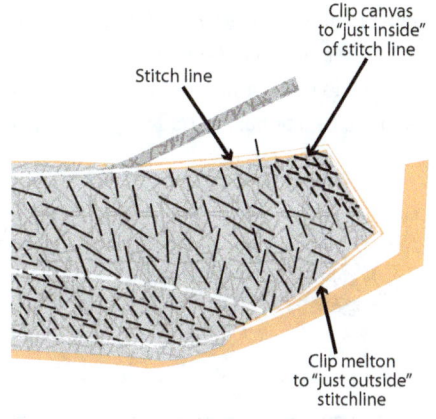

Figure 10.9

7. The undercollar is now pressed into shape. Fold the undercollar on the roll line, right sides to right side, and pin to a tailor's ham. Steam into shape, without pressing a crease in the roll line. Let the collar dry completely before removing from the ham (See Figure 10.10).

8. If shaping the undercollar without a tailor's ham, fold the undercollar on the roll line with the right sides together. Steam press the roll line in a curve or arc to shrink it and then stretch the outer edge at center back (Figure 10.11). The slope of the shoulders determines the height of the curve. In Figure 10.11, the height of the curve is 2 inches (5 cm); this is appropriate for someone with normal shoulders. If the shoulders are square, curve the collar higher approximately 2¾ inch (7 cm); this will require more shrinking and stretching than if the shoulders are sloped, where the curve is going to be lower about 1½ inches (3.8 cm).

Figure 10.10

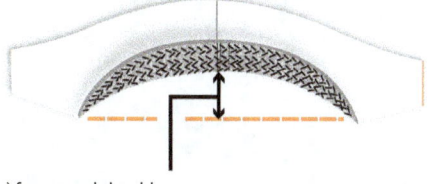

Figure 10.11

2" (5 cm) for normal shoulders
- Curve the collar higher approximately 2 3/4" (7 cm) for square shoulders.
- Curve the collar lower approximately 1 1/2" (3.8 cm) for sloped shoulders.

9. Hold the neck edge back for a couple of inches (approx. 5 cm) at each end of the roll, and press the crease out (Figure 10.12).

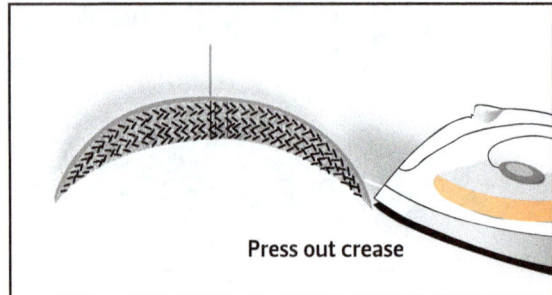

Press out crease

Figure 10.12

10. Finish the neck edge by folding the seam allowance back onto the interfacing, and catch stitch into place if you are working in fabric and the traditional method (Figure 10.13).

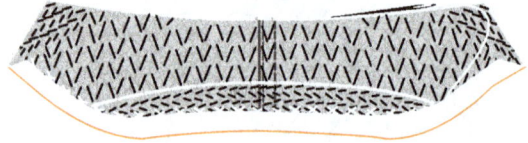

Figure 10.13

11. This is a good point to baste stitch your undercollar to the neckline of your jacket using whichever method you have chosen. Your undercollar should be about ½ inch (1.3 cm) longer than the jacket neckline. Pin together at the center back, at the shoulder seams, and then ease the excess between these two points. Pin down the gorge line, and baste stitch your collar into place (Figure 10.14). You are now ready for a fitting.

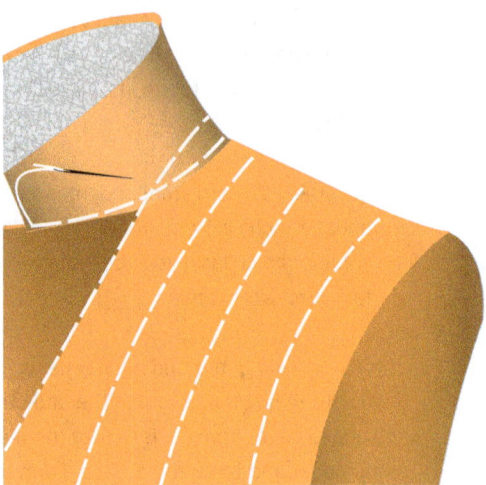

Figure 10.14

Evaluating Undercollar Fit

Fit the jacket on a body or a stand and ensure that:
- The roll line hugs the back of the neck.
- The fall of the collar at center back covers the neck line seam.
- The neckline seam is not showing below the outer edge of the collar, the edge is not too tight, and the shoulders are not square. If any of these problems exist, stretch the edge more so that it covers the neckline seam.
- The outer edge of the collar lies smoothly without rippling.
- The ease in the roll line is evenly distributed and sits smoothly.
- The roll line on the lapels hugs the body.

Make any alterations if needed.

ATTACHING THE UNDERCOLLAR TO THE NECKLINE

As previously noted, we will look at three methods for attaching the undercollar to the neckline: traditional, machine, and fusible, starting with machine, which in contemporary tailoring is often the most efficient method for this job.

Machine Method for Attaching the Undercollar to the Neckline

You can attach the undercollar to the neckline in four steps:

1. When attaching your undercollar by machine, begin by pinning the undercollar to the jacket body, right sides together, starting at the center back (Figure 10.15).

2. When you come to the gorge line you are going to have to make a clip into the seam allowance of the jacket so that the collar will shape around the corner onto the lapel (Figure 10.16).

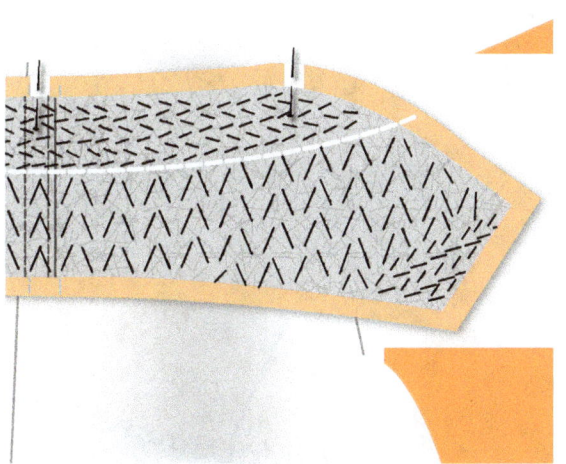

Figure 10.15

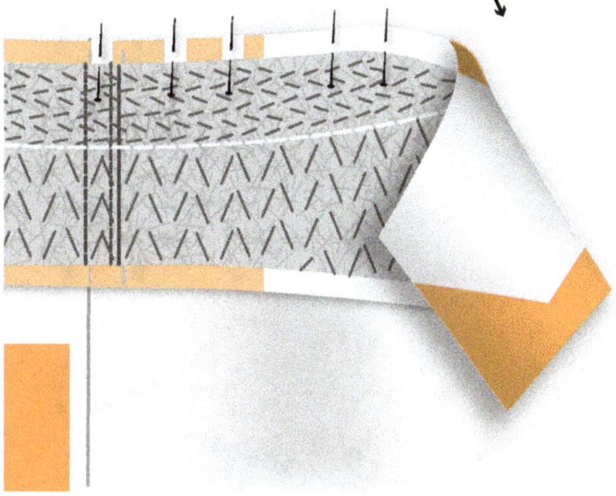

Figure 10.16 — Chip seam allowance for shaping

3. Attach the undercollar by machine stitching along the seam allowance. Be careful not to stitch into the seam allowance at the point of the collar (Figure 10.17).

4. Clip the seam allowance, and press seam allowance open (Figure 10.18).

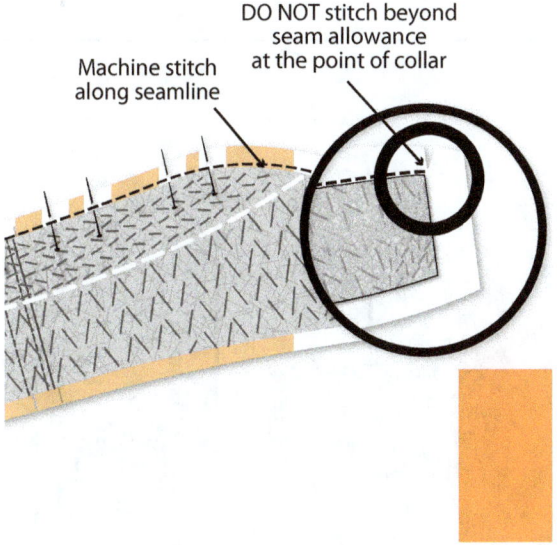

Machine stitch along seamline — DO NOT stitch beyond seam allowance at the point of collar

Figure 10.17

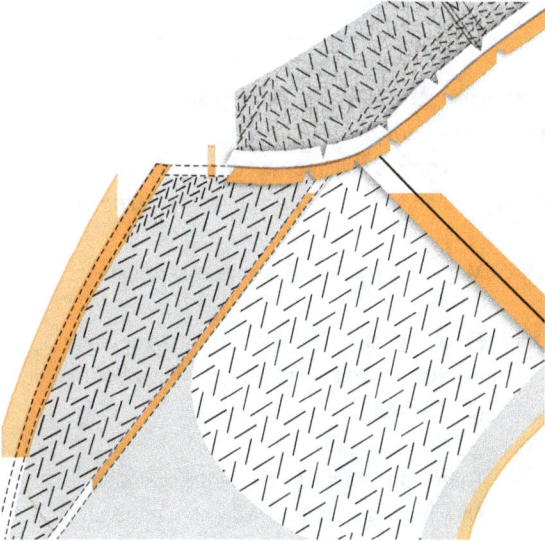

Figure 10.18

THE UNDERCOLLAR

147

Traditional Method for Attaching Undercollar to Neckline

You can attach the undercollar by hand in two steps:

1. Catch stitch the neckline seam allowance to the collar on the wrong side (Figure 10.19).

2. Catch stitch or slip stitch the undercollar to the right side of your jacket (Figure 10.20).

In contemporary tailoring, you could alternatively attach the collar onto the jacket body, right side facing, by machine zigzag stitch (Figure 10.21).

Figure 10.19

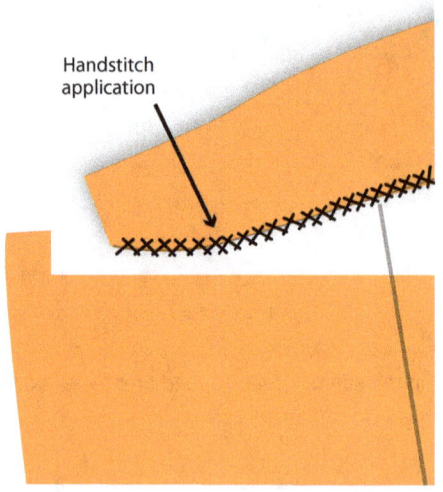

Figure 10.20

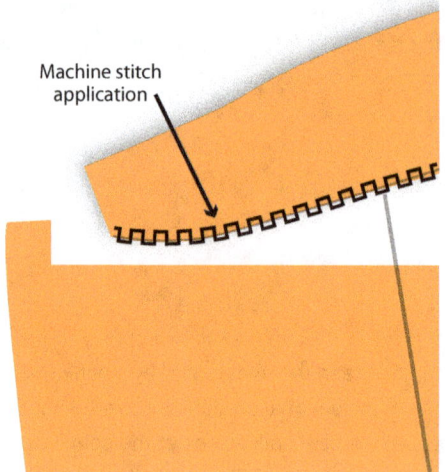

Figure 10.21

Machine Method for Stitching the Undercollar

The undercollar is still interfaced with hair canvas, but the pad stitching is done using machine stitching.

1. Mark in the seam allowance and roll line.

2. Following the curve of the roll line, machine stitch the stand in lines of stitching about ¼ inch (6 mm) apart.

3. Then mark the fall following the grainline as shown in Figure 10.24. Now shape the undercollar (Figure 10.22).

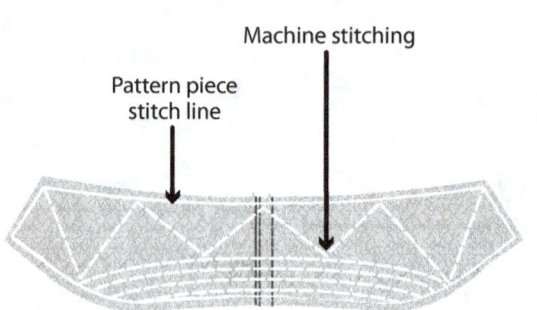

Figure 10.22

148

Fusible Method for Constructing the Undercollar

Select a suitable fusible interfacing for the fabric and collar design.

1. Cut two undercollars in fusible weft interfacing on the bias. Trim off the seam allowance at center back. Cut the collar stand from fusible weft interfacing on the crossgrain, or use a non-woven fusible interfacing. Fuse the interfacing to the undercollar, and stitch the center back seam. Press the seam open. Fuse the interfacing to the collar stand (Figure 10.23).

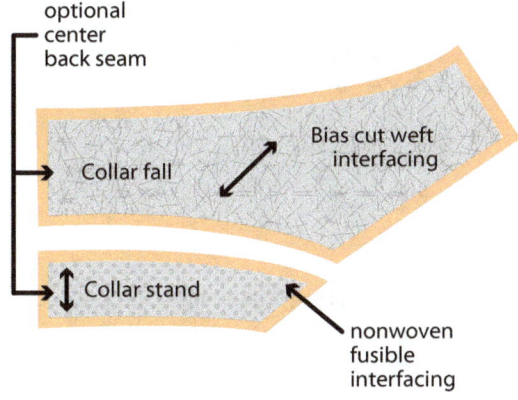

Figure 10.23

2. Shape the collar (refer to Figure 10.13).

3. Figure 10.24 shows a separate undercollar stand and one- or two-piece collar.

4. Figure 10.25 shows how the undercollar fall is cut on the bias grain.

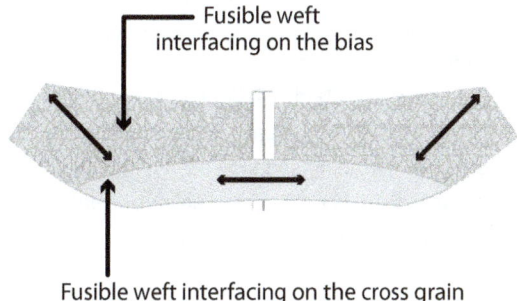

Figure 10.25

5. For the undercollar stand, cut on the straight of grain (refer to Figure 10.25). The undercollar is fused with a bias weft interfacing and the stand with a non-woven fusible interfacing. The center back seam can also be eliminated.

6. When the roll line is replaced with a seam, machine stitch the undercollar stand to the undercollar fall (Figure 10.26).

Figure 10.26

7. Clip the seam allowance and then press the seam allowance open (Figure 10.27).

Figure 10.27

The shaping of this seam will reduce the amount of pressing with the iron. Your undercollar is now ready to be attached to your jacket body.

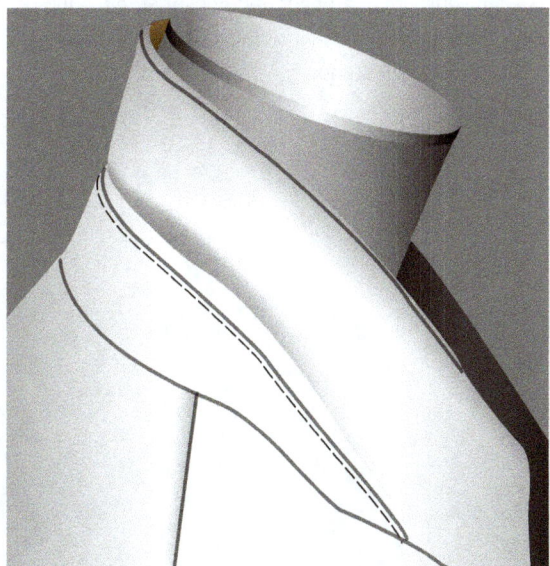

Figure 10.24 How the undercollar fall is cut on the bias grain.

CONSTRUCTING THE SHAWL COLLAR

The shawl collar (Figure 10.28) gives you a softer look than the notched collar and is not as complicated to construct. You can even design your shawl collar to look like a notched collar.

In the shawl collar both the undercollar and upper collar have a center back seam. The undercollar is shaped with interfacing and tape as in a notched collar. You can choose to work the shawl collar by traditional, machine, or fusible method (Figure 10.29).

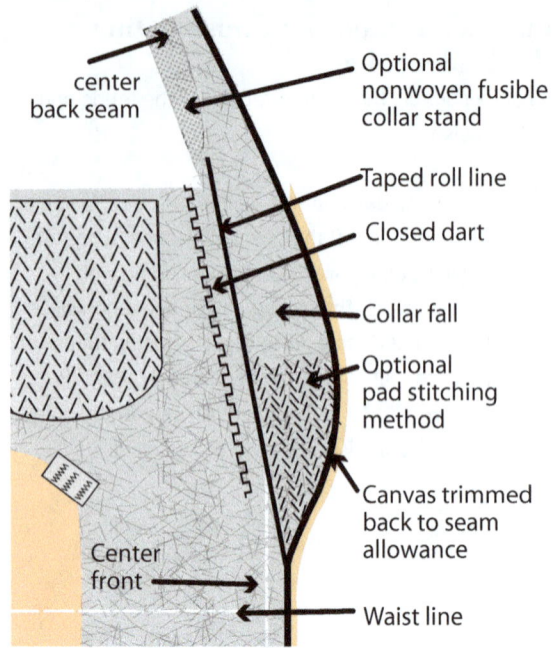

Figure 10.29

Figure 10.28

1. Begin by applying interfacing to the undercollar in the traditional or machine method. Right side to right side, join the collar at center back and press open.

2. Tape the roll line from the shoulder seam and down the center front to the hemline.

3. If working in fusible method, fuse weft interfacing, matching the grainline to the undercollar.

4. If you want a stronger undercollar stand, cut a strip of non-woven interfacing and fuse to the undercollar stand.

Figure 10.30 Alberta Ferretti, Fall/Winter, 2005–'06.

CONSTRUCTING A CONVERTIBLE OR FLAT UNDERCOLLAR

The jacket shown in Figure 10.30 buttons to the neckline with no front lapels and has a convertible, or flat, collar.

Work the undercollar interfacing and shaping from one of the techniques previously shown and then attach the collar to the neckline as follows:

1. Attach the undercollar to the jacket body (Figure 10.31).

2. Clip seam allowance and press open (Figure 10.32).

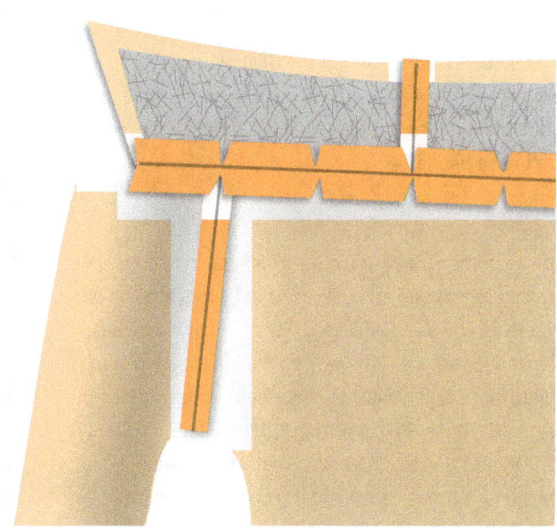

Figure 10.31

Figure 10.32

CHAPTER CHECKLIST

Before moving on to the next chapter, be sure to check that:

- ☐ You are pleased with the collar shape.
- ☐ The neckline seam is smooth and flat.
- ☐ The collar covers the back neck seam line.
- ☐ The collar is consistent in size and shape from one end to the other.
- ☐ The outer edges are smooth, even, and flat, and the corners do not curl up or under.
- ☐ Your collar is balanced and working with the shape of your lapels.
- ☐ If you were unsure of the design of your collar and cut your collar larger than needed, you have redrawn the collar and trimmed away the excess.
- ☐ You have referred back to the points under evaluating the fit of the undercollar and checked that each point is covered.

Make any alterations before moving on to the next stage.

REFERENCES

Wilson, E. (2009, March 12) "Front row, Gigli is himself again," *New York Times*.

BOX 10.1 Romeo Gigli

Figure Box 10.1a
Romeo Gigli, Fall, 2009.

The first time I stepped inside the Romeo Gigli boutique in South Molton Street, London, I was sold. There was a jacket in the boutique that I had to have; yes, I could have made the jacket myself, but it wouldn't have been Gigli.

A GRAND TOUR TOWARDS FASHION DESIGN

Romeo Gigli was born in 1949 at Castelbolognese in Faenza, Italy. He studied architecture at university, but by this time he had acquired a taste for travel. He collected objects from his travels, mostly cloths and jewels, and little by little his passion was drawn towards design, fabrics, and color. Romeo Gigli comes from a wealthy aristocratic family. He drew from a rich culture, imbibed from the 20,000 rare antiquarian books that were located in his father's library and his many travels to the East. His creativeness was also inspired by his muse, Empress Theodora from Byzantium, the young and beautiful women depicted in the mosaics of Ravenna's Byzantine churches and Piero Della Francesca's virginal beauties. This love of rich muted colors found in old paintings, mixed with a fluid sense of cut and drape, gives a feeling of balance and harmony to all his designs. As are some of Gigli's coats in velvet, so richly embroidered that they could only become treasured garments to be passed on as heirlooms.

In 1979, he traveled to New York to design a collection of menswear for Piertro Dimitri and remained in New York for only one season. He returned to Italy to begin work as a design consultant for several Italian clothing companies, including Timmi.

Figure Box 10.1b
Romeo Gigli, Fall, 2009.

CATERING TO THE FORGOTTEN ROMANTIC

In 1986 he presented his first collection: the cloths were heralded and acclaimed throughout fashion news worldwide. The exaggerated shoulder pads were all the rage, his deconstructed jackets and coats with only the faintest hint of a shoulder were the prelude to the natural lines he was to design in the future. In essence, he created a range of clothing where he removed the shock of severity and, instead, catered to the forgotten romantic.

Throughout Romeo Gigli's menswear collections run a pallet of simple muted colors and subtle cuts that are the structure for his success. The clothes are constructed to work with the shape of the body rather than against it. His jackets are often high buttoned, with depth and texture that came from rich wools, offering elegance and luxury to his customers and creating a cult following.

When interviewed by Derek Allen in 1999 for the Italian website Yes Please, Romeo Gigli said, "All the pieces I create must be beautiful in character, and that means they must process beauty outside the context of the overall project. If I remove a piece from the collection and it doesn't function in alternative contexts, then it lacks the necessary sense of balance."

STEPPING INTO THE FUTURE

Romeo Gigli's name was sold in 1999 to IT Holdings, an Italian manufacturer who filed for bankruptcy protection. Then in 2004 he left IT Holdings after a battle with its owners. Since then the brand of the company ROMEO GIGLI ceased to have any connection with fashion designer Romeo Gigli.

Romeo Gigli is currently launching a comeback, showing a collection under the name *io ipse idem,* which can loosely be translated from Latin as "myself, more than myself." It will be financed by IP Investimenti e Partecipazioni SPA, a private independent investment company. Catherine Vautrin, who was formerly with Emilio Pucci, will be chief executive of the company.

Romeo Gigli is quoted as saying, "I was watching out of the window for the last five years, thinking what I did wrong and what I did right. I wanted to think about what I could do now."

In March 2009, Eric Wilson wrote in the *New York Times:*

> So far the new collection is filled with languid day suits in jewel tones, some with soft round shoulders and others with the pointed origami shapes of the season. Many of the models in the shows wore boots with a diamond cutout pattern that was repeated on the back of a black suit, or in notches cut into the lapel of a jacket to reveal flashes of a red blouse underneath. Ah, nostalgia.

"For me, that is a big emotion," Romeo Gigli said. "I was thinking I would like my dress to be free of time (Wilson, 2009).

Figure Box 10.1c
Romeo Gigli, Spring/Summer, 2009.

CHAPTER 11

The Shoulder Pads

The essence of style is a simple way of saying something complex.

—Giorgio Armani

CHAPTER OBJECTIVES

After reading this chapter, you should be able to:

Recognize different shoulder pad shapes for the tailored jacket.

Evaluate the size and thickness needed for both design and wearer.

Set the pads so that they are unnoticeable when the jacket is worn.

Create the correct shape or reshape existing pads.

This chapter is all about the horror of the shoulder pad!

We will answer the question, "Why must your design include shoulder pads?" And no, you don't have to make the shoulders look like a pro football player's uniform or a costume for a character from the cast of that 1980s television phenomenon called *Dallas* (Figure 11.1).

A well-fitted shoulder pad, correctly made and adjusted to both the jacket and the wearer, plays a key role in shaping tailored garments. Tailors have been adding shoulder padding for centuries in an endeavor to reshape the body into the current fashion trend.

Today, shoulder pads still follow the current fashion. But you can also use pads to correct body faults by (a) broadening the shoulders, which also makes the waist appear smaller; (b) adjusting drooping or sloping shoulders; and (c) correcting posture. Shoulder pads can even start from under the arm to give a very rounded bust line, as Vivienne Westwood did in her collection "five centuries ago," which was based on Elizabeth 1.

Should pads are available in a wide variety of shapes and sizes. It is very easy to construct your own shoulder pads. A viable option is to take the wadding from ready-made pads and reshape them.

Figure 11.1
Thierry Mugler 1981: Conceiving women as fetishes or goddesses, he gave them curves along with exaggerated padded shoulders.

Figure 11.2 Dandies in 1820. Illustration by Barbosa.

CONSTRUCTING THE SHOULDER PAD

Shoulder pads are built to the desired thickness by layering wadding or cotton batting onto a hair canvas and muslin base. To make the pattern for your shoulder pads, pin the shoulder seams of your toile together (Figure 11.3).

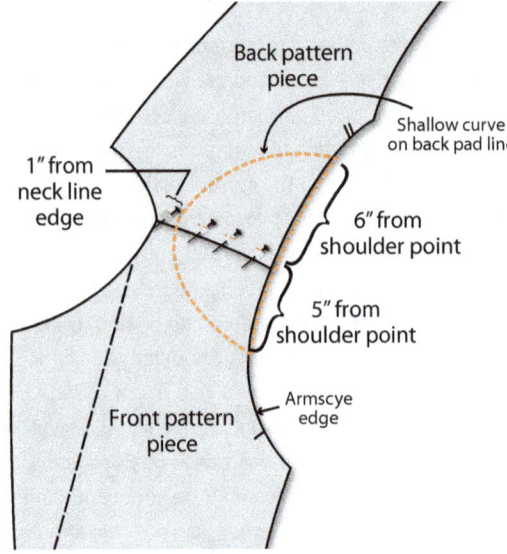

Figure 11.3

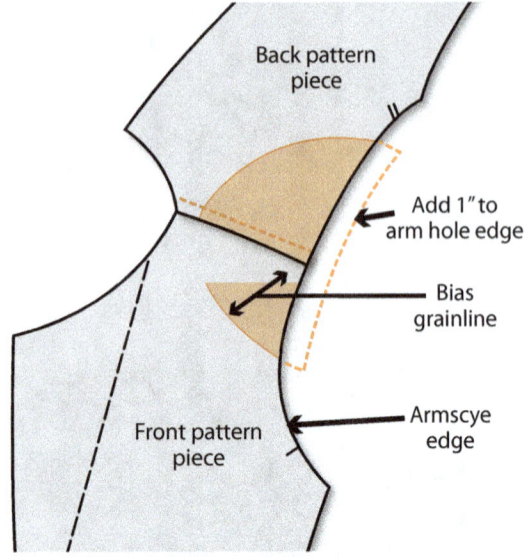

Figure 11.4a

1. Mark a point on the shoulder seam 1 inch in from the neckline edge. On the front, measure down from the shoulder point 5 inches (12.5 cm) and make a mark. On the toile back, measure down from the shoulder point on the armhole edge 6 inches (15 cm). Draw the pad shape, beginning at the marked point on the shoulder seam. Draw a deep curve on the front from the marked point in the shoulder seam to the mark on the armhole. And on the back, draw a shallow curve from the armhole marking up to the shoulder line. (Refer to Figure 11.3.)

2. Transfer these markings on to paper drawing in the shoulder line. Working on your pattern, add 1 inch (2.5 cm) at the armhole edge. Mark in the true bias at the shoulder line (Figure 11.4a and b).

3. From this pattern, cut two muslin and one hair canvas pieces for each pad. Cut five to six layers of wadding or cotton batting for each pad. Separate the wadding into thin layers. Starting with the muslin topped with the hair canvas, layer the wadding with each layer about 3/8 inch (1 cm) shorter than the lower layer, and feather out the edges. Finish with a layer of muslin (Figure 11.5).

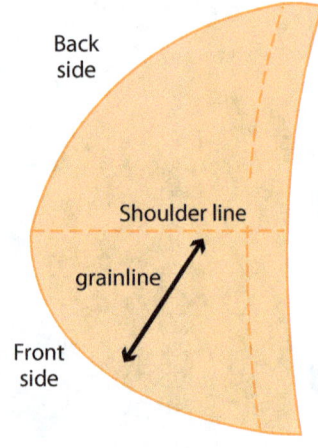

Figure 11.4b

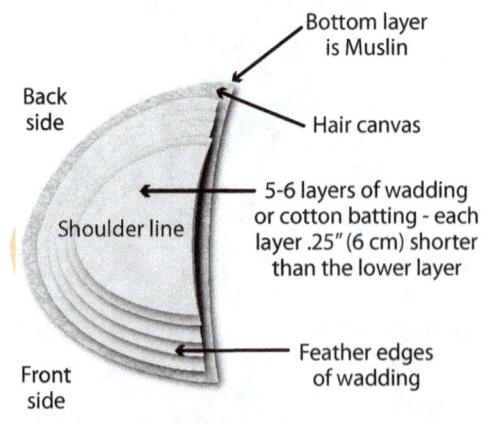

Figure 11.5

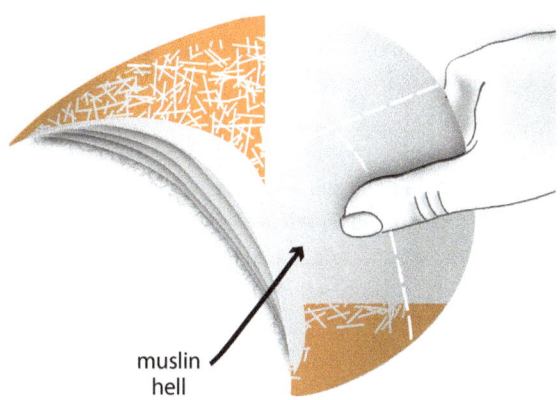

muslin hell

Figure 11.6

Figure 11.8

4. Baste stitch down the shoulder line and across the layers to hold them together (Figure 11.6). If you want a square shoulder line as in the 1940s, add more layers of wadding to build up the outer edge to approximately 1 inch (2.5 cm).

5. Hold the pad over your hand so that the pad will shape as you stitch. Pad stitch the pad from end to end working in rows. The stitches go right through all the layers of filling, and there should be no pulling (Figure 11.7).

6. Press the pad, maintaining the shape you have created (Figure 11.8).

7. Setting the shoulder pads can be a little difficult because they have been shaped to fit the shoulder; when you turn your jacket wrong side out to set the pads, the shoulder curve will be reversed. Place the pad onto the shoulder seam starting at the shoulder point seam allowance.

8. Matching the shoulder seam to shoulder line, hold in place with your hand and turn your jacket to the right side. Pin along the shoulder seam and at the sides of the pad at the armhole edge.

9. Baste stitch the pad into place down the shoulder seam and around the outer edge (Figure 11.9).

When pad stitching go through all layers

Figure 11.7

Figure 11.9

10. Before the shoulder pad is permanently attached into the jacket, put the jacket onto a body or dress form to check your shoulder (Figures 11.10 and 11.11).

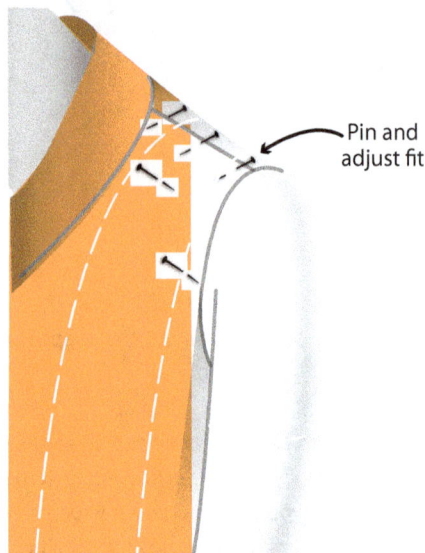

Figure 11.10

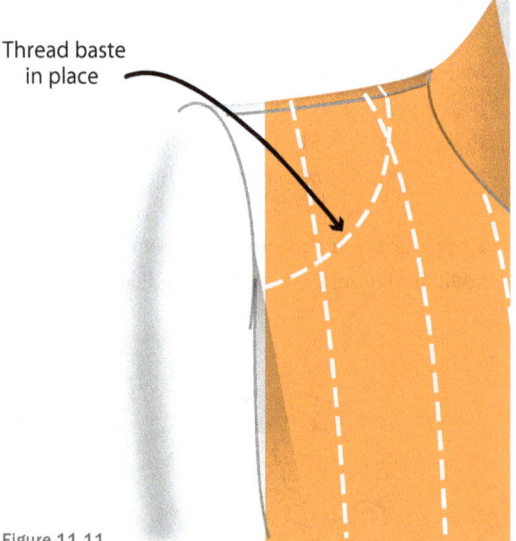

Figure 11.11

11. Make the following adjustments as necessary:
    - If the shoulder pad is extending out into the sleeve head, you may have to trim back the pads.
    - If there is a ridge forming between the shoulder head and pad, you will have to extend the pad out into the sleeve head.
    - If the shoulder pads look too bulky, remove some of the fullness.
    - If the wearer has round shoulders, you can correct this by moving the pads back slightly.
    - Check that both shoulders look the same; you may have to build up one shoulder more than the other.

12. Undo the baste stitching around the edge of the pad and slip stitch the pad into place along the shoulder seam allowance. Be careful that your stitches do not go through to the right side of the jacket (Figure 11.12).

Figure 11.12

13. Now slip stitch loosely across the pad at the armhole edge, being careful to keep the shape of the pad (Figure 11.13).

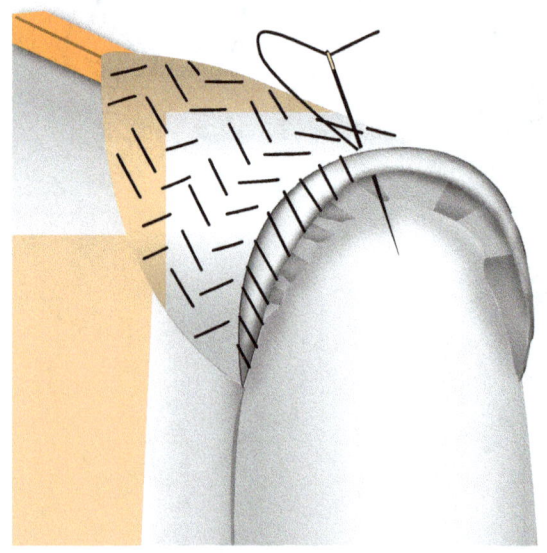

Figure 11.13

Raglan, or Rounded, Shoulder Pad

1. Measure out from the shoulder line 1 to 1½ inch (2.5 to 3 cm) and make a mark. Draw a curved line from the back edge of the pad to the mark and repeat from the front edge (Figure 11.14a and b).

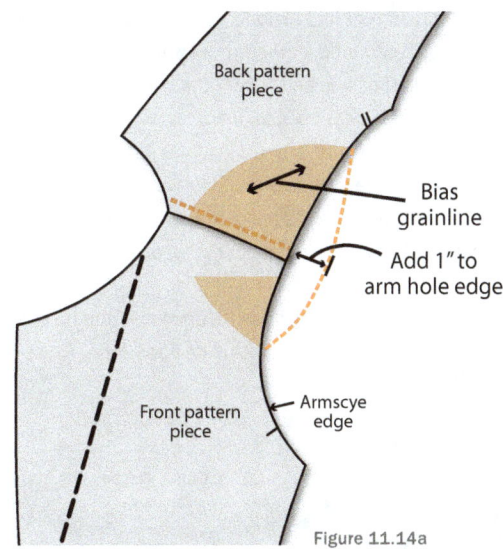

Figure 11.14a

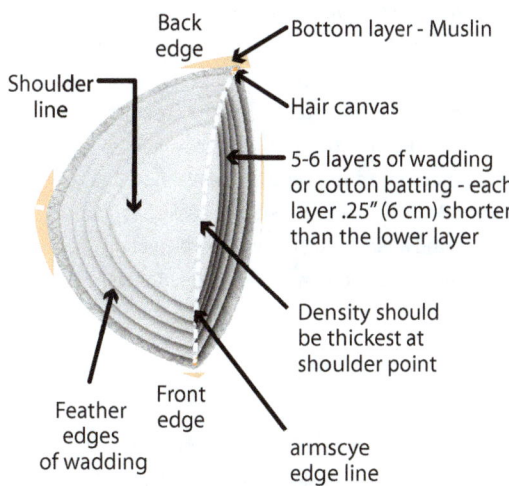

Figure 11.15

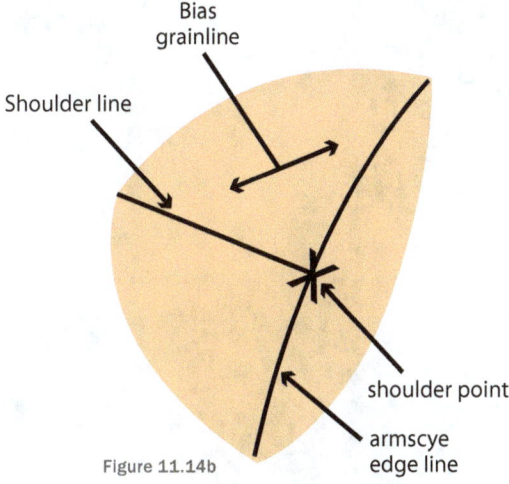

Figure 11.14b

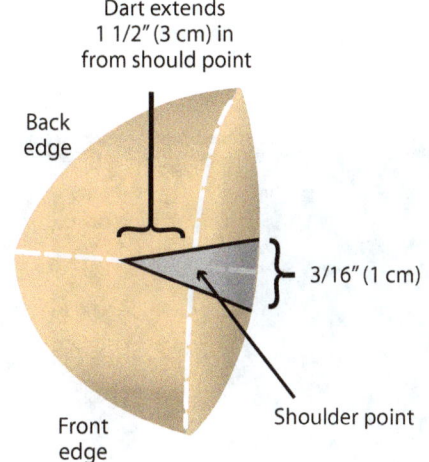

Figure 11.16

2. Cut five to six layers of wadding or cotton batting for each pad. Separate the wadding into thin layers. Starting with the muslin topped with the hair canvas layer the wadding, with each layer about ⅜ inch (1 cm) shorter than the lower layer and feathering out the edges. Finish with a layer of muslin. The pad will be thickest at the armhole shoulder point (Figure 11.15).

3. Make a small dart along the shoulder line, and machine stitch through all layers (Figure 11.16). This will give the shoulder seam line a slight curve.

4. For more curve and a rounder shoulder, make two small darts on either side of the shoulder seam dart and machine stitch (Figure 11.17).

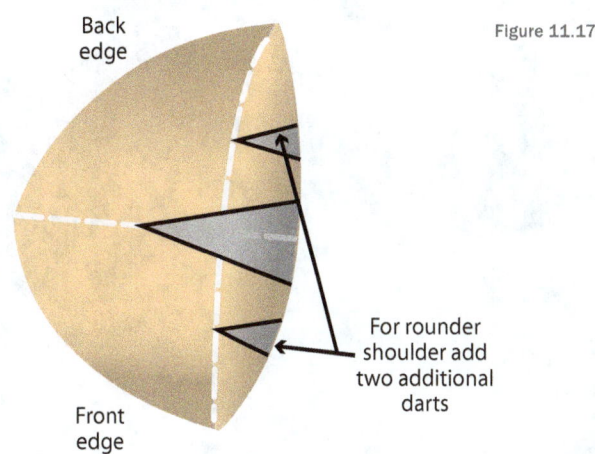

Figure 11.17

BOX 11.1 Gianni Versace

In an interview with Carla Fendi, president of the board of directors for the Fendi Group, Fendi spoke of art and memories of Gianni Versace. When asked to identify Versace's strengths, Fendi replied:

> The courage to do what he believed in and the creativity that pushed him to dare. Result: young fashion, rock, beauty that passed from tradition to a shameless modernism. In this he was a magician. Because being classic can easily become musty. But he forged ahead. A bit like we do, respecting the past but always projected toward the future. Always. (Pisa, 1997)

EXCELLENCE, ATTENTION TO DETAIL, AND IMPECCABLE SKILL

Born in Reggio, Calabria, on December 2, 1946, Versace was to learn the arts of dressmaking and design from his mother. In 1972 he went to work for Lucca, followed by Genny and Callaghan. He was to go on to help with the launch of the Complice label in 1974.

In March 1978, Versace presented his first signature women's wear collection at the Palazza della Permanente Art Museum of Milan. This was quickly followed by his first menswear collection in September of the same year.

His work was marked by his unique use of color; his incredible prints could include up to 27 different color combinations with sea shells, roses, and animal prints mixed together. The use of surreal and poster art embroideries and beading, inspired from world events both current and historic, gave a new meaning to surface decoration. Studded leather mixed with prints and draped fabric that followed the lines and curved the body gave elegant black evening gowns a clever sense of eroticism that showed up in both his men's and women's wear.

Elegance, impeccable skill, attention to detail, and his love of the arts and music gave him the belief that art and fashion went together, and this was a factor that set him apart from other designers.

Versace's look was young, aggressive, and sexy, and he quickly became the designer of the stars, including Elton John, Bruce

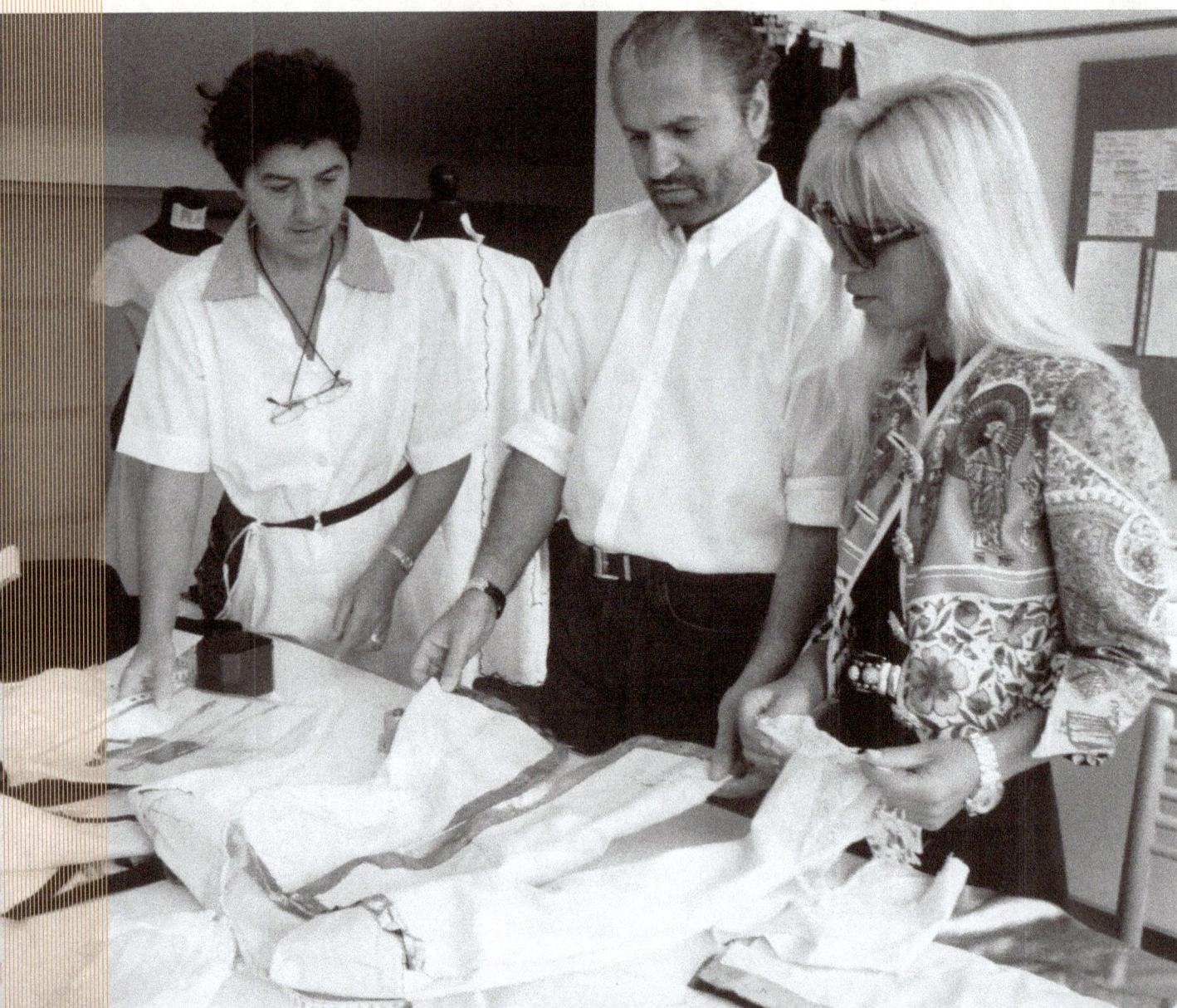

Figure Box 11.1a Gianni Versace with his niece.

Figure Box 11.1b Gianni Versace takes a bow at a fashion show in Los Angeles in 1991.

Springsteen, and Phil Collins. He also dressed celebrity royalty such as Princesses Diana and Caroline of Monaco.

Versace's mentor was Karl Lagerfeld, of whom he was very fond and had a very close friendship. Versace always liked to think of himself as a tailor rather than a designer because he knew how to cut and make garments. In 1989, the Atelier Versace was born when he showed his first "Atelier" collection in Paris. For his first show in America, which he called "simple," he said that he had to work in a great rush, trying to be imaginative and as quick as possible. He knew that he was being watched by Gloria Vreeland, but he said that he was so carried away by his work that he forgot she was there. At the end of the show, she hugged him and said, "I have never seen anyone drape a dress so well and in such little time."

Versace wrote that she had given him the greatest compliment that remained in his heart.

Gianni Versace hired the top photographers such as Richard Avedon, Bruce Webber, and Herb Ritts, and the top supermodels to interpret his visions for his advertising campaigns. He paid special attention in promoting his name and image.

He won a Stanley award, two Cutty Sacks, and the C.F.D.A. award from the Council of Fashion Designers of America throughout what became an illustrious career. He first designed theater costumes in 1983 for La Scala in Milan, and went on to collaborate with Robert Wilson, Maurice Béjart, Roland Petit, and Twyla Tharp on projects such as operas and ballets around the world.

As fashion journalist and devotee Andre Leon Talley puts it, "The world of Gianni Versace gives an optimistic view to the human spirit. If it is self indulgent to some, so be it."

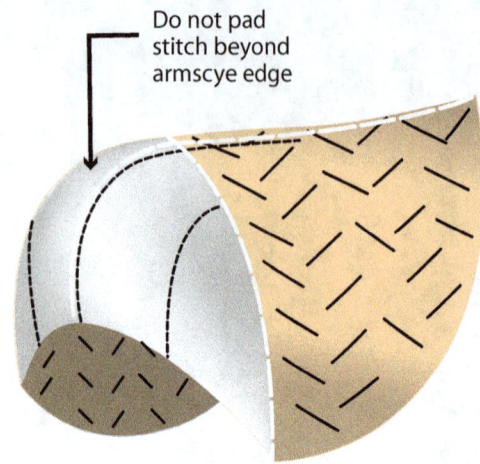

Figure 11.18

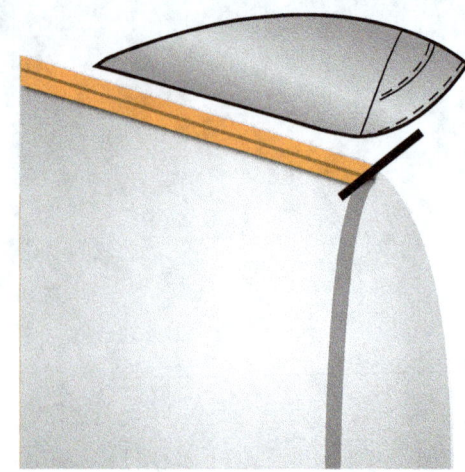

Figure 11.19

5. Hold the pad over your hand so that the pad will shape as you stitch (Figure 11.18).

6. Pad stitch the pad from end to end working in rows. The stitches go right through all the layers of filling; there should be no pulling. Do not stitch out past the armhole edge (Figure 11.18). Press the pad, maintaining the shape you have created (Figure 11.19).

7. Place the pad onto the shoulder seam starting at the shoulder point seam allowance. Match the shoulder seam to shoulder line, hold in place with your hand, and turn your jacket to the right side. Pin along the shoulder seam and at the sides of the pad at the armhole edge.

8. Baste stitch the pad in place around the outer edge (Figure 11.20).

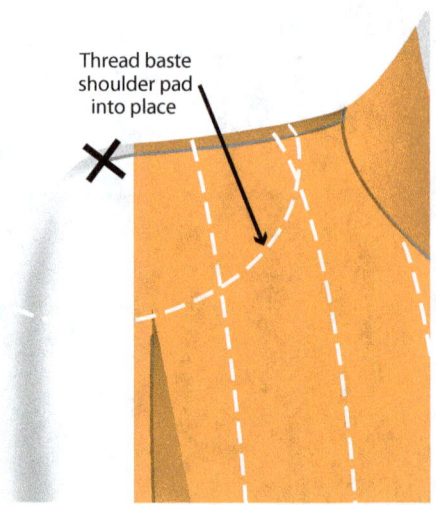

Figure 11.20

Before the shoulder pad is permanently attached into the jacket, put the jacket onto a body or dress form and check the shoulder. Make any adjustments and slip stitch the shoulder pads into your jacket.

CHAPTER CHECKLIST

Before you are ready to begin construction, be sure to check that:

☐ Your shoulder pads are the right size and shape for the design of your jacket.
☐ They are sitting in the correct position for the wearer of the jacket.
☐ Your stitching from attaching the shoulder pad into the jacket does not through to the right side of the jacket.
☐ The jacket shoulder is sitting smooth and rounded with no pulling or wrinkling.

REFERENCES

Versace, G. (1994) *Vanitas: Design.* New York: Abbeville Press.

Pisa, P. (1997, July 18) "A Tribute to Gianni Versace," Made in Italy Online. Retrieved on December 16, 2009, from www.made-in-italy.com/tribute/versace/fendi.htm

CHAPTER 12

Top Collar, Back Neck Facing, and Front Lapel Facing

Fashion is very important, it is life enhancing and, like everything that gives pleasure, it is worth doing well.

—*Vivienne Westwood*

CHAPTER OBJECTIVES

After reading this chapter, you should be able to:

Construct a top collar for your jacket:

Evaluate the size of the top collar.

Determine the correct shape of the top collar.

Evaluate the fit of the top collar.

Determine the construction method.
- Add structure to the back neck facing.
- Construct a front lapel facing:

Determine the correct shape and cut of the front facing.

Evaluate the fabric and pattern to decide which strip will be the front edge of the facing.

Determine the lower grain of the facing.

Attach the back neck facing.

Evaluate the ease needed for the facing to turn without pulling or rolling back.

The thickness, weight, texture, and pattern of your fabric all play an important role in the construction of both your top collar and lapel facing. Here, you have the opportunity to use a contrast color, print, stripe, plaid, leather/suede, and embellishments for the fabric of your jacket.

We begin this chapter with the top collar and then move to the back neck and the front facings. You can choose to work in this order, or construct the front facings and back neck before the top collar.

Figure 12.1 John Galliano, Fall/Winter, 2003.

Figure 12.2 Prada, Fall/Winter, 2005–'06.

THE TOP COLLAR

Whenever two or more layers of fabric are held together in a curved position, the upper layer must be slightly bigger than the under layer to allow for the curve or turn of the cloth. The thickness and weight of your fabric will determine the size of your top collar piece because it has to go up and over the roll of the undercollar. From shoulder to shoulder across the back, it has to cover the back neckline without pulling or rolling out.

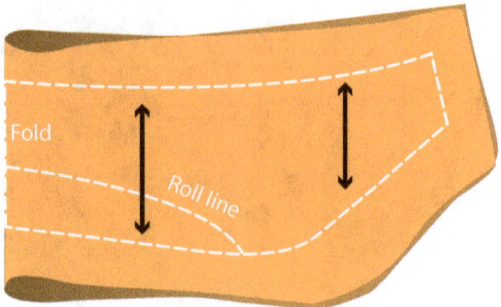

Figure 12.3

1. Using the top collar or undercollar pattern piece, cut a rectangular piece of fabric that is approximately 2 inches (5 cm) longer and wider. The center back of the collar will be on the grainline and should match the grain of the jacket both vertically and horizontally. If you are working with a plaid or stripe, make sure that both edges of your collar are the same (Figure 12.3).

2. Using a steam iron and working on the wrong side up, press in a circular motion, stretching the edges and shrinking the center as in Figure 12.4. This will make the top collar fit the undercollar smoothly without any pulling. The crossgrain will be the outer edge.

4. Right side to right side, match and pin the top collar to the undercollar along the roll line.

5. Pin the seam line together at the outer edge, easing the top collar onto the undercollar, beginning at the center back and stopping at the notch. Repeat on other side (Figure 12.6).

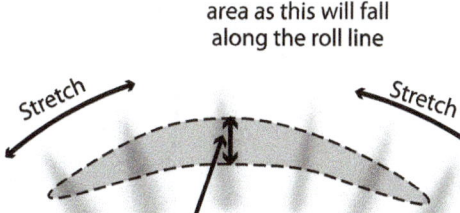

Figure 12.4

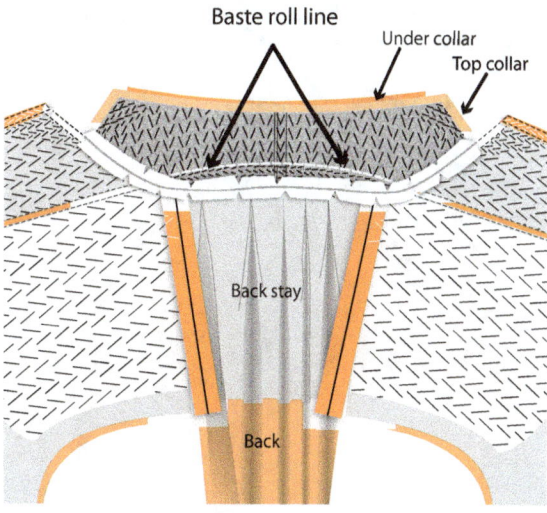

Figure 12.6

3. To check that you have shaped the collar enough, place the collar over the undercollar, with your jacket on a shaped hanger or dress form (Figure 12.5).

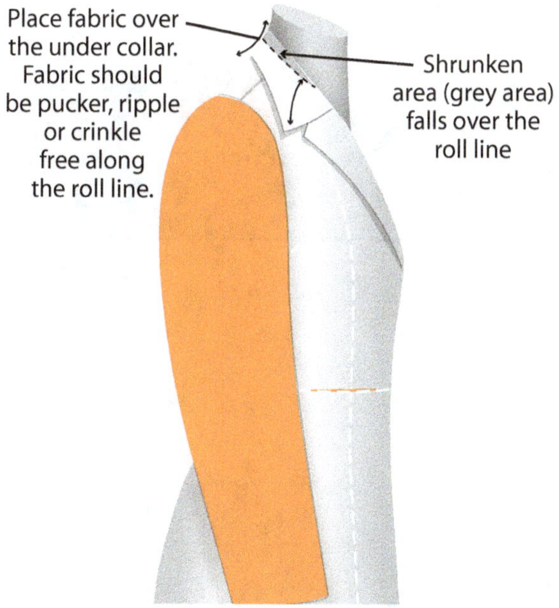

6. Trim back the excess on the top collar as shown in Figure 12.7. Remove the pins across the roll line.

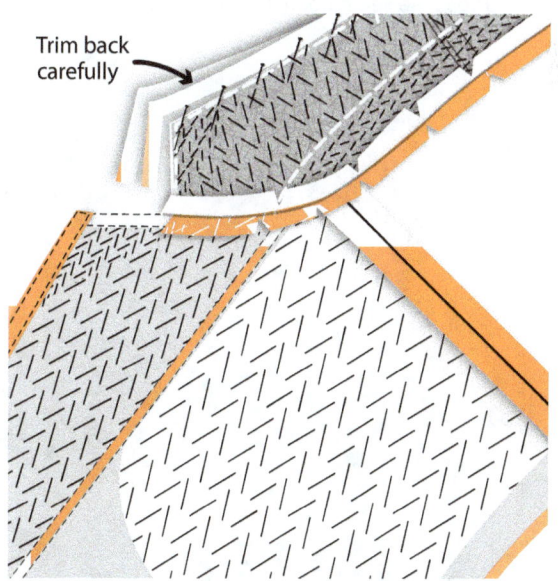

Figure 12.5

Figure 12.7

7. Permanently stitch the edges, being careful to start and stop at the notch and not stitching onto the seam allowance where the undercollar is attached to the jacket neckline (12.8).

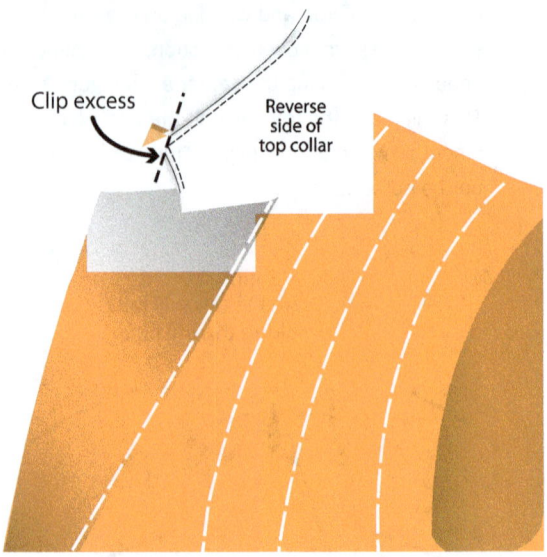

Figure 12.9

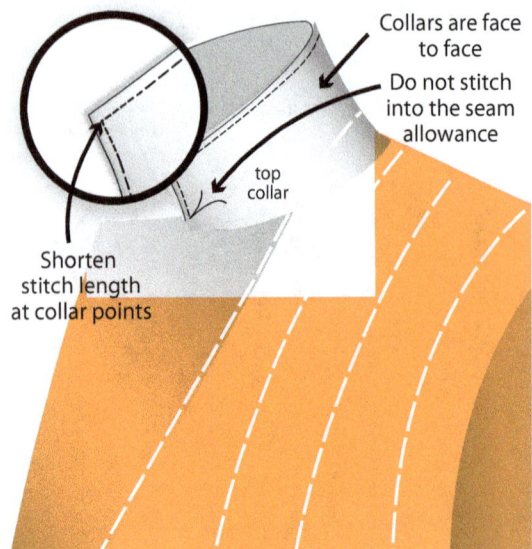

Figure 12.8

8. Shorten the stitch length around the collar points to give them strength and to get a better point. Cut away the excess seam allowance at the collar points (Figure 12.9).

9. Press the seam open (Figure 12.10).

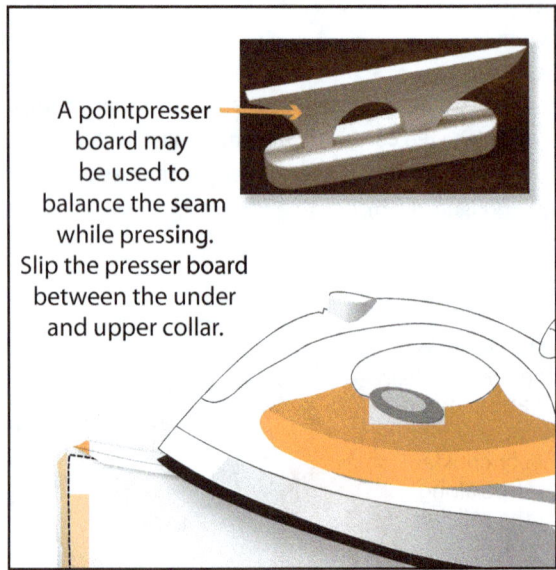

Figure 12.10

Traditional Method for Constructing the Top Collar

Follow the previous instructions to shape and fit your collar to the undercollar. Then:

1. Wrong side to wrong side, pin the top collar to the undercollar roll line and baste. Baste across the top of the undercollar approximately 1 inch (2.5 cm) in from the outer edge (Figure 12.11).

2. Trim the top collar so that you have a ⅜ inch (1 cm) seam allowance visible above the edge of the undercollar and 1 inch (2.5 cm) at the sides. Fold the seam allowance of the top collar to the inside leaving an extension of about 1/8 inch (3 mm) and baste. Catch- or slip stitch together.

3. The excess fabric at each end of the collar is now folded back and pressed into place. The two sides are slip stitched while the end is cross stitched across the raw edge (Figure 12.13).

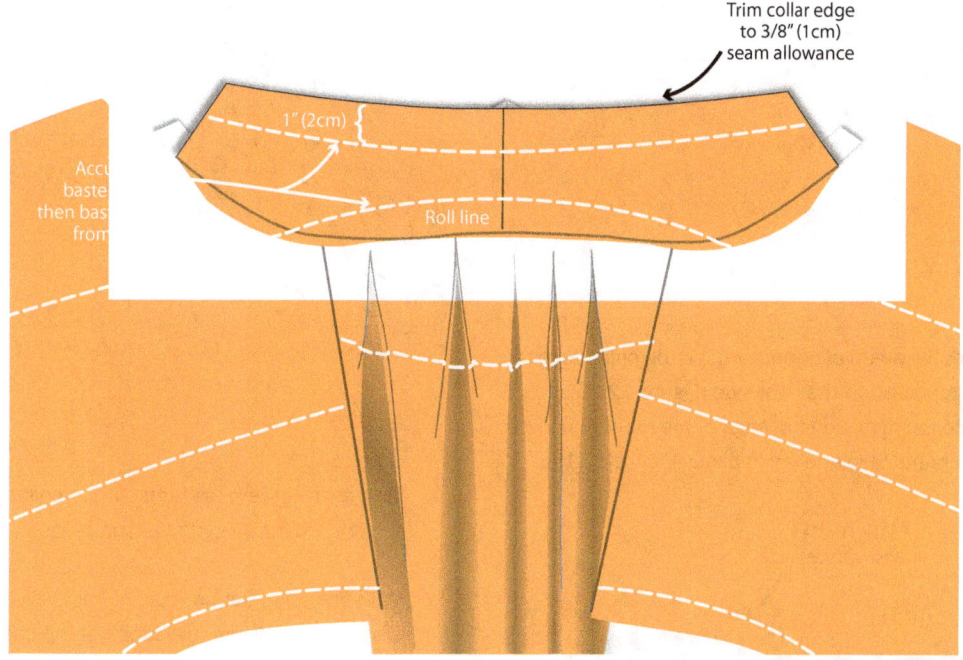

Figure 12.11

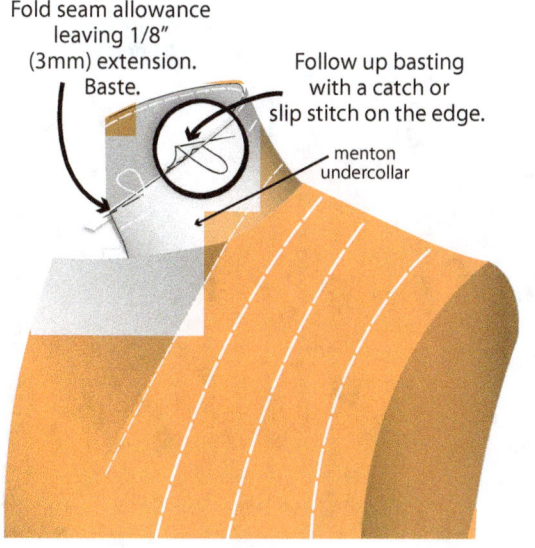

Figure 12.12

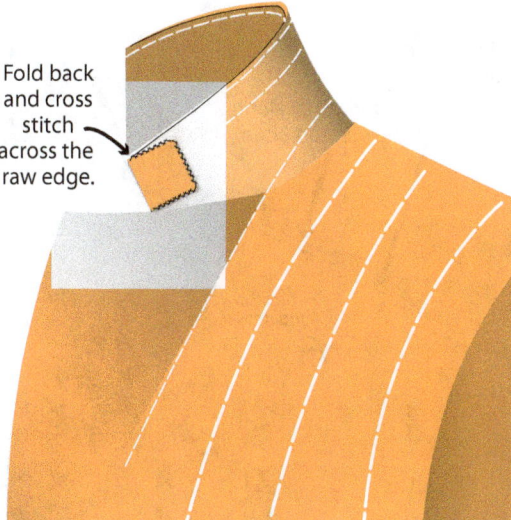

Figure 12.13

Attaching the Top Collar by Machine

You can use the zigzag stitch on your machine to attach the top collar to the undercollar (Figure 12.14).

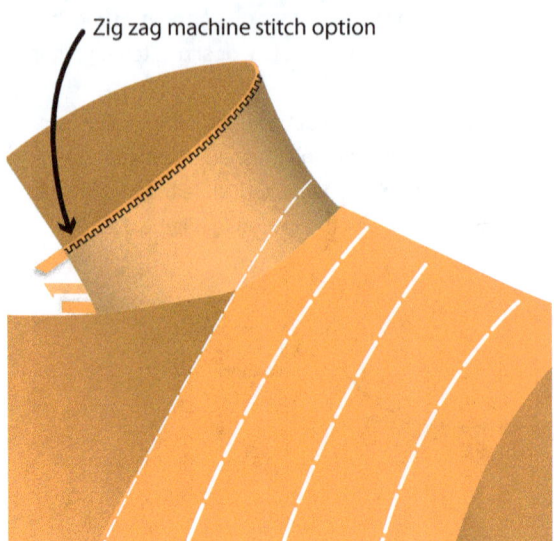

Figure 12.14

1. Mark the seam allowance on the top collar across the top edge on the right side (Figure 12.15), place the right side top edge of the menton undercollar onto this, and pin in place (Figure 12.16).

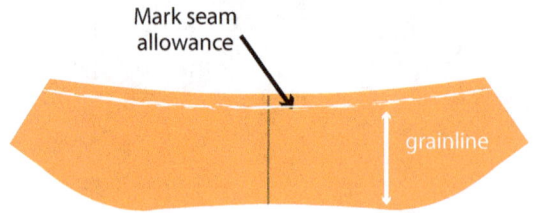

Figure 12.15

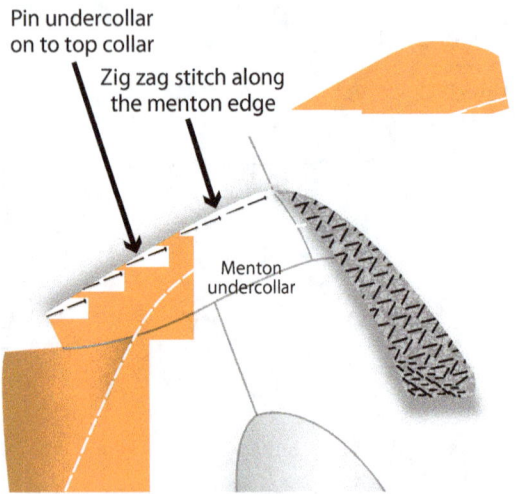

Figure 12.16

2. Machine zigzag stitch across the collar, catching both the menton undercollar and the top collar. Turn the collar so that the two right sides are together; sew across the ends of the collar (Figure 12.17).

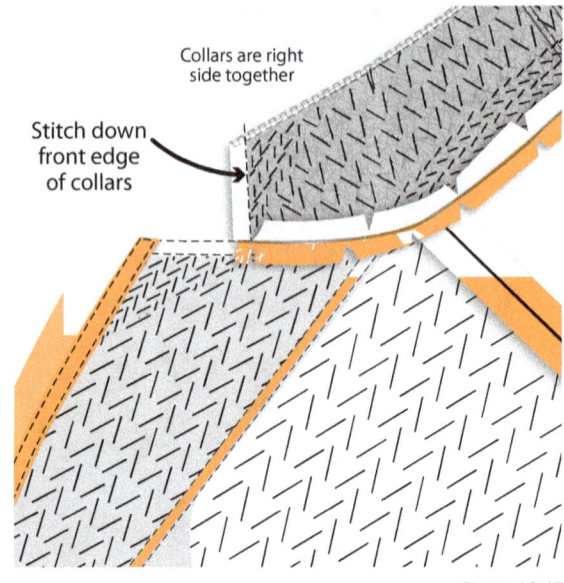

Figure 12.17

3. Trim away any excess fabric at the collar point; turn the collar to right side and press.

4. With the collar flat on a table, baste across the undercollar roll line, catching the top collar fabric underneath (Figure 12.18).

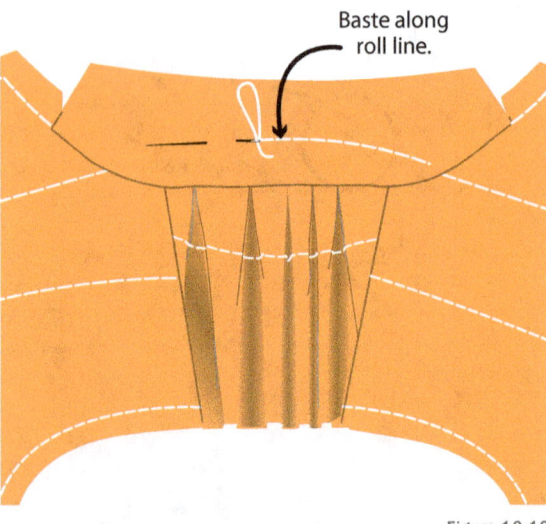

Figure 12.18

As shown in Figure 12.19, carefully trim back to the edge of the seam allowance. If you are attaching a neck facing to your jacket, remove the pins and move on to working the lapel. If your jacket has no neck facing, baste along the back neck facing, catching the undercollar. These stitches will remain in the jacket, so make sure they don't show through to the right side.

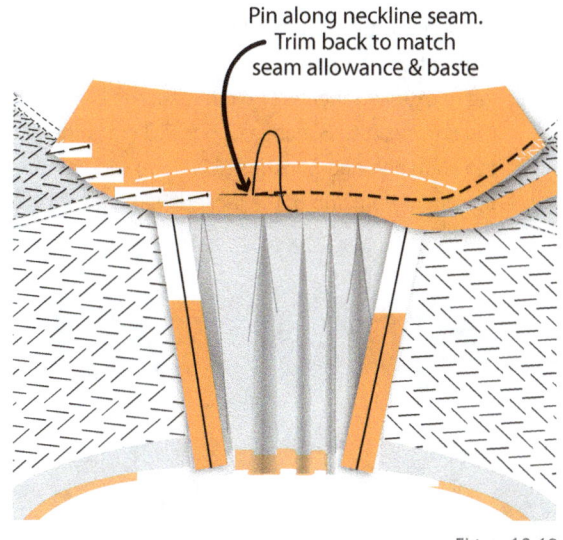

Figure 12.19

CONSTRUCTING THE FRONT LAPEL FACING

The front lapel facing plays an important role in the finished jacket. It must be carefully cut and shaped so that the lapel will roll freely with no pulling or strain on the front of your jacket.

1. Begin by drafting the facing pattern or revising the facing pattern. As shown in Figure 12.20, add ¼ inch (.5 cm) to the lapel from points A to B.

2. Working from the muslin (toile) of the jacket front; trace onto paper the jacket front leaving a ⅜-inch (1 cm) margin at the shoulder, neck and top of lapel. The front edge of the facing is the straight of grainline. Continue the ⅜-inch (1 cm) margin down the front edge and below the bottom of the jacket front (Figure 12.21).

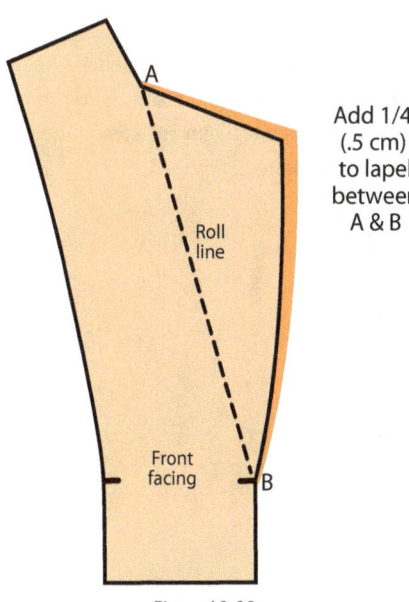

Figure 12.20

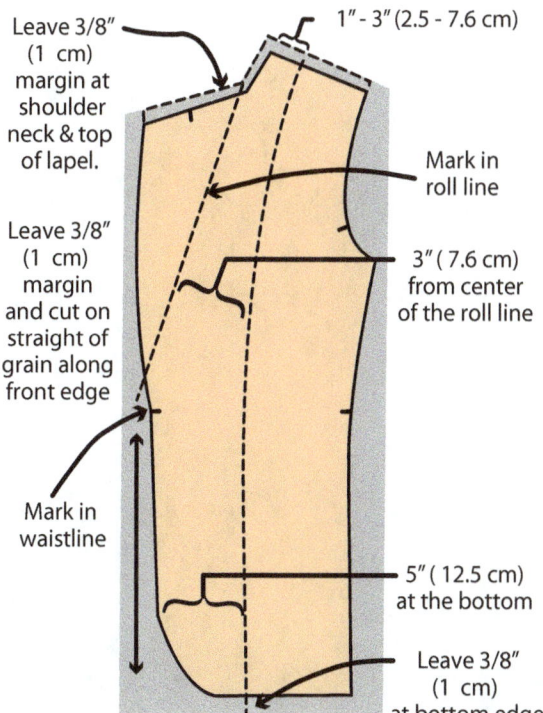

Figure 12.21

3. Mark in waistline and roll line before removing muslin from the paper pattern. The facing is going to extend 3 inches (7.6 cm) past the center of the roll line, 1 to 3 inches (2.5 to 7.6 cm) wide at the shoulder, and 5 inches (12.5 cm) wide at the bottom or hem line of the jacket (Figure 12.22).

4. If you are working with a striped, patterned, or plaid fabric, decide which section of the pattern or which color strip of the plaid will be the finished edge before cutting the fabric. The dominant color will be the most attractive (Figure 12.23).

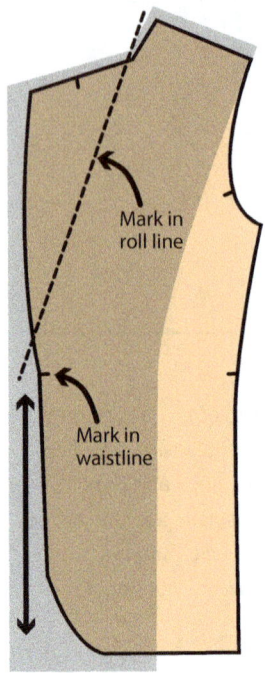
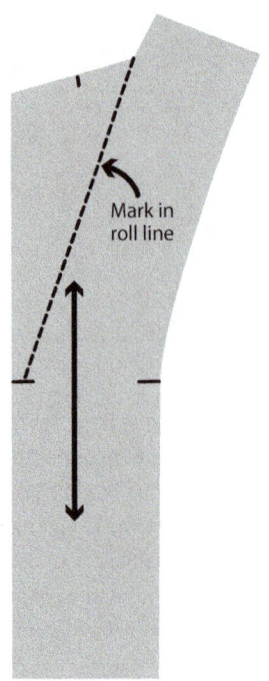

Figure 12.22

Figure 12.23

In Figure 12.22, the lapel on the left is cut with the dominant stripe as the front edge of the facing before being shaped, whereas the lapel on the right is cut using the straight of grainline on the facing pattern. It has not been shaped.

Cut the facing into two sections, placing a seam between the first and second buttons. If your jacket has bound buttonholes you can cut across the facing behind the top buttonhole (Figure 12.27).

Shaping the Lapel

The facing is now pressed into a curve that matches the jacket lapel.

1. Begin by stretching and curving the front edge. Fill your fabric with steam and begin pressing, moving the iron in a counter clockwise arc as you gently pull the front edge of the facing into a curve. Use your pattern piece as a guide (Figure 12.24).

2. Ripples will have appeared at the center and inner edge of the facing. You need to shrink these ripples away, doing so carefully to avoid making any unwanted creases. Trim back your seam allowances to ⅜ inch (1 cm) (Figure 12.25).

3. When working with some worsteds, linens, and cottons, the fabric will not shrink or stretch enough to fit the shape of the lapel edge. You can shape the lapel, but then the grainline below the break point is off; you can also opt to ignore this as your design dictates (Figure 12.26).

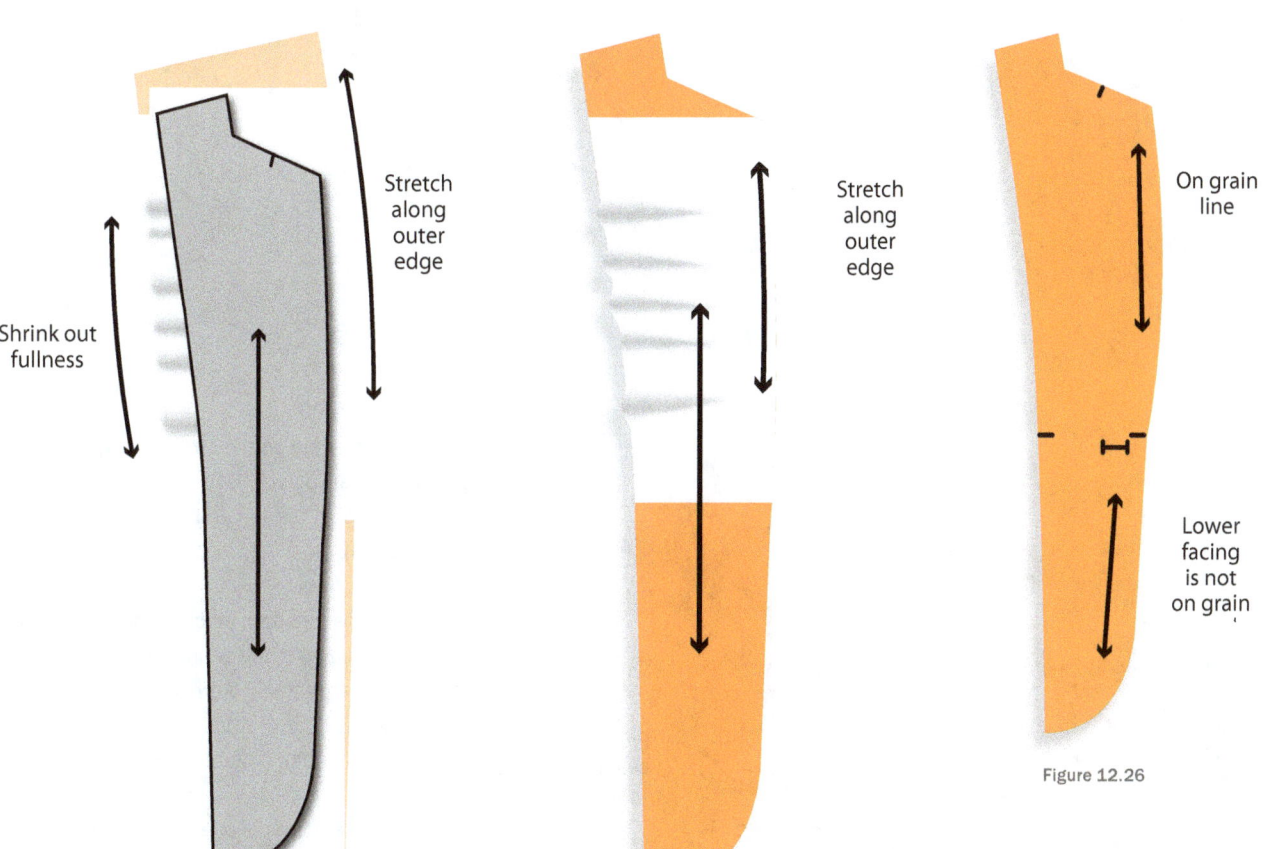

Figure 12.24

Figure 12.25

Figure 12.26

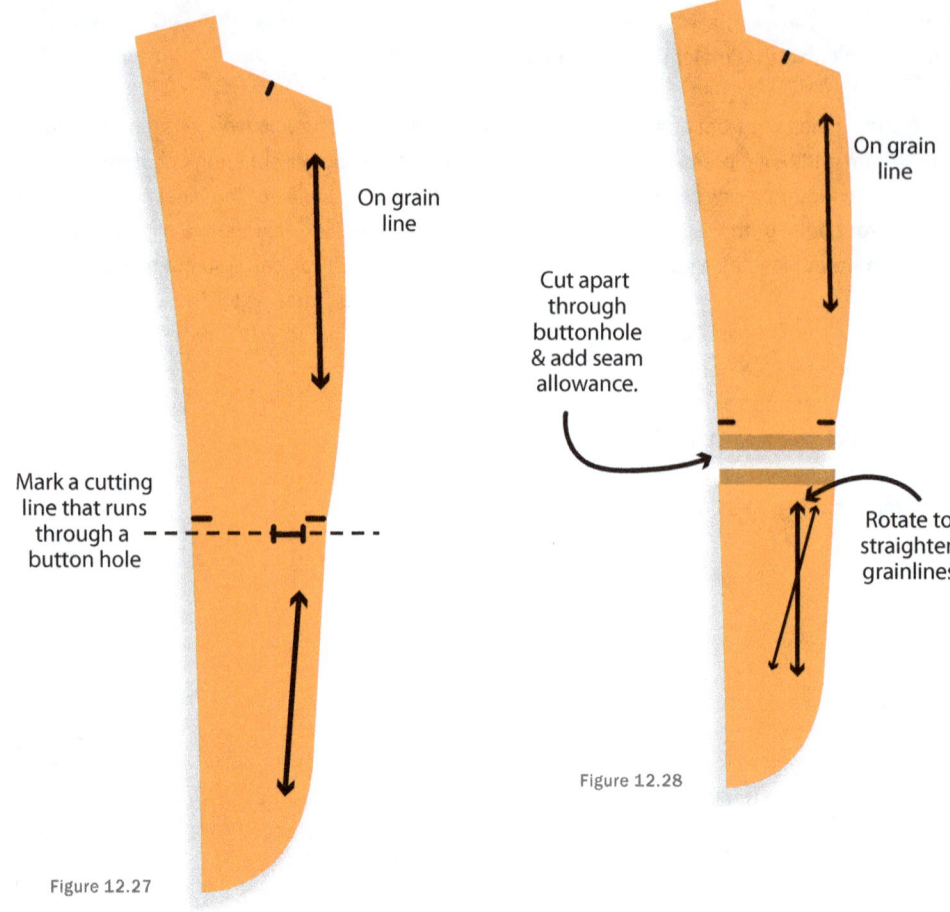

Figure 12.27

Figure 12.28

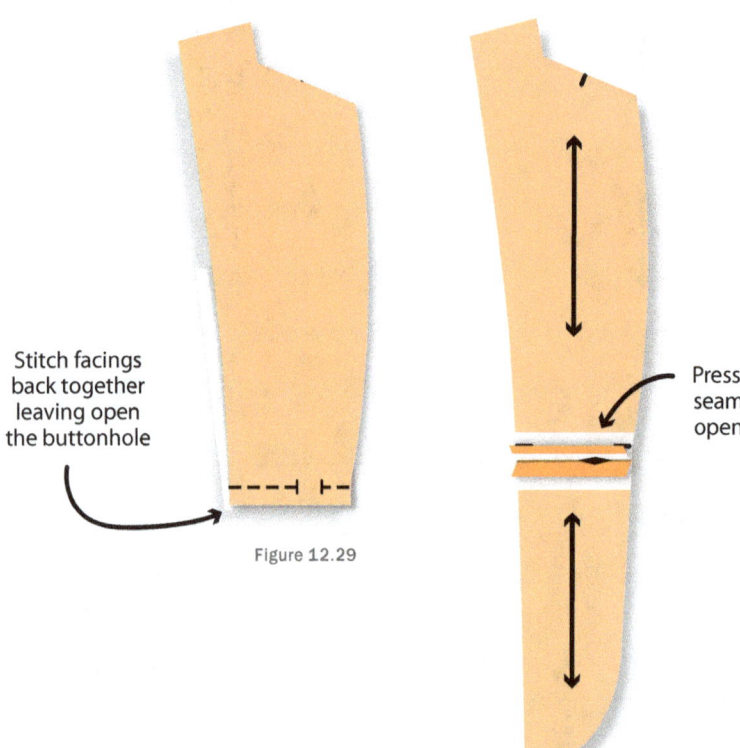

Figure 12.29

Figure 12.30

5. Cut the lower facing on the straight of grain. Remember that you will have to add seam allowance to both the top and lower facings (Figure 12.28).

6. With right sides together, stitch across the facing leaving an opening in the seam that will be the back of the buttonhole (Figure 12.29).

7. Press the seam open (Figure 12.30).

If you want to make the lapel in a contrasting fabric, color, or pattern, it is better to cut the lapel as described so that the lower lapel is the same fabric as your jacket. Doing this can also eliminate any bulk, if you are making a fur or bulky fabric lapel.

If you are working the traditional tailoring method, you now attach your facing to your jacket front. At this point, you can attach the back neck facing.

Figure 12.31 shows a lapel that has been made into a design element in this Vivienne Westwood jacket. The lapel here has been cut, and the buttonhole and button have become an important feature. Refer to Figure 12.27 for how to cut your lapel facing; in this case it has not been cut because of the fabric straight of grain, but rather as a design detail.

Figure 12.31 The lapel has been made into a design element in this Vivienne Westwood jacket.

CONSTRUCTING THE BACK NECK FACING

Cut a piece of fusible interfacing the same size as the back neck facing, and fuse into place. With right side to right side, matching notches, stitch the back neck facing to the front facings at the shoulder seam and press seam allowance open (Figure 12.32).

1. Place the right side of the facing to the right side of the jacket front. Beginning at the tip of the lapel, baste down though the center of the tape, attaching the facing to the jacket. Just below the roll line, add in ¼-inch (6 mm) ease to the facing to accommodate the roll of the lapel (Figure 12.33).

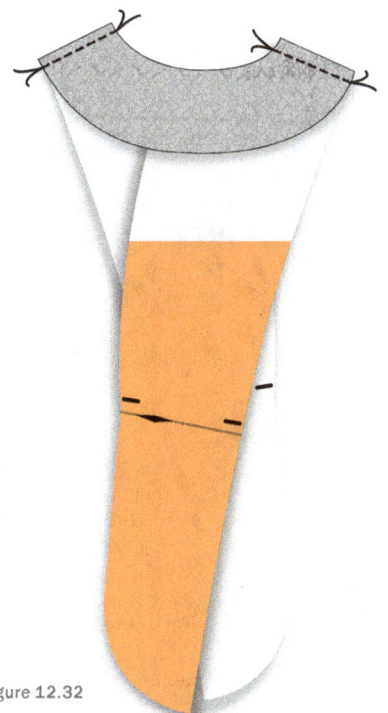

Figure 12.32

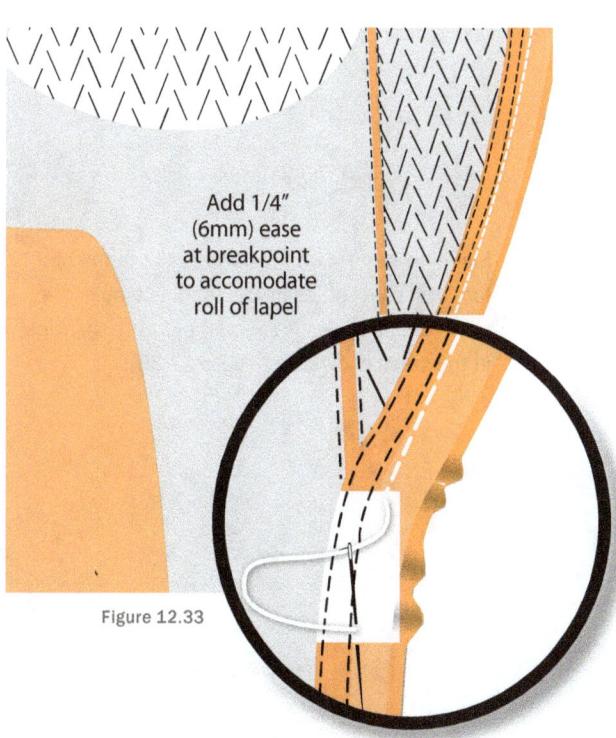

Add 1/4" (6mm) ease at breakpoint to accomodate roll of lapel

Figure 12.33

173

2. If the front of the jacket curves in at the hem, the facing should be basted to the curve using a slightly different technique. To stop the curve from curling outwards in the finished jacket, away from the body, roll the bottom of the jacket towards the facing as you baste, as shown in Figure 12.34. This will shorten the facing slightly and ensure that in the finished jacket the curved edge will incline towards the body, rather than curl out.

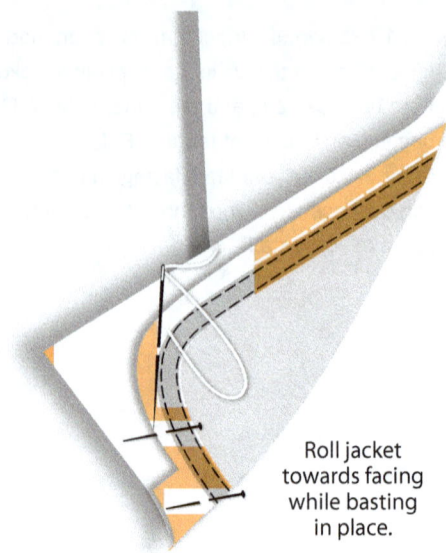

Roll jacket towards facing while basting in place.

Figure 12.34

3. The tip of the lapel should also incline towards the body and not curl upwards. Ease is now placed at the tip of the lapel. At the top of the lapel, lower the facing slightly to create about ¼ inch (6 mm) of ease. When a slight excess of fabric is visible at the lapel tip, baste across the lapel, from the tip to just beyond the collar notch (Figure 12.35).

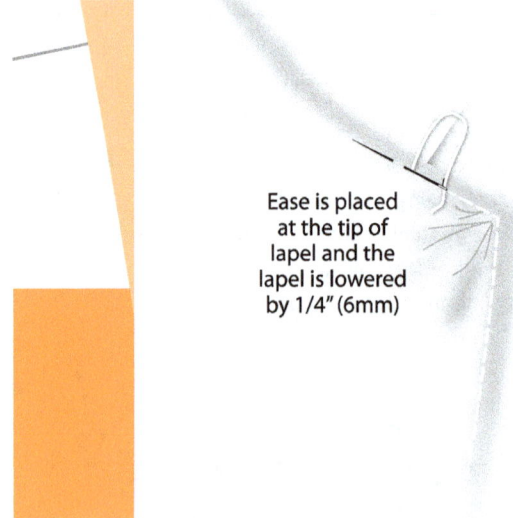

Ease is placed at the tip of lapel and the lapel is lowered by 1/4" (6mm)

Figure 12.35

4. Machine stitch from the collar notch to the bottom of the jacket, using the tape as a guideline stitch about 1/16 inch (1.5 mm) out from the tape in the seam allowance (Figure 12.36).

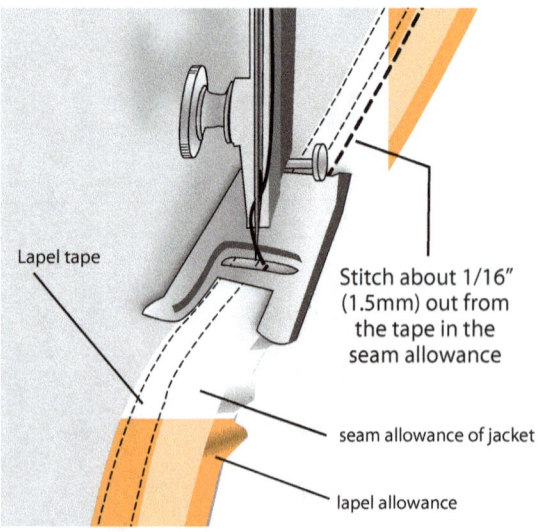

Lapel tape

Stitch about 1/16" (1.5mm) out from the tape in the seam allowance

seam allowance of jacket

lapel allowance

Figure 12.36

5. Shorten the stitch length as you stitch around the corner. It is also better to stitch the lapel point as a curve because a shape pivot point can result in a misshapen lumpy lapel tip. Cut away excess seam allowance at collar points to reduce bulk (Figure 12.37).

7. If your jacket has a back neck facing, pin the top collar to the back neck facing the right sides together from collar notch to collar notch. Machine stitch (Figure 12.39).

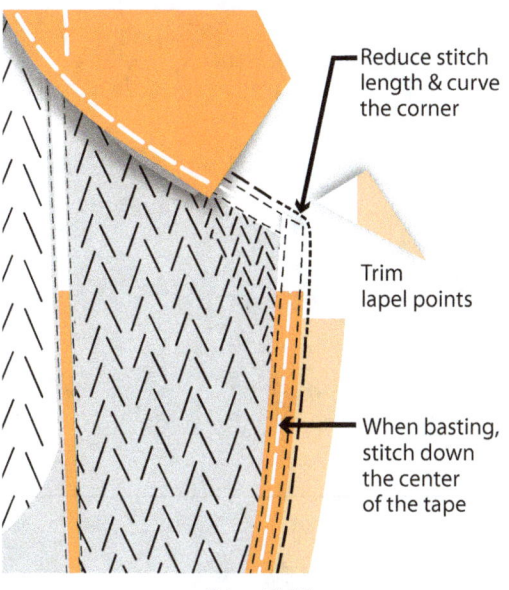

Reduce stitch length & curve the corner

Trim lapel points

When basting, stitch down the center of the tape

Figure 12.37

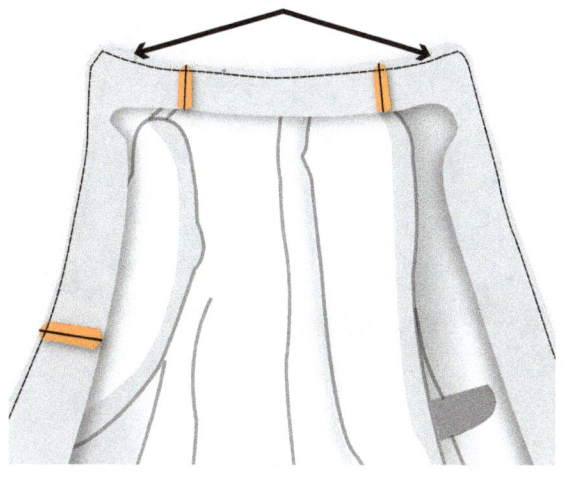

Machine stitch from collar notch to collar notch to the top collar.

Figure 12.39

6. Press seam allowance open using a point presser board (Figure 12.38).

8. Press open seam allowance and loosely slip stitch between the top collar and the undercollar from shoulder seam to shoulder seam (Figure 12.40).

Press the lapel seams open. Use a point presser board

Figure 12.38

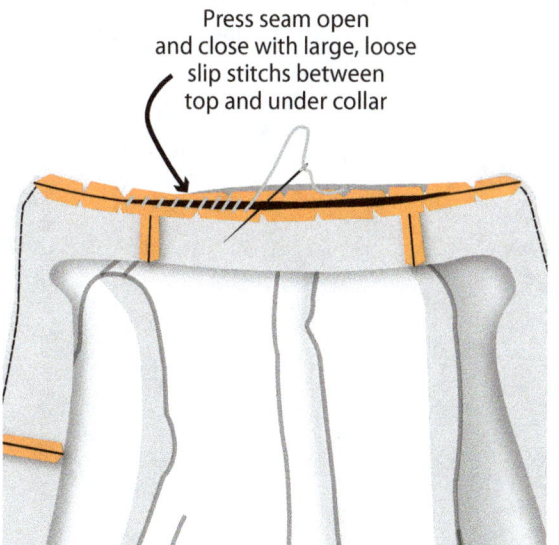

Press seam open and close with large, loose slip stitchs between top and under collar

Figure 12.40

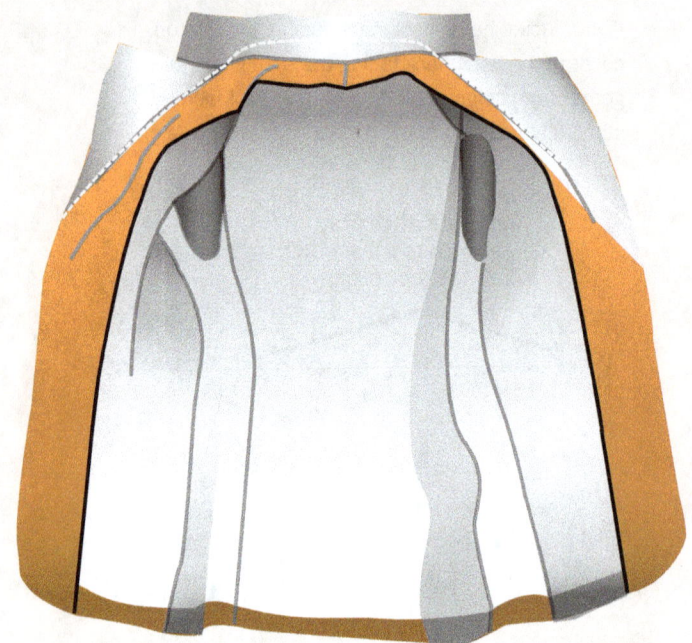

The collar and facings are now attached (Figure 12.41).

The back of the bound buttonhole can now be finished before setting the lining. Refer back to "Bound Buttonhole" in Chapter 6 for instructions. Then put your jacket on a stand or body and make any adjustments to the collar and lapels.

Figure 12.41

CHAPTER CHECKLIST

Before moving on to the next chapter, be sure that:
- ☐ The collar is covering the back neckline seam.
- ☐ The front lapel is rolling back from the roll line.
- ☐ The tip of the lapel inclines towards the body and does not curl upwards.
- ☐ Both lapels are the same size and shape.
- ☐ The tips of the collar and lapel have no lumps and don't look bulky.
- ☐ The collar is fitting around the neckline.
- ☐ The bottom of the jacket at the hemline curves in towards the body and doesn't curl outwards.

BOX 12.1 Create-A-Marker, Inc.

Create-A-Marker, Inc. is one of the leading computerized grading and marking companies serving the fashion industry. The company is owned and operated by Paul Cavazza. A family-owned business, Create-A-Marker, Inc. has been in operation since 1993.

Cavazza grew up in the fashion industry. His grandmother owned a sewing factory in Brooklyn for more than 25 years. His mother owned a sewing factory and cutting room in Marlboro, New York, for over 30 years. Cavazza attended The Fashion Institute of Technology (FIT) in New York City, and after working in production for a few years, opened his own grading and marking service.

Grading and marking are essential parts of producing a garment. If the measurements are off, the whole garment can be cut and sewn completely wrong, thereby ruining your garments.

GRADING

Grading is the process of adding various sizes from an original single-sized pattern. For example, a customer brings Cavazza a size 8 pattern, and his company creates it into a pattern that includes sizes 2, 4, 6, 8, 10, 12, 14, and 16. Precision pattern grading requires an in-depth knowledge of sophisticated computer technology run by people who are specifically trained to operate these systems. Create-A-Marker, Inc. also generates spec sheets to give the customer an accurate sample that improves the manufacturing of a garment. Spec sheets consist of important construction information such as trim, material details, and fabric yields.

Grading begins after patterns have been approved for production. A production marker is then prepared.

MARKER MAKING

A marker is a blueprint to cut garments in mass production. Markers maximize the fabric utilization based on widths and fabric types. There are three types of markers: yield markers, sample markers, and production markers.

A sample marker is a full-size plot of your pattern used to help establish your production budget. A yield marker (also called a mini marker) is recommended before a garment gets produced. A yield marker lets you know how to optimize any fabric width to achieve the highest profit margin. Markers can be plotted or emailed all over the world.

MIDTOWN PAPER, INC.

In addition to grading and marking, Cavazza also owns a company called Midtown Paper, Inc., which distributes paper directly to fashion companies. Examples of products sold are: plotter paper, dotted paper, pattern paper, sensitized paper, tissue paper, Kraft paper, and wax paper. They also distribute sewing and pattern supplies.

Both companies are located at 254 West 35th Street, 10th Floor, New York, NY 10001, in the heart of the city's fashion industry. To contact Create-A-Marker, Inc., call (212) 730-5615 or visit them online at createamarkernyc.com. To reach Midtown Paper Inc., call (212) 302-0021 or online at midtownpaper.com.

CHAPTER 13

The Lining

Knowledge is not a passion from without the mind, but an active exertion of the inward strength vigor and power of the mind, displaying itself from within.

—Ralph Lauren

CHAPTER OBJECTIVES

After reading this chapter, you should be able to:

Determine the different types of linings for the tailored jacket.

Define the different methods of setting a lining.

Determine the amount of ease to be added to the lining and adjust your pattern accordingly.

Construct and insert the lining.

Construct pockets into the lining.

Although the lining is not always visible, there are both aesthetic and practical reasons for lining your jacket or coat. The prime reason for the lining is that it covers the inner construction of your garment so that your garment feels and looks better and is easier to slip on and off. The lining should never pull the garment out of shape or cause wrinkling. More importantly, the lining takes some of the wear and strain off areas of stress as well as eliminates the need for seam finishes.

But just because the lining is functional doesn't mean it can't also be fun. Think of using a contrasting color, jacquard, or print to add interest and to personalize the design with your creative signature as shown in Figure 13.1a–d.

Figure 13.1a–d Think of using a contrasting color, jacquard, or print to add interest and personalize the design with your creative signature.

TYPES OF LININGS

The most common lining in a jacket is the full lining. There is also a partial or half lining that performs some of the same functions as a full lining. A full lining can also be detachable—this type is usually worked over a permanent lining. These are usually zip-out linings that make your jacket or coat an all-weather garment.

CONSTRUCTING THE LINING

You can set your lining by machine stitching the lining body pieces together and then hand stitching it to the jacket body. Then you make the lining sleeves and attach them by hand to the armhole of the jacket.

A faster method is to both make and set the lining by machine. Or you can choose to do a combination of both methods.

Full Lining Pattern

To construct the full lining pattern, you will cut all of the lining hems along the hem fold line of the jacket pattern.

1. Working from the jacket pattern pieces and beginning with the center back, make a 1-inch (2.5 cm) pleat from the neck to the waistline. This is added to ensure that there is enough ease across the shoulders. Add ⅛ inch (0.3 mm) at the shoulder. Add ¼ inch (0.6 mm) to both the front and back side seam allowances starting at the underarm and tapering down to the waist. Position the front facing pattern under the front pattern, matching the outer edges and notches. The inner edge of the front facing is the reference for cutting the lining as shown in Figure 13.2.

2. If your jacket has a back neck facing, the pleat will start from the facing as shown in Figure 13.3.

3. If the jacket has a center back vent, trim back 1 inch (2.5 cm) lengthwise from the left side for women and the right side for men (Figure 13.4).

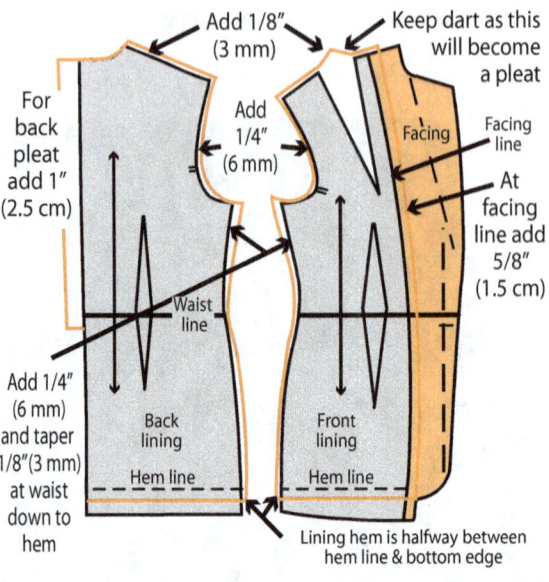

Figure 13.2

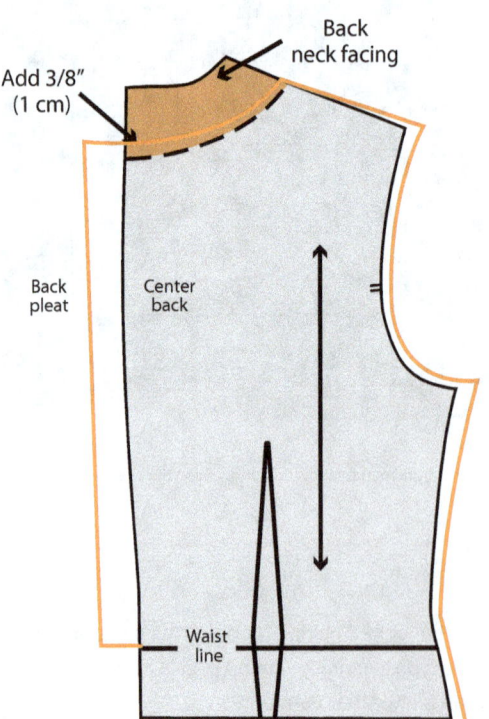

Figure 13.3

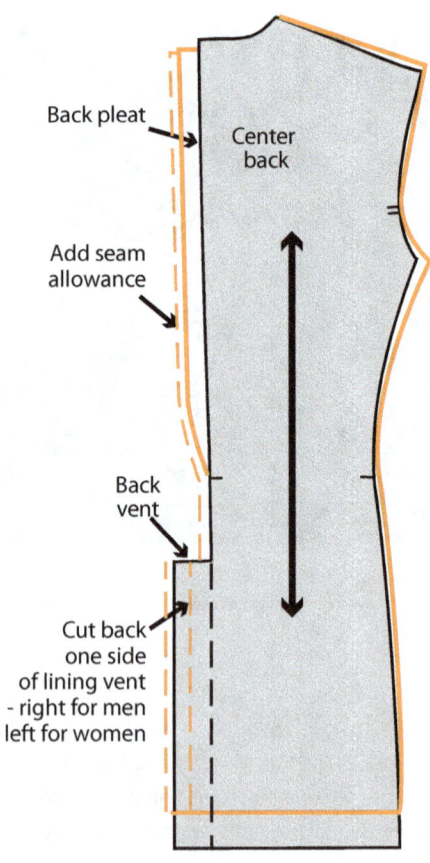

Figure 13.4

4. Figure 13.5 shows a jacket with both front and back side panels. Here you are going to add ⅛ inch (0.6 mm) to each seam allowance (Figure 13.5).

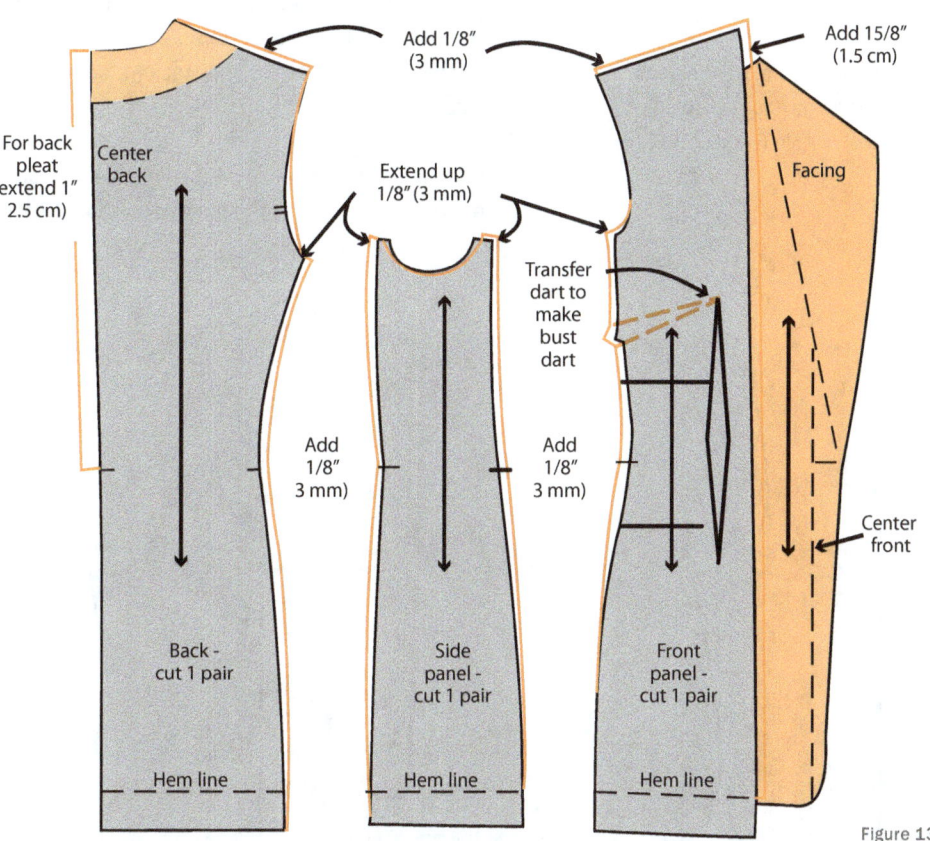

Figure 13.5

5. Figure 13.6 shows transferring the front dart to the bust line. To do this, make a slash about 3 inches (7.5 cm) down from the armhole on the front pattern piece to the bust point. Close the front dart, and the bust dart will open as shown in Figure 13.6.

6. Add ⅜ inch (0.5 mm) to the top sleeve at the shoulder point, ⅝ inch (1.5 cm) and ⅛ inch (0.3 mm) out. Rise the underarm ⅝ inch (1.5 cm) at the underarm and add ⅝ inch up and ⅛ inch (0.3 mm) out, as shown in Figure 13.7.

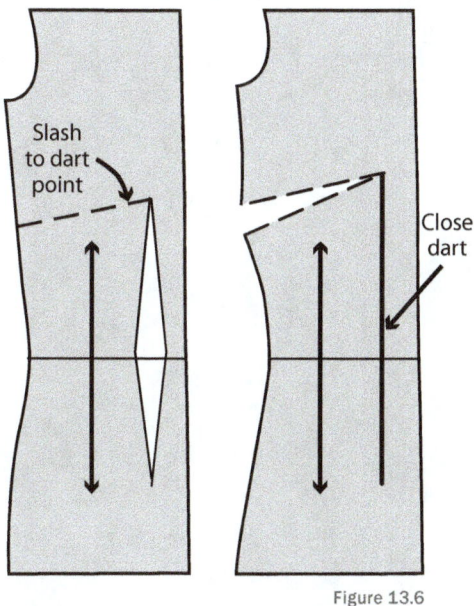

Figure 13.6

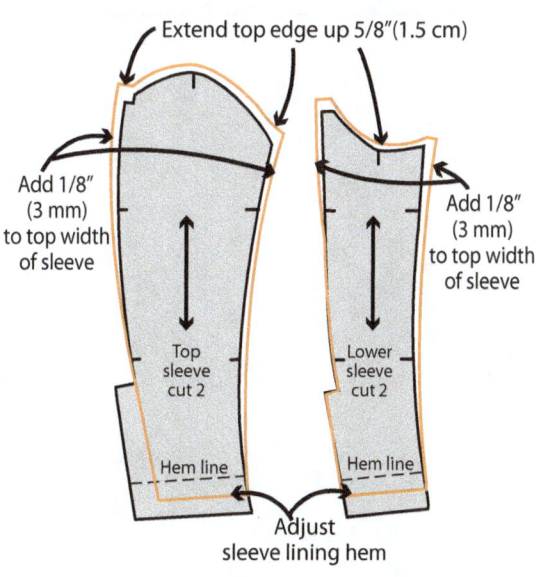

Figure 13.7

The Lining

After you have completed the lining pattern, you are ready to start constructing the lining.

1. Begin with the center back seam, right side to right side, machine stitch down to the notch at the top of the vent, as shown in Figure 13.8.

2. If your jacket does not have a vent, stitch down to the bottom of the seam. Machine stitch down the center back pleat line for approximately 4 inches (10 cm), finishing with a back tack (refer to Figure 13.8).

3. Clip the seam allowance on the left side for women's wear and right for men's wear (Figure 13.9).

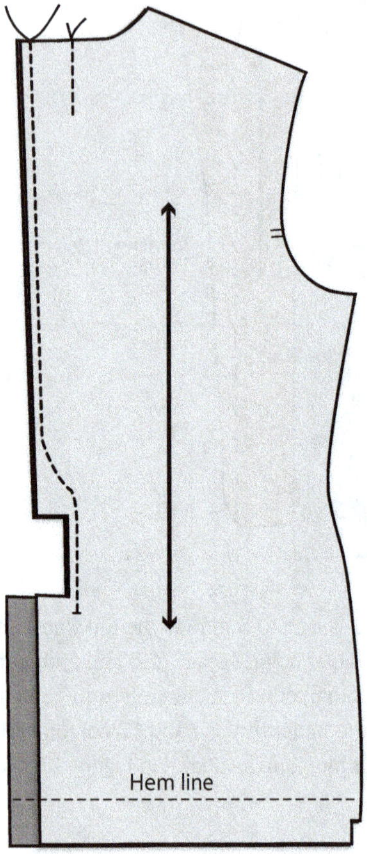

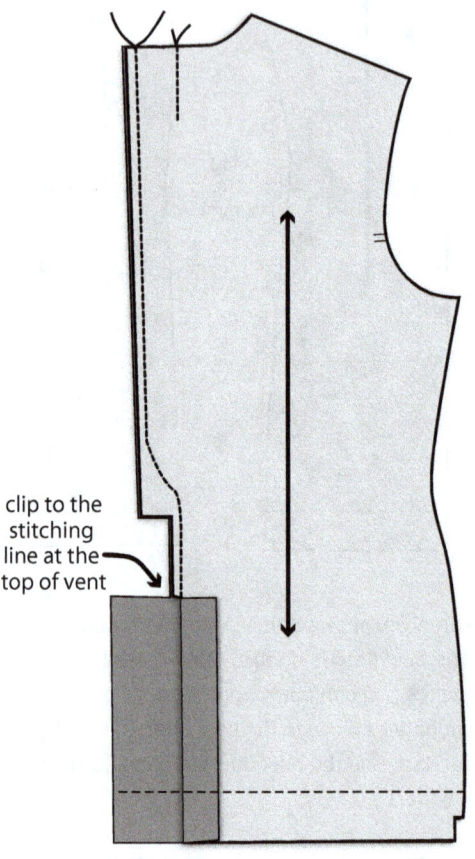

Hem line

Figure 13.8

clip to the stitching line at the top of vent

Figure 13.9

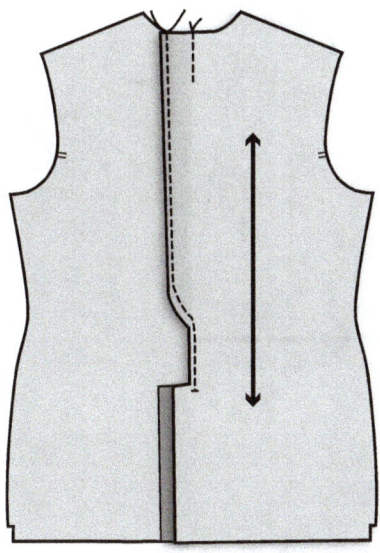

Figure 13.10

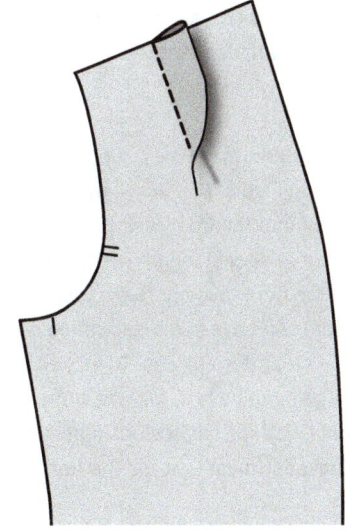

Figure 13.11

4. Press the seam toward the left for women's wear and right for menswear (Figure 13.10).

5. If your jacket lining looks like Figure 13.11 and you have a dart in the shoulder line, stitch down this dart for 2 inches (5 cm) so that it becomes a pleat. Press the dart towards the neck edge (Figure 13.11).

Inside Lining Pocket

In women's wear, the lining or inside pocket is placed on the left side of the jacket front just lower than the armhole. In a man's jacket, there can be more than one pocket on both lining fronts. It's a simple way to add both function and polish to any jacket lining. Figure 13.12 is showing the lining pocket placements.

1. Measure down from the chest/bust line on your pattern 1½ inches (3.75 cm) and draw a line 5 inches (12.5 cm) wide for your inside or lining pocket. If you are adding a second pocket, measure down 1 inch (2.5 cm) from the top pocket placement line and draw in the second

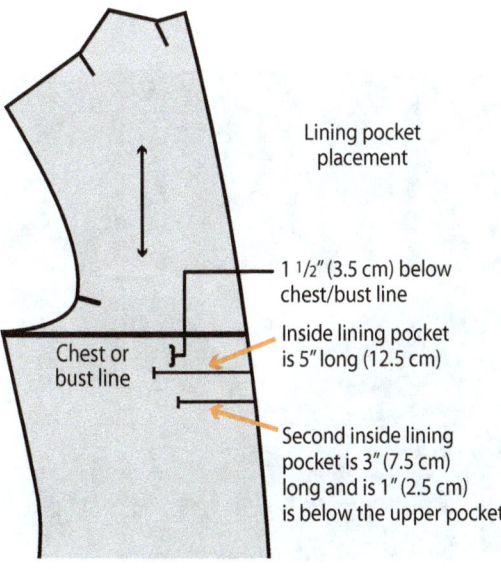

Figure 13.12

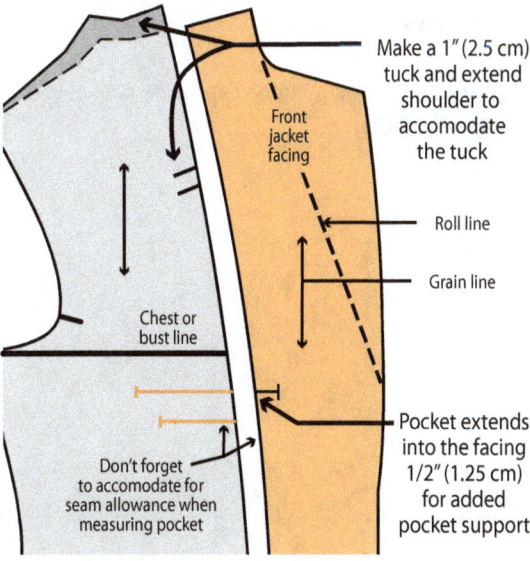

Figure 13.13

pocket 3 inches (7.5 cm) wide (Figure 13.12). This pocket can also extend into the jacket front facing as shown in Figure 13.13.

2. On your pattern, mark the top pocket placement as shown in Figure 13.12, but this time extend the pocket into the front facing ½ inch (1.25 cm) and draw the pocket length 4½ inches (11.5 cm) long on the front lining pattern piece. Do not forget that you have seam allowance added on both of your pattern pieces. To make the pocket you are going to have to join the front facing to the front lining with right sides together. Press the seam allowance towards the front facing.

3. Men tend to use the inside lining pocket more than women, and to counterbalance the weight of objects that are placed in this pocket extra ease can be added into the lining front above the pocket placement by adding a small tuck (Figure 13.14).

4. Make a small 1 inch (2.5 cm) tuck approximately half way between the shoulder and the chest/bust line. Bring the tuck together at the seam allowance and baste stitch in place. Press the tuck down towards the hem (Figure 13.15).

5. Make a 5-inch (12.5 cm) double-piped pocket following the instructions in Chapter 7. The jacket facing seam line is going to form one end of the pocket, but do not catch the pocket bag into this seam. To help support the pocket, work over a piece of pocketing 6 inches (15 cm) long by 2 inches (5 cm) wide.

Figure 13.16 shows a button-flap inside pocket in a ready-to wear jacket.

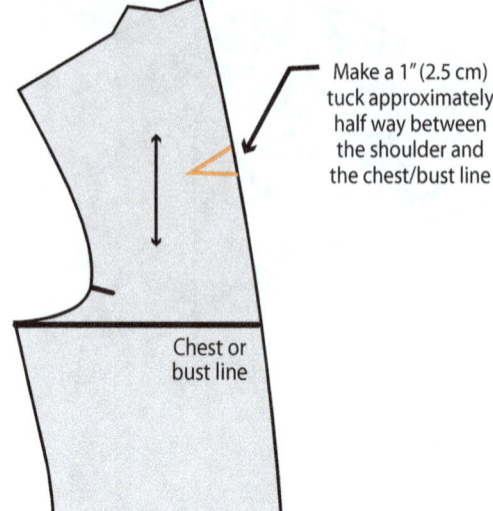

Figure 13.14

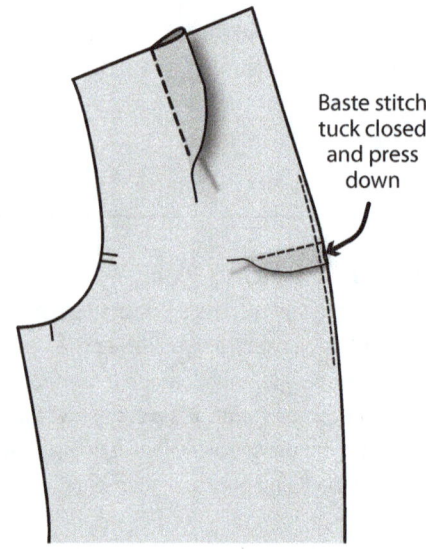

Figure 13.15

Figure 13.15

"Bagging" the Jacket Lining or Set by Machine

This ready-to-wear technique of attaching a lining is the fastest and gives a professional-looking result. This method is standard in the industry and almost eliminates all hand work. But you have to have a back neck facing to make "bagging" the lining work.

1. Turn the garment right side out through an opening in the sleeve or center back vent. Leave an opening in the sleeve underarm of 10 to 12 inches (25.5 to 30.5 cm) and starting about 1½ inch (2 cm) down from the armhole (Figure 13.17).

Figure 13.17

2. At this point you have both an entire jacket and lining shell. With the jacket wrong side out, and right sides together, match the lining to the entire front and back neck facing, and pin in place.

3. With one continuous seam, sew together starting and finishing about 4 inches (10 cm) up from the hem (refer to Figure 13.17). Press the seam allowance towards the lining.

4. Keep the right sides together and flip the jacket's basted hem open, but don't remove any basting stitches along the hem. Align the edge of the jacket's hem to the lining's hem, matching all of the seams in the lining with corresponding seams in the jacket. Pin together, taking care not to stretch the pinned fabrics machine stitch across the hem (Figure 13.18).

5. Catch stitch hem into place.

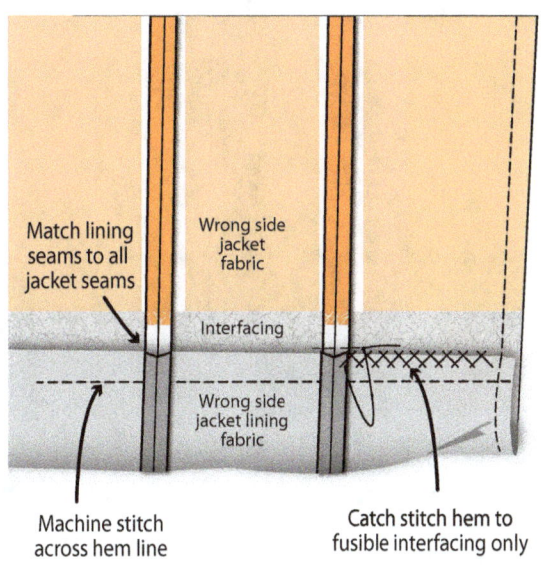

Figure 13.18

Jacket Vent and Hem

Before you begin, be sure that the seam allowance is pressed out on the right vent underlap for the women's jacket, and opposite for men's.

1. Line up and pin or baste the top of the right lining vent to the top of the right jacket vent with right sides facing (Figure 13.19).

2. Pin the left vent lining to the left vent jacket facing, fold up the raw edges of the jacket hem, and pin in place, matching all of the seams in the lining with corresponding seams in the jacket (refer to Figure 13.19).

Figure 13.19

185

3. Machine stitch down the left vent, pivoting at the corner; sew across the jacket hem to the front facing (refer to Figure 13.20).

4. Turn right side out and press a soft crease at the lining hem.

5. Working through the opening in the sleeve lining, pin the remaining lining hem to the jacket hem, with right sides together. Machine stitch down the under vent and across the hem. Figure 13.21 shows how the jacket hem and lining should look.

6. Catch stitch the jacket hem in place, catching only the interfacing (Figure 13.22).

7. Return to the front facing and the 4 inches (10 cm) of unfinished stitching. Fold up the hemline, as shown in Figure 13.23, and stitch. The lining will form a small pleat or crease.

8. Catch stitch the front jacket facing to the fusible interfacing (Figure 13.24).

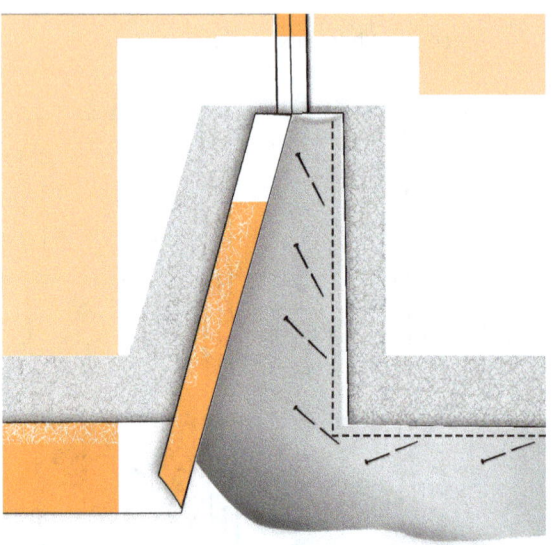

Figure 13.20

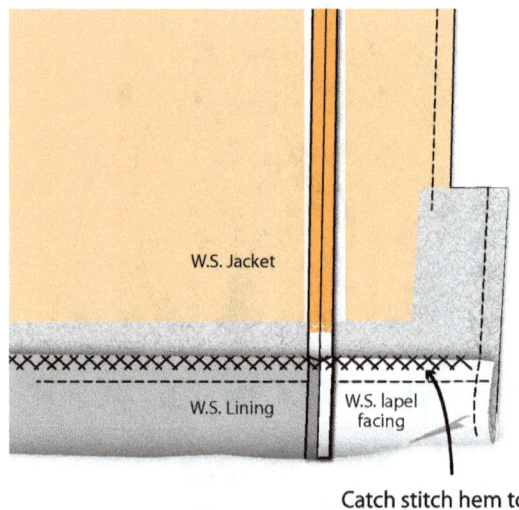

Catch stitch hem to fusible interfacing

Figure 13.22

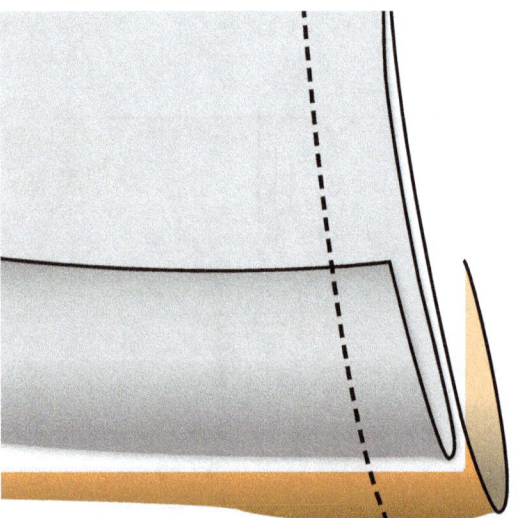

Figure 13.21

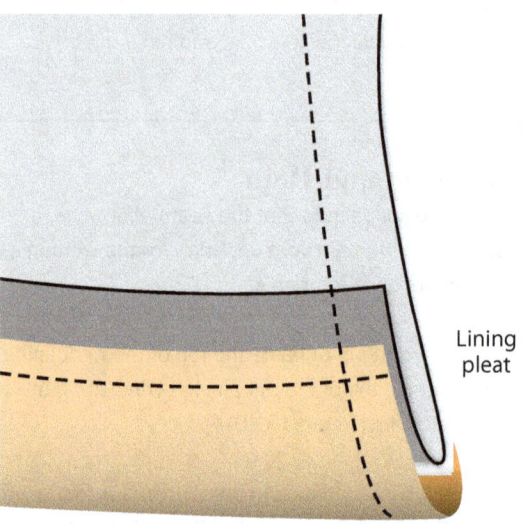

Lining pleat

Figure 13.23

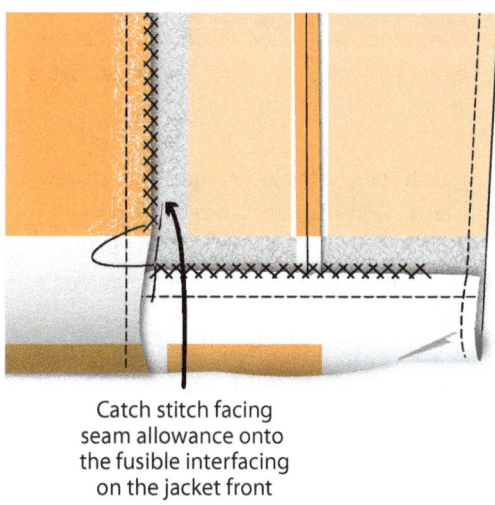

Catch stitch facing seam allowance onto the fusible interfacing on the jacket front

Figure 13.24

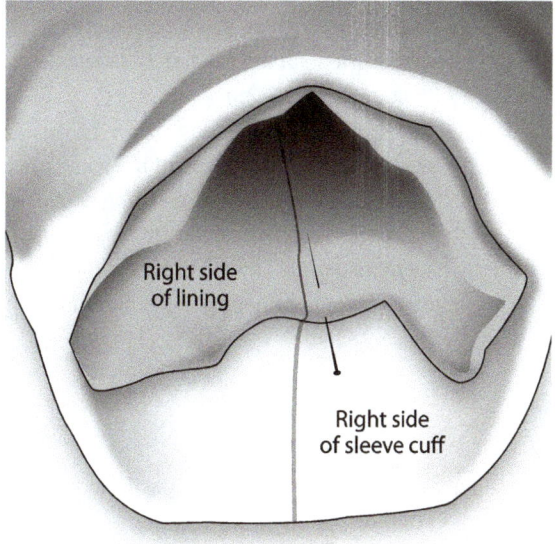

Figure 13.26

9. Turn the jacket to the right side out, and push the sleeve lining down the jackets sleeve. Now working thought the gap in the lining sleeve or back vent, attach the sleeve hem lining to the jacket (Figure 13.25).

10. Fold up the seam allowance at the lining sleeve hem and pin to the jacket hem, making sure that all your seams are aligned (i.e., the way you would wear the jacket). Pin the underarm seam, making sure that the sleeves are not twisted (Figure 13.26).

11. Pull the hem out through the opening in the lining, and transfer the pins so that you have right side to right side. Re-pin and stitch as shown in Figure 13.27.

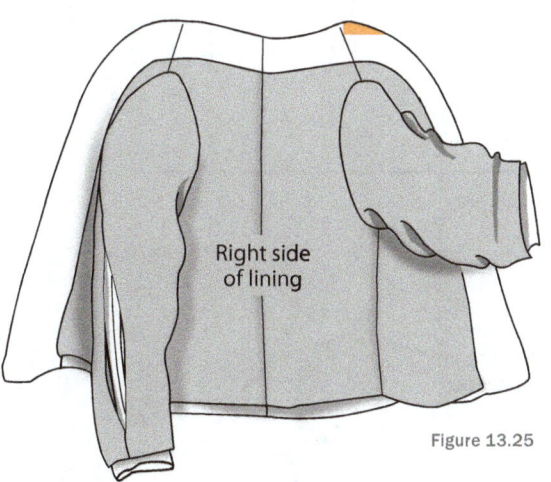

Figure 13.25

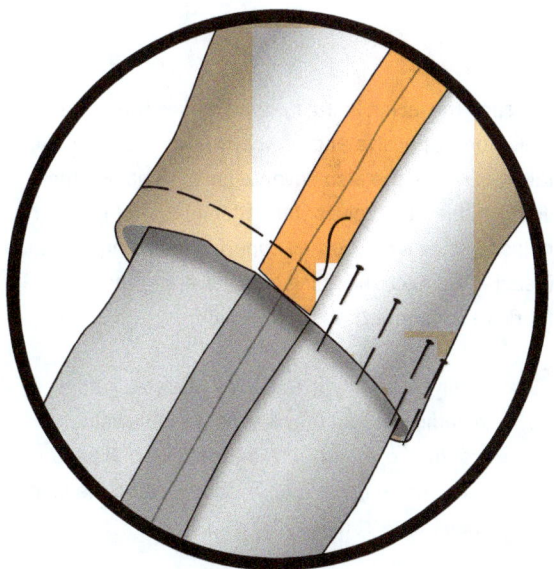

Figure 13.27

12. Hand stitch or machine stitch across the top of the back vent(s) for approximately 1½ inches (3.25 cm) (Figure 13.28).

13. This stitching will hold the top of the vents in place. Be accurate with your stitching because this is going to be seen as topstitching if done with a machine. This stitching almost disappears if you work by hand using a pickstitch.

14. Attach the lining to the shoulder point of the jacket with a 1/10-inch (.3 cm) bar tack (Figure 13.29).

15. Attach lining to the jacket underarm sleeve with a 1/10-inch bar tack, as shown in Figure 13. 29. Then slip stitch or machine stitch closed the opening in the jacket underarm or back vent.

16. Turn jacket right side out and press.

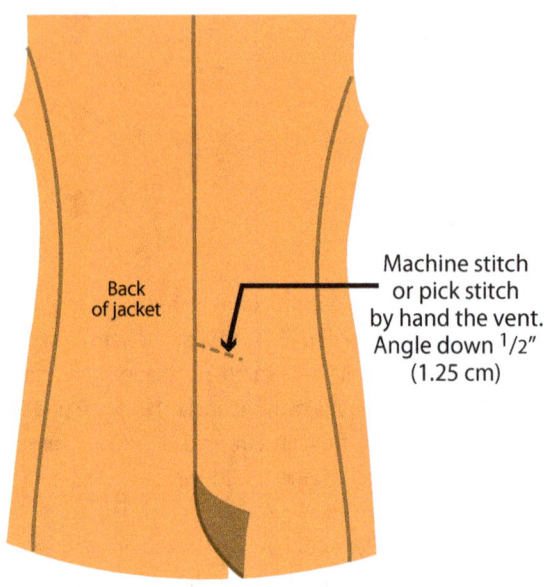

Figure 13.28

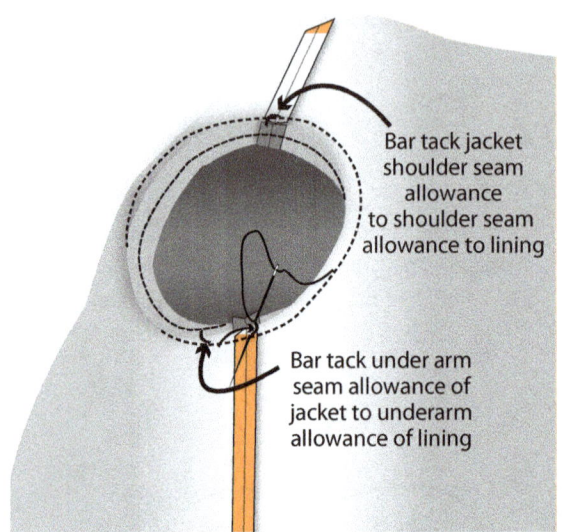

Figure 13.29

INSERTING THE LINING BY HAND

Inserting the jacket lining by hand makes the jacket look more expensive and is synonymous with bespoke tailoring. There are also advantages to attaching the lining in this way. It gives you better control of the fabric, helps to cover small sewing imperfections, and makes it easier to attach the lining onto velvet or other pile fabrics and fabrics that slip and slide.

1. Begin by sewing all the lining pieces together, including setting the sleeves. Then staystitch around the edge of the lining shell on the seam allowance (Figure 13.30). This will stop the lining shell from stretching.

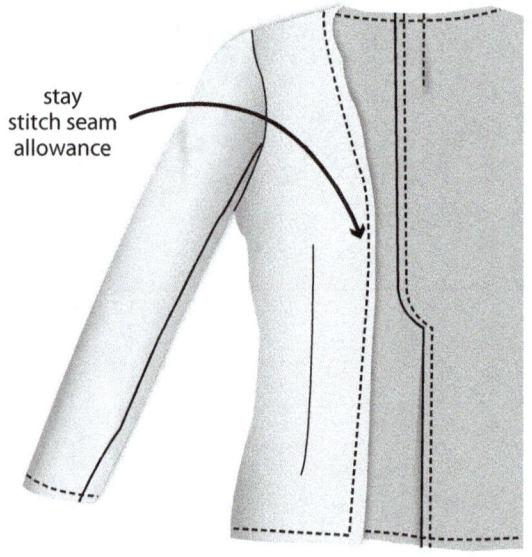

Figure 13.30

2. Press the seam allowance back using the stay-stitching as a guide.

3. Pin the lining shell to the jacket facing, matching the center back and shoulder seams. You may have to clip the lining seam allowance to make it easier to pin to the curve of the neck edge facing (Figure 13.31).

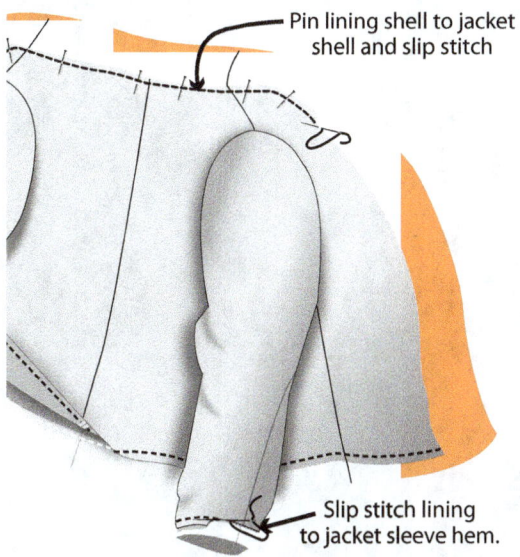

Figure 13.31

4. Working from the hemline back up to the shoulder, pin in place, as shown in Figure 13.31, and slip stitch in place beginning at the center back seam across to the shoulder seam and down the front facing, finishing about 4 inches (10 cm) up from the hem. Repeat on the other side (Figure 13.32).

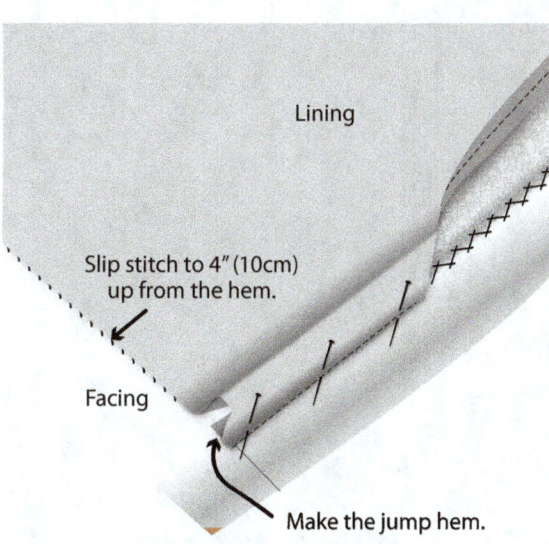

Figure 13.32

5. Place the raw edge of the lining hem to the raw edge of the jacket hem, making sure that all your seams are aligned. Pin in place and slip stitch (Figure 13.33).

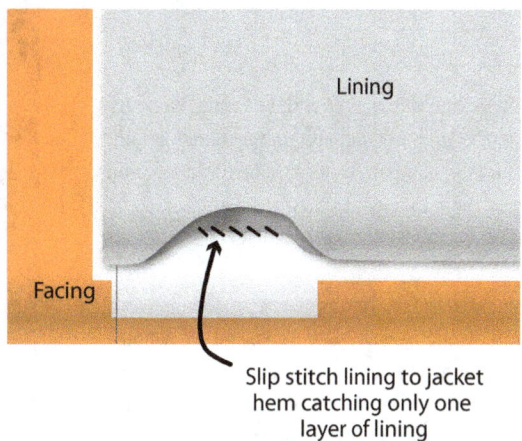

Figure 13.33

6. Figure 13.32 shows the ease that is created by making the jump hem on the lining. Smooth down the excess lining towards the hem, and finish slip stitching the front edge of the lining to the jacket facing as shown in Figure 13.33. This will form what is called a jump hem.

7. Finish the sleeve hems in the same way as the lining hem, as shown in Figure 13.34.

8. Secure the lining shoulders to the shoulder pads and the undersleeve at the seam line to the armhole of the jacket with pickstitches. Do not let these stitches show through to the right side of the jacket.

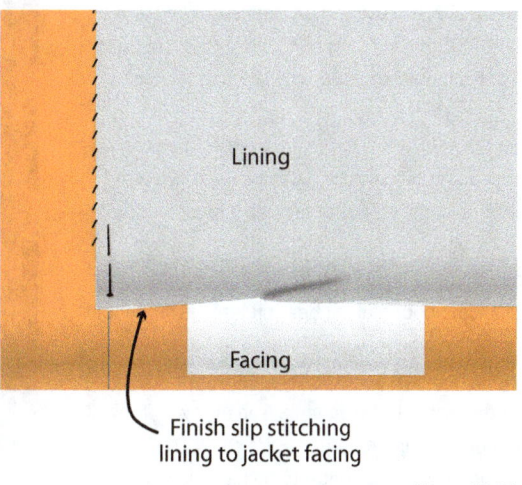

Figure 13.34

BOX 13.1 John Rocha

In the 1970s John Rocha moved from a cramped 11th-floor apartment in his native Hong Kong to take a nursing job in London. His mother and neighbors paid for his ticket. "It was the only way I could get out of Hong Kong, but I switched careers at 21 and entered the Croydon College of Art and Design to study fashion" (Walsh, 2001).

IRISH INSPIRATION

While visiting Ireland with a girlfriend, he found a length of what he called "big old beautiful hand-woven Irish tweed." He approached the company that manufactured the fabric and convinced them to sponsor him for his graduation final collection, which was all done with the Irish fabric (Walsh, 2001).

Rocha moved to Ireland and continued to develop and refine his own distinctive style, inspired by fabric, silhouette, and technique, and combined with Chinese and Celtic design details. He is known for his beautiful hand-painted fabrics, embellishments, classic tailoring, crochet, and hand knits that he shows twice a year at London Fashion Week. "This twelve-minute show has to show everything you did for the last six months, it has to make a big impression" he explains (Hourican, 2009).

Rocha was named British designer of the year in 1994 and again in 2002.

BRANCHING OUT

In 2000, Rocha walked away from the catwalks of Europe for a season because he said he was too busy with other things.

Those other things included John Rocha at Waterford Crystal, which was launched in 1997 and has achieved worldwide acclaim. His first architectural project was the Morrison Hotel, which opened in 1999. He has since worked on both interior design and structural architecture projects. A jewelry collection followed in 2002 as well as a move into mass marketing with Debenhams department store in the UK, with the diffusion label, Rocha.John Rocha.

In February 2002, he received a Commander of the British Empire (CBE) award from Her Majesty the Queen in recognition of his long-standing contribution to the fashion industry.

"Whatever I design, it has to please my eye," he said. "If I go to work on an office block, I'll draw the office that I want to walk into. If it's a piece of crystal, it must feel the way I want it to feel in my hand. If it's women's wear, it must be something I'd like to see my wife dressed in.... It's all about balance, about making beautiful things for people to enjoy. What I like, you may hate. What you hate, my darling wife might love. It's a definition of my own. It's not what I learned at school. The balance is in my eyes. They tell me that things are in proportion" (Walsh, 2001).

Rocha considers his wife Odette to be his muse (as well as his business partner). His design company is called Three Moons Design, located at Dublin's Ely, and John Rocha, lifestyle boutique, which was opened in 2006, at 15A Dover Street, London, W1.

Figure Box 13.1 "When I design menswear, I always think to myself, 'What would Jack Nicholson like from this collection?'" says John Rocha (Hourican, 2009).

ATTACHING THE JACKET LINING WITHOUT A BACK NECK FACING

Follow the previous instructions until your lining is attached into the jacket, except for around the back neck and the shoulder facing. Then do the following:

1. Pin the lining to the back neckline, turning under the seam allowance and making sure that you align to the center back seam. Turn under the back shoulder seam allowance, and lap over the front jacket facing. Pin in place and baste stitch. Slip stitch the neckline and shoulder seam in place (Figure 13.35).

2. If you want a high-end look to your jacket, you can also hand attach the sleeve to the jacket body, as shown in Figure 13.36. Because of the ease at the sleeve head, it is easiest to work from the underarm up to the shoulder seam. Slip stitch the sleeve lining to the armhole, being careful to only catch the lining shell and not the jacket in the stitches.

3. Now that you have the lining attached to the jacket, put the jacket on a body or stand. Make sure that the lining is not pulling, but is sitting smoothly and comfortably inside the jacket.

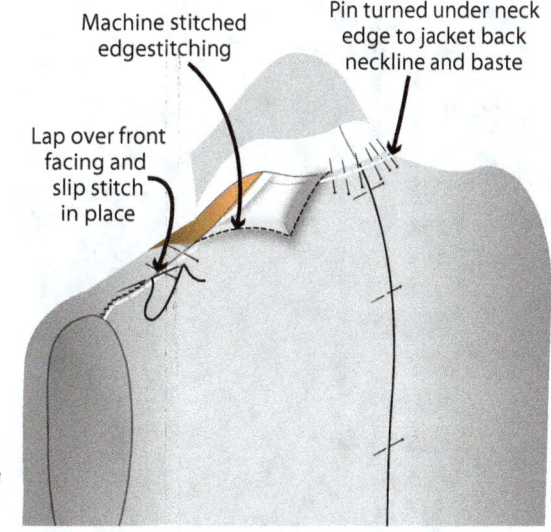

Figure 13.35

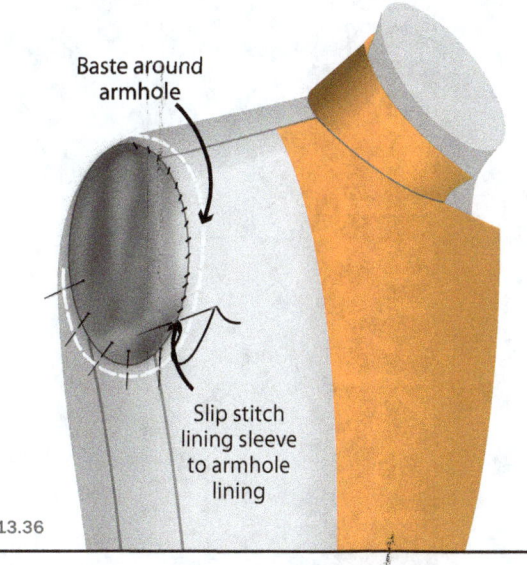

Figure 13.36

CHAPTER CHECKLIST

Before moving onto the next chapter, make sure that:
- [ ] The lining is not showing below the hem of the jacket.
- [ ] The lining inside the sleeves is not twisted.
- [ ] You make any necessary adjustments.

REFERENCES

Hourican, E. (2009, October 11) "The House of Rocha," *The Independent*. Retrieved on December 22, 2009 from http://www.independent.ie/lifestyle/the-house-of-rocha-1910395.html

Wash, J. (2001, January 4) "Death, My Greatest Career Move," *The Independent*. Retrieved on December 22, 2009 from http://www.independent.co.uk/news/people/profiles/death-my-greatest-career-move-695670.html

CHAPTER 14

Finishing the Jacket

> If you ask any lady, they want to be taller, they want to be slimmer, you know, and they want a waist. I'm not here to make people look like a sack of potatoes.
>
> —Alexander McQueen

CHAPTER OBJECTIVES

After reading this chapter, you should be able to:

Evaluate the jacket button to match the design—is the button functional or ornamental?

Decide which buttonhole to construct, and determine its correct placement.

Hand work a keyhole buttonhole.

Give the jacket its final press.

Add topstitching to the jacket.

Determine where to place the buttons.

Determine if you need to shank the button or work two buttons together.

Give your completed jacket a final evaluation.

The jacket is now almost finished, but you may still have the buttonholes to make and the buttons to attach.

Figure 14.1 Balmain.

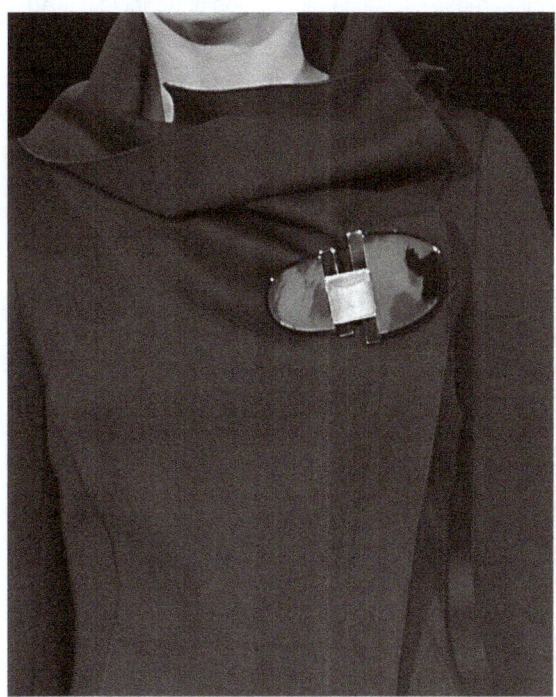

Figure 14.2 Look at the fastening on this Giorgio Armani jacket. Sometimes it is the unexpected detail like this that makes the garment.

BUTTONS

Traditionally dull horn or bone buttons close in color to the jacket fabric were used on tailored jackets in keeping with the high quality and a conservative tone that *high quality* implied. Today this choice is more about fashion; the button as well as the buttonhole can be part of the design statement. Buttons come in all shapes and sizes, so they can serve as both decorative accents as well as functional fasteners (Figure 14.2).

Buttonhole placement is important because you do not want to lose the balance of the jacket. In Chapter 6, we discussed how to mark the buttonhole placement. Follow these directions with the top buttonhole placed approximately ⅝ to 1 inch (1.6 to 2.5 cm) below the bottom of the lapel roll line. The lapel will begin to roll back just above the button. In a three-button jacket, the next button will be placed at the waistline. I prefer the bottom button to finish just above or level with the pockets (Figure 14.4).

You may also add a lapel buttonhole, which would be placed parallel to the top of the lapel. If your lapel is peaked, the buttonhole will slant upwards. On a square lapel, it will slant downwards (Figure 14.3).

Measuring the Button

For a flat button, the buttonhole is equal to the diameter of the button. If the button is not flat, the length of the buttonhole should equal one half the circumference of the button.

Figure 14.3
Carlo Pignatelli Cerimonia, 2005.

Figure 14.4

Hand-Worked Buttonholes

Hand-worked buttonholes are found on traditional men's tailored suits and jackets. There is also a Chanel jacket with a hand-worked buttonhole constructed on the jacket front and a bound buttonhole constructed behind this in the jacket facing. In such a case, the two are simply slip stitched together.

Hand-worked buttonholes are cut before they are worked. It can be easier to machine stitch around each buttonhole rectangle before cutting the opening. This helps stop fraying, acts as a guide, and holds all the layers of fabric together (Figure 14.5).

1. Cut the buttonhole precisely down the mark, using a small, very sharp pair of scissors or a knife (Figure 14.6). Trim back the canvas.

2. To make the keyhole, cut away a small triangle with the one straight edge parallel to the jacket edge, or clip very short lines that radiate around the end of the buttonhole and use a stiletto to form the eyelet as shown in Figure 14.6.

3. Overcast or buttonhole stitch around the edge of the opening (Figure 14.7).

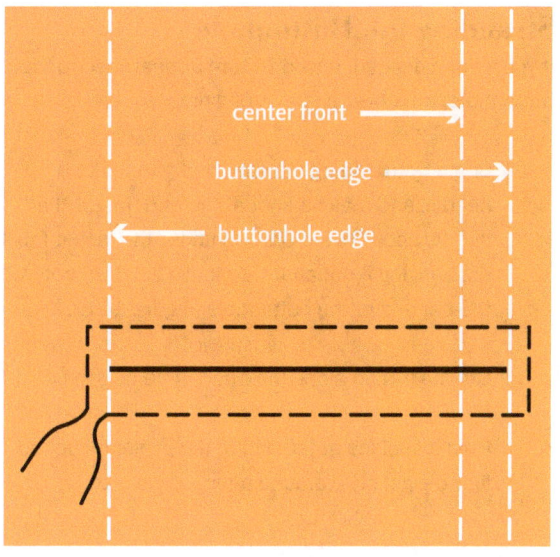

Figure 14.5

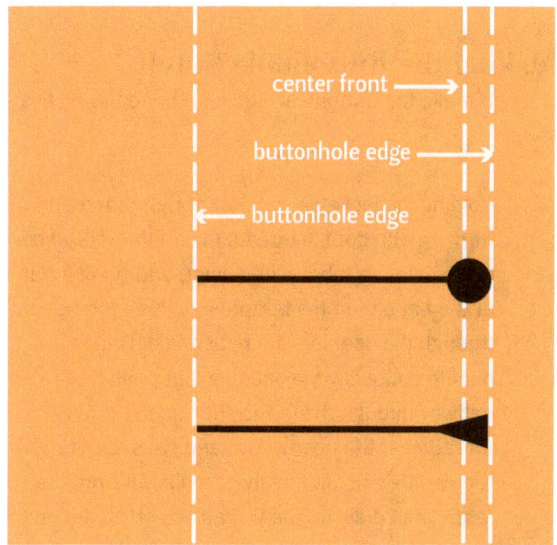

Figure 14.6

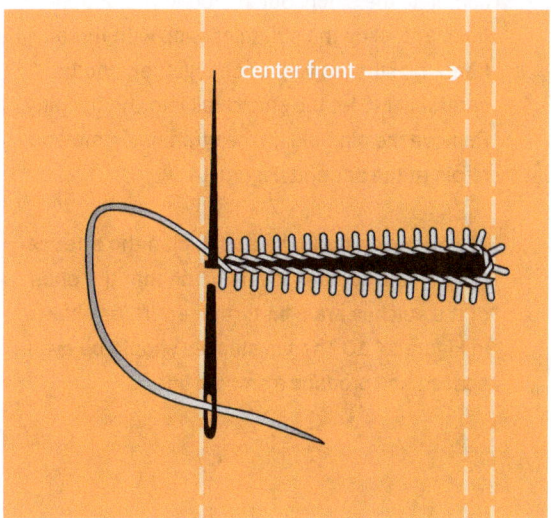

Figure 14.7

Stranding the Buttonhole

If you want a defined, raised texture appearance to the buttonhole, work over a strand of gimp.

1. Begin by threading the strand of gimp onto a needle, and make a knot at the end. Insert the needle about ⅜ inch (1 cm) under the jacket fabric, bringing it out about 1/16 inch (1.5 mm) before the bar end of the buttonhole (Figure 14.8).

2. Lay the thread along the buttonhole edge.

3. Hold it in place at the end of the eyelet, wrapped figure-eight style around a pin.

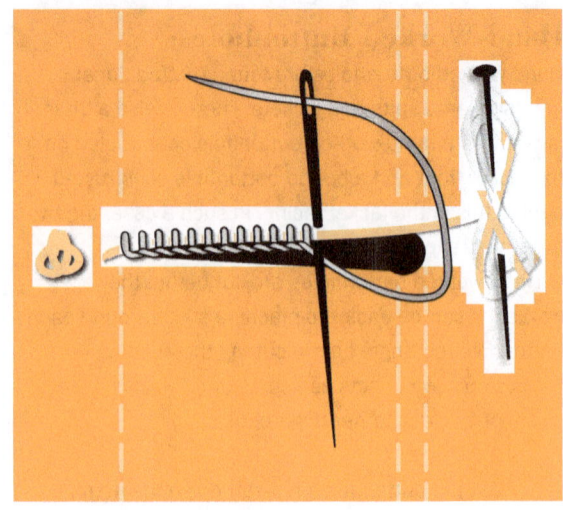

Figure 14.8

Making the Buttonhole Stitch

You can make the buttonhole stitch in the following five steps.

1. Holding the jacket in your left or right hand and working with double thread, fasten the thread securely into the fabric with a knot, and bring it out at the bar end of the buttonhole. Push the needle through the opening at a right angle. Bring the needle out below the opening, but push it only halfway through the fabric. Pick up the double thread near the needle eye, and pass it under the needle's point. Pull the needle out from the fabric, and draw up the thread almost to the end. Use your thumb or index figure to set the purl on the edge of the buttonhole. Setting the purl will complete the stitch. Stitch around the buttonhole, encircling the strand or gimp with thread. Keep the stitches very close together, and be careful not to let the strand fall into the opening. Remove the pin holding the stranding gimp and re-pin at the bar end (Figure 14.9).

2. As you work around the eyelet, plan the arrangement of the stitches to fan out so that the ends of the stitches are a bit further apart, as shown in Figure 14.10 The fan stitches should be evenly spaced and produce a smooth line.

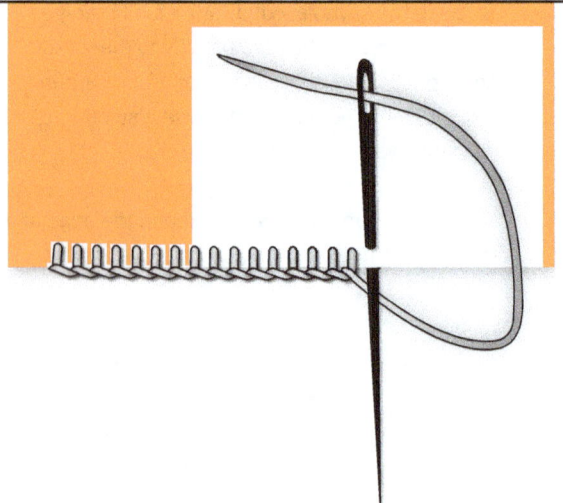

Figure 14.9

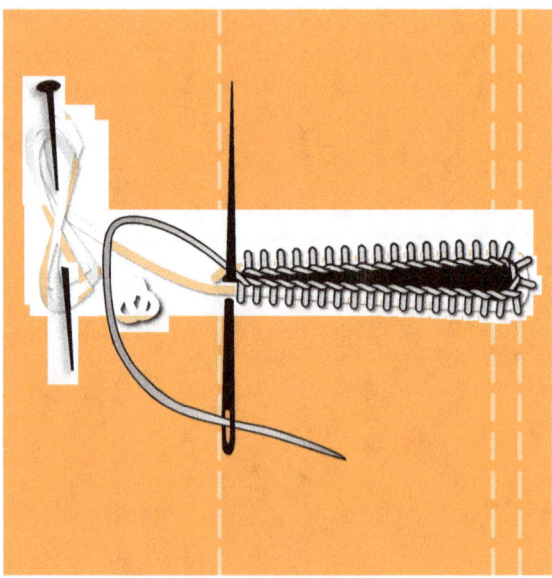

Figure 14.10

3. Continue to stitch down the other side of buttonhole, making the final stitch exactly opposite the first stitch. Bring the needle and thread through the purl of the first stitch, and draw the first and last stitches closely together (Figure 14.11). Drop the needle and thread out of the way.

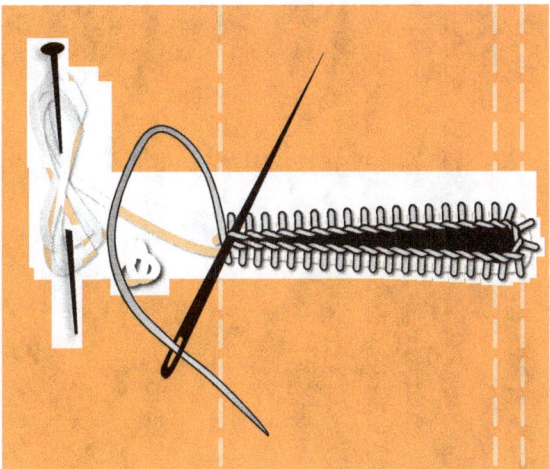

Figure 14.11

4. Draw up the stranding thread to make the buttonhole firm and smooth at the edge. Do not draw it up too tightly. Place a stiletto in the eyelet, and hold it there as you draw up the stranding thread. The use of the stiletto will prevent the stranding from being drawn up too tightly and will improve the appearance of your buttonhole. Thread the stranding thread onto a needle, thread it through to the wrong side of the jacket, and cut close to your fabric. Push them under the canvas (Figure 14.12).

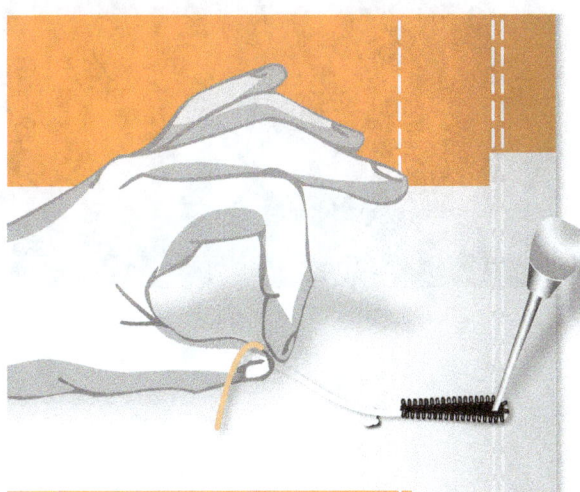

Figure 14.12

5. Across the end of the buttonhole, make a small bar by pushing the needle down through the fabric at the edge of the buttonhole and up through the fabric at the other end. Repeat this three to four times, or work three to four purled stitches over the bar end, setting the purl inwards towards the buttonhole as shown in Figures 14.13 and 14.14 a and b.

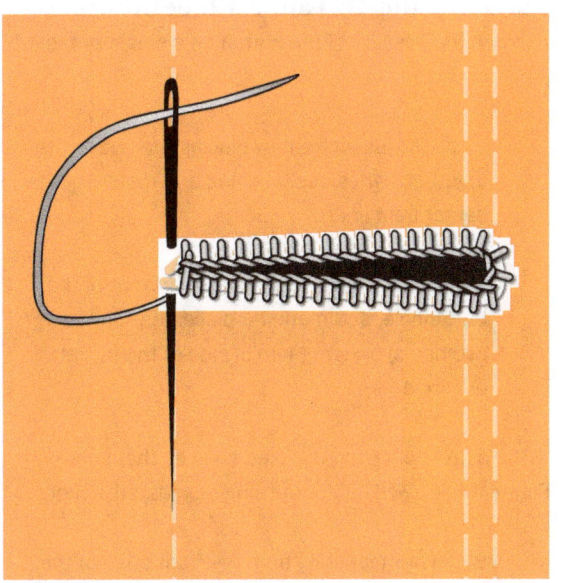

Figure 14.13

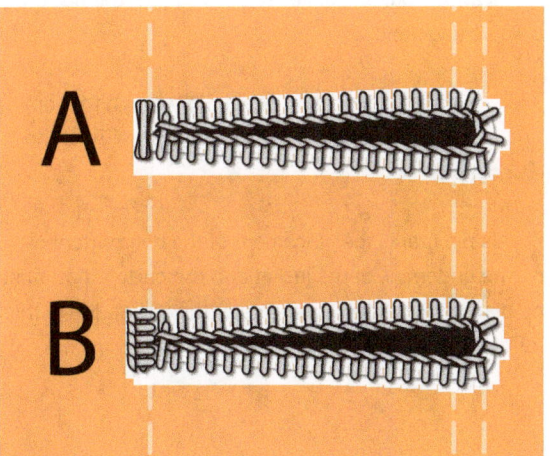

Figure 14.14a and b

197

Machine-Stitched Buttonholes

Machine-stitched buttonholes are also worked after the jacket is finished. For ready-to-wear, these are the buttonholes of choice because they are quick and easy to make.

Begin by marking the buttonhole placement as previously described and then use the buttonhole attachment or program on your machine to make the buttonholes. These buttonholes can be worked over cord for a more distinctive look. To do this, follow the instructions in your sewing machine manual.

Marking the Button's Placement

To mark the position of the button on a single-breasted jacket:

1. Close the jacket front by placing the two fronts together, right sides touching and matching the center front line.

2. Push a pin through the keyhole or front of the buttonhole, and mark the placement on the left (women's) or right (men's) side of the jacket (Figure 14.15).

For a double-breasted jacket, such as that shown in Figure 14.15, work as for the single-breasted jacket.

1. Begin by measuring from the front edge of the button hole to the center front line. Now apply this measurement from the center front line away from the jacket edge and mark the button placement.

2. With the jacket still closed, pin through the top button mark, and mark on the underside of the jacket front.

This pin marks the placement of the one buttonhole on the underside of the jacket and the button that must be placed inside the upper side of the jacket. Make this buttonhole.

Figure 14.15
Christian Dior
ready to wear, 2009.

FINAL PRESSING

Note that buttons are attached to the jacket after the final pressing. Also, remember to remove all the basting stitches from the jacket because you do not want them to mark the jacket during pressing.

1. First, using a clapper and cloth press, press around the edge of the jacket with the jacket facing side up. Start about 1 inch (2.5 cm) down from the lapel roll line. Press down the front edge along the hemline and up the other side of the jacket to just below the roll line. Be careful not to stretch the edges. Press the underside of the front lapels and undercollar. Work over a tailor's ham to keep the shape (Figure 14.16).

2. Turn the jacket over so that the right side is up, and press the lapel edges. Work from the bottom of the roll line, around the collar edge and down to the bottom of the roll line on the other lapel. Lay the lapel and collar into position, and press the crease line. Pressing over a ham, lightly press the jacket body, being careful not to alter the shaping. Working with a pressing cloth, press the jacket on the right side from the shoulders to the hem and down the side seams (Figure 14.17).

3. Press the sleeves over a sleeve board, first the front seam and then the undersleeve seam. Using a pressing mitt or ham inside the sleeve head, press each shoulder and sleeve cap on the right side of the jacket. Finish by lightly pressing the top or right side of the lapel, keeping it curved over the ham and only pressing the body part and not the edge.

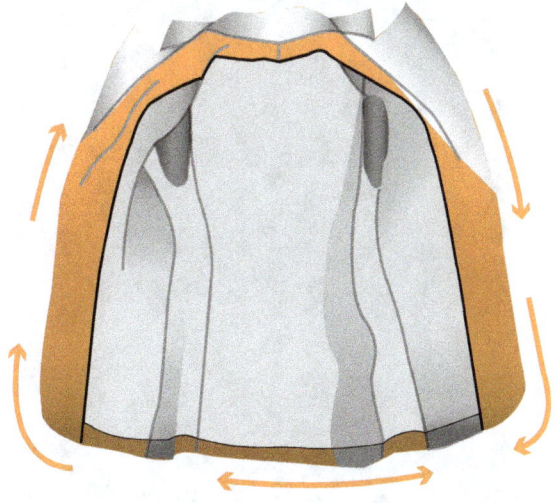

Figure 14.16

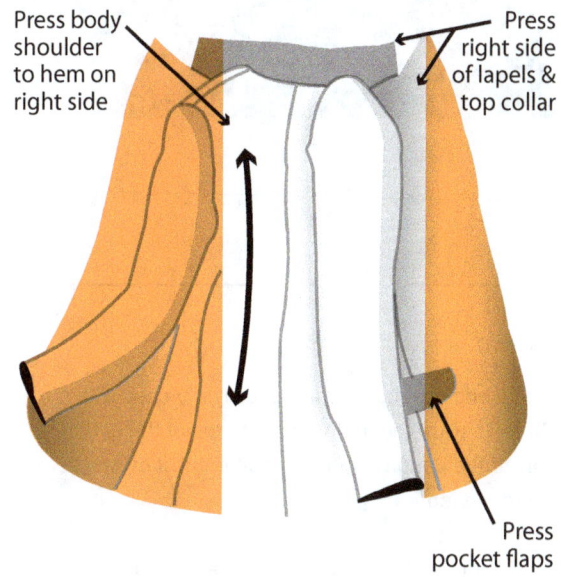

Figure 14.17

Figure 4.18
John Galliano for Christian Dior,
Fall/Winter, 2003.

TOPSTITCHING

Topstitching is added for decoration, but it can also hold the collar and lapel edges flat. It can also be worked around cuffs, pockets, pocket flaps, belts, and other areas. Figure 14.18 shows a decorative topstitched hem on a coat.

Work the topstitching before attaching the buttons. On a jacket, the topstitching is worked ¼ inch (6 mm) in from the jacket edge, and you can work more than one row of topstitching. You can edgestitch the topstitching onto a linen or lightweight woolen jacket; this will make a stronger, harder-wearing outer edge.

Use a heavier matching or contrasting thread to topstitch. Lengthen the stitch length of your machine for more definition. Do not back tack, but when you are finished pull the threads through to the facing side and tie off before burying them back between the garment layers.

Topstitching can also be worked by hand, as can pickstitching (Figure 14.19).

Figure 14.19

ATTACHING THE BUTTONS

Jacket and coat buttons are usually attached with a shank to allow the button to sit on top of the buttonhole. If the button is purely ornamental, it can be sewn flat to the fabric.

1. Double the thread in your needle; take a small stitch in the mark on the jacket front. Keep the button about ¼ inch (6 mm) away from the fabric so that a small shank in made. You can place a pin or match between the button and the fabric to help create the shank. The needle will pass though each hole in the button no more than three times, and will not go through all of the fabric layers. You do not want these stitches to show on the jacket facing (Figure 14.20).

2. When you have completed these stitches, remove the pin or match and wind the thread around the shank three times, as shown in Figure 14.21.

Figure 14.20

Figure 14.21

3. Then make a small knot at the base of the shank to finish (Figure 14.22).

4. If your buttons are very large or heavy, place a small clear or fabric-matched button on the jacket facing and work the stitches through both buttons. This will help adjust the weight and stop the button from drooping.

5. Add any embellishments.

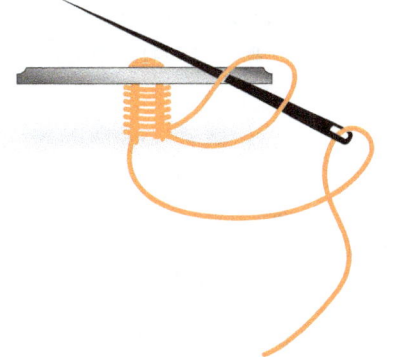

Figure 14.22

GIVING YOUR COMPLETED JACKET A FINAL EVALUATION

The most important parts of a jacket, as far as general appearance is concerned, are located within the area above the chest or bust line. However, attention to every detail is the hallmark of the well-tailored jacket.

The parts of your completed tailored jacket should include the following qualities.

The Collar
The collar should lie smoothly and fit to the neck over the shoulder and across the back. The fall of the collar should lie flat against the undercollar and fully cover the stand of the collar. The ends of the collar should lie flat with no curling.

The Lapels
There should be a soft roll along the crease line without an actual crease being pressed into this line. The lapels should lie in position with no curling points. The seam line along the outer edge should be concealed. The lappets should form the "V" of the front opening with no bulges or broken lines (wrinkling).

The Front Edge
Seams at the edges should be concealed. Curves and corners should lie smooth with no curling up.

The Sleeves
The sleeves should fall vertically from the top of the sleeve to the elbow, and to the wrist following the line of the arm. Stitches should not be visible at the top of the sleeve hem, and no lining should show.

The Waist and Hip Area
The waist and hip areas in a fitted jacket should sit smoothly over the body with no pulling or diagonal wrinkling.

The Lower Hem Line
No stitches should show at the top of the hem. The hem should not be pulled up by a lining set too tight. The lining should not be longer than the jacket.

The Fabric Design: Plaids, Stripes, or Checks
The design of the fabric should be carried across the jacket seam lines and openings, adding to the final effect of the jacket.

Be sure to check that the edges of the lapels lie flat and softly roll back over the chest area. The crease line of the collar and fold line of the lapel should form an unbroken line that runs from the top button up, around the back of the neck, and down to the top buttonhole. The shoulders and tops of the sleeves should give a nice trim line to the silhouette.

Finally, the jacket should look like it belongs to its wearer.

Box 14.1 Savile Row Jargon

Over its centuries of history, Savile Row has developed a colorful language of its own. Here are a selection of words and phrases most of which are still in use.

On the cod Gone drinking.

Baby Stuffed cloth pad on which the tailor works his cloth.

Balloon/having a balloon A week without work or pay.

Banger Piece of wood with handle, used to draw out steam and smooth cloth during ironing.

Board Tailor's workbench.

Bodger Crude worker; common to other trades.

Boot Loan until payday.

Bunce A trade perk, like mungo or a crib.

Bushelman Journeyman who alters or repairs.

Can you spare the boot? Can you give me a loan? Dates from "crossed-leg days," when a tailor recorded the loan by chalking it on the sole of his boot.

Cat's face A small shop opened by a cutter starting out on his own.

Chuck a dummy To faint; allusion is to a tailor's dummy tumbling over.

Clapham Junction A paper design draft with numerous alterations or additions.

Codger Tailor who does up old suits.

Cork The boss.

Crib Large scrap of cloth left over from a job, usually enough to make a pair of trousers or a skirt.

Crushed beetles Badly made buttonholes.

Cutting turf Clumsy, unskilled working.

Doctor Alteration tailor.

Dolly Roll of wet material used as a sponge to dampen cloth.

Drag/in the drag Working behind time.

Drummer Trousermaker.

Goose iron Hand iron heated on a naked flame.

Have you been on the board? Are you experienced?

Hip stay Old-time name for wife.

Jeff A small master; one who cuts out his garments and also makes them up.

Kicking your heels No work to do.

Kicking Looking for another job.

Kill A spoiled job that has to be thrown away.

Kipper A tailoress. So called because they sought work in pairs to avoid unwelcome advances.

Log/on the log Piecework; the traditional and complex system of paying out-workers.

Mangle Sewing machine.

Mungo Cloth cuttings that, by custom, the tailor would retain to sell to a rag merchant for a little extra income.

Pig An unclaimed garment.

Pigged A lapel that turns up after some wear.

Pinked/pink a job Making with extra care.

Skiffle A job needed in a hurry.

Skipping it Making the stitches too big

Small seams Warning call when someone being discussed enters workroom.

Soft sew An easily worked cloth.

Tab Fussy, difficult customer.

Trotter Fetcher and carrier; messenger.

Tweed merchant Tailor who does the easy work; a poor workman.

Whipping the cat Traveling around and working in private houses; common practice in old days when a tailor would be given board and lodging while he made clothes for a family and their servants.

Glossary

Armscyle—Armhole.

Back—Wrong side of the fabric.

Basting—Sewing temporary stitches into a garment for making or holding fabric together until the permanent stitching.

Bespoke—English term describing a garment made to the client's measurements.

Bias (true bias)—Refers to a hypothetical line at a 45-degree angle to the warp of the fabric.

Breakpoint—Beginning of the roll line on the front edge of the jacket.

Bridle—Another name for the roll line and the tape applied to the roll line.

Canvas—Hair canvas interfacing, made from horse or goat hair and cotton. Also see Hymo.

Catchstitch—Hand-sewn stitch that looks like the letter X. It is used to sew one edge flat against the other.

CB—Center back.

CF—Center front.

Collar fall—The section of collar between the roll line and outer edge.

Collar stand—The section of collar between the roll line and neck line.

Crease line—Another term for roll line.

Crossgrain—The weft yarns of the fabric that run horizontal across the fabric from the selvage edge.

Domette—Made from lambs' wool, used in the chest piece or sleeve head.

Ease—Used to provide shaping in a sleeve, back shoulder, and bust area. Working in extra fabric when stitching two garment pieces together of unequal length without gathers or pleating.

Face—Right side of the fabric.

Fitting—Trying the jacket on a body shape to check fit and make adjustments.

Garment body—Garment front and back excluding the sleeves.

Gorge line—Seam line that joins the collar and lapel.

Grainline—When the lengthwise and crosswise yarn lies at perfect right angles, the fabric is grain perfect. The grainline usually refers to the lengthwise or warp grain.

Hymo—Type of hair canvas.

Interfacing—Layer of support fabric between the garment and the facing. Can be inserted for warmth.

Linen tape—See Stay.

Lining—A suitable fabric constructed in the shape of the jacket to cover and finish the inside of the garment.

Literal inspiration—Inspiration derived from social influences tempered by one's opinion or objectively interpreted.

Melton—Heavily felted wool fabric used for undercollars.

Miter—The angle formed when the excess fabric has been removed from the corner by a diagonal seam.

Muslin—Inexpensive, plain weave cotton fabric used for making the toile.

Notch—Angle formed where the collar joins the lapel.

Pad stitch—Small diagonal stitches used in tailoring to sew two layers together for the purpose of shaping and adding body to a garment section.

Personal inspiration—Inspiration based on one's own tastes, personality, background, social standing, and experience.

Press—To apply heat to a seam, hem, or garment section in order to flatten or press open.

Revers—Lapel.

Roll line—Crease line that separates the jacket front from the lapel.

Shank—The space between button and fabric; used to give room for the buttonhole.

Shape—To shrink or stretch a garment section with both heat and moisture.

Shell—Outside part of the garment, not including the lining.

Shoulder point—Point on the body at the end of the shoulder.

Sleeve cap—The section of the sleeve above the underarm seam.

Sleeve head—Strip of padded interfacing used to support the sleeve cap.

Slipstitch—A concealed hand stitch that can be used only on an area where there is a folded edge, such as a hem.

Stay—Tape sewn to the edge or seam of a garment to stop it from stretching.

Style line—Outside edge of the collar, lapel, or hemline.

Toile—A fitting garment made of muslin to check a new design or fit.

Topstitch—Row of stitches that shows on the outside of the garment. Usually decorative.

Tuck—A fold of fabric stitched to give shape to that garment section.

Underlining—A backing layer of fabric applied to the wrong side of the garment section that can be added to increase strength.

Vent—Finished opening at one end of a seam.

Design

Aldrich, W. (2002) *Pattern Cutting for Women's Tailored Jackets: Classic and Contemporary.* New York: Blackwell Publishing.

Chenoune, F. (2007) *Christian Dior.* New York: Assouline.

Evans, C. (2007) *Fashion at the Edge.* New Haven: Yale University Press.

Flusser, A. J. (1991), *Clothes and the Man: The Principles of Fine Men's Dress.* New York: Villard Books.

Gavenas, M. L. (2007) *The Fairchild Encyclopedia of Menswear.* New York: Fairchild Books.

Giorgetti, C. (1995) *Brioni: Fifty Years of Style.* Florence: Cantini Octavo Franc.

Golbin, P., & Baron, F. (2006) *Balenciaga Paris.* London: Thames and Hudson.

Kyoto Costume Institute, Eds. (2002) *Fashion: A History from the Eighteenth to the Twentieth Century.* Cologne: Taschen.

Mauries, P. (1996) *Christian Lacroix, The Diary of the Collection.* London: Thames and Hudson.

McDowell, C. (1997) *The Man of Fashion: Peacock Males and Perfect Gentlemen.* London: Thames and Hudson.

Molyneux, M. (1997) *Vivienne Westwood (Fashion Memoir).* London: Thames and Hudson.

Schoeffler, O. E., & Gale, W. (1974) *Esquire's Encyclopedia of Twentieth Century Men's Fashions.* New York: McGraw Hill Books.

Seeling, C. (2000) *Fashion, the Century of the Designer 1900–1999.* Cologne: Konemann.

Shaeffer, C. (2001) *Couture Sewing Techniques.* New Towne, CT: Taunton Press.

Udale, J., & Sorger, R. (2006) *The Fundamentals of Design.* West Sussex, UK: AVA Publishing.

Versace, G. (1994) *Vanitas Designs.* New York: Abbeville Press.

Wilson, E., & Taylor, L. (1991) *Through the Looking Glass: A History of Dress From 1860 to the Present Day.* London: BBC Books.

Techniques

Aldrich, W. (2002) *Pattern Cutting for Women's Tailored Jackets: Classic and Contemporary.* New York: Blackwell Publishing.

Aldrich, W. (2006) *Metric Pattern Cutting for Menswear.* New York: Blackwell Publishing.

Amaden C. (2000) *A Guild to Fashion Sewing.* New York: Fairchild Books.

Bane, A. (1968) *Tailoring.* New York: McGraw Hill.

Bishop, E. B. (1966) *Bishop Method of Clothing Construction.* New York: Lippincott.

Cabrera, R., & Meyers, P. H. (1984) *Tailoring Techniques: A Construction Guide for Women's Wear.* New York: Fairchild Books.

Cabrera, R., & Meyers, P. H. (1984) *Tailoring Techniques: A Construction Guide for Men's Wear.* New York: Fairchild Books.

Eds. (1993) *Jackets, Coats and Suits.* New Towne, CT: Taunton Press.

Eds. (2005) *Tailoring: The Classic Guide to Sewing the Perfect Jacket.* Minneapolis: Creative Publishing International.

Flury, M. E. (1996) *Tailoring Ladies' Jackets: Step by Step Instructions.* Upper Saddle River, NJ: Parker Publishing Company.

Kawashima, M. (1980) *Fundamentals of Men's Fashion Design.* New York: Fairchild Books.

Long, C. (1988) *Easy Guide to Sewing Linings.* New Towne, CT: Taunton Press.

Mauck, F. F. (1949) *Modern Tailoring for Women.* New York: Macmillian.

Palmer, P., & Pletsch, S. (1978) *Easy Easier Easiest Tailoring.* Portland, OR: Palmer.

Shaeffer, C. (2000) *Sewing for the Apparel Industry.* New Towne, CT: Taunton Press.

Shaeffer, C. (2001) *Couture Sewing Techniques.* New Towne, CT: Taunton Press.

Note: All illustrations by Pamela Powell, with graphic design by Thom Olson.

Chapter 1
Part I opener: © WWD
Chapter 1 opener: © WWD
Figure 1.1: © Hulton-Deutsch Collection/CORBIS
Figure 1.2: The Art Archive/Bibliothèque des Arts Décoratifs Paris/Gianni Dagli Orti
Figure 1.3: © Hulton-Deutsch Collection/CORBIS
Figure 1.4: Réunion des Musées Nationaux/Art Resource, NY ART154813
Figure 1.5: Collection of The Kyoto Costume Institute, photo by Toru Kogure
Figure 1.6: © WWD
Figure 1.7: © Everett Collection
Figure 1.8: © Bettmann/CORBIS
Figure 1.9a: © United Artists/Everett Collection
Figure 1.9b: © WWD
Figure 1.10: © Tommy Nutter for Kilgour
Figure 1.11: © WWD/Thomas Iannaccone
Figure 1.12: © firstVIEW
Figure 1.13: imaxtree.com/Alessandro Lucioni
Figure 1.14: © WWD

Chapter 2
Chapter 2 opener: © WWD
Figure 2.1: © WWD
Figure 2.2: © WWD
Figure 2.3: © firstVIEW
Figure 2.4: © WWD
Figure 2.5: Courtesy Musée des Tissus de Lyon/photo Stephan Guillermond
Figure 2.6: www.renegruau.com
Figure 2.7: Tony Barson/Wireimage
Figure 2.8: © firstVIEW
Figure 2.9: © WWD
Figure 2.10: © WWD
Figure 2.11: © WWD
Figure 2.12: © WWD
Figure 2.13: © WWD
Figure 2.14: © WWD
Figure 2.15: © Wendelien Daan Photography
Figure 2.16: © WWD
Figure 2.17: © WWD
Figure 2.18: © firstVIEW
Figure 2.19: © WWD
Figure 2.20: © WWD
Figure 2.21: Photo: Courtesy of Alexander McQueen
Figure 2.22: © WWD
Figure 2.23: © WWD
Figure 2.24: © WWD
Figure 2.25: © WWD
Figure 2.26: © WWD
Figure 2.27: © WWD
Figure 2.28: © WWD
Box 2.1a: © Vivienne Westwood, The Navy Wool Double Breasted Jacket with Square Cut Sleeves and Cotton Jersey Tube Skirt with Navy Wool Pleats are from the Autumn/Winter 1983/84 Witches collection.
Box 2.1b: © Vivienne Westwood, The Navy Wool Double Breasted Jacket with Square Cut Sleeves and Cotton Jersey Tube Skirt with Navy Wool Pleats are from the Autumn/Winter 1983/84 Witches collection.

Chapter 3
Part II opener: © WWD
Chapter 3 opener: © WWD
Figure 3.1: WWD
Figure 3.2: © firstVIEW
Figure 3.3: Courtesy of YSL
Figure 3.4: © WWD
Figure 3.5: © WWD
Box 3.1a: Courtesy www.lintondirect.co.uk
Box 3.1b: Courtesy www.lintondirect.co.uk
Table 3.2a: © WWD
Table 3.2b: © WWD
Table 3.2c: © WWD
Table 3.2d: © WWD
Table 3.2e: © WWD/Thomas Iannaccone
Table 3.2f: © WWD
Table 3.2g: © firstVIEW
Table 3.2h: © WWD
Table 3.2i: © WWD
Table 3.2j: © firstVIEW
Table 3.2k: © WWD
Table 3.2l: © WWD
Table 3.2m: © WWD
Table 3.2n: © WWD

Chapter 4
Chapter 4 opener: © WWD
Box 4.1: © WWD

Chapter 5
Chapter 5 opener: © WWD
Box 5.1: Courtesy of Joe, http://00o00.blogspot.com

Chapter 6
Part III opener: © WWD
Chapter 6 opener: © WWD
Figure 6.1: © firstVIEW

Box 6.1a: © firstVIEW
Box 6.1B: © firstVIEW

Chapter 7
Chapter 7 opener: © WWD
Figure 7.48: © WWD
Figure 7.49: Image copyright © The Metropolitan Museum of Art/Art Resource, NY
Figure 7.50: © WWD
Figure 7.59: © WWD
Box 7.1: © WWD

Chapter 8
Chapter 8 opener: © WWD
Figure 8.1: © WWD
Figure 8.2: Charles Frederick Worth Visite c. 1885 Collection of The Kyoto Costume Institute, photo by Takashi Hatakeyama
Box 8.1: © firstVIEW

Chapter 9
Chapter 9 opener: © WWD
Figure 9.1: © WWD
Figure 9.2: Pierre Cardin Suit, Autumn/Winter 1966, Collection of The Kyoto Costume Institute, photo by Takashi Hatakeyama
Figure 9.3: © The Metropolitan Museum of Art/Art Resource, NY, Image Reference : ART348625
Figure 9.4: Photo B.D.V./CORBIS
Figure 9.5: Martin Margiela Jacket, Spring/Summer 1998, Collection of The Kyoto Costume Institute, photo by Takashi Hatakeyama
Figure 9.6: © The Metropolitan Museum of Art/Art Resource, NY
Figure 9.35: © WWD
Box 9.1: © WWD

Chapter 10
Chapter 10 opener: © WWD
Figure 10.2: © firstVIEW
Figure 10.24: Carolyn Mandarano
Figure 10.30: © WWD
Box 10.1a: © WWD
Box 10.1b: © WWD
Box 10.1c: © firstVIEW

Chapter 11
Chapter 11 opener: © WWD
Figure 11.1: © firstview
Figure 11.2: Three Elegant Young Men, 1841 (colour engraving), French School, (19th century)/ Bibliotheque des Arts Decoratifs, Paris, France/ Archives Charmet/The Bridgeman Art Library International
Box 11.1a: © Fairchild Archive
Box 11.1b: George Rose/Getty Images

Chapter 12
Chapter 12 opener: © WWD
Figure 12.1: © WWD
Figure 12.2: © WWD
Figure 12.41: © Vivienne Westwood, Metropolitan Jacket from Autumn/Winter 1995/96 Vive La Cocotte collection

Chapter 13
Chapter 13 opener: © WWD
Figure 13.1a: Photo: Jack Duetch
Figure 13.1b: Photo: Jack Duetch
Figure 13.1c: Photo: Jack Duetch
Figure 13.1d: Photo: Jack Duetch
Figure 13.16: T. Olson
Figure 13.26: Carolyn Mandarano
Box 13.1: © firstVIEW

Chapter 14
Chapter 14 opener: © WWD
Figure 14.1: © WWD
Figure 14.2: © WWD
Figure 14.4: © WWD/Thomas Iannaccone
Figure 14.16: © WWD
Figure 14.18: © WWD

Index

Page numbers in italics refer to figures.

A
Ackermann, Haider, 116
Armani, Giorgio, 11–12, 154, 193

B
back neck facings, 173–76
Balenciaga, Christóbal, 39, 126
   profile, 138
basting stitches, 72
The Beatles, 3
bespoke tailoring, 4
Boateng, Ozwald, 13
Brioni, 9, *10*
buttons and buttonholes, 84–85, 193–98, 200–1
   attaching buttons, 200–1
   buttonhole stitch, 196–97
     machine-stitched, 198
   marking buttons placement, 198
   measuring the button, 194
   hand-worked buttonholes, 195
   stranding the buttonhole, 196

C
Cardin, Pierre. *See* Pierre Cardin
Cassini, Oleg, 90
catch stitching and basting, 72
Cavalli, Roberto, *39*
Chanel, 5, *26*
collars, undercollars, and top collars, 54–55, 143–53
   anatomy of the undercollar, 143
   attaching undercollar to neckline
     machine method, 147
     traditional method, 148
   constructing the undercollar, 144
     fusible method, 149
     machine method, 148
     traditional method, 144–46
   convertible or flat undercollar, 151
   evaluating undercollar fit, 146
   notched collars, 143
   shawl collars, 143
     constructing, 150
   top collars, 164–69
color, 27
construction
   back neck facing, 173–76
   buttonholes, 84–85, 194–98, 200–1
   collars, undercollars, top collars, 143–53

anatomy of the undercollar, 143
attaching undercollar to neckline
   machine method, 147
   traditional method, 148
constructing the undercollar, 144
   fusible method, 149
   machine method, 148
   traditional method, 144–46
convertible or flat undercollar, 151
evaluating undercollar fit, 146
notched collars, 143
shawl collars, 143
   constructing, 150
top collars, 164–69
jacket back, 118–24
   attaching to jacket front, 122
   back vent, 121–22
   back yoke, 120–21
   half belt addition, 123–24
   stabilizing back, neck, and armhole edges, 119
jacket front, 74–87
   applying fusible interfacing, 74
   bound buttonholes, 84–85
   canvas preparation, 77–78
   chest piece, 79–80
   darts, tucks, and pleats, 76–77
   facing, attachment of, 86–87
   joining canvas and jacket front, 80
   pad stitching and shaping lapels, 81–82
   roll line, taping and shaping of, 82–84
   waist darts, stitching of, 76
lapels
   front lapel facings, 169–70
   shaping, 171–73
linings, 179–89, 91
   attaching without back neck facing, 191
   "bagging," or attaching, 185
   full lining, 182–83
   full lining pattern, 180–81
   inserting by hand, 188–89
   inside lining pocket, 183–84
   jacket vent and hem, 185–88
pockets, 91–115
   double-piped pockets, 97–101
     with a flap, 102–5
   inseam pockets, 114–15
   patch pockets, 106–11
     inside-stitched, 112–13
   placement, 91
   welt pockets, 92–96

shoulder pads, 155–59, 162
    constructing, 156–58
    raglan, or rounded, 159, 162
sleeves, 52–54, 127–41
    one-piece sleeves, 128–29
    raglan sleeves, 140–41
    sleeve heads, 137
    two-piece, or tailored, sleeves, 129
        with a mitered vent, 130–37, 139
top collars, 164–69
    attaching top collar by machine, 168–69
    constructing, traditional method, 167
contrast, 27
Create-A-Marker, Inc., 177

D

dandies, *155*
darts, tucks, and pleats
    jacket front, 76–77
details, 24–25, *26*, 27
Dior, Christian, 18, *21*, *34*, 33
Dior's 1947 Bar suit, 18, *21*

E

Edward VII, Prince of Wales, 5
Edward VIII, Prince of Wales, 7
Eisenhower jackets, 8–9
Esterel, Jacques, 3, 12
evaluation of jacket construction, final, 201

F

fabric, 28, 34–42
    choosing, 34–35
    interfacings, 41–42
    linings, 41
    Linton tweed, 40–41
    nap fabrics, 37
    plaids and stripes, 36–37
fashion design
    Hollywood's influence, 8
    inspiration for, 15–18
    Italian influence, 9
    and tailoring, 3–5
    see *also* tailored fashion design
Ferretti, Alberta, *37*
Feruch, Gilbert, 3
finishing the jacket, 193–201
    buttons and buttonholes, 84–85, 194–98, 200–1
    final evaluation, 201
    final pressing, 199
    top stitching, 200

G

Galliano, John, 16–17, 18, *34*, 45
Gaultier, Jean Paul, 12
Gigli, Romeo, 152–53
Grès, Madame, *127*

I

interfacings, 41–42, 74

J

jacket back, 118–24
    attaching to jacket front, 122
    back vent, 121–22
    back yoke, 120–21
    constructing, 119–22
    half belt addition, 123–24
    stabilizing back, neck, and armhole edges, 119
jacket design
    back neck facing, 173–76
    bust
        fitting, 66–67, 69
        adding bust dart on a woman's jacket, 78
    buttons and buttonholes, 84–85, 194–98, 200–1
    collars and undercollars, 54–55, 143–53
    color, 27
    contrast, 27
    details, 24–25, *26*, 27
    fabric, 28, 34–42
    finishing the jacket, 193–201
        buttons and buttonholes, 84–85, 194–98, 200–1
        final evaluation, 201
        final pressing, 199
        top stitching, 200
    fitting the jacket, 48, 60–67, 69–70
        adjusting for individual backs and bust lines, *62*, 63
        bust, 66–67, 69
        lapels, 60
        proportions, 70
        shaping the jacket, 70
        shoulder line, 64–66
        waistline, 60
    inspiration for, 15–18
    interfacings, 41–42, 74
    jacket back, 118–24
    jacket front, 51, 74–87
    lapels, 60, 81
        front lapel facings, 169–70
        shaping, 171–73
    linings, 41, 179–89, 91
    patterns, 46–55, 58

pockets, 91–115
proportion and line, 22, *23*
scale and volume, 20, *21*, 22
shoulder pads, 155–59, 162
    constructing, 156–58
    raglan, or rounded, 159, 162
silhouette, 19–20
sleeves, 52–54, 127–41
tailoring methods, *75*
texture, 28, *29*
top collars, back neck facings, front lapel facings, 164–76
top stitching, 200
types of design by characteristics and fabric choices, *38–39*
waistline, fitting of, 60
jacket front, 51, 74–87
    applying fusible interfacing, 74
    bound buttonholes, 84–85
    canvas preparation, 77–78
    chest piece, 79–80
    darts, tucks, and pleats, 76–77
    facing, attachment of, 86–87
    joining canvas and jacket front, 80
    pad stitching and shaping lapels, 81–82
    roll line, taping and shaping of, 82–84
    waist darts, stitching of, 76
jargon from Savile Row, 202

K
Kenzo, 38

L
La Croix, Christian, 15, *16*
Lanvin, *21*, 25
Lanvin jacket, *21*
lapels, 60, 81
    front lapel facings, 169–70
    shaping, 171–73
Lauren, Ralph. *See* Ralph Lauren
linings, 41, 179–89, 91
    attaching without back neck facing, 191
    "bagging," or attaching, 185
    full lining, 182–83
    full lining pattern, 180–81
    inserting by hand, 188–89
    inside lining pocket, 183–84
    jacket vent and hem, 185–88
Linton tweed, 40–41

M
Madame Grès, *127*
marker making, 177
McCartney, Stella, 20
McLaren, Malcolm, 31
McQueen, Alexander, 13, 16, *17*, *18*, *38*, *39*, *57*, 192
    profile, 56
measurements, 46–47
    men's standard body, *46*
    women's standard body, *47*
Mugler, Thierry, 155
muslin, 36, 44

N
nap fabrics, 37
Nutter, Tommy, 9, *10*

O
off-the-peg, 9, 10
Oldfield, Bruce, 73

P
pad stitching, 72, 81–82
patterns, 46–55, 58
    collars, 54–55
    double-breasted jacket, front, 51
    fit of the jacket, 48
    jacket front, 51
    making, 49–50
    measurements, 46–47
    sleeves, 52–54
    toile construction, 58
Pierre Cardin, 3, 12
plaids and stripes, 36–37
pockets, 91–115
    double-piped pockets, 97–101
        with a flap, 102–5
    inseam pockets, 114–15
    patch pockets, 106–11
        inside-stitched, 112–13
    placement, 91
    welt pockets, 92–96
Poole, Henry, 5
Posen, Zac, 38
Potter, James, 5
Prada, 38
proportion and line, 22, *23*

R
raglan sleeves, 54, 140–41
    shoulder pad, 159, 162

Ralph Lauren, 10, *11*, 178
ready-to-wear, 9, *10*
Redfern, John, 7
Rocha, John, 190
roll line, taping and shaping of, 82–84

S
Saint Laurent, Yves. *See* Yves Saint Laurent
Sander, Jil, 125
Satyenkummer (Satyen Patel), 68
Savile Row, 3, 4, 9
   jargon, 202
Savile Row Bespoke Association, 4
scale and volume, 20, *21*, 22
Schiaperelli, Elsa, 8
The Sex Pistols, 31
shoulder line, 64–66
shoulder pads, 155–59, 162
   constructing, 156–58
   raglan, or rounded, 159, 162
silhouette, 19–20
Simons, Raf, *39*
sleeves, 52–54, 127–41
   one-piece sleeves, 128–29
   raglan sleeves, 140–41
   sleeve heads, 137
   two-piece, or tailored, sleeves, 129
      with a mitered vent, 130–37, 139
slip stitching, 72
stitchings, 72

T
tailored fashion design
   evolution of, 5–13
   Hollywood's influence, 8
   inspiration for, 15–18
tailoring overview
   contemporary, 3, 5, *75*
   equipment, 44
   and fashion design, 3–5
   fusible, *75*
   history of, 5–13
   Italian influence, 9
   jargon, 202
   methods, *75*
   stitchings, 72
   traditional, 4, *75*
   for women, 6–7
   see also tailored fashion design
texture, 28, *29*
toiles, 36, 58
top collars, 164–69
top stitching, 200
tuxedos, 5–6

V
Valentino, *39*
vent of jacket and hem, 185–88
Versace, Gianni, 142, 160–61

W
Watanabe, Junya, *38*
Westwood, Vivienne, 17, *30*, 31, *127*, 163
Worth, Charles Frederick, 7

Y
Yves Saint Laurent, 6, 88–89

Z
zoot suit, *8*

www.ingramcontent.com/pod-product-compliance
Lightning Source LLC
Chambersburg PA
CBHW080745250426

43673CB00062B/1895